DEATH AND DYING
END-OF-LIFE CONTROVERSIES

ISSN 1532-2726

DEATH AND DYING
END-OF-LIFE CONTROVERSIES

Erin Brown

INFORMATION PLUS® REFERENCE SERIES
Formerly Published by Information Plus, Wylie, Texas

GALE
A Cengage Company

Farmington Hills, Mich • San Francisco • New York • Waterville, Maine
Meriden, Conn • Mason, Ohio • Chicago

Death and Dying: End-of-Life Controversies

Erin Brown

Kepos Media, Inc.: Steven Long and Janice Jorgensen, Series Editors

Project Editor: Laura Avery

Rights Acquisition and Management:
 Ashley M. Maynard, Carissa Poweleit

Composition: Evi Abou-El-Seoud,
 Mary Beth Trimper

Manufacturing: Rita Wimberley

Product Design: Kristin Julien

For product information and technology assistance, contact us at
Gale Customer Support, 1-800-877-4253.
For permission to use material from this text or product,
submit all requests online at **www.cengage.com/permissions.**
Further permissions questions can be e-mailed to
permissionrequest@cengage.com

Cover photograph: © clearimages/Shutterstock.com.

While every effort has been made to ensure the reliability of the information presented in this publication, Gale, a Cengage Company, does not guarantee the accuracy of the data contained herein. Gale accepts no payment for listing; and inclusion in the publication of any organization, agency, institution, publication, service, or individual does not imply endorsement of the editors or publisher. Errors brought to the attention of the publisher and verified to the satisfaction of the publisher will be corrected in future editions.

Gale
27500 Drake Rd.
Farmington Hills, MI 48331-3535

ISBN-13: 978-0-7876-5103-9 (set)
ISBN-13: 978-1-5730-2696-3

ISSN 1532-2726

This title is also available as an e-book.
ISBN-13: 978-1-4103-3271-4 (set)
Contact your Gale sales representative for ordering information.

Printed in the United States of America
1 2 3 4 5   22 21 20 19 18

TABLE OF CONTENTS

rising. Attempts to address cost and expand coverage through the Patient Protection and Affordable Care Act are considered, as is the continued viability of Medicare, which is imperiled by the dual pressures of an aging population and rising medical costs.

PREFACE

Death and Dying: End-of-Life Controversies is part of the *Information Plus Reference Series*. The purpose of each volume of the series is to present the latest facts on a topic of pressing concern in modern American life. These topics include the most controversial and studied social issues of the 21st century: abortion, capital punishment, care for the elderly, crime, the environment, gambling, health care, immigration, race and ethnicity, social welfare, women, youth, and many more. Although this series is written especially for high school and undergraduate students, it is an excellent resource for anyone in need of factual information on current affairs.

By presenting the facts, it is the intention of Gale, a Cengage Company, to provide its readers with everything they need to reach an informed opinion on current issues. To that end, there is a particular emphasis in this series on the presentation of scientific studies, surveys, and statistics. These data are generally presented in the form of tables, charts, and other graphics placed within the text of each book. Every graphic is directly referred to and carefully explained in the text. The source of each graphic is presented within the graphic itself. The data used in these graphics are drawn from the most reputable and reliable sources, such as from the various branches of the U.S. government and from private organizations and associations. Every effort has been made to secure the most recent information available. Readers should bear in mind that many major studies take years to conduct and that additional years often pass before the data from these studies are made available to the public. Therefore, in many cases the most recent information available in 2017 is dated from 2014 or 2015. Older statistics are sometimes presented as well, if they are landmark studies or of particular interest and no more-recent information exists.

Although statistics are a major focus of the *Information Plus Reference Series*, they are by no means its only content. Each book also presents the widely held positions and important ideas that shape how the book's subject is discussed in the United States. These positions are explained in detail and, where possible, in the words of their proponents. Some of the other material to be found in these books includes historical background, descriptions of major events related to the subject, relevant laws and court cases, and examples of how these issues play out in American life. Some books also feature primary documents or have pro and con debate sections that provide the words and opinions of prominent Americans on both sides of a controversial topic. All material is presented in an evenhanded and unbiased manner; readers will never be encouraged to accept one view of an issue over another.

HOW TO USE THIS BOOK

Death is one of the universal human experiences. This and its ultimately unknowable nature combine to make it a topic of great interest to most Americans. How we die and how we deal with the deaths of others evokes profound religious or ethical issues, or both, about which many people hold strong beliefs. When these beliefs are in conflict with those of others, this can result in some of the most serious and divisive controversies in the United States. This book examines how Americans deal with death, with a particular focus on the highly charged political and moral issues of living wills, life-sustaining treatments, funding for end-of-life care, and physician-assisted suicide.

Death and Dying: End-of-Life Controversies consists of 10 chapters and three appendixes. Each chapter is devoted to a particular aspect of death and dying in the United States. For a summary of the information that is covered in each chapter, please see the synopses that are provided in the Table of Contents. Chapters generally begin with an overview of the basic facts and background information on the chapter's topic, then proceed to examine subtopics of particular interest. For example,

Chapter 7: Suicide, Euthanasia, and Assisted Suicide begins with an examination of suicide rates among various demographic groups and considers factors such as age, gender, race, and sexual orientation. An assessment of historical and contemporary attitudes toward suicide follows, with a focus on the ethical and moral repercussions of physician-assisted suicide, notably from the perspective of medical professionals. The chapter concludes by analyzing the impact of "death with dignity" legislation in Oregon and Washington, while providing an overview of notable assisted-suicide and euthanasia laws overseas. Readers can find their way through a chapter by looking for the section and subsection headings, which are clearly set off from the text. They can also refer to the book's extensive Index if they already know what they are looking for.

Statistical Information

The tables and figures featured throughout *Death and Dying: End-of-Life Controversies* will be of particular use to readers in learning about this issue. These tables and figures represent an extensive collection of the most recent and important statistics on death, as well as related issues—for example, graphics cover the death rates for the 15 leading causes of death, the percentage of high school students who attempt suicide, the growth in Medicare expenditures, and public opinion on the moral acceptability of physician-assisted suicide. Gale, a Cengage Company, believes that making this information available to readers is the most important way to fulfill the goal of this book: to help readers understand the issues and controversies surrounding death and dying in the United States and reach their own conclusions.

Each table or figure has a unique identifier appearing above it, for ease of identification and reference. Titles for the tables and figures explain their purpose. At the end of each table or figure, the original source of the data is provided.

To help readers understand these often complicated statistics, all tables and figures are explained in the text. References in the text direct readers to the relevant statistics. Furthermore, the contents of all tables and figures are fully indexed. Please see the opening section of the Index at the back of this volume for a description of how to find tables and figures within it.

Appendixes

Besides the main body text and images, *Death and Dying: End-of-Life Controversies* has three appendixes. The first is the Important Names and Addresses directory. Here, readers will find contact information for a number of government and private organizations that can provide further information on aspects of death and dying. The second appendix is the Resources section, which can also assist readers in conducting their own research. In this section, the author and editors of *Death and Dying: End-of-Life Controversies* describe some of the sources that were most useful during the compilation of this book. The final appendix is the detailed Index. It has been greatly expanded from previous editions and should make it even easier to find specific topics in this book.

COMMENTS AND SUGGESTIONS

The editors of the *Information Plus Reference Series* welcome your feedback on *Death and Dying: End-of-Life Controversies*. Please direct all correspondence to:

Editors
Information Plus Reference Series
27500 Drake Rd.
Farmington Hills, MI 48331-3535

CHAPTER 1
DEATH THROUGH THE AGES: A BRIEF OVERVIEW

Strange, is it not? That of the myriads who
Before us pass'd the door of Darkness through,
Not one returns to tell us of the Road,
Which to discover we must travel too.

—Omar Khayyám, *Rubáiyát of Omar Khayyám*

Death is the inevitable conclusion of life, a universal destiny that all living creatures share. Although all societies throughout history have realized that death is the certain fate of human beings, different cultures have responded to it in different ways. Death is central to all major world religions, all of which address the fate of the individual after the body ceases to function. Individual religions answer the challenges posed by death in different ways, however. Many promise an afterlife in which the soul survives bodily death, but there is little agreement among religions about the nature of that afterlife, and this diversity of views has centrally shaped the customs and attitudes of cultures, nations, and individuals. Philosophical inquiry into the nature of death has likewise varied from culture to culture over time, ensuring an ongoing diversity of beliefs and customs. Increased scientific understanding in the 19th and 20th centuries has not made earlier religious and philosophical approaches to death obsolete, but in some cases it has diminished the universality of these traditional modes of understanding, and it has complicated the overall approach to death at the societal level. The medical advances of the 20th and 21st centuries, by prolonging life dramatically, have further reshaped some of humanity's most basic assumptions about the relation between life and death, raising a host of ethical issues that would have been unimaginable to past generations.

ANCIENT TIMES

Archaeologists have found that as early as the Paleolithic period, around 2.5 million to 3 million years ago, humans held metaphysical beliefs about death and dying—those beyond what humans can know with their senses. Tools and ornaments excavated at burial sites suggest that the earliest human ancestors believed that some element of a person survived the dying experience.

Continuity between life and death formed the foundation of what was central to traditional religious beliefs in Africa. Specific ideas about death varied widely, but in most indigenous African religions the deceased individual continued to exist in the afterlife. The ultimate purpose of death, for the individual, was to achieve the status of an ancestor, a being with the ability to communicate with and influence the visible world. Families and communities typically observed elaborate funeral rituals when one of their members died, both to ease the dead person's passage into the afterlife and to ensure that ancestors did not wield too much power over the living. Although the earliest African religions originated sometime between 200,000 to 100,000 BC, many practices and beliefs continue to survive in the 21st century.

The earliest civilizations typically believed in the existence of an eternal soul or something like it. For example, the ancient Egyptians (c. 3100–332 BC) believed that a person had a dual soul: the *ka* and the *ba*. The *ka* was the spirit that dwelled near the body, whereas the *ba* was the vitalizing soul that lived on in the netherworld (the world of the dead) but that could not survive without the body. Accordingly, early ancient Egyptians left their deceased loved ones in the open air of the desert, the aridity of which allowed bodies to be preserved long after they would have decomposed in wetter environments. Later Egyptians relied on a more active form of bodily preservation, mummification, to allow their loved ones access to a happy afterlife.

The mummification process, which may have taken more than two months to complete, included the ritual washing of the corpse and the removal of the brain and organs, with the exception of the heart, which was believed to be vital for the deceased person's continued existence. The body was then dried, padded for the retention of its lifelike shape, and preserved through the use of embalming chemicals. After being blessed by a priest, the mummified body was wrapped in bandages, decorated, and entombed. Mummification remained a common practice in Egypt for approximately 3,000 years.

The ancient Mesopotamians (c. 3100–539 BC), whose civilization flourished near present-day Iraq at roughly the same time as the ancient Egyptian civilization, also believed in an afterlife, but in their cosmology the afterlife was uniformly dismal. After the death of the body, the immortal element of the spirit was believed to exist in a dark underworld, where it ate dust and clay and had no access to water. The dead could find relief from this onerous existence only when their living relatives ritually contributed food and other offerings to them. Thus, the living had a significant responsibility toward their dead loved ones and ancestors, and one of the worst fates that could befall a person who had died was for his or her remains to be removed from the care of the living family. It was believed, however, that the dead would haunt the living if they were not given a proper burial. As a result, even the bodies of fallen enemies were typically buried so as to prevent the spirit's vengeful return.

The ancient Chinese (c. 2100–256 BC) believed in an afterlife that in most respects represented a continuation of the individual's worldly life. The dead were thus buried with possessions they would need in the afterlife, and living relatives were expected to continue making offerings and attending to the needs of their deceased loved ones. Royal and noble people were buried with particular extravagance, in some cases in houses complete with stables and grounds rivaling those that they had enjoyed in life. Beginning in the Shang dynasty (1600–1046 BC), some royal or noble people were buried not only with vast amounts of riches and material possessions but also with their servants and concubines, who may have possibly been buried alive. By the end of the ancient period, this practice had largely been discontinued, and human figures made of pottery were used in their place. The burial of possessions and figures continued well into the second millennium AD.

The Vedic tradition (c. 1500–500 BC) is the earliest religion in India and the foundation of classical Hinduism. In the Hindu belief system, the human soul, or *atman*, experiences existence in the material world, or *samsara*, as a continuous cycle of birth, life, death, and reincarnation. Although the physical body is subject to constant change, the *atman* remains eternal and represents the permanent essence of the individual. For Hindus, the ultimate goal of life is to achieve a state of enlightenment, or *moksha*, thereby gaining liberation from the endless cycle of birth and death. The path to

moksha varies, with some Hindu traditions emphasizing virtuous deeds (*karma*) and others stressing devotion (*bhakti*), meditation (*raja*), or knowledge (*jnana*). The concepts of *samsara* and *moksha* later formed the core tenets of Buddhism, although Buddhists deny the existence of *atman*, and consider freedom from *samsara* to be a state of self-annihilation (*nirvana*).

In ancient Greece (1200 BC–AD 600), it was believed that the souls of the dead passed into an underworld ruled by Hades and his wife, Persephone. Depending on the life that the individual had lived, the soul might be remanded to the Fields of Asphodel or to Tartarus. The Fields of Asphodel were the abode of those whose lives had been neither excessively good nor excessively evil. Tartarus was a pit where those who had been wicked suffered in torment. Some accounts of the Greek afterlife also refer to Elysium, an idyllic part of the underworld reserved for heroes and others who had lived exceptional lives. The ancient Romans (c. 800 BC–AD 476) derived many of their religious and cultural traditions from their Greek predecessors, including those parts of their cosmology relating to the afterlife.

Greek and Roman attitudes toward death were strongly influenced by the mythological epic poems of Homer (c. eight century–c. seventh century BC), the *Iliad* and the *Odyssey*. Greek mythology was freely interpreted by writers after Homer, and belief in eternal judgment and retribution evolved throughout the ancient period. Certain Greek philosophers also influenced conceptions of death. For example, Pythagoras of Samos (c. 570–c. 490 BC) opposed euthanasia ("good death" or mercy killing) because it might disturb the soul's journey toward final purification as planned by the gods. On the contrary, Socrates (469–399 BC) and Plato (428–347 BC) believed that people could choose to end their life if they were no longer useful to themselves or the state.

Like Socrates and Plato, the classical Romans (c. 509–264 BC) believed that a person suffering from intolerable pain or an incurable illness should have the right to choose a "good death." They considered euthanasia a "mode of dying" that allowed a person to take control of an intolerable situation. The Romans distinguished euthanasia from suicide, an act considered to be a shirking of responsibilities to one's family and to humankind.

The historical sense and attitudes of the ancient Hebrews (c. 1800 BC–AD 363) toward death are described in the Tanakh, or Hebrew Bible (which also constitutes the Old Testament of the Christian Bible). The ancient Jewish people, whose destinies overlapped with those of the ancient Egyptians, Mesopotamians, Greeks, and Romans, did not generally live in the expectation of an immediate individual afterlife. They lived according to the commandments of their god, to whom they entrusted their eternal destiny. The Tanakh describes the end of days, a time when the world will end. At that time, according to ancient prophets, God will return the Jewish people to the Land of Israel, resurrect the dead, and create a new heaven and a new earth. The Tanakh also includes references to the coming of the Messiah, a human leader who will unite the people of Israel and bring about an age of peace and well-being for the living and the dead.

THE MIDDLE AGES AND THE RENAISSANCE

During the European Middle Ages (500–1485) the tenets of Christianity, as adjudicated by the medieval Roman Catholic Church, established many of the cultural and social conventions relating to death and dying. Although the Christian Bible references an afterlife in which believers will be united with God, concrete descriptions of heaven and hell have been more the creation of various interpreters of the Bible than of the text itself. In the medieval view, to ascend to heaven after death, one had to be not only a believer but also an observer of proper Christian behavior. Those who were impious or guilty of sin risked eternal damnation if they did not confess their sins prior to death.

Because life expectancy during this period commonly extended to little more than 30 years, death and the necessity of being prepared for it were a constant and looming presence in the lives of many. Because medical practices during this era were crude and imprecise, the ill or dying person often endured prolonged suffering. This long period of suffering gave the dying individual an opportunity to feel forewarned about impending death, to put his or her affairs in order, and to confess his or her sins.

The spread of Islam (AD 610–800) in the Middle East and North Africa introduced a somewhat different notion of death. Like Christians, Muslims viewed earthly existence as a preparation for the afterlife. As a person was dying, Malak al-Maut, the angel of death, descended onto the individual to extract the soul from the body. This extraction was painless for Muslims who had lived a life of virtue and piety, but a cause of great anguish for those who had sinned. Following death, a Muslim was interrogated by the angels Munkar and Nakir, who tested the individual's faith in God (Allah) to determine whether he or she deserved to go to heaven (*Jannat*) or hell (*Jahannam*).

By the late Middle Ages, the fear of death had intensified because of the Black Death—the great plague of 1347 to 1351. The Black Death killed more than 25 million people in Europe alone. Commoners watched not only their neighbors but also church officials and royalty struck down: King Alfonso XI (1311–1350) of Castile met with an untimely death, as did many at the papal court in Avignon, France. With their perceived "proper order" of existence shaken, the common people became increasingly preoccupied with their own death and with

the Last Judgment—God's final and certain determination of the character of each individual.

From the 14th through the 16th centuries Europe experienced a cultural rebirth, the Renaissance, in which Christian doctrine and art forms were supplemented by notions of earthly beauty and the good life derived from the cultures of ancient Greece and Rome. New directions emerged in economics, the arts, and social, scientific, and political thought. This flowering occurred especially in the city-states of what is now Italy but also in the rest of Continental Europe and the British Isles. Despite a renewed focus on the things of this world, medicine remained rudimentary, and life expectancy was low by modern standards. Outbreaks of plague continued to erupt periodically, especially in the urban centers of art, intellectual life, and commerce.

Furthermore, the new self-awareness and emphasis on humans as the center of the universe may have fueled the fear of dying. In *The Hour of Our Death*, an influential study of Western attitudes toward death first published in France in 1977, the French historian Philippe Ariès (1914–1984) suggests that whereas the ancient and medieval attitude toward death involved casual acceptance, the increasing rationalism and individualism characteristic of the Renaissance brought an increased focus on death as a moment of fear and crisis.

The Catholic Church remained a dominant influence on perceptions of death and dying during the Renaissance. The generally accepted Christian attitude was that believers should continually meditate on death as a means of staying mindful of their soul's destiny and their duty to God. By the 16th century, however, the Protestant Reformation had begun, representing a diminution of the church's power, including its authority to dictate what Christians believed about death and dying. In general, the doubt cast on the Roman Catholic Church's cosmology translated into increased uncertainty about death and dying.

THE 17TH AND 18TH CENTURIES

Although Christianity remained the dominant arbiter of Western attitudes toward death throughout the 17th and 18th centuries, science progressed, bringing about an increasing reliance on reason. As such, death became an object for medical and scientific study as well as for religious meditation. Increasing rationalism, however, did not result in an immediate break with historical beliefs in an afterlife. René Descartes (1596–1650), the philosopher most responsible for inaugurating the period of modern philosophy (from the 17th century to the early 20th century), was both a committed rationalist and a believer in the immortality of the soul. His *Meditations on First Philosophy* (1641), one of the most influential works of philosophy in history, is famous for formulating the idea of mind–body dualism, as encapsulated in the phrase *Cogito ergo sum* (I think, therefore I am), which Descartes had first used several years earlier. This suggestion that the mind, as distinct from all aspects of the body, is the starting point for all identity and existence has been one of the central preoccupations of Western thought in the centuries since Descartes advanced the idea. Less commonly discussed is the fact that Descartes's stated reason for establishing the mind as the seat of existence in this way was to prove that it "is immortal by its very nature."

Also during the 17th and 18th centuries, people began questioning the medical definition of death. Reports of unconscious patients mistakenly believed to be dead and hurriedly prepared for burial by the clergy, only to "come back to life" during transport to the cemetery or burial, led to an increased focus on understanding the physiological processes of death. Some physicians believed that the body retained some kind of "sensibility" after death. Thus, many people preserved cadavers so that the bodies could "live on." Alternatively, some physicians applied the teachings of the Catholic Church to their medical practice and believed that once the body was dead, the soul proceeded to its eternal fate and the body could no longer survive. These physicians did not preserve cadavers and pronounced them permanently dead.

The fear of "apparent death," a condition in which people appeared to be dead but were not, increased in intensity during the 18th century. Coffins were built with contraptions that enabled any prematurely buried person to survive and communicate from the grave. Figure 1.1, which dates from the 19th century, shows such a device. In some cases Christianity was blamed for the hasty burial of those who were only apparently dead because religious authorities had actively deemphasized such pagan burial traditions as protracted mourning rituals. In the wake of apparent death incidents, some older burial traditions were revived.

THE 19TH CENTURY

Throughout most of the 19th century, as in previous eras, death typically took place in the home following a long deathbed watch. Family members then prepared the corpses of their loved ones for viewing in the home. During the late 19th century, however, a new class of professional undertakers emerged, and they began taking over the job of preparing and burying the dead. Undertakers provided services such as readying the corpse for viewing and burial, building the coffin, digging the grave, and directing the funeral procession. Professional embalming and cosmetic restoration of bodies became widely available, all carried out in a funeral parlor, where bodies were then viewed.

FIGURE 1.1

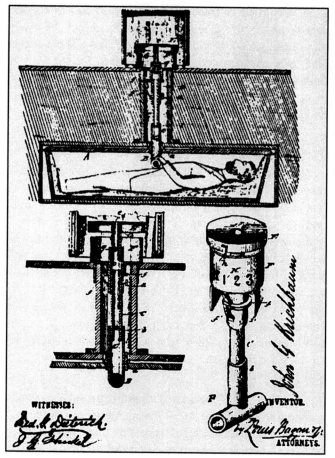

Device for indicating life in buried persons, 1882. *U.S. Government Printing Office.*

Cemeteries changed as well. Before the early 19th century U.S. cemeteries were unsanitary, overcrowded, and weed-filled places that bore an odor of decay. The graveyard environment began to change in 1831, when the Massachusetts Horticultural Society purchased 72 acres (29 ha) of fields, ponds, trees, and gardens in Cambridge and built Mount Auburn Cemetery. This cemetery became a model for the landscaped garden cemetery in the United States. Such cemeteries were tranquil places where mourners could visit the graves of loved ones and find comfort in the beautiful surroundings.

Literature of the time often focused on and romanticized death. Death poetry, consoling essays, and mourning manuals became available after 1830. These works comforted the grieving with the concept that the deceased were in heaven—released from worldly cares and reunited with other deceased loved ones. During the 19th century the deadly lung disease tuberculosis was pervasive in Europe and the United States. The disease caused sufferers to develop a certain appearance—an extreme pallor and thinness, with a look often described as haunted—that actually became a kind of fashion statement. The fixation on the subject by writers such as Edgar Allan Poe (1809–1849) and the English romantic poets helped fuel the public's fascination with death and dying.

Spiritualism

In the mid-19th century one of the most notable trends in attitudes about the end of life was the rise of spiritualism. This belief system centered on the idea that certain "mediums" could communicate with the dead. In 1848 in the United States, the sisters Margaret Fox (1833–1893) and Kate Fox (1839–1892) of Hydesville, New York, became celebrated for their supposed ability to receive messages from the dead. The sisters claimed to have communicated with the spirit of a man who had been murdered by a former tenant in their house. The practice of conducting "sittings" to contact the dead gained instant popularity. Mediums such as the Fox sisters were supposedly sensitive to "vibrations" from the disembodied souls who temporarily lived in that part of the spirit world just outside Earth's limits.

Efforts to communicate with the dead have been practiced for millennia in cultures all over the world. For example, many Native Americans believe that shamans (priests or medicine men) have the power to communicate with the spirits of the dead. In the Judeo-Christian tradition, the first book of Samuel in the Old Testament of the Christian Bible recounts the visit of King Saul to a medium at Endor. The medium summoned the spirit of the prophet Samuel, who predicted the death of Saul and his sons. The outbreak of spiritualism in the United States is noteworthy, however, because the country was among the most rapidly modernizing in the world and because increased scientific understanding had begun to extinguish many of humanity's lingering beliefs in the supernatural.

During the 1860s and 1870s the mood in the United States was ripe for spiritualist séances. Most people had lost a son, a husband, or another loved one during the U.S. Civil War (1861–1865). Some survivors wanted assurances that their loved ones were all right; others were simply curious about life after death. Those who had drifted away from traditional Christianity embraced this new spiritualism, which claimed scientific evidence of survival after physical death. This so-called evidence included table rapping, levitation, and materialization that occurred during the séances. In May 1875 a 12-member commission organized by the Russian chemist and inventor Dmitry Ivanovich Mendeleyev (1834–1907) concluded that spiritualism had no scientific basis and that the séance phenomena resulted from fraud—from mediums consciously deceiving those in attendance by using tricks to create illusions.

Nineteenth-century spiritualism was not a purely American philosophy. In 1882 the British poet and classicist Frederic William Henry Myers (1843–1901), who coined the word *telepathy* to describe the supposed phenomenon of two minds communicating without words or any sensory interactions, established the Society for Psychical Research. The organization, which was devoted to the "scientific" investigation of paranormal phenomena — especially those providing evidence for the continued existence of deceased individuals — attracted some of the most prominent intellectuals of the late 19th and early 20th centuries. Among them were the American philosopher and psychologist William James (1842–1910), the French philosopher Henri Bergson (1859–1941), the Nobel Prize-winning French physiologist Charles Robert Richet (1850–1935), the British writers John Ruskin (1819–1900) and Alfred, Lord Tennyson (1809–1892), and leading British politicians, including William Gladstone (1809–1898) and Arthur James Balfour (1848–1930). *The Immortalization Commission* (2011), by the British political philosopher John Gray (1948–), describes the outbreak of such belief in the supernatural at a time otherwise characterized by the dominance of science-based views of death. Gray argues that the burgeoning of spiritualism was not merely a continuation of a previous era's superstitions but a desperate response to scientific rationalism, which had "disclosed a world in which humans were no different from other animals in facing final oblivion when they died and eventual extinction as a species."

THE 20TH AND 21ST CENTURIES

In the 20th century advances in medicine and public health revolutionized humans' relationship with death, at least in the developed world. People continued to wrestle with the idea of death and to look to religion and philosophy for ways of understanding and coping with it. By the end of the 20th century, however, vaccines and other public health initiatives had eradicated or brought under control many previously fatal diseases, and few developed countries were regularly ravaged by war in the decades after World War II (1939–1945). In this environment it became the norm, for the first time in human history, for most people to expect to live into old age. No longer an imminent threat to most young and middle-aged people, death became less interwoven into the fabric of daily life than it had been in other periods of history.

Moreover, whereas death throughout history most commonly resulted from unexpected diseases for which there was no treatment, in the late 20th and early 21st centuries most people were able to stave off disease through preventive care or to manage illness through treatment. Thus, people were more likely to die of a chronic illness, treated by medical professionals, over a protracted period. As a consequence, most deaths began occurring in hospitals or other institutionalized settings, rather than in the home. This fact, as well as the fact that burial and funerary rituals were still largely managed by professional undertakers, resulted in what many observers characterize as a depersonalization of death.

The removal of death from daily life, from the home, and from community life posed challenges for individuals. Death remained as inevitable as ever, of course, but in the absence of the cultural and community structures that once helped people cope with loss and with the eventuality of their own death, many people were left alone to grieve and to prepare for their own death. New societal institutions have, to some extent, arisen to compensate for these absences and to address the challenges death poses for the modern individual. For example, death has become the subject of intense sociological and psychological study, much of which has resulted in new forms of understanding the ways humans cope with the deaths of loved ones and with the prospect of their own death. Many of the insights from such research are used by grief counselors (mental health professionals who specialize in helping bereaved people navigate the challenges of mourning).

One of the most influential theoreticians of death in the modern world was Elisabeth Kübler-Ross (1926–2004), an American psychologist. Her pioneering first book, *On Death and Dying* (1969), established the widely accepted notion that individuals confront death (either their own death or the death of a loved one) in five distinct stages, commonly called the five stages of grief: denial, anger, bargaining, depression, and acceptance. In the denial stage, the individual refuses to admit the reality of the situation, believing, for example, that a loved one's death is not final or that one's own terminal illness can be cured. As the reality of the situation becomes evident, the individual feels pain and responds with anger. Often, this anger is directed inappropriately, such as at the loved one who has died or at other grieving family members or friends. The bargaining stage may involve attempts to make a deal with God, or it may include a reassessment of past choices ("If I had not done X, my mother would still be alive"), both of which represent attempts to regain control. These attempts at control typically give way to depression, as the individual faces the inconsolable nature of the loss and regrets practical mistakes made in relationships with those from whom he or she is being permanently separated. The last phase, acceptance, is not reached by all who are facing their own death or who are mourning a loved one. Acceptance does not suggest happiness or forgetting but an integration of memories into the process of going about daily life.

The "five stages" model is not meant to imply that all individuals respond to death in exactly these ways or that all people move through the stages in order. Rather, the theory suggests that people move back and forth through the first four stages prior to reaching the stage of acceptance and a renewed commitment to life. Still, many

researchers and analysts have contested Kübler-Ross's model, noting that it has never been substantiated in scientific studies, that it may suggest a normative model for grief that can be counterproductive for those who experience loss differently, and that the very concept of dividing grief into discrete "stages" bears little relation to reality.

Alternative models of the grief process include Margaret Stroebe and Henk Schut's "dual process" model, which is presented in "The Dual Process Model of Coping with Bereavement: Rationale and Description" (*Death Studies*, vol. 23, no. 3, April–May 1999). Stroebe and Schut suggest that, rather than moving through distinct stages, grief is a process characterized by alternating confrontation and avoidance of the loss and the feelings associated with it. The periods of avoidance provide needed respite from the difficult periods of confrontation and allow the individual to progress toward integration of the loss in a piecemeal fashion.

Another influential theory of the grief process is the "four tasks of mourning" model pioneered by the psychologist J. William Worden (1932–), the author of *Grief Counseling and Grief Therapy* (4th ed., 2009), an influential textbook for grief counselors. Worden maintains that an individual must accomplish four tasks before completing the grieving process: accepting the reality of the loss, working through the pain of grief, adjusting to the environment characterized by the absence of the loved one, and finding a way to relocate the emotions related to the deceased so that the living person can form new relationships.

Common Attitudes toward Death and Dying

RELIGION AND THE AFTERLIFE. In the United States, attitudes toward death and dying are strongly tied to the country's persistent religiosity as compared with other developed countries, most of whose populations are far less likely to claim religious affiliation of any kind. According to Frank Newport of Gallup, Inc., in *Five Key Findings on Religion in the US* (December 23, 2016, http://www.gallup.com/poll/200186/five-key-findings-religion.aspx), in 2016 a majority (53%) of U.S. adults claimed that religion was "very important" in their life, which was a slight decrease from the percentage (59%) who gave the same answer in 1992. Gallup finds that 48.9% of respondents were Protestant or some other form of Christianity, 23% were Roman Catholic, 2.1% were Jewish, 1.8% were Mormon, and 0.8% were Muslim. Another 2.5% of Americans were believers in other religions, and 18.2% were affiliated with no religion.

Surveys undertaken by the Pew Research Center largely confirm these findings. In *America's Changing Religious Landscape* (May 12, 2015, http://assets.pew research.org/wp-content/uploads/sites/11/2015/05/RLS-08-26-full-report.pdf), Pew notes that more than three-quarters (76.5%) of Americans belonged to some religious group in 2014. This figure actually represented a decline compared with 2007, when more than four out of five (83.1%) of respondents claimed affiliation with some religion.

ANXIETIES ABOUT DEATH. Medical researchers in the late 20th and early 21st centuries have often found that young adults are typically more fearful of death than are older adults and that women typically report higher levels of anxiety about death than do men. In "Death Anxiety across the Adult Years: An Examination of Age and Gender Effects" (*Death Studies*, vol. 31, no. 6, July 2007), R. J. Russac et al. confirm these findings, noting that anxiety about death peaks around age 20 and that women report higher levels of concern about death than do men. However, the researchers also show that the decline in death anxiety after age 20 differed between men and women. Concern about death declined after age 20 in both sexes, but in women a secondary peak in anxiety about death occurred during their early 50s.

In attempting to explain these differences in attitudes toward death by age and sex, Russac et al. note that other researchers argue that older Americans come to terms with death as they age. Other hypotheses suggest that death is more appealing to older people (especially those with chronic conditions and illnesses) than to younger people, that older people are more religious and that their beliefs affect their views, and that older people have more experience with death over their lifetime and are thus less anxious about it. Russac et al. suggest that the differences might have to do with the concurrent peak in younger people's reproductive years. People of this age are likely concerned about their children and might wonder what would happen to their children if they died. Likewise, some researchers suggest that women report more anxiety about death than do men because women are the primary caretakers, not only of children but also of the elderly and those who might be dying. One hypothesis for women's secondary peak of anxiety about death in their 50s is that women reach menopause during those years, and this change of life may remind them that they are getting older and closer to death.

Ann Bowling et al. observe in "Fear of Dying in an Ethnically Diverse Society: Cross-Sectional Studies of People Aged 65+ in Britain" (*Postgraduate Medical Journal*, vol. 86, no. 1014, April 2010) that fears about dying differ among social and ethnic groups. The researchers find that in an ethnically diverse sample of study participants aged 65 years and older, Pakistani participants expressed the greatest fear of dying, whereas Chinese participants expressed the least fear. Bowling et al. conclude that when the combined ethnically diverse group of older participants was compared with an ethnically homogeneous group of older British participants, the "older people from ethnic minorities had more anxieties about dying than others, and were more likely to express fears the more extensive their family support."

CHILDREN. Prior to the 20th century, when it was the norm for people to die at home surrounded by their families and for bodies to be prepared for burial by loved ones, children experienced death as part of daily life and were part of the communal grieving that took place. In the 20th and 21st centuries, however, as death was moved into hospitals and bodies were prepared for burial by professional undertakers, children became less likely to spend time in the presence of dying people and to become acquainted with the process of grieving. Thus, children are often left to develop their attitudes toward death on their own, in accordance with their stages of development and their individual experiences (e.g., witnessing the deaths of pets and insects or characters on television). Mental health professionals strongly encourage parents to learn to communicate with their children about death. Parents must be sensitive to their children's readiness to communicate on the subject, allowing them to feel free to discuss their concerns, being attentive to children's feelings, explaining situations honestly within the limits of their understanding, and being careful not to overwhelm children with answers that are too long, elaborate, or sophisticated.

THE SERIOUSLY ILL. In "What Matters Most in End-of-Life Care: Perceptions of Seriously Ill Patients and Their Family Members" (*Canadian Medical Association Journal*, vol. 174, no. 5, February 28, 2006), Daren K. Heyland et al. explain that when patients with advanced chronic illnesses and advanced cancer were asked whether they agreed or strongly agreed about the importance of various end-of-life issues, their concerns were quite different from those of the general population. Although dying at home appears to be a priority for many Americans, dying in the location of choice (home or hospital) was 24th on the chronically ill patients' ranked list of concerns. Their top priorities (very or extremely important) were trusting their physician (ranked first), not being kept on life support when there is little hope (ranked second), having their physician communicate with them honestly (ranked third), and completing tasks and preparing for death (such as resolving conflicts and saying good-bye; ranked fourth). Seriously ill patients also revealed that they did not want to be a physical or emotional burden on their families (ranked fifth), they wanted to have an adequate plan of home care and health services when discharged from the hospital (ranked sixth), and they wanted to have relief from their symptoms (ranked seventh).

REGRETS. In *The Top Five Regrets of the Dying: A Life Transformed by the Dearly Departing* (2013), Bronnie Ware, an Australian palliative-care nurse, reports that the most common regrets of her dying patients were as follows:

1. I wish I'd had the courage to live a life true to myself, not the life others expected of me.

2. I wish I hadn't worked so hard.

3. I wish I'd had the courage to express my feelings.

4. I wish I had stayed in touch with my friends.

5. I wish I had let myself be happier.

Public Health Advances and an Aging Population

Between 1900 and 1999 the average life span of U.S. residents increased more than 30 years. According to the Centers for Disease Control and Prevention, in "Ten Great Public Health Achievements—United States, 1900–1999" (*Morbidity and Mortality Weekly Report*, vol. 48, no. 12, April 2, 1999), the most recent publication on this topic as of September 2017, "25 years of this gain are attributable to advances in public health." The introduction of compulsory vaccination led to the eradication or control of a number of life-threatening diseases, such as smallpox, polio, and measles. Expanded access to clean water and improved sanitation contributed to the prevention of other deaths resulting from infectious diseases. Elevated standards for motor-vehicle and workplace safety led to large reductions in deaths on the road and on the job, and improvements in food safety and nutrition led to decreases in harmful food-borne illnesses as well as the elimination of nutritional deficiencies. Better understanding of heart disease and stroke risks, as well as advances in treatment and early detection, led to dramatic decreases in the death rates for these conditions. Improvements in prenatal and neonatal care transformed the risks associated with pregnancy and birth: infant mortality decreased 90% over the course of the 20th century, and maternal mortality decreased 99%. With the 1964 U.S. surgeon general's report on the dangers of smoking, tobacco use began to decline, and by the early 21st century smoking-related deaths had declined dramatically.

According to Donna L. Hoyert of the National Center for Health Statistics, in *75 Years of Mortality in the United States, 1935–2010* (March 2012, http://www.cdc.gov/nchs/data/databriefs/db88.pdf), the age-adjusted rate of death (the chance that a person of any age will die in a given year, measured in terms of deaths per 100,000 people) dropped 60% between 1935 and 2010, from 1,860.1 to 746.2. (See Figure 1.2.) Death rates for all age groups except those aged 85 years and older fell more than 50%, and the risk of dying declined most dramatically for the young. (See Figure 1.3.) For individuals under the age of one year, aged one to four years, and aged five to 14 years, death rates fell more than 80%.

As Figure 1.4 shows, the gap between death rates in men and women peaked between 1975 and 1981, when there were 1.7 male deaths for every female death. This gap steadily narrowed over the next three decades, falling to 1.4 male deaths for every female death by 2010.

The major strides made in protecting the health of children represent one of the signature features of modernity in the developed world. Throughout human history, low life expectancy was intimately linked with high rates of infant and child mortality, and until the mid-20th century, the loss of a child was a commonplace experience within families. By the early 21st century the death of a child had become a rarity for families in the United States and other similarly developed countries.

These public health trends, together with the enormous size of the baby boom generation (people born between 1946 and 1964, the first of whom reached retirement age in 2011), have transformed the nature of the U.S. population. Carrie A. Werner of the U.S. Census Bureau notes in *The Older Population: 2010* (November 2011, http://www.census.gov/prod/cen2010/briefs/c2010br-09.pdf) that there were more people aged 65 years and older in the United States in 2010 than in any previous decennial census and that this sector of the population was growing more rapidly (at a rate of 15.1%) than the population at large (9.7%). As Figure 1.5 shows, in 1900 only around 3 million people in the United States were aged 65 years and older, and they accounted for a little over 4% of the population. By 2010, 40.3 million Americans were aged 65 years and older, and they accounted for 13% of the total population. These trends were expected to continue. As Figure 1.6 shows, the Census Bureau projects the over-65 population to more than double between 2014 and 2060, from 46 million to 98 million. According to Figure 1.7, the over-65 cohort is expected to increase steadily as a share of the total population, from 15% in 2014 to 24% in 2060.

The growing population of older people and the medical ability to prolong life far beyond historical norms have generated a host of societal changes and pressing issues. These issues are, for the most part, unique to the late 20th and early 21st centuries, and many of them are far from being conclusively settled. Given the ability to keep people's bodies alive through medical technology even when they are in a nonresponsive state, how do we define death? How much medical intervention should be harnessed when extending life? How should people be cared for at the end of life? Who will pay for their care? What role should the government take? Is it ethical, and should it be legal, for a terminally ill person to stop medical treatment or even actively end his or her life? At what point in the illness can such judgments be made? These are just some of the questions that this book seeks to address.

FIGURE 1.2

Number of deaths, crude death rate, and age-adjusted death rate, 1935–2010

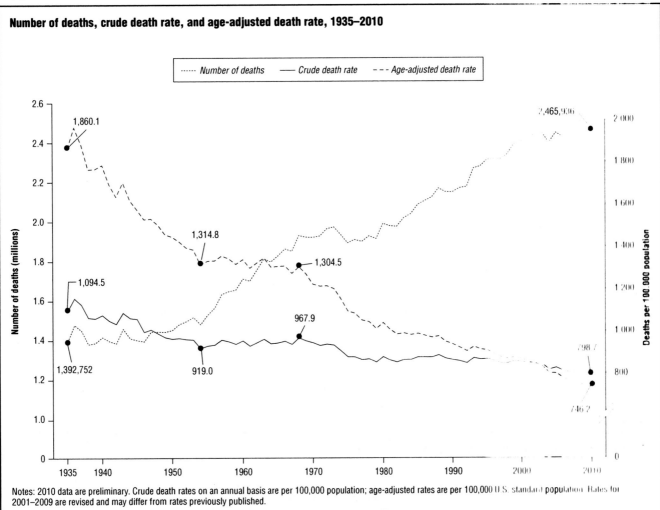

Notes: 2010 data are preliminary. Crude death rates on an annual basis are per 100,000 population; age-adjusted rates are per 100,000 U.S. standard population. Rates for 2001–2009 are revised and may differ from rates previously published.

SOURCE: Donna L. Hoyert, "Figure 1. Number of Deaths, Crude and Age-Adjusted Death Rates: United States, 1935–2010," in *75 Years of Mortality in the United States, 1935–2010,*" *NCHS Data Brief*, no. 88, Centers for Disease Control and Prevention, National Center for Health Statistics, March 2012, https://www.cdc.gov/nchs/data/databriefs/db88.pdf (accessed July 13, 2017)

FIGURE 1.3

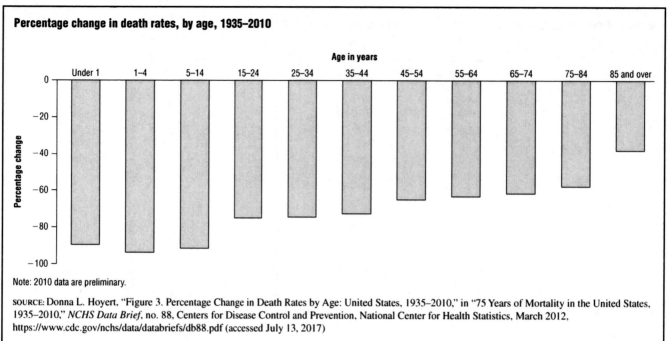

Percentage change in death rates, by age, 1935–2010

Note: 2010 data are preliminary.

SOURCE: Donna L. Hoyert, "Figure 3. Percentage Change in Death Rates by Age: United States, 1935–2010," in "75 Years of Mortality in the United States, 1935–2010," *NCHS Data Brief*, no. 88, Centers for Disease Control and Prevention, National Center for Health Statistics, March 2012, https://www.cdc.gov/nchs/data/databriefs/db88.pdf (accessed July 13, 2017)

FIGURE 1.4

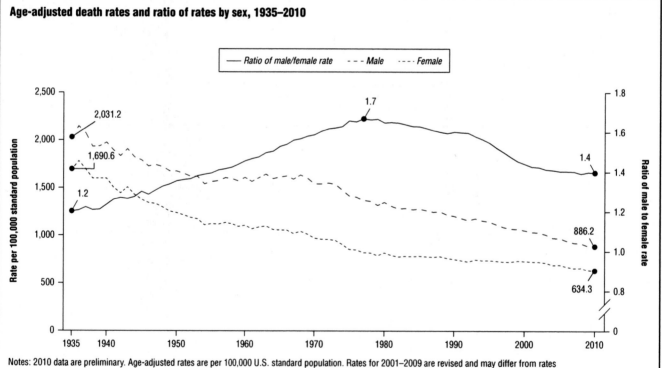

Age-adjusted death rates and ratio of rates by sex, 1935–2010

Notes: 2010 data are preliminary. Age-adjusted rates are per 100,000 U.S. standard population. Rates for 2001–2009 are revised and may differ from rates previously published.

SOURCE: Donna L. Hoyert, "Figure 4. Age-Adjusted Death Rates and Ratio of Rates by Sex: United States, 1935–2010," in "75 Years of Mortality in the United States, 1935–2010," *NCHS Data Brief*, no. 88, Centers for Disease Control and Prevention, National Center for Health Statistics, March 2012, https://www.cdc.gov/nchs/data/databriefs/db88.pdf (accessed July 13, 2017)

FIGURE 1.5

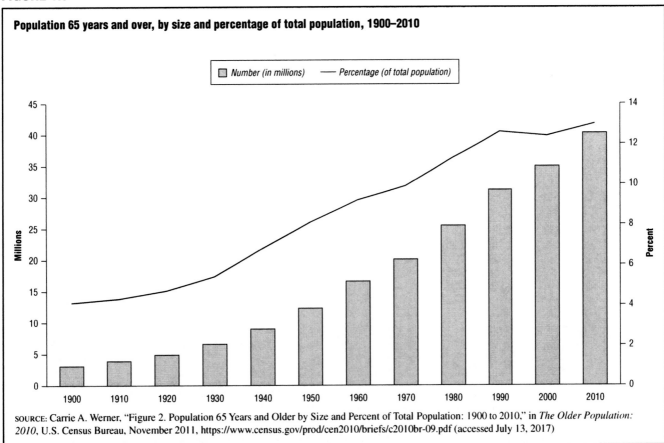

Population 65 years and over, by size and percentage of total population, 1900–2010

[Legend] Number (in millions) — Percentage (of total population)

SOURCE: Carrie A. Werner, "Figure 2. Population 65 Years and Older by Size and Percent of Total Population: 1900 to 2010," in *The Older Population: 2010*, U.S. Census Bureau, November 2011, https://www.census.gov/prod/cen2010/briefs/c2010br-09.pdf (accessed July 13, 2017)

FIGURE 1.6

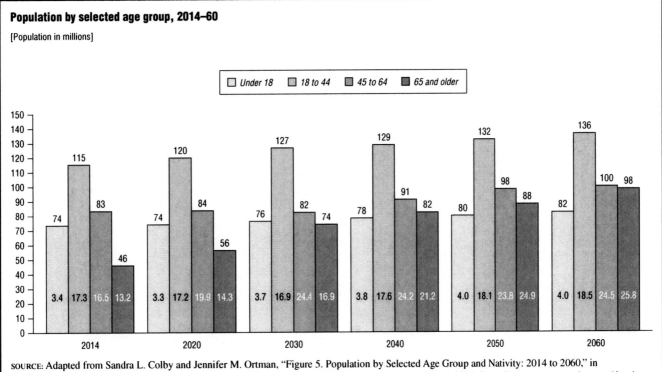

Population by selected age group, 2014–60

[Population in millions]

[Legend] Under 18   18 to 44   45 to 64   65 and older

SOURCE: Adapted from Sandra L. Colby and Jennifer M. Ortman, "Figure 5. Population by Selected Age Group and Nativity: 2014 to 2060," in *Projections of the Size and Composition of the U.S. Population: 2014 to 2060*, U.S. Census Bureau, March 2015, https://www.census.gov/content/dam/Census/library/publications/2015/demo/p25-1143.pdf (accessed July 14, 2017)

FIGURE 1.7

Age distribution of the population, 2014–60

[Percent of group's total population]

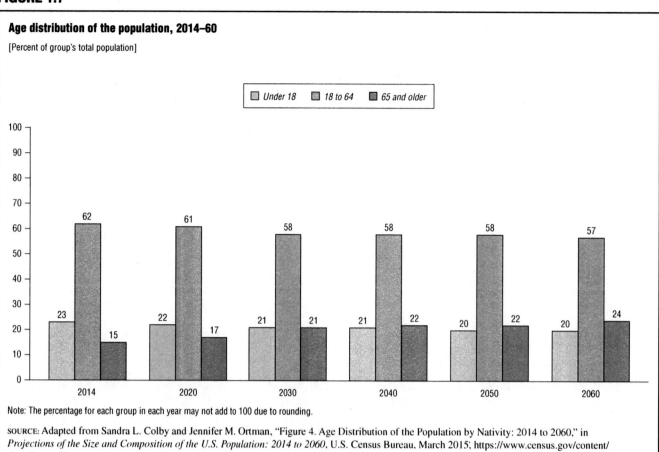

Note: The percentage for each group in each year may not add to 100 due to rounding.

SOURCE: Adapted from Sandra L. Colby and Jennifer M. Ortman, "Figure 4. Age Distribution of the Population by Nativity: 2014 to 2060," in *Projections of the Size and Composition of the U.S. Population: 2014 to 2060*, U.S. Census Bureau, March 2015; https://www.census.gov/content/dam/Census/library/publications/2015/demo/p25-1143.pdf (accessed July 14, 2017)

CHAPTER 2
REDEFINING DEATH

THE CHANGING DEFINITION OF DEATH

Prior to the age of modern medicine, determining that a person was dead consisted of determining whether he or she was breathing or had a detectable heartbeat. Respiration and blood circulation provide the body's cells with the oxygen that is needed to perform their life functions. When injury or disease prevents these operations and the supply of oxygen to the body is interrupted, the body's cells deteriorate and life ceases.

Modern life-saving measures such as cardiopulmonary resuscitation or defibrillation (electrical shock) can restart cardiac activity, however, and modern medical technologies such as the mechanical respirator, which was developed during the 1950s, can breathe on behalf of a patient whose respiratory functions would otherwise have ceased. Based on the heart and lung criteria, then, many people who would have been declared dead in prior eras can continue to live and, in some cases, recover from their injuries and diseases.

Further complicating the traditional definition of death was the development of the capacity to transplant the human heart. Experimental organ transplantations were first performed during the early decades of the 20th century, and by the 1960s transplantation of organs such as kidneys became routine practice. Kidneys could be harvested from a patient whose heart had stopped and who therefore could be declared legally dead. By contrast, a successful heart transplant required a beating heart from a "dead" donor.

On December 3, 1967, the South African surgeon Christiaan Barnard (1922–2001) transplanted a heart from a fatally injured accident victim, who was being kept alive by mechanical means, into the South African businessman Louis Washkansky (1913–1967). The transplanted heart functioned in Washkansky's body, but the drugs required to prevent his body from rejecting the organ weakened his immune system, and he died of pneumonia 18 days later. Following Barnard's success, dozens of transplant teams globally tried to improve on the transplantation process. By the end of the decade, approximately 150 patients had received transplanted hearts, but few patients lived longer than one year after the surgery due to the difficulties of suppressing the body's tendency to reject the organ. The 1980s saw improvements in the drugs needed to prevent rejection of the transplanted heart, and the increased ability to keep patients alive after surgery led to increased numbers of heart transplants across the world. In "A Brief History of Heart Transplants" (Time.com, November 16, 2009), Laura Fitzpatrick indicates that by the early 21st century more than 2,000 heart transplants were being performed annually, and over 85% of patients survived more than one year after surgery.

Because heart donors must be both fatally injured or otherwise compromised at the same time that their heart continues to function and respirators breathe on their behalf, a new definition of death was necessary to ensure that a patient was truly dead before his or her heart was removed. During the late 1960s physicians first proposed a new criterion: irreversible cessation of brain activity, or what many called brain death.

The Harvard Criteria

In 1968 the Ad Hoc Committee of the Harvard Medical School to Examine the Definition of Brain Death was organized. The goal of the Harvard Brain Death Committee, as it was also known, was to redefine death. In August 1968 the committee published the report "A Definition of Irreversible Coma" (*Journal of the American Medical Association*, vol. 205, no. 6). This landmark report, known as the Harvard Criteria, listed the following guidelines for identifying irreversible coma:

- Unreceptivity and unresponsivity—the patient is completely unaware of externally applied stimuli and inner need. He or she does not respond even to intensely painful stimuli.

- No movements or breathing—the patient shows no sign of spontaneous movements and spontaneous respiration and does not respond to pain, touch, sound, or light.

- No reflexes—the pupils of the eyes are fixed and dilated. The patient shows no eye movement even when the ear is flushed with ice water or the head is turned. He or she does not react to harmful stimuli and exhibits no tendon reflexes.

- Flat electroencephalogram (EEG)—this shows lack of electrical activity in the cerebral cortex.

The Harvard Criteria could not be used unless reversible causes of brain dysfunction, such as drug intoxication and hypothermia (abnormally low body temperature—below 90 degrees Fahrenheit [32.2 degrees C] core temperature), had been ruled out. The committee further recommended that the four criteria be repeated 24 hours after the initial test.

The Harvard committee stated, "Our primary purpose is to define irreversible coma as a new criterion for death." Despite this, the committee in effect reinforced brain death (a lack of all neurological activity in the brain and brain stem) as the legal criterion for the death of a patient. A patient who met all four guidelines could be declared dead, and his or her respirator could be withdrawn. The committee added, however, "We are concerned here only with those comatose individuals who have no discernible central nervous system activity." Brain death differs somewhat from irreversible coma; patients in deep coma may show brain activity on an EEG, although they may not be able to breathe on their own. People in a persistent vegetative state are also in an irreversible coma; however, they show more brain activity on an EEG than patients in deep coma and are able to breathe without the help of a respirator. Such patients were not considered dead by the committee's definition because they still had brain activity.

Criticisms of the Harvard Criteria

In 1978 Public Law 95-622 established the ethical advisory body called the President's Commission for the Study of Ethical Problems in Medicine and Biomedical and Behavioral Research. President Ronald Reagan (1911–2004) assigned the commission the task of defining death. In *Defining Death: A Report on the Medical, Legal and Ethical Issues in the Determination of Death* (July 1981, https://repository.library.georgetown.edu/bitstream/handle/10822/559345/defining_death.pdf?sequence=1&isAllowed=y), the commission reported that "the 'Harvard criteria' have been found to be quite reliable. Indeed, no case has yet been found that met these criteria and regained any brain functions despite continuation of respirator support."

However, the commission noted the following deficiencies in the Harvard Criteria:

- The phrase "irreversible coma" is misleading. Coma is a condition of a living person. A person lacking in brain function is dead and, therefore, beyond the condition called coma.

- The Harvard Brain Death Committee failed to note that spinal cord reflexes can continue or resume activity even after the brain stops functioning.

- "Unreceptivity" cannot be tested in an unresponsive person who has lost consciousness.

- The committee had not been "sufficiently explicit and precise" in expressing the need for adequate testing of brain stem reflexes, especially apnea (absence of the impulse to breathe, leading to an inability to breathe spontaneously). Adequate testing to eliminate drug and metabolic intoxication as possible causes of the coma had also not been spelled out explicitly. Metabolic intoxication refers to the accumulation of toxins (poisons) in the blood resulting from kidney or liver failure. These toxins can severely impair brain functioning and cause coma, but the condition is potentially reversible.

- Although all people who satisfy the Harvard Criteria are dead (with irreversible cessation of whole-brain functions), many dead individuals cannot maintain circulation long enough for retesting after a 24-hour interval.

THE GOVERNMENT REDEFINES DEATH

The president's commission proposed in *Defining Death* a model statute, the Uniform Determination of Death Act, the guidelines of which would be used to define death:

- [Determination of Death.] An individual who has sustained either (1) irreversible cessation of circulatory and respiratory functions, or (2) irreversible cessation of all functions of the entire brain, including the brain stem, is dead. A determination of death must be made in accordance with accepted medical standards.

- [Uniformity of Construction and Application.] This act shall be applied and construed to effectuate its general purpose to make uniform the law with respect to the subject of this act among states enacting it.

Brain Death

In *Defining Death*, the president's commission incorporated two formulations or concepts of the "whole-brain definition" of death. It stated that these two concepts were "actually mirror images of each other. The Commission has found them to be complementary; together they enrich one's understanding of the 'definition' [of death]."

The first whole-brain formulation states that death occurs when the three major organs (heart, lungs, and brain) suffer an irreversible functional breakdown. These organs are closely interrelated, so that if one stops functioning permanently, the other two will also stop working. Although traditionally the absence of the "vital signs" of respiration and circulation have signified death, this is simply a sign that the brain, the core organ, has permanently ceased to function. Individual cells or organs may continue to live for many hours, but the body as a whole cannot survive for long. Therefore, death can be declared even before the whole system shuts down.

The second whole-brain formulation "identifies the functioning of the whole brain as the hallmark of life because the brain is the regulator of the body's integration." Because the brain is the seat of consciousness and the director of all bodily functions, when the brain dies, the person is considered dead.

Reason for Two Definitions of Death

The president's commission claimed in *Defining Death* that its aim was to "supplement rather than supplant the existing legal concept." The brain-death criteria were not being introduced to define death in a new way. In most cases the cardiopulmonary definition of death would be sufficient. Only comatose patients on respirators would be diagnosed using the brain-death criteria.

Criteria for Determination of Death

The president's commission did not include in the proposed Uniform Determination of Death Act any specific medical criteria for diagnosing brain death. Instead, it had a group of medical consultants develop a summary of currently accepted medical practices. The commission stated in *Defining Death* that "such criteria—particularly as they relate to diagnosing death on neurological grounds—will be continually revised by the biomedical community in light of clinical experience and new scientific knowledge." These Criteria for Determination of Death read as follows (with medical details omitted here):

1. An individual with irreversible cessation of circulatory and respiratory functions is dead. A) Cessation is recognized by an appropriate clinical examination. B) Irreversibility is recognized by persistent cessation of functions during an appropriate period of observation and/or trial of therapy.

2. An individual with irreversible cessation of all functions of the entire brain, including the brainstem, is dead. A) Cessation is recognized when evaluation discloses findings that cerebral functions are absent and brainstem functions are absent. B) Irreversibility is recognized when evaluation discloses findings that the cause of coma is established and is sufficient to account for the loss of brain functions; the possibil-

ity of recovery of any brain functions is excluded; and the cessation of all brain functions persists for an appropriate period of observation and/or trial of therapy.

The Criteria for Determination of Death further warn that conditions such as drug intoxication, metabolic intoxication, and hypothermia may be confused with brain death. Physicians should practice caution when dealing with young children and people in shock. Infants and young children, who have more resistance to neurological damage, have been known to recover brain function. Shock victims might not test well due to a reduction in blood circulation to the brain.

Since the development of brain-death criteria in the United States, most countries have adopted the brain-death concept. Nevertheless, determining brain death varies worldwide. One reason has to do with cultural or religious beliefs. For example, in Japan it is believed that the soul lingers in the body for some time after death. Such a belief may influence the length of time the patient is observed before making the determination of death.

There is no federally mandated definition for brain death or method for certifying brain death. Thus, states have adopted the previously described Uniform Determination of Death Act. Within each hospital, however, clinical practice is determined by the medical staff and administrative committees. A simplified list of criteria for brain death, which was current as of September 2017, is listed in Table 2.1.

Although the practice parameter was published, several questions arose regarding the American Academy of Neurology's (AAN) guidelines, which were established in 1995. These questions are based on historical criteria. In "Evidence-Based Guideline Update: Determining

TABLE 2.1

Criteria for brain death

Coma
Absence of motor responses
Absence of pupillary responses to light and pupils at midposition with respect to dilatation (4–6 mm)
Absence of corneal reflexes
Absence of caloric responses
Absence of gag reflex
Absence of coughing in response to tracheal suctioning
Absence of respiratory drive at $PaCO_2$ that is 60 mm Hg or 20 mm Hg above normal baseline values

SOURCE: Eelco F. M. Wijdicks and Ronald E. Cranford, "Table 3. Clinical Criteria for Brain Death," in "Clinical Diagnosis of Prolonged States of Impaired Consciousness in Adults," *Mayo Clinic Proceedings*, vol. 80, no. 8, August 2005, http://download.journals.elsevierhealth.com/pdfs/journals/0025-6196/PIIS0025619611615863.pdf (accessed July 14, 2017).
Data from E. F. M. Wijdicks, "The Diagnosis of the Brain," *New England Journal of Medicine*, no. 344, 2001: 1215-21.

Brain Death in Adults" (*Neurology*, vol. 74, no. 23, June 8, 2010), Eelco F. M. Wijdicks et al. articulate the questions and seek to answer them. The questions are:

1. Are there patients who fulfill the clinical criteria of brain death who recover neurologic [nervous system] function?

2. What is an adequate observation period to ensure that cessation of neurologic function is permanent?

3. Are complex motor movements that falsely suggest retained brain function sometimes observed in brain death?

4. What is the comparative safety of techniques for determining apnea?

5. Are there new ancillary [secondary] tests that accurately identify patients with brain death?

The researchers reviewed studies between January 1996 and May 2009, and they limited their focus to adults aged 18 years and older. The answers that Wijdicks et al. report, which are endorsed by the Neurocritical Care Society, the Child Neurology Society, the Radiological Society of North America, and the American College of Radiology, are:

1. The criteria for the determination of brain death given in the 1995 AAN practice parameter have not been invalidated by published reports of neurologic recovery in patients who fulfill these criteria.

2. There is insufficient evidence to determine the minimally acceptable observation period to ensure that neurologic functions have ceased irreversibly.

3. Complex-spontaneous motor movements and false-positive triggering of the ventilator may occur in patients who are brain dead.

4. There is insufficient evidence to determine the comparative safety of techniques used for apnea testing.

5. There is insufficient evidence to determine if newer ancillary tests accurately confirm the cessation of function of the entire brain.

Wijdicks et al.'s results confirm that the parameters described in Table 2.1 remain accurate guidelines for diagnosing brain death. Moreover, these guidelines are widely accepted in developed countries throughout the world. Even so, researchers have observed considerable variation in international practices for diagnosing and documenting brain death. In the editorial "The Clinical Criteria of Brain Death throughout the World: Why Has It Come to This?" (*Canadian Journal of Anesthesia*, vol. 53, no. 6, June 2006), Wijdicks notes that a survey of medical practices in 80 countries throughout the world revealed "stunning" differences in diagnostic procedure, which were generally related to the qualification of the medical examiner, the time of observation, and the use of confirmatory tests. According to Wijdicks, there was no evidence to suggest that variations in procedure were linked to differences in religious or cultural attitudes

between countries or regions. In fact, there was no clear explanation for the disparities. To improve the accuracy and consistency of brain death diagnoses around the work, Wijdicks argues, "what is required is standardization of policy, appropriate education of staff, introduction of checklists in intensive care units, and brain death examination by designated, experienced physicians who have documented proficiency in brain death examination." In 2012 Wijdicks joined an international panel of medical experts, in collaboration with the World Health Organization, to begin the complex process of establishing International Guidelines for the Determination of Death. As of September 2017, this effort was still in progress.

Diagnosing Brain Death in Children

The American Academy of Pediatrics first issued guidelines for diagnosing brain death in children in 1987. They were updated in 2011, in keeping with the recommendations of Thomas A. Nakagawa et al. in "Clinical Report—Guidelines for the Determination of Brain Death in Infants and Children: An Update of the 1987 Task Force Recommendations" (*Pediatrics*, vol. 128, no. 3, September 2011).

Diagnosing brain death in children corresponds to the process for making diagnoses in adults, but there are variations in protocol and guidelines specific to newborns, in whom diagnosis differs from older children and adults. Whereas only one examination is required to determine brain death in adults, determination of brain death in children requires two examinations that are conducted by two different doctors. The first exam is to determine that the child has met the standard neurologic criteria for brain death. Upon the second examination, if the child's condition is determined to be unchanged and irreversible, brain death is confirmed. For term newborns (those born at or after 37 weeks of gestational age) up to 30 days of age, the exams should be separated by a 24-hour observation period. For infants 31 days old and children up to 18 years of age, the recommended observation period between exams is 12 hours.

Brain Death and Persistent Vegetative State

In the past, when someone suffered an injury that caused them to stop breathing—such as a severe head injury—they typically died shortly thereafter. Beginning in the 20th century, however, the development of rapid emergency medical interventions makes it possible to place individuals in these dire situations onto respirators before they die. Sustained by respirators, some of these people go on to recover from their condition to various degrees. In other cases, however, lack of oxygen has already caused serious, irreversible brain damage.

FIGURE 2.1

Parts of the brain

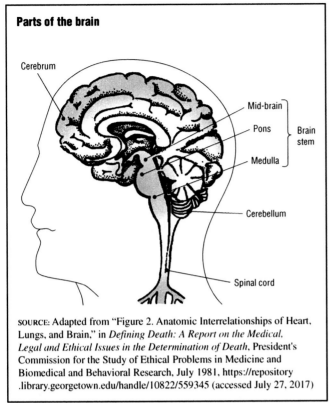

SOURCE: Adapted from "Figure 2. Anatomic Interrelationships of Heart, Lungs, and Brain," in *Defining Death: A Report on the Medical, Legal and Ethical Issues in the Determination of Death*, President's Commission for the Study of Ethical Problems in Medicine and Biomedical and Behavioral Research, July 1981, https://repository.library.georgetown.edu/handle/10822/559345 (accessed July 27, 2017)

TABLE 2.2

Criteria for persistent vegetative state (PVS)

- Unaware of surroundings or self
- Exhibits eye-opening and eye-closing cycles
- Has enough autonomic nervous system and hypothalamus function to allow long-term survival with medical care
- Unable to interact with others
- Does not respond in a sustained, reproducible, or purposeful way to sights, sounds, touches, or smells
- Does not provide evidence of understanding language nor an ability to communicate with language
- Cannot control bladder and bowel functions
- May exhibit certain cranial nerve reflexes, such as dilation and constriction of pupils and the gag reflex

SOURCE: Created by Sandra Alters for Gale, © 2017

The brain stem, traditionally called the lower brain, is usually more resistant to damage from anoxia (oxygen deprivation). Thus, oxygen deprivation may cause irreversible damage to the cerebrum, or higher brain, but may spare the brain stem. (See Figure 2.1.) When the cerebrum is irreversibly damaged yet the brain stem still functions, the patient goes into a persistent vegetative state. Persistent vegetative state patients, lacking in the higher-brain function, are awake but unaware. They swallow, grimace when in pain, yawn, open their eyes, and may even breathe without a respirator.

Table 2.2 lists the criteria for the diagnosis of the persistent vegetative state, which is also called unresponsive wakefulness syndrome. Steven Laureys et al. explain in "Unresponsive Wakefulness Syndrome: A New Name for the Vegetative State or Apallic Syndrome" (*BMC Medicine*, vol. 8, no. 68, November 1, 2010) that the use of the term *unresponsive wakefulness syndrome* is more appropriate, neutral, and descriptive. According to the researchers:

> Our proposal offers the medical community the possibility to adopt a neutral and descriptive name, unresponsive wakefulness syndrome, as an alternative to vegetative state (or apallic syndrome) which we view as outdated. We feel this is a real necessity, given that the term [persistent vegetative state] continues to have strong negative connotations after over 35 years of use, while inadvertently risking comparisons between patients and vegetables and implying persistency from the moment of

diagnosis. It should be stressed that [unresponsive wakefulness syndrome] is a clinical syndrome describing patients who fail to show voluntary motor responsiveness in the presence of eyes-open wakefulness which can be either transitory on the way to recovery from (minimal) consciousness or irreversible.

Patients in a persistent vegetative state are not dead, so the brain-death criteria do not apply to them. They can survive for years with artificial feeding and antibiotics for possible infections. In *Defining Death*, the president's commission reported on a patient who remained in a persistent vegetative state for 37 years: Elaine Esposito (1934–1978) lapsed into a coma after surgery in 1941 and died in 1978.

The case of Karen Ann Quinlan (1954–1985) called attention to the ramifications of the persistent vegetative state. In 1975 Quinlan suffered a cardiopulmonary arrest after ingesting a combination of alcohol and drugs. In 1976 Joseph Quinlan was granted court permission to discontinue artificial respiration for his comatose daughter. Even after life support was removed, Karen remained in a persistent vegetative state until she died of multiple infections in 1985.

A more recent case that refocused national attention on the persistent vegetative state was that of Terri Schiavo (1963–2005), who entered a persistent vegetative state in 1990, when her brain was deprived of oxygen during a heart attack that was brought on by an eating disorder. Michael Schiavo, her husband, argued that she would never recover and that she would not want to be kept alive by artificial means. He petitioned a Florida court to remove her feeding tube. In October 2003 a Florida judge ruled that the tube should be removed. However, Schiavo's parents believed their daughter would recover and requested that Jeb Bush (1953–), the governor of Florida, intervene. The Florida legislature subsequently gave Governor Bush the authority to override the courts, and the feeding tube was reinserted six days after its removal. In May 2004 the law that allowed

Governor Bush to intervene in the case was ruled unconstitutional by a Florida appeals court. The case was then appealed to the U.S. Supreme Court, which in January 2005 refused to hear the appeal and reinstate the Florida law. In March 2005 doctors removed Terri's feeding tube. She died 13 days later. An autopsy showed extensive damage throughout the cerebrum.

A similar case followed four years later, in 2009, when Eluana Englaro (1970–2009) died in Italy. She had been in a vegetative state for 17 years after a car accident resulted in her irreversible brain damage. Eluana's father, Beppino, tried for a decade to have his daughter's feeding tube removed, because she did not want to be kept alive by artificial means. He finally succeeded in spite of protests by the Catholic Church. Eluana died four days into the process of having her food and water diminished.

That same year the case of Rom Houben (1963–) was publicized worldwide. When Houben was 20, he was injured in an automobile accident, and his doctors eventually determined that he fell into a persistent vegetative state. Twenty-three years later he was suddenly able to communicate. Houben's doctors were convinced that he had been misdiagnosed and that he had not really been in a persistent vegetative state for all those years. However, experts questioned the man's method of communication, which is called facilitated communication. Maria Cheng explains in "Belgian Coma Patient Can't Talk after All" (Associated Press, February 19, 2010) that facilitated communication is a method by which a speech therapist helps the patient type out his or her thoughts by having the patient guide the therapist's hand. In response to questions raised about the technique, one of Houben's doctors performed tests on the method and determined that it did not work. Further tests have revealed that facilitated communication does not work with patients such as Houben. Claims that Houben could communicate were proven to be false.

Martin M. Monti et al. reveal in "Willful Modulation of Brain Activity in Disorders of Consciousness" (*New England Journal of Medicine*, vol. 362, no. 7, February 18, 2010) that they used functional magnetic resonance imaging technology to determine whether patients in a persistent vegetative state or a minimally conscious state (patients with partial preservation of conscious awareness) had brain activity that reflected "some awareness and cognition." The researchers scanned the brains of 54 previously unresponsive patients. Five of the patients showed brain activity (responsiveness) when researchers asked the patients to imagine themselves playing tennis. One of those five patients was also able to respond to questions with brain activity that is consistent with yes or no answers. Monti et al. expect that using such techniques

with patients in a persistent vegetative or minimally conscious state may help to better refine the diagnosis of their condition, provide more appropriate treatment to those who show responsiveness, and establish basic communication with patients who otherwise appear to be unresponsive. See Chapter 4 for more information on disorders of consciousness and the minimally conscious state.

THE NEAR-DEATH EXPERIENCE

The term *near-death experience* was first used by Raymond A. Moody Jr. in *Life after Life: The Investigation of a Phenomenon—Survival of Bodily Death* (1976), a compilation of interviews with people who claimed to have come back from the dead. A decade earlier, the American psychiatrist Elisabeth Kübler-Ross (1926–2004) investigated out-of-body episodes that were recounted by her patients.

The near-death experience is not a phenomenon limited to modern times. It has been recounted in various forms of mysticism and by well-known historical figures such as the Greek philosopher Plato (428–347 BC) and the Benedictine historian and theologian St. Bede the Venerable (c. 673–c. 735). It appears, however, that the development and administration of emergency resuscitation has contributed to widespread reports of near-death experiences.

Some people who were revived after having been declared clinically dead have recounted remarkably similar patterns of experiences. They report leaving their body and watching, in a detached manner, while others tried to save their life. They felt no pain and experienced complete serenity. After traveling through a tunnel, they encountered a radiant light. Some claim to have met friends and relatives who had already died; many attest to seeing their whole life replayed and of being given a choice or a command to return to their body. Many people who have had such an experience believe it to be a spiritual event of great importance. For example, they may believe that they saw, or even entered, the afterlife.

Scientists have investigated whether there are potential physical explanations for near-death experiences. Studies conducted during the 1990s indicated that the near-death experience might be related to one or more physical changes in the brain. These changes include the gradual onset of anoxia in the brain, residual electrical activity in the brain, the release of endorphins in response to stress, or drug-induced hallucinations produced by drug therapies that are used during resuscitation attempts or resulting from previous drug abuse. In "Near-Death Experiences and the Temporal Lobe" (*Psychological Science*, vol. 15, no. 4, April 2004), Willoughby B. Britton and Richard R. Bootzin of the University of Arizona discuss the results of their study of temporal lobe functioning in 43 individuals who had experienced life-threatening events. Of the 43 participants, 23 reported having had near-death experiences during these events. The researchers find that people who reported near-death experiences had more of certain types of temporal lobe activity than those who did not have such experiences. Britton and Bootzin conclude that "altered temporal lobe functioning may be involved in the near-death experience and that individuals who have had such experiences are physiologically distinct from the general population."

C. van Tellingen describes in "Heaven Can Wait—or Down to Earth in Real Time: Near-Death Experience Revisited" (*Netherlands Heart Journal*, vol. 16, no. 10, October 2008) a neurophysiological explanation for near-death experiences. Van Tellingen suggests that as the body's nerve cells and their connections break down, "reminiscences, memories and building stones of the personal identity are 'released' and strengthen a feeling of time travel and life review. Perhaps this situation is more or less comparable with the situation in old age when literally loss of neurons and their connections bring back 'buried' memories and reminiscences." Dean Mobbs and Caroline Watt agree and conclude in "There Is Nothing Paranormal about Near-Death Experiences: How Neuroscience Can Explain Seeing Bright Lights, Meeting the Dead, or Being Convinced You Are One of Them" (*Trends in Cognitive Sciences*, vol. 15, no. 10, August 18, 2011) that "near-death experiences are the manifestation of normal brain function gone awry, during a traumatic, and sometimes harmless, event."

Jimo Borjigin et al. shed further light on what may occur in the brain as the body approaches death in "Surge of Neurophysical Coherence and Connectivity in the Dying Brain" (*Proceedings of the National Academy of Sciences of the United States of America*, vol. 110, no. 28, July 9, 2013). In research conducted on dying rats, the authors found that, contrary to the conventional wisdom maintaining that the brain became inactive at the point of clinical death, brain activity spikes at the point of death, exceeding comparable activity during periods of wakefulness. Furthermore, the researchers found increased levels of gamma oscillations (a form of high-frequency brainwave) near the visual cortex, the part of the brain responsible for the processing of visual sensations, which could be linked to the reports of near-death experiences involving radiant light. Experts noted that these findings were extremely preliminary, however. "This is an interesting and well-conducted piece of research," Chris Chambers of Cardiff University told Rebecca Morelle in "Near-Death Experiences Are Electrical Surge in Dying Brain" (BBC.co.uk, August 12, 2013). "We know precious little about brain activity during death, let alone conscious brain activity.... [But] we should be extremely cautious before drawing any conclusions about human near-death experiences: it is one thing to measure brain activity in rats during cardiac arrest, and quite another to relate that to human experience."

Pam Reynolds, a singer-songwriter who had a near-death experience while undergoing brain surgery in Arizona in 1991, lived to tell a compelling story of her experience. Barbara Bradley Hagerty reports in "Decoding the Mystery of Near-Death Experiences" (NPR.org, May 22, 2009) that Reynolds was undergoing a rare form of neurosurgery to remove an aneurysm, that involved "chilling her body, draining the blood out of her head like oil from a car engine, snipping the aneurysm and then bringing her back from the edge of death." As part of the procedure, the medical team placed special headphones in her ears and played deafening sounds that they believed would make it impossible for Reynolds to hear anything else. They also taped her eyes shut. Reynolds, who was deeply comatose during the procedure, with a stopped heart and no brain activity, later described a near-death experience in which she "popped out" of the top of her head and watched her body being attended to by 20 physicians, accompanied by her deceased grandmother and uncle. She heard the sound of a drill and observed the saw that her neurosurgeon was using to perform the surgery; she heard a female voice say, "Her arteries are too small" in reference to her groin area; and she heard the classic rock song "Hotel California" by the Eagles.

Reynolds initially took these sensations for a hallucination, but a year after the operation, she discussed the details of her experience with the neurosurgeon who had led the surgery, and her account matched his own memory of the procedure. Years later, Michael Sabom, a cardiologist who was researching near-death experiences, examined the records from Reynolds's surgery and found that her account of what had happened matched the records with startling exactitude. There were 20 doctors in the room, there was a conversation about the veins in her left leg, "Hotel California" was playing on the stereo, and the saw that the neurosurgeon used matched Reynolds's description. "She could not have heard [it]," Sabom told Hagerty, "because of what they did to her ears.... In addition, both of her eyes were taped shut, so she couldn't open her eyes and see what was going on. So her physical sensory perception was off the table." Although some see Reynolds's experience and others like it as evidence that consciousness—and, by extension, an entity such as the soul or spirit—can exist outside of the body, anecdotes such as hers do not rise to the level of scientific evidence. Furthermore, critics charge that there are other possible explanations for her experience. The anesthesiologist Gerald Woerlee, who studied Reynolds's case, told Hagerty that he believes she experienced "anesthesia awareness," a condition in which a person is conscious but cannot move, and that she heard parts of the operation because her headphones did not work as intended. In any case, scientific proof of what happens in near-death experiences such as Reynolds's may be impossible to achieve given the moral, ethical, and legal issues that would be involved in experimentally inducing death or near-death in human beings.

CHAPTER 3
THE END OF LIFE: ETHICAL CONSIDERATIONS

Difficulties in defining death present but one of the many ethical dilemmas related to end-of-life care and decision making. Decisions concerning the withdrawal of life-support efforts for people who are in persistent vegetative states are often even more controversial. Because of the diversity of religious and other belief systems that influence people's opinions about such matters of life and death, there exist no universal standards for making determinations about when, and for whom, such measures are appropriate. Besides the fact that the intentional discontinuation of life support is itself controversial, in many cases such decisions must be made by the spouses, parents, or adult children of the individuals involved, complicating matters still further. How much weight should be given to the patient's wishes versus the ethical convictions of the decision makers and the physicians and other personnel charged with carrying out the decision? Who should determine when medical care is futile and no longer benefits the dying patient?

RELIGIOUS TEACHINGS

All major religions consider life sacred. When it comes to death and dying, they take seriously the fate of the soul, be it eternal salvation (as in Christian belief) or reincarnation (as in Buddhist philosophy). Much of the debate surrounding end-of-life issues centers on the strongly held beliefs of people and institutions with religious affiliations.

Roman Catholicism

According to Catholic teachings, death is contrary to God's plan for humankind. When God created the first human beings, Adam and Eve, he did not intend for them to die. When Adam and Eve, however, disobeyed God in the Garden of Eden, physical death was the consequence of their sin. The New Testament of the Bible explains that Jesus was the son of God who, out of love for humankind, was born into the world and died as a man.

God raised Jesus from the dead after his crucifixion to live eternally with him in heaven, and Jesus promised humankind the same opportunity. The Vatican notes in *Catechism of the Catholic Church* (August 23, 2002, http://www.vatican.va/archive/ccc_css/archive/catechism/ccc_toc.htm) that according to Christian doctrine, Jesus "transformed the curse of death into a blessing."

HISTORY. Early Christians believed that God was the giver of life and that he alone could take life away. They viewed euthanasia (hastening the death of a dying, suffering patient who requests death) as usurping that divine right. The Christian philosopher St. Augustine of Hippo (354–430) taught that people must accept suffering because it comes from God. According to Augustine, suffering not only helps Christians grow spiritually but also prepares them for the eternal joy that God has in store for them. Moreover, the healthy were exhorted to minister to the sick not for the purpose of helping to permanently end their suffering, but to ease their pain.

St. Thomas Aquinas (c. 1225–1274), the most influential Catholic thinker after Augustine, taught that ending one's suffering by ending one's life was sinful. To help another take his or her life was just as sinful. Not all Catholic thinkers have always agreed. In 1516 Sir Thomas More (1478–1535), an English statesman, humanist, and loyal defender of the Catholic Church, published *Utopia*, which described an ideal country governed by reason. If a disease is not only incurable but also causes pain that is hard to control, in More's *Utopia* it is permissible to free the sufferer from his or her painful existence. This was a major departure from the medieval acceptance of suffering and death as the earthly price to be paid for eternal life.

RULE OF DOUBLE EFFECT. Thomas Aquinas is believed to have first formulated the ethical principle of "double effect," which has been influential among Catholic theologians and other moral philosophers. According to this principle, an action that might be wrong if committed intentionally is acceptable if committed unintentionally. Thomas Aquinas introduced the idea in the context of killing an assailant in self-defense, a situation that creates two effects: the saving of one's life and the ending of the life of another. The rule of double effect was not unconditional, however. Even a well-intentioned person who killed in self-defense might err in moral terms if his response was disproportionate, for example by being excessively violent.

The rule of double effect has been applied by Catholics to discussions surrounding end-of-life care. For example, a physician may prescribe an increased dosage of the painkiller morphine to ease a patient's pain, even if the physician reasonably foresees that it might bring about the patient's death. Pain relief, not death, is the intent, although both effects may result from the administration of the drugs. In *Catechism of the Catholic Church*, the Vatican states that "the use of painkillers to alleviate the sufferings of the dying, even at the risk of shortening their days, can be morally in conformity with human dignity if death is not willed as either an end or a means, but only foreseen and tolerated as inevitable."

ON EUTHANASIA. Since the mid-20th century Catholic theologians have debated balancing the preservation of God-given life with the moral issue of continuing medical treatments that are of no apparent value to patients. In "The Prolongation of Life" (1957), Pope Pius XII (1876–1958) states that if a patient is hopelessly ill, physicians may discontinue heroic measures "to permit the patient, already virtually dead, to pass on in peace." He adds that if the patient is unconscious, relatives may request withdrawal of life support under certain conditions.

The Vatican's 1980 *Declaration on Euthanasia* (http://www.vatican.va/roman_curia/congregations/cfaith/documents/rc_con_cfaith_doc_19800505_euthanasia_en.html) outlines the official Catholic Church stance on euthanasia today. It defines the term thus: "By euthanasia is understood an action or an omission which of itself or by intention causes death, in order that all suffering may in this way be eliminated." The declaration notes that a person cannot ask for euthanasia no matter what the situation, because it is a "violation of the divine law" and it is almost always an "anguished plea for help and love." The declaration indicates, however, that a dying patient may be administered painkilling medications at the end of life to help him or her be more comfortable.

The Committee for Pro-Life Activities of the National Conference of Catholic Bishops states in *Nutrition and Hydration: Moral and Pastoral Reflections* (April 1992, http://www.priestsforlife.org/magisterium/bishops/92-04nutritionandhydrationnccbprolifecommittee.htm) that "in the final stage of dying one is not obliged to prolong the life of a patient by every possible means:

'When inevitable death is imminent in spite of the means used, it is permitted in conscience to take the decision to refuse forms of treatment that would only secure a precarious and burdensome prolongation of life, so long as the normal care due to the sick person in similar cases is not interrupted.'" However, the Vatican's Congregation for the Doctrine of the Faith ruled in 2007 that a person in a persistent vegetative state must receive nutrition and hydration. Pope Benedict XVI (1927–) approved the ruling. Pope Francis (1936–), who succeeded Benedict in 2013, maintained a strict opposition to euthanasia in keeping with the *Catechism of the Catholic Church*, which states that "direct euthanasia" is "morally unacceptable" in any situation under the Fifth Commandment.

The Eastern Orthodox Church

The Eastern Orthodox Church, which resulted from the division between eastern and western Christianity during the 11th century, does not have a single worldwide leader such as the Roman Catholic pope. Instead, national jurisdictions called sees are each governed by a bishop. Accordingly, Eastern Orthodoxy relies on the scriptures, traditions, and decrees of the first seven ecumenical councils to regulate its daily conduct. Concerning matters of morality in the 21st century, such as the debates on end-of-life issues, contemporary Orthodox ethicists explore possible courses of action that are in line with the "sense of the church." The sense of the church is deduced from church laws and dissertations of the church fathers, as well as from previous council decisions. Their recommendations are subject to further review.

In "The Stand of the Orthodox Church on Controversial Issues" (2014, https://www.goarch.org/-/the-stand-of-the-orthodox-church-on-controversial-issues), the Reverend Stanley S. Harakas of the Greek Orthodox Archdiocese of America (a branch of the larger Eastern Orthodox faith), states "the Orthodox Church has a very strong pro-life stand which in part expresses itself in opposition to doctrinaire advocacy of euthanasia." However, Harakas notes that "as current Orthodox theology expresses it: 'The Church distinguishes between euthanasia and the withholding of extraordinary means to prolong life. It affirms the sanctity of human life and man's God-given responsibility to preserve life. But it rejects an attitude which disregards the inevitability of physical death.'"

Protestantism

The different denominations of Protestantism have varying positions on end-of-life care. Many hold that euthanasia is morally wrong, but they also believe that prolonging life by extraordinary measures is not necessary. In other words, few leaders of any Protestant church would condone active euthanasia, but many consider the withdrawal of life support from a dying patient to be morally acceptable. Among the Protestant denominations that support this latter view are the Jehovah's Witnesses, the Church of Jesus Christ of Latter-Day Saints (Mormons), the Lutheran Church, the Reformed Presbyterians, the Presbyterian Church in America, the Christian Life Commission of the Southern Baptist Convention, and the General Association of the General Baptists.

Some denominations have no official policy on euthanasia. However, many individual ethicists and representatives within these churches agree with other denominations that euthanasia is morally wrong but that futile life support serves no purpose. Among these churches are the Seventh-Day Adventists, the Episcopal Church, and the United Methodist Church.

Christian Scientists believe that prayer heals all diseases. They claim that illnesses are mental in origin and therefore cannot be cured by outside intervention, such as medical help. Some also believe that seeking medical help while praying diminishes or even cancels the effectiveness of the prayers. Because they feel that God can heal even those diseases that others see as incurable, withholding medical care has no practical significance among Christian Scientists.

The Unitarian Universalist Association, a union of the Unitarian and Universalist Churches, is perhaps the most liberal when it comes to the right to die. The association states in "The Right to Die with Dignity: 1988 General Resolution" (2017, http://www.uua.org/action/statements/right-die-dignity) that "human life has inherent dignity, which may be compromised when life is extended beyond the will or ability of a person to sustain that dignity." Furthermore, "Unitarian Universalists advocate the right to self-determination in dying, and the release from civil or criminal penalties of those who, under proper safeguards, act to honor the right of terminally ill patients to select the time of their own deaths."

Judaism

There are three main branches of Judaism in the United States. The Orthodox tradition adheres strictly to Jewish laws. Conservative Judaism advocates adapting Jewish precepts to a changing world, but all changes must be consistent with Jewish laws and tradition. Reform Judaism, while accepting the ethical laws as coming from God, generally considers the other laws of Judaism as "instructional but not binding."

Like the Roman Catholics, Jews believe that life is precious because it is a gift from God. No one has the right to extinguish life, because one's life is not his or hers in the first place. Generally, rabbis from all branches of Judaism agree that euthanasia is not morally justified. It is tantamount to murder, which is forbidden by the Torah. Moreover, Jewish teaching holds that men and women are stewards entrusted with the preservation of God's gift of life and therefore are obliged to hold on to that life as long as possible.

PROLONGING LIFE VERSUS HASTENING DEATH. Although Jewish tradition maintains that a devout believer must do everything possible to prolong life, this admonition is subject to interpretation even among Orthodox Jews.

The Torah and the Talmud (the definitive rabbinical compilation of Jewish laws, lore, and commentary) provide the principles and laws that guide Jews. The Talmud offers continuity to Jewish culture by interpreting the Torah and adapting it to the constantly changing situations of Jewish people.

On the subject of prolonging life versus hastening death, the Talmud narrates a number of situations that involve people who are considered "goses" (literally, "the death rattle is in the patient's throat" or "one whose death is imminent"). Scholars often refer to the story of Rabbi Hanina ben Teradyon, who, during the second century, was condemned to be burned to death by the Romans. To prolong his agonizing death, the Romans wrapped him in some wet material. At first, the rabbi refused to hasten his own death; however, he later agreed to have the wet material removed, thus bringing about a quicker death.

Some Jews interpret this Talmudic narration to mean that in the final stage of a person's life it is permissible to remove any hindrance to the dying process. In this modern age of medicine, this may mean implementing a patient's wish, such as a do-not-resuscitate order or the withdrawal of artificial life support.

Islam

Islam was founded by the prophet Muhammad (c. 570–632) during the seventh century. The Koran, which is composed of Allah's (God's) revelations to Muhammad, and the sunna, Muhammad's teachings and deeds, are the sources of Islamic beliefs and practice. Although there are many sects and cultural diversities within the religion, all Muslims (followers of Islam) are bound by a total submission to the will of Allah. The basic doctrines of Allah's revelations were systematized into definitive rules and regulations that now make up the sharia (the religious law that governs the life of Muslims).

Muslims look to the sharia for ethical guidance in all aspects of life, including medicine. Sickness and pain are part of life and must be accepted as Allah's will. They should be viewed as a means to atone for one's sins. By contrast, death is simply a passage to another existence in the afterlife. Those who die after leading a righteous life will merit the true life on Judgment Day. The Koran states, "How do you disbelieve in God seeing you were dead and He gave you life and then He shall cause you to die, then He shall give you life, then unto Him you shall be returned?"

Islam teaches that life is a gift from Allah; therefore, no one can end it except Allah. Muhammad said, "Whosoever takes poison and thus kills himself, his poison will be in his hand; he will be tasting it in Hell, always abiding therein, and being accommodated therein forever" (compiled in *Sahih Bukhari*). Although an ailing person does not have the right to choose death, even if he or she is suffering, Muslims heed the following admonition from the *Islamic Code of Medical Ethics* (1981): "[The] doctor is well advised to realize his limit and not transgress it. If it is scientifically certain that life cannot be restored, then it is futile to diligently [maintain] the vegetative state of the patient by heroic means.... It is the process of life that the doctor aims to maintain and not the process of dying. In any case, the doctor shall not take a positive measure to terminate the patient's life."

Hinduism

The Eastern religious tradition of Hinduism is based on the principle of reincarnation (the cycle of life, death, and physical rebirth). Hindus believe that death and dying are intricately interwoven with life and that the individual soul undergoes a series of physical life cycles before uniting with Brahman (God or the ultimate reality). Karma refers to the ethical consequences of a person's actions during a previous life, which determine the quality of his or her present life. A person can neither change nor escape his or her karma. By conforming to dharma (religious and moral law), an individual is able to fulfill obligations from the past life. Life is sacred because it offers one the chance to perform good acts toward the goal of ending the cycle of rebirths.

Therefore, a believer in Hinduism views pain and suffering as personal karma, and serious illness as a consequence of past misdeeds. Death is simply a passage to another rebirth, which brings one closer to Brahman. Artificial medical treatments to sustain life are not recommended, and medical intervention to end life is discouraged. Euthanasia simply interrupts one's karma and the soul's evolution toward final liberation from reincarnation.

Buddhism

Buddhism, like Hinduism, has a cosmology involving a cycle of reincarnation. To Buddhists, the goals of every life are the emancipation from samsara (the compulsory cycle of rebirths) and the attainment of nirvana (enlightenment or bliss). Like the Hindus, Buddhists believe that sickness, death, and karma are interrelated. The followers of Buddha (563–480 BC), the founder of Buddhism, claim that Buddha advised against taking too strict a position when it comes to issues such as the right to die.

Tenzin Gyatso (1935–), the 14th Dalai Lama, the spiritual leader of Tibetan Buddhism, has commented on the use of mechanical life support when the patient has no chance of recovery. Sogyal Rinpoche explains in *The Tibetan Book of Living and Dying* (1992) that the Dalai Lama advises that each case be considered individually: "If there is no such chance for positive thoughts [Buddhists believe that a dying person's final thoughts determine the circumstances of his or her next life], and in addition a lot of money is being spent by relatives simply to keep someone alive, then there seems to be no point. But each case must be dealt with individually; it is very difficult to generalize."

SECULAR PERSPECTIVES

Atheists and others whose moral beliefs are human-centered, or secular, rather than based on divine law or religious dogma, share no single set of beliefs on end-of-life issues such as the prolongation of life and euthanasia. Nevertheless, secular belief systems are generally more likely to privilege human dignity and the wishes of the individual person, rather than adhering to one-size-fits-all rules regarding the sanctity of life. Secularists are more likely than most religious people to agree with the idea that every case must be considered individually rather than in accordance with belief systems that cannot, in a modern world characterized by a diversity of religions and moral systems, claim universal applicability. Many of the strongest arguments in favor of allowing people to make their own choices regarding the end of life are rooted in secular viewpoints.

There are a number of secular, rights-based arguments in favor of ending life either through the withdrawal of life support or through active euthanasia. One argument is that humans have the right to die at a time and in the manner of their choosing; another, similar argument is that the right to life implies a right to die; still others argue that the rights to privacy and to determine one's own belief system imply a right to die. Many secular thinkers, however, would place limits on each of these arguments by maintaining that these rights must be balanced with the individual's obligations. For example, a terminally ill person may not have an unconditional right to die when and how he or she wishes when dependent children or other loved ones will be affected by the death. In such cases, the individual's rights should be balanced against the obligations he or she has to those other people.

Other secular thinkers argue that it is immoral to require people to suffer against their will and in situations in which they have no hope for meaningful life. Against religious arguments maintaining that life in all its manifestations is sacred and must be defended, some secularists maintain that forcing people to prolong a life that presents them only with agony represents a degradation of life.

MEDICAL ETHICS AND THE PERSPECTIVES OF HEALTH CARE PROFESSIONALS

Medical practice has always been governed by ethical codes and concerned with ethical issues that arise in matters of life, death, and illness. Physicians since the mid-20th century, however, have been faced with far more—and far more complicated—ethical dilemmas than their counterparts in earlier eras of human history.

The Hippocratic Oath

The earliest written document to deal with medical ethics is generally attributed to Hippocrates (460–377 BC), an ancient Greek physician traditionally considered the father of medicine. For more than 2,000 years the Hippocratic oath has stood as the centerpiece of medical ethics in the Western world, defining the conduct of health care providers in the discharge of their duties. In part, the oath states: "I will follow that method of treatment, which, according to my ability and judgment, I consider for the benefit of my patients, and abstain from whatever is deleterious [harmful] and mischievous. I will give no deadly medicine to anyone if asked, nor suggest any such counsel."

Some scholars claim that the giving of "deadly medicine" does not refer to euthanasia. During the time of Hippocrates, helping a suffering person end his or her life was common practice. Therefore, the oath might have been a commitment to avoid acting as an accomplice to murder, rather than a promise to refrain from the practice of euthanasia.

Most physicians, moreover, believe that a literal interpretation of the oath is not necessary. It simply offers guidelines that allow for adaptation to 21st-century situations. In fact, in 1948 the World Medical Association modified the Hippocratic oath to call attention to the atrocities that were committed by Nazi physicians. Known as the Declaration of Geneva (2017, http://www.cirp.org/library/ethics/geneva/), the document reads in part: "I will practice my profession with conscience and dignity; the health of my patient will be my first consideration.... I will not permit considerations of religion, nationality, race, party politics or social standing to intervene between my duty and my patient. I will maintain the utmost respect for human life from the time of conception, even under threat, I will not use my medical knowledge contrary to the laws of humanity."

The Changing Patient–Physician Relationship

In all periods of human history, the practice of medicine has presupposed that physicians are able to determine what is best for their patients, often more effectively than the patients themselves. Prior to the mid-20th century, it was common for patients to rely on their doctors' abilities and judgment without question. Doctors were not even required to tell their patients the details of their illnesses or to disclose that an illness was terminal. Beginning in the 1960s, however, patients generally began to assume a more active role in their medical care. An emphasis on preventive medicine encouraged people to take responsibility for their own health, and physicians encouraged patients to be active participants in the health care process. Patients have also generally become more attentive to technologies and procedures that have changed the practice of medicine. As a result of this new patient–physician relationship, health care providers have become responsible for fully informing and educating patients, and increasingly they have been found legally liable for failing to inform patients of the consequences of medical treatments and procedures.

To compound the complexity of the changing patient–physician relationship, modern technology can prolong death as well as life. Historically, physicians had been trained to prevent and combat death, rather than to deal with dying patients, communicate with the patient and the family about a terminal illness, prepare them for an imminent death, or respond to a patient requesting assisted suicide.

Contemporary Ethical Guidelines for Physicians

For most of history, physicians' training has been focused on the saving of lives, not on the process of dying. Ira R. Byock, a well-known palliative care physician (palliative care is focused on relieving pain and stress in seriously ill patients) and a former president of the American Academy of Hospice and Palliative Medicine, admits in one of his early books, *Dying Well: The Prospect for Growth at the End of Life* (1997), that "a strong presumption throughout my medical career was that all seriously ill people required vigorous life-prolonging treatment, including those who were expected to die, even patients with advanced chronic illness such as widespread cancer, end stage congestive heart failure, and kidney or liver failure. It even extended to patients who saw death as a relief from suffering caused by their illness."

More recent medical education, however, has changed the focus from life-prolonging treatment for all patients to one of understanding the futility of prolonging the life, and process of dying, of a terminally ill and actively dying patient. Medical ethics now recognizes the obligation of physicians to shift the intent of care for dying patients from that of futile procedures that may only increase patient distress to that of comfort and closure.

The AMA provides ethical guidelines to help educate and support physicians in such end-of-life care. In *Code of Medical Ethics* (2016, https://www.ama-assn.org/delivering-care/ama-code-medical-ethics), the AMA provides end-of-life ethical guidelines in the following areas:

5.1 "Advance Care Planning"; 5.2 "Advance Directives"; 5.3 "Withholding or Withdrawing Life-Sustaining Medical Treatment"; 5.4 "Orders Not to Attempt Resuscitation (DNAR)"; 5.5 "Medically Ineffective Interventions"; 5.6 "Sedation to Unconsciousness in End-of-Life Care"; 5.7 "Physician-Assisted Suicide"; and 5.8 "Euthanasia." For example, the section on "Withholding or Withdrawing Life-Sustaining Medical Treatment" (2016, https://www.ama-assn.org/sites/default/files/media-browser/code-of-medical-ethics-chapter-5.pdf) states in part: "a patient who has decision-making capacity appropriate to the decision at hand has the right to decline any medical intervention or ask that an intervention be stopped, even when that decision is expected to lead to his or her death and regardless of whether or not the individual is terminally ill.... While there may be an emotional difference between not initiating an intervention at all and discontinuing it later in the course of care, there is no ethical difference between withholding and withdrawing treatment. When an intervention no longer helps to achieve the patient's goals for care or desired quality of life, it is ethically appropriate for physicians to withdraw it."

Sameera Karnik and Amar Kanekar note in "Ethical Issues Surrounding End-of-Life Care: A Narrative Review" (*Healthcare*, vol. 4, no. 2, 2016) that continuing advancements in medical science, which enable doctors to extend life in ways that were not previously possible, have brought end-of-life care decision making to the forefront of medical ethics debates. The authors emphasize that health care clinicians have a duty to "promote communication, education and discussion related to end-of-life care preferences and their implications among the patient, and their families in order to facilitate improved decision making."

MEDICAL EDUCATION IN DEATH AND DYING. Training in end-of-life care was not widely recognized as an important component of medical education until the late 20th century. In "Educating Medical Students about Death and Dying" (*Archives of Disease in Childhood*, vol. 64, no. 5, May 1989), D. Black, D. Hardoff, and J. Nelki note that, in a review of the medical literature between 1960 and 1971, they found no articles about the teaching of death and dying to medical students. This began to change in the 1970s.

George E. Dickinson of the College of Charleston (South Carolina) studied medical school offerings on end-of-life issues and palliative care by mailing brief questionnaires to all accredited U.S. medical schools every five years from 1975 to 2010. His findings, published in "Thirty-Five Years of End-of-Life Issues in U.S. Medical Schools" (*American Journal of Hospice and Palliative Medicine*, vol. 28, no. 6, 2011) provide an overview of the growing attention paid to these issues. By 2000, all of the responding schools provided some

content on death and dying; by 2010, 99% offered some palliative care education. Student participation in end-of-life and palliative care content increased from 71% in 1975 to 100% in 2010. Even so, this content was usually delivered as short modules within larger courses, rather than as separate, dedicated courses. On average, schools offered only 12 teaching hours in palliative care over the term of their degree programs.

In "Improving Medical Graduates' Training in Palliative Care: Advancing Education and Practice" (*Advances in Medical Education and Practice*, vol. 7, 2016), Barbara A. Head et al. note that despite improvements in palliative care education, "new doctors continue to report palliative care as the area in which they experience distress and feel unprepared." Reviewing a number of other recent studies of palliative education in U.S. medical schools, the researchers report a general consensus that the curriculum remains "variable and underdeveloped.... largely due to an already overstrained curricula, insufficient time, lack of faculty expertise, and inadequate funding." In conclusion, the authors recommend that "a comprehensive palliative care curriculum focused on competency development and integrated throughout the 4 years of medical education should be the goal of every medical school across the world."

PATIENT AUTONOMY

Principles of patient autonomy have increasingly informed the physician–patient relationship and influenced the process of end-of-life care. Competent patients, as defenders of personal autonomy argue, have the right to self-rule—to choose among medically recommended treatments and to refuse any treatment they do not want. To be truly autonomous, a patient has to be told about the nature of his or her illness, the prospects for recovery, the course of the illness, alternative treatments, and treatment consequences. After thoughtful consideration, a patient makes an informed choice and grants "informed consent" to treatment or decides to forgo treatment. Decisions about medical treatment may be influenced by the patient's psychological state, family history, culture, values, and religious beliefs.

Cultural Differences

Although patient autonomy is a fundamental aspect of medical ethics, not all patients want to know about their illnesses or be involved in decisions about their terminal care. In their widely cited study, "Cultural Diversity at the End of Life: Issues and Guidelines for Family Physicians" (*American Family Physician*, vol. 71, no. 3, February 1, 2005), H. Russell Searight and Jennifer Gafford of the Forest Park Hospital Family Medicine Residency Program in St. Louis, Missouri, point out that the concept of patient autonomy is not easily applied to members of some racial and ethnic groups. Searight and Gafford explain the three basic dimensions in end-of-life treatment that vary culturally: communication of bad news, locus of decision making, and attitudes toward advance directives and end-of-life care.

Members of some ethnic groups, including a variety of people from African nations and people from Japan, soften bad news with terms that do not overtly state that a person has a potentially terminal condition. For example, the term *growth* or *blood disease* may be used rather than telling a person he or she has a cancerous tumor or leukemia. This concept is taken one step further in many Hispanic, Chinese, and Pakistani communities, in which the terminally ill are generally protected from knowledge of their condition. Many reasons exist for this type of behavior, such as viewing the discussion of serious illness and death as disrespectful or impolite, not wanting to cause anxiety or eliminate hope in the patient, or believing that speaking about a condition makes it real. Many people of Asian and European cultures believe that it is cruel to inform a patient of a terminal diagnosis.

Another excellent study on multiculturalism in death and dying issues is Jessica Doolen and Nancy L. York's "Cultural Differences with End-of-Life Care in the Critical Care Unit" (*Dimensions of Critical Care Nursing*, vol. 26, no. 5, September–October 2007). In this study the researchers add similar cultural scenarios in communication about death and dying to those outlined by Searight and Gafford. Doolen and York note that South Koreans generally do not talk about the dying process because it fosters sadness and because such discussions may quicken the dying process. According to the authors Filipinos similarly believe that such discussions may hasten death and interfere with God's will.

The phrase "locus of decision making" refers to the network of people who make end-of-life decisions together: the physician, the family, and/or the patient. Searight and Gafford explain that the locus of decision making varies among cultures. For example, in North America the patient typically plays the primary role in the decision-making process. South Koreans and Mexicans often approach end-of-life decision making differently, abiding by a collective process in which relatives may make treatment choices for a family member without that person's input. Eastern Europeans and Russians often look to the physician as the expert in end-of-life decision making. In Indian, Pakistani, and other Asian cultures, physicians and family members may share decision making. Doolen and York note that among Afghans, health care decisions are made by the head of the family, possibly in consultation with an educated younger family member.

An advance directive (often called a living will) is a written statement that explains a person's wishes about end-of-life medical care. Completion of advance directives varies among cultures. For example, Searight and Gafford note that approximately 40% of elderly whites have completed advance directives, whereas only 16% of elderly African Americans have done the same. Doolen and York add that Mexican Americans, African Americans, Native Americans, and Asian Americans do not necessarily share the typical American philosophy that end-of-life decisions are the individual's responsibility and are much less likely than the general American population to sign advance directives or do-not-resuscitate orders.

The quality of end-of-life care may be compromised in countries where antiquated or ambiguous laws can place doctors and other medical professionals in legal jeopardy if they attempt to deliver palliative care. For example, in "End-of-Life Care: Indian Perspective" (*Indian Journal of Psychiatry*, vol. 55, supplement 2, January 2013) Himanshu Sharma et al. note the legal complexities associated with withdrawing life support for patients in India given the prohibitions against suicide and assisted suicide that are outlined in Supreme Court decisions and the Indian Penal Code.

In "Cultural Relevance in End-of-Life Care" (Ethnomed.org, May 1, 2012), clinician Phyllis R. Coolen highlights numerous studies that emphasize the need for medical caregivers to conduct a thorough cultural assessment to understand a patient's beliefs, values, and practices. This cultural assessment can serve as the basis for respectful, appropriate, and effective communication and decision making with the patient and his or her family.

Health Care Proxies and Surrogate Decision Makers

When a patient is not competent to make informed decisions about his or her medical treatment, a proxy or a surrogate must make the decision for that patient. Some patients, in anticipation of being in a position of incompetence, will execute a durable power of attorney for health care by designating a proxy. Most people choose family members or close friends who will make all medical decisions, including the withholding or withdrawal of life-sustaining treatments.

When a proxy has not been named in advance, health care providers usually involve family members in medical decisions. Most states have laws that govern surrogate decision making. Some states designate family members, by order of kinship, to assume the role of surrogates.

THE DESIRE TO DIE: EUTHANASIA AND ASSISTED SUICIDE

The prospect of being allowed to end one's own life by active means, with the help of a physician, has become more relevant in an age when life can often be prolonged past the point when an individual wants to continue living. Euthanasia became a topic of mainstream conversation in the 1990s, thanks in large part to the activities of Jack Kevorkian (1928–2011), a physician who publicized his role in administering lethal injections to more than 130 terminally ill people. Kevorkian, an advocate for the right to die, attempted to further his cause by euthanizing a terminally ill man on videotape in 1998 and providing the footage to the CBS television show *60 Minutes*. After the show broadcast the footage, Kevorkian was arrested and charged with second-degree murder. In 1999 he was convicted and sentenced to 10 to 25 years in prison, in spite of emotional pleas on his behalf from the widow and the brother of the man who had sought out Kevorkian's services. He was paroled in 2007, and he died in 2011.

Although the type of active euthanasia championed by Kevorkian remains illegal everywhere in the United States, some states have legalized physician-assisted suicide in which the patient takes the dominant role in death. Oregon became the first U.S. state to legalize physician-assisted suicide in 1997, when it enacted the Death with Dignity Act. Under the law, terminally ill adults are allowed to obtain prescriptions for lethal doses of medication to be self-administered. In 2009 Washington enacted its own Death with Dignity Act, closely modeled on Oregon'. Three states subsequently followed suit: Vermont in 2013; and California and Colorado in 2016. The District of Columbia passed the D.C. Death with Dignity Act in 2017, but the law's implementation was jeopardized by the proposed 2018 federal budget, which would block funding for the act's reporting requirements. In Montana the state Supreme Court ruled in 2009 that state law permitted physician-assisted suicide, but as of 2017 no legislation or regulatory framework had been created to implement the practice.

CHAPTER 4
THE END OF LIFE: MEDICAL CONSIDERATIONS

TRENDS IN CAUSES OF DEATH AND IN DEATH RATES

The public-health advances that are described in Chapter 1 have brought about a change in the primary causes of death in the United States. During the 19th and early 20th centuries infectious (communicable) diseases such as influenza, tuberculosis, and diphtheria (a potentially deadly upper respiratory infection) were leading causes of death. Vaccinations, antibiotics, increased public awareness, improved sanitation, and advances in treatment have eliminated or drastically circumscribed the effects of these conditions. Progress has also been made at reducing the fatality of chronic noninfectious conditions, such as heart disease, cancer (often referred to as "malignant neoplasms"), and chronic lower respiratory diseases, but the impact on their effects has been more modest. Thus, as rates of infectious diseases have fallen, chronic noninfectious diseases, although they are less likely to strike any given person in any given year, have come to account for a majority of deaths in the United States. (See Figure 4.1.)

As Figure 4.1 shows, in every year since the mid-20th century heart disease and cancer have accounted for half or more of all deaths in the United States; furthermore, heart disease, cancer, and stroke were among the five leading causes of death every year between 1935 and 2010. Some conditions appeared and then disappeared from the ranks of the five leading causes of death over this time. For example, kidney disease was among the five leading causes of death from 1935 to 1948; influenza and pneumonia were among the five leading causes from 1935 to 1945, in 1963, and between 1965 and 1978; and diseases of early infancy were among the five leading causes from 1949 to 1962 and in 1964. All of these conditions have since fallen out of the top five, due to the effectiveness of prevention and treatment. Meanwhile, chronic lower respiratory diseases appeared as one of the five leading causes in 1979 and have remained there in the decades since.

Table 4.1 shows the top 15 causes of death in 2014 for residents of the United States. Heart disease accounted for 614,348 deaths and cancer (malignant neoplasms) accounted for 591,700 deaths, making both conditions more than four times as deadly as the third-leading cause of death, chronic lower respiratory diseases (147,101). Accidents (135,928) and strokes (cerebrovascular diseases; 133,103) accounted for similar numbers of deaths. Alzheimer's disease, the sixth-leading cause of death in 2014, took the lives of 93,541 people, and diabetes took the lives of 76,488.

Not surprisingly, the leading causes of death vary by age. (See Table 4.2.) For the six youngest age groups (children under one year old, children between one and four years old, children five to 14 years old, young people 15 to 24 years old, adults 25 to 34 years old, and adults 35 to 44 years old) tracked by the Centers for Disease Control and Prevention, accidents were the leading cause of death in 2014. Older Americans' causes of death more closely tracked the overall national trends. This is unsurprising, because those aged 45 years and older had considerably higher death rates than those aged 44 years and younger in 2014. The two leading causes of death for adults aged 45 to 84 years were cancer and heart disease, in that order. The same causes of death were most common for adults aged 85 years and older, but for this age group heart disease was more than twice as common than cancer. Chronic lower respiratory disease, strokes, and Alzheimer's disease were much more common causes of death for the over-65 cohort than for any other age group.

Age-adjusted death rates differed significantly by sex, race, and ethnicity in the early 21st century. As Table 4.3 shows, the 2014 age-adjusted death rate for men was 855.1 deaths per 100,000 people, whereas the rate for women was 616.7. The death rate for African American men (1,034), however, far exceeded that of white men (853.4). Meanwhile, the death rate for African American women (713.3)

FIGURE 4.1

Percentage of all deaths due to five leading causes of death, by year, 1935–2010

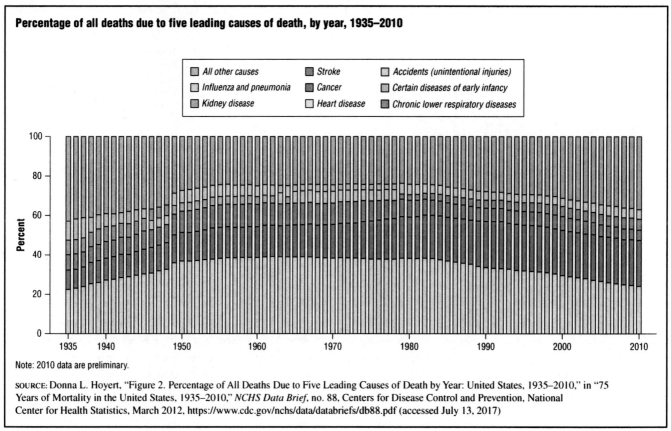

Note: 2010 data are preliminary.

SOURCE: Donna L. Hoyert, "Figure 2. Percentage of All Deaths Due to Five Leading Causes of Death by Year: United States, 1935–2010," in "75 Years of Mortality in the United States, 1935–2010," *NCHS Data Brief*, no. 88, Centers for Disease Control and Prevention, National Center for Health Statistics, March 2012, https://www.cdc.gov/nchs/data/databriefs/db88.pdf (accessed July 13, 2017)

exceeded that for white women (617.6) but was lower than that of white men. The infant mortality rate was much higher for African Americans (11.05 per 1,000 live births) than for whites (4.93). (See Table 4.4.)

These disparities translate into differences in life expectancy. Non-Hispanic African American men had the lowest life expectancy of any demographic subgroup in 2013–14, followed by non-Hispanic white men. (See Figure 4.2.) Non-Hispanic African American women had a slightly lower life expectancy during this period than Hispanic men. Non-Hispanic white women had a life expectancy of over 81 years throughout this period, and Hispanic women had a life expectancy of 84 years in 2013–14, the highest of any demographic subgroup in the United States.

As of 2014, there were also significant disparities in death rates by geography. As Table 4.5 shows, that year the age-adjusted death rate was highest in Mississippi (937.6 per 100,000 people), followed by West Virginia (929.1), Alabama (909.1), Kentucky (906.3), and Oklahoma (897.5). Of the 50 states, Hawaii (588.7) had the lowest age-adjusted death rate, followed by California (605.7), New York (636.5), Connecticut (646.5), and Minnesota (647).

LIFE-SUSTAINING TREATMENTS

As people succumb to the chronic, noninfectious diseases that are the leading causes of death in the United

States, life-sustaining treatments, commonly called life support, are often used. Such treatments are not controversial when a patient suffers from a treatable illness, in which cases life support is a temporary measure used until the body can function on its own. Debate arises when life-sustaining treatments are used in cases involving the incurably ill and permanently unconscious. These treatments prolong life, but they can also prolong the process of dying. In many cases, moreover, they may even add to a patient's suffering.

The following sections describe the types of life-sustaining medical interventions used in end-of-life care.

Cardiopulmonary Resuscitation

Traditional cardiopulmonary resuscitation (CPR) consists of two basic life-support skills that are administered in the event of cardiac or respiratory arrest: artificial circulation and artificial respiration. Cardiac arrest may be caused by a heart attack, which occurs when the blood flow to the heart is interrupted. A coronary artery that is clogged with an accumulation of fatty deposits is a common cause of interrupted blood flow to the heart. By contrast, respiratory arrest may be the result of an accident (such as drowning) or the final stages of a pulmonary disease (such as emphysema—a disease in which the alveoli [microscopic air sacs] of the lungs are destroyed).

TABLE 4.1

Deaths and death rates for the 15 leading causes of death, 2014, and percentage change, 2013–14

Rank[a]	Cause of death (based on ICD–10[c])	Number	Percent of total deaths	2014 crude death rate	Age-adjusted death rate 2014	Percent change 2013 to 2014	Ratio Male to female	Ratio Black[b] to white
. . .	All causes	2,626,418	100.0	823.7	724.6	−1.0	1.4	1.2
1	Diseases of heart	614,348	23.4	192.7	167.0	−1.6	1.6	1.2
2	Malignant neoplasms	591,700	22.5	185.6	161.2	−1.2	1.4	1.1
3	Chronic lower respiratory diseases	147,101	5.6	46.1	40.5	−3.8	1.2	0.7
4	Accidents (unintentional injuries)	135,928	5.2	42.6	40.5	2.8	2.0	0.8
5	Cerebrovascular diseases	133,103	5.1	41.7	36.5	0.8	1.0	1.4
6	Alzheimer's disease	93,541	3.6	29.3	25.4	8.1	0.7	0.8
7	Diabetes mellitus	76,488	2.9	24.0	20.9	−1.4	1.5	1.9
8	Influenza and pneumonia	55,227	2.1	17.3	15.1	−5.0	1.3	1.1
9	Nephritis, nephrotic syndrome and nephrosis	48,146	1.8	15.1	13.2	0.0	1.5	2.0
10	Intentional self-harm (suicide)	42,826	1.6	13.4	13.0	3.2	3.6	0.4
11	Septicemia	38,940	1.5	12.2	10.7	0.0	1.2	1.8
12	Chronic liver disease and cirrhosis	38,170	1.5	12.0	10.4	2.0	2.0	0.6
13	Essential hypertension and hypertensive renal disease	30,221	1.2	9.5	8.2	−3.5	1.1	2.1
14	Parkinson's disease	26,150	1.0	8.2	7.4	1.4	2.3	0.5
15	Pneumonitis due to solids and liquids	18,792	0.7	5.9	5.1	−1.9	1.9	1.0
. . .	All other causes	535,737	20.4	168.0	NA	NA	NA	NA

. . .Category not applicable.
[a]Based on number of deaths.
[b]Multiple-race data were reported by 46 states and the District of Columbia in 2014. The multiple-race data for these reporting areas were bridged to the single-race categories of the 1977 Office of Management and Budget (OMB) standards for comparability with other reporting areas.
[c]International Classification of Diseases, Tenth Revision
Notes: Crude death rates on an annual basis per 100,000 population; age-adjusted rates per 100,000 U.S. standard population.
Rates are based on populations estimated as of July 1 using postcensal estimates.
Race categories are consistent with the 1977 Office of Management and Budget (OMB) standards.

SOURCE: Kenneth D. Kochanek et al., "Table B. Number of Deaths, Percentage of Total Deaths, Death Rates, and Age-Adjusted Death Rates for 2014, Percentage Change in Age-Adjusted Death Rates in 2014 from 2013, and Ratio of Age-Adjusted Death Rates by Sex and by Race for the 15 Leading Causes of Death for the Total Population in 2014: United States," in "Deaths: Final Data for 2014," *National Vital Statistics Reports*, vol. 65, no. 4, June 30, 2016, https://www.cdc.gov/nchs/data/nvsr/nvsr65/nvsr65_04.pdf (accessed July 14, 2017)

In CPR, artificial circulation is accomplished by compressing the chest rhythmically to cause blood to flow sufficiently to give a person a chance for survival. Artificial respiration (rescue breathing) is accomplished by breathing into the victim's mouth. Research indicates that in the case of cardiac arrest, providing chest compressions alone is more effective than providing chest compressions and rescue breathing. Medical researchers have determined that taking the time to give rescue breaths to heart attack victims reduces the effectiveness of chest compressions, and effective chest compressions are vital in helping the heart retain its ability to beat after being shocked with a defibrillator (a device that delivers an electrical shock to the heart, hopefully causing it to restart). Nevertheless, if someone has experienced respiratory arrest, rescue breathing must be performed to keep that person alive until an ambulance arrives.

The American Heart Association (AHA) states in "CPR & First Aid: Emergency Cardiovascular Care" (2017, http://cpr.heart.org/AHAECC/CPRAndECC/General/UCM_477263_Cardiac-Arrest-Statistics.jsp) that survival rates differ significantly depending on whether one experiences cardiac arrest in a hospital or away from a hospital. Among the more than 350,000 instances of out-of-hospital cardiac arrest the AHA counted in 2016, CPR was performed by bystanders in 46.1% of cases and the overall survival rate was 12%. By comparison, among the 209,000 instances of cardiac arrest that occurred in hospitals (where CPR and other life-saving techniques were routinely used), the overall survival rate was 24.8% for adults (the survival rate for children was unavailable for this period).

The low survival rate for those who experience cardiac arrest away from a hospital is to a substantial degree attributable to the fact that less than half of all such people receive CPR. Steven M. Bradley and Tom D. Rea suggest in "Improving Bystander Cardiopulmonary Resuscitation" (*Current Opinion in Critical Care*, vol. 17, no. 3, June 2011) that changing the emphasis in CPR education to focus on chest compressions alone in cases of heart attack would likely save lives, because it is easier for a bystander to administer chest compressions without rescue breathing when he or she notices a person who is unconscious and not breathing normally.

REFUSAL OF CPR WITH A DO-NOT-RESUSCITATE ORDER. CPR is intended for generally healthy individuals who unexpectedly suffer a heart attack or other trauma, such as drowning. Usually, following CPR, survivors

TABLE 4.2

Death rates by age for the 15 leading causes of death in 2014

Cause of death	All ages[a]	Under 1 year[b]	1–4	5–14	15–24	25–34	35–44	45–54	55–64	65–74	75–84	85 and over
							Age group (years)					
All causes	823.7	588.0	24.0	12.7	65.5	108.4	175.2	404.8	870.3	1,786.3	4,564.2	13,407.9
Diseases of heart	192.7	8.0	0.9	0.5	2.2	7.7	25.6	80.1	185.8	385.2	1,070.2	3,920.9
Malignant neoplasms	185.6	1.3	2.0	2.1	3.6	8.3	27.8	103.2	287.6	603.1	1,125.9	1,632.9
Chronic lower respiratory diseases	46.1	d	0.3	0.3	0.4	0.8	1.9	10.1	41.2	134.9	349.0	670.5
Accidents (unintentional injuries)	42.6	29.4	7.6	3.6	26.8	39.8	39.6	47.4	44.9	45.1	108.7	349.1
Cerebrovascular diseases	41.7	2.4	0.2	0.2	0.4	1.3	4.3	12.3	29.3	74.5	265.7	929.7
Alzheimer's disease	29.3	d	d	d	d	d	d	0.2	2.1	19.6	185.6	1,006.8
Diabetes mellitus	24.0	d	d	0.1	0.4	1.6	4.9	13.9	33.3	69.0	141.8	268.6
Influenza and pneumonia	17.3	4.7	0.7	0.2	0.5	1.3	2.8	6.3	13.4	29.8	96.4	385.9
Nephritis, nephrotic syndrome and nephrosis	15.1	2.3	d	d	0.2	0.5	1.7	4.7	126.6	343.3	98.6	282.4
Intentional self-harm (suicide)	13.4	—	—	1.0	11.6	15.1	16.6	20.2	18.8	15.6	17.5	19.3
Septicemia	12.2	4.0	0.3	0.2	0.3	0.8	2.1	5.8	14.2	31.1	73.1	176.9
Chronic liver disease and cirrhosis	12.0	d	d	d	0.1	1.7	6.4	19.9	31.9	29.6	30.4	23.4
Essential hypertension and hypertensive renal disease	9.5	d	d	d	0.0[c]	0.2	1.1	3.3	8.4	16.9	51.3	217.0
Parkinson's disease	8.2	d	d	d	d	d	d	0.2	1.4	13.0	79.2	182.0
Pneumonitis due to solids and liquids	5.9	d	d	d	0.1	0.2	0.4	1.2	3.3	9.4	36.7	147.8

NA = Category not applicable.

[a]Figures for age not stated included in "All ages" but not distributed among age groups.

[b]Death rates for "Under 1 year" (based on population estimates) differ from infant mortality rates (based on live births).

[c]0.0 quantity more than zero but less than 0.05.

[d]Figure does not meet standards of reliability or precision.

Notes: Rates on an annual basis per 100,000 population in specified group; age-adjusted rates are per 100,000 U.S. standard population, estimated as of July 1.

SOURCE: Adapted from Kenneth D. Kochanek et al., "Table 9. Death Rates by Age, and Age-Adjusted Death Rates, for the 15 Leading Causes of Death in 2014: United States, 1999–2014," in "Deaths: Final Data for 2014," *National Vital Statistics Reports*, vol. 65, no. 4, June 30, 2016, https://www.cdc.gov/nchs/data/nvsr/nvsr65/nvsr65_04.pdf (accessed July 14, 2017)

TABLE 4.3

Deaths and age-adjusted death rates, by race and sex, 2010–14

Year	All races Both sexes	Male	Female	White[a] Both sexes	Male	Female	Black[a] Both sexes	Male	Female	American Indian or Alaska Native[a,b] Both sexes	Male	Female	Asian or Pacific Islander[a,c] Both sexes	Male	Female
							Number								
2014	2,626,418	1,328,241	1,298,177	2,237,880	1,128,993	1,108,887	308,960	157,733	151,227	18,008	9,829	8,179	61,570	31,686	29,884
2013	2,596,993	1,306,034	1,290,959	2,217,103	1,110,956	1,106,147	302,969	154,767	148,202	17,052	9,331	7,721	59,869	30,980	28,889
2012	2,543,279	1,273,722	1,269,557	2,175,178	1,085,250	1,089,928	295,222	150,586	144,636	16,527	9,067	7,460	56,352	28,819	27,533
2011	2,515,458	1,254,978	1,260,480	2,156,077	1,071,966	1,084,111	290,100	146,884	143,216	15,945	8,638	7,307	53,336	27,490	25,846
2010	2,468,435	1,232,432	1,236,003	2,114,749	1,051,514	1,063,235	286,959	145,802	141,157	15,565	8,516	7,049	51,162	26,600	24,562

[a]Multiple-race data were reported by 46 states and the District of Columbia in 2014, by 42 states and the District of Columbia in 2012 and 2013, by 38 states and the District of Columbia in 2011, by 37 states and the District of Columbia in 2010. The multiple-race data for these reporting areas were bridged to the single-race categories of the 1977 OMB standards for comparability with other reporting areas.

[b]Includes Aleut and Eskimo persons.

[c]Includes Chinese, Filipino, Hawaiian, Japanese, and other Asian or Pacific Islander persons.

Notes: Crude rates are on an annual basis per 100,000 population in specified group; age-adjusted rates are per 100,000 U.S. standard population. Rates are based on populations enumerated as of April 1 for census years and estimated as of July 1 for all other years. Excludes deaths of nonresidents of the United States. Data for specified races other than white and black should be interpreted with caution because of inconsistencies between reporting race on death certificates and on censuses and surveys. Race categories are consistent with the 1977 Office of Management and Budget (OMB) standards.

SOURCE: Adapted from Kenneth D. Kochanek et al., "Table 1. Number of Deaths, Death Rates, and Age-Adjusted Death Rates, by Race and Sex: United States, 1940, 1950, 1960, 1970, and 1980–2014," in "Deaths: Final Data for 2014," *National Vital Statistics Reports*, vol. 65, no. 4, June 30, 2016, https://www.cdc.gov/nchs/data/nvsr/nvsr65/nvsr65_04.pdf (accessed July 14, 2017)

eventually resume a normal life. Outcomes are quite different, understandably, for patients who suffer cardiac arrest in the final stages of a terminal illness. In "Life-Support Interventions at the End of Life: Unintended

TABLE 4.4

Number of infant and neonatal deaths and mortality rates, by race and sex, 2014

	Infant deaths						Neonatal deaths					
	All races[a]		White[b]		Black[b]		All races[a]		White[b]		Black[b]	
Sex and area	Number	Rate	Number	Rate	Number	Rate	Number	Rate	Number	Rate	Number	Rate
United States[c]	23,215	5.82	14,883	4.93	7,076	11.05	15,720	3.94	10,170	3.37	1,686	7.32
Male	12,886	6.31	8,297	5.36	3,900	12.01	8,671	4.25	5,624	3.63	2,578	7.94
Female	10,329	5.30	6,586	4.47	3,176	10.06	7,049	3.62	4,546	3.09	2,108	6.68

[a]Includes races other than white and black.
[b]Race categories are consistent with the 1977 Office of Management and Budget (OMB) standards. In 2014, multiple-race data were reported by 46 states and the District of Columbia for deaths and by 49 states and the District of Columbia for births. The multiple-race data for these reporting areas were bridged to the single-race categories of the 1977 OMB standards for comparability with other reporting areas.
[c]Excludes data for Puerto Rico, Virgin Islands, Guam, American Samoa, and Northern Marianas.
Notes: Rates are infant (under 1 year) and neonatal (under 28 days) deaths per 1,000 live births in specified group. Infant deaths are based on race of decedent; live births are based on race of mother.

SOURCE: Adapted from Kenneth D. Kochanek et al., "Table 22. Number of Infant and Neonatal Deaths and Mortality Rates, by Race for the United States, Each State, Puerto Rico, Virgin Islands, Guam, American Samoa, and Northern Marianas, and by Sex for the United States, 2014," in "Deaths: Final Data for 2014," *National Vital Statistics Reports*, vol. 65, no. 4, June 30, 2016, https://www.cdc.gov/nchs/data/nvsr/nvsr65/nvsr65_04.pdf (accessed July 14, 2017)

FIGURE 4.2

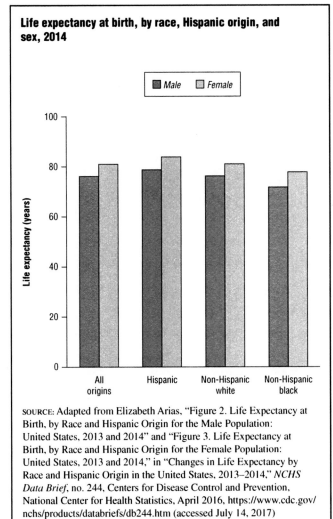

Life expectancy at birth, by race, Hispanic origin, and sex, 2014

SOURCE: Adapted from Elizabeth Arias, "Figure 2. Life Expectancy at Birth, by Race and Hispanic Origin for the Male Population: United States, 2013 and 2014" and "Figure 3. Life Expectancy at Birth, by Race and Hispanic Origin for the Female Population: United States, 2013 and 2014," in "Changes in Life Expectancy by Race and Hispanic Origin in the United States, 2013–2014," *NCHS Data Brief*, no. 244, Centers for Disease Control and Prevention, National Center for Health Statistics, April 2016, https://www.cdc.gov/nchs/products/databriefs/db244.htm (accessed July 14, 2017)

"fewer than 5% of terminally ill patients survive CPR to leave the hospital. Even if they do survive, they may require mechanical ventilation indefinitely. Depending on how long a patient's brain was deprived of oxygen, there may be brain damage significant enough to result in coma or leave the patient in a persistent vegetative state. Quality of life may be considerably diminished, and the prolonged dying process will likely add to the stress the family is already experiencing." Scott adds that during CPR a dying patient may experience a broken rib or ribs, which can puncture the lungs and necessitate the insertion of a chest tube. The chest tube is usually uncomfortable and is a common site of infection. CPR may also result in a ruptured liver or spleen, which would require surgery.

A terminally ill person not wishing to be resuscitated in case of cardiac or respiratory arrest may ask a physician to write a do-not-resuscitate (DNR) order on his or her medical chart. This written order instructs health care personnel not to initiate CPR. Even if a patient's living will (a written document outlining one's wishes regarding medical and end-of-life care and granting decision-making authority to others in the case that the patient becomes incapacitated) includes refusal of CPR, emergency personnel hurrying to respond to a heart attack or other incident may be unable to check a living will before initiating the procedure. This underscores the necessity of having the DNR order noted on the chart.

NONHOSPITAL DNR ORDERS. People who do not want CPR performed in case of an emergency that occurs away from a hospital can request a nonhospital DNR order from their physician. Also called a prehospital DNR order, it instructs emergency medical personnel to withhold CPR. The DNR order may be on a bracelet or necklace or on a wallet card. Although this is the best method of ensuring that one's end-of-life wishes are carried out in a nonhospital setting, there is no guarantee

Consequences" (*American Journal of Nursing*, vol. 110, no. 1, January 2010), Shirley A. Scott of the Orlando Regional Medical Center in Orlando, Florida, notes that

TABLE 4.5

Deaths, death rates, and age-adjusted death rates, by state and territory, 2014

Area	All causes Number	Rate	Age-adjusted rate[a]
United States[b]	2,626,418	823.7	724.6
Alabama	50,215	1,035.5	909.1
Alaska	4,128	560.3	736.8
Arizona	51,538	765.6	661.7
Arkansas	30,467	1,027.1	883.7
California	245,929	633.8	605.7
Colorado	35,237	657.9	664.4
Connecticut	29,860	830.2	646.5
Delaware	8,260	882.8	734.0
District of Columbia	4,723	716.8	743.8
Florida	185,956	934.8	662.0
Georgia	76,887	761.5	801.9
Hawaii	10,767	758.5	588.7
Idaho	12,613	771.7	723.8
Illinois	105,293	817.5	726.0
Indiana	60,940	923.8	822.3
Iowa	29,190	939.5	722.9
Kansas	25,793	888.2	759.3
Kentucky	44,838	1,015.9	906.3
Louisiana	43,869	943.5	894.2
Maine	13,510	1,015.7	739.0
Maryland	45,867	767.5	699.5
Massachusetts	55,200	818.3	663.0
Michigan	93,914	947.7	783.7
Minnesota	41,445	759.5	647.0
Mississippi	30,557	1,020.6	937.6
Missouri	58,320	961.8	807.0
Montana	9,381	916.5	732.1
Nebraska	15,978	849.2	718.2
Nevada	21,793	767.6	749.2
New Hampshire	11,516	867.9	706.2
New Jersey	71,316	797.9	665.7
New Mexico	17,579	842.9	749.6
New York	149,944	759.4	636.5
North Carolina	85,367	858.5	775.9
North Dakota	6,184	836.3	692.7
Ohio	114,509	987.6	810.0
Oklahoma	38,464	991.8	897.5
Oregon	34,151	860.2	706.7
Pennsylvania	128,434	1,004.4	750.2
Rhode Island	9,770	925.9	700.9
South Carolina	45,454	940.6	829.1
South Dakota	7,507	879.9	710.4
Tennessee[c]	64,661	987.3	880.0
Texas	183,912	682.2	745.3
Utah	16,719	568.1	709.6
Vermont	5,623	897.4	694.8
Virginia	63,598	763.8	717.5
Washington	52,099	737.8	672.9
West Virginia	22,186	1,199.0	929.1
Wisconsin	50,291	873.5	712.1
Wyoming	4,666	798.8	742.4
Puerto Rico	30,152	849.7	677.1
Virgin Islands	NA	NA	NA
Guam	939	583.2	814.3
American Samoa	246	451.2	935.3
Northern Marianas	202	392.4	923.7

NA = data not available.

[a]Death rates are affected by the population composition of the area. Age-adjusted death rates should be used for comparisons between areas.

[b]Excludes data for Puerto Rico, Virgin Islands, Guam, American Samoa, and Northern Marianas.

[c]In Tennessee, an increase in the number of certificates with a blank entry for "Manner of Death" in 2014 may have significantly impacted the coding of some reported conditions, resulting in more deaths being assigned to select unintentional injuries.

Notes: Rates per 100,000 population; age-adjusted rates per 100,000 U.S. standard population. Populations used for computing death rates are postcensal estimates based on the 2010 census estimated as of July 1, 2014.

SOURCE: Adapted from Kenneth D. Kochanek et al., "Table 19. Number of Deaths, Death Rates, and Age-Adjusted Death Rates for Major Causes of Death: United States, Each State, Puerto Rico, Virgin Islands, Guam, American Samoa, and Northern Marianas, 2014," in "Deaths: Final Data for 2014," *National Vital Statistics Reports*, vol. 65, no. 4, June 30, 2016, https://www.cdc.gov/nchs/data/nvsr/nvsr65/nvsr65_04.pdf (accessed July 14, 2017)

that bystanders will not perform CPR in contravention of a DNR order. Laypeople cannot be held liable for performing CPR on an individual with a nonhospital DNR order.

Mechanical Ventilation

When a patient's lungs are not functioning properly, a ventilator (or respirator) can breath for the patient. Most ventilators are positive-pressure ventilators. That is, they deliver gas under pressure to the patient's lungs. The pressure is relieved when gas is exhaled via an exhalation pathway. Negative-pressure ventilators, known colloquially as iron lungs, were common prior to the 1960s. They are tank-shaped devices that enclose much of a patient's body. By lowering air pressure inside the machine a patient's chest could be made to expand, drawing air into the lungs. Increasing pressure in the iron lung would then force the lungs to compress and cause the air to be exhaled. Iron lungs were largely phased out with the rise of positive-pressure ventilators, which do not obstruct patients' movements, or doctors' and nurses' ability to examine their bodies, nearly as much. In positive-pressure ventilators, oxygen is supplied to the lungs via a tube that is inserted through the mouth or nose into the windpipe. Mechanical ventilation is generally used to temporarily maintain normal breathing in those who have been in serious accidents or who suffer from a serious illness, such as pneumonia. In some cases, if the patient needs ventilation indefinitely, the physician might perform a tracheotomy to open a hole in the neck for placement of the breathing tube in the windpipe.

Ventilators are also used on terminally ill patients. In these cases the machine keeps the patient breathing but does nothing to cure the disease. Once ventilation is started, it raises the question of when ventilation will be stopped. Those preparing a living will are advised to give clear instructions about their desires regarding continued use of an artificial respirator that could prolong the process of dying.

Artificial Nutrition and Hydration

Artificial nutrition and hydration (ANH) is another medical technology that has complicated the dying process. It is a process where nutrients and fluids are supplied to a patient intravenously or through a stomach or intestinal tube, fully meeting the nutritional and hydration needs of people who are either not capable of, or interested in, eating and drinking normally. This can save the life of someone who is temporarily unable to eat or drink because of illness or injury; it can also meet the nutritional needs of permanently comatose or terminally ill patients who would otherwise die.

ANH has a strong emotional impact because it relates to basic sustenance. The prospect of withholding food and water from a loved one can be so powerful that even families who know that the patient would not want to be kept alive may still struggle to fulfill his or her wishes. Nevertheless, the National Hospice and Palliative Care Organization (NHPCO) explains in "Artificial Nutrition (Food) and Hydration (Fluids) at the End of Life" (2015, http://www.caringinfo.org/files/public/brochures/Artificial NutritionAndHydration.pdf) that it is often not as cruel as it might seem to stop ANH. The organization reports that appetite loss is common in dying patients and that the withdrawal of ANH does not prolong death or make it more painful. By contrast, continuing ANH for a patient whose body is shutting down in preparation for death can increase discomfort. The Academy of Nutrition and Dietetics supports this view of ANH, as Julie O'Sullivan Maillet, Denise Baird Schwartz, and Mary Ellen Posthauer write in "Position of the Academy of Nutrition and Dietetics: Ethical and Legal Issues in Feeding and Hydration" (*Journal of the Academy of Nutrition and Dietetics*, vol. 113, no. 6, June 2013). The researchers state that "loss of appetite is common with terminally ill individuals and it does not reduce quality of life except for reducing the enjoyment of food. Withholding or minimizing hydration can have the desirable effect of reducing disturbing oral and bronchial secretions, and reduced cough from diminished pulmonary congestion. Withholding nutrition has been studied closely and the majority of reports indicate that physiological adaptation allows individuals not to suffer from the absence of food."

ANH has traditionally been used in end-of-life care when patients experience a loss of appetite and difficulty swallowing. Health care practitioners use ANH to prolong life, prevent aspiration pneumonia (inflammation of the lungs due to inhaling food particles or fluid), maintain independence and physical function, and decrease suffering and discomfort. However, ANH does not always accomplish these goals. Tube feeding does not always prolong life, and insertion or placement of the tube can result in complications that themselves cause death. Neither does ANH always protect against aspiration pneumonia.

Kidney Dialysis

Kidney dialysis is a medical procedure in which a machine takes over the function of the kidneys, removing waste products from the bloodstream. Dialysis can be used when an illness or injury temporarily impairs kidney function. It may also be used by patients with irreversibly damaged kidneys who are awaiting organ transplantation.

Kidney failure may also occur as an end stage of a terminal illness. In such cases, dialysis may cleanse the body of waste products, but it cannot cure the disease. Dialysis patients may suffer from various side effects, including chemical imbalances in the body, low blood pressure, nausea and vomiting, headache, itching, and fatigue. Dialysis must be performed several times a week in the absence of functioning kidneys. Those terminally ill patients who wish to let their illness take its course may choose to stop dialysis. Death might follow within a day, or the patient might live for several weeks more, depending on the state of the kidneys and the patient's underlying health. As waste products build up in the body, the patient may experience drowsiness, difficulty breathing, and fluid weight gain. In most cases doctors can help such patients manage their discomfort as the body approaches death.

DISORDERS OF CONSCIOUSNESS

A coma is a deep state of unconsciousness that is caused by damage to the brain, often from illness or trauma. The patient is neither awake nor aware; his or her eyes are always closed. A coma rarely lasts for more than one month, and most people in a coma recover quickly, die, or progress to a vegetative state within that time.

Most often, patients who do not recover quickly from a coma progress to a vegetative/unresponsive state: they experience periods of wakefulness (eyes open) but without awareness. Those in a vegetative/unresponsive state for one month are then considered to be in a persistent vegetative state, and eventually, if they remain unresponsive, they are considered to be in a permanent vegetative state/unresponsive wakefulness state (PVS/UWS). The word *permanent* intentionally refers to the absence of any medical grounds for believing that there is a chance of recovery.

PVS/UWS patients are unaware of themselves or their surroundings. They do not respond to stimuli, understand language, or have control of bowel and bladder functions. They may intermittently open their eyes but are not conscious—a condition often referred to as eyes-open unconsciousness.

Some PVS/UWS patients do recover and regain partial consciousness. This condition is called a minimally conscious state (MCS). The perception of the minimally conscious patient is severely altered, but the patient is awake and shows an awareness of self or the environment, exhibiting behaviors such as following simple commands and smiling or crying at appropriate times. Some patients eventually emerge from an MCS, while some remain in an MCS permanently. Table 4.6 lists the criteria for the diagnosis of an MCS.

TABLE 4.6

Criteria for a minimally conscious state (MCS)

Impaired responsiveness
Limited by perceptible awareness of surroundings or self evidenced by one or more of the following:

MCS−	MCS+
Following someone with the eyes	Following commands
Crying or smiling appropriately to emotional stimuli	Using words understandably
Localization of unpleasant stimuli	Non-functional communication

MCS− = low-level behavioral responses.
MCS+ = high-level behavioral responses.

SOURCE: Created by Sandra Alters for Gale, © 2017

Locked-in syndrome is another disorder of consciousness that can occur after a coma. In this rare condition, the patient is awake and has full consciousness, but all the voluntary muscles of the body are paralyzed except (usually) for those that control vertical eye movement and blinking. People with locked-in syndrome communicate primarily with eye or eyelid movements.

In "From Unresponsive Wakefulness to Minimally Conscious PLUS and Functional Locked-In Syndromes: Recent Advances in Our Understanding of Disorders of Consciousness" (*Journal of Neurology*, vol. 258, no. 7, July 2011), Marie-Aurélie Bruno et al. propose splitting the category of MCS into MCS+ (high-level behavioral responses) and MCS− (low-level behavioral responses). High-level behavioral responses include following commands and saying words that are understandable. (See Table 4.6.) Low-level behavioral responses include following someone with the eyes and smiling or crying appropriately to emotional stimuli. A person with MCS+ can exhibit lower-level behaviors as well as higher-level behaviors.

PVS/UWS and MCS patients cannot, of course, make decisions about their own health care. Many of the highest-profile court cases and public controversies surrounding end-of-life care have involved individuals with these conditions, in some cases pitting different family members against one another in their attempts to determine what is best for their loved one, and in other cases pitting family members against the state or politicians. One of the reasons that most health care professionals urge individuals to create a living will or advance directive is to spare their loved ones the heartache and stress associated with making life-and-death decisions in cases such as these.

ORGAN TRANSPLANTATION

Most organ and tissue donations are from the bodies of people who are deceased. In particular, people who have suffered a brain injury and subsequent brain death often have other healthy bodily organs that may be successfully donated to patients in need. In these cases, once death is pronounced the body is kept on mechanical support (if possible) to maintain the organs until it is determined whether the person will be a donor. In addition, living people may donate a kidney; parts of a lung, liver, or pancreas; or bone marrow. Most living donors make their donations to help a family member or close friend. Whatever their source, donated organs must usually be transplanted within six to 48 hours of harvest, although some tissue may be stored for future use.

Organ transplantation has come a long way since the first kidney was transplanted from one identical twin to another in 1954. The introduction in 1983 of cyclosporine, an immuno-suppressant drug that helps prevent the body's immune system from rejecting a donated organ, made it possible to successfully transplant a variety of organs and tissues.

FIGURE 4.3

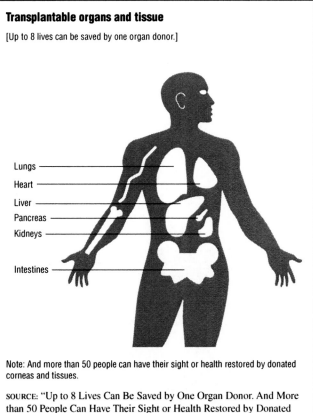

Transplantable organs and tissue

[Up to 8 lives can be saved by one organ donor.]

Lungs
Heart
Liver
Pancreas
Kidneys

Intestines

Note: And more than 50 people can have their sight or health restored by donated corneas and tissues.

SOURCE: "Up to 8 Lives Can Be Saved by One Organ Donor. And More than 50 People Can Have Their Sight or Health Restored by Donated Corneas and Tissues," in *The Gift of Life*, U.S. Department of Health and Human Services, Health Resources and Services Administration, March 2015, https://organdonor.gov/awareness/pdfs/english-process-brochure.pdf (accessed July 14, 2017)

Figure 4.3 shows the organs and tissues that are transplantable with 21st-century immunosuppressant drugs and technologies. The organs that may be donated and transplanted are the heart, intestines, kidneys, liver, lungs, and pancreas. One person who dies in conditions conducive to organ donation can save the lives of up to eight people. Transplantable tissues include blood vessels, bone, cartilage, corneas, heart valves, ligaments, middle ears, skin, and tendons. These tissues can be used in a variety of ways, such as the repair of hearts or connective tissues, or the restoration of sight or hearing. Although tissue donation does not save lives, it can immeasurably improve life for many people in addition to the recipients of organs.

Soon after organ transplantation began, the demand for donor organs exceeded the supply. In 1984 Congress passed the National Organ Transplant Act to create "a centralized network to match scarce donated organs with critically ill patients." In the 21st century organ transplant is an accepted medical treatment for a number of end-stage illnesses, but many people who might see their lives extended through transplants do not live long enough to receive the organs that they need.

The U.S. Department of Health and Human Services reports in "The Gift of Life" (2012, http://organdonor.gov/images/pdfs/giftoflifegeneralbrochure.pdf) that in 2012 more than 100 million people in the United States were registered organ donors. Nevertheless, very few people die from brain injuries or from other causes that make donation possible. As a result, the number of people in need of transplanted organs has for decades grown faster than the number of donors, creating conditions of permanent shortage and long waiting lists for those who need transplants. Figure 4.4 shows the widening gap between the number of people in need of transplants and the number of donors between 1992 and 2014. In 2014 there were 14,412 donors, who accounted for 29,532 transplants. That same year 123,851 people in need of transplants remained on waiting lists. As of September 2016, more than two out of five (41.9%) people waiting for organ transplants were white, while 29.7% were African American, 19% were Hispanic, 7.5% were Asian American, and 2.2% belonged to other races and ethnicities. (See Figure 4.5.)

The Department of Health and Human Services' Organ Procurement and Transplantation Network (https://optn.transplant.hrsa.gov/) reports that as of July 2017 there were 117,232 people on the transplant waiting list in the United States. As Table 4.7 shows, 97,132 (82.9%) of these people were waiting for kidney transplants. Another 12.2% (14,301) of those on the waiting list were in need of liver transplants, and 3.4% (3,954) were waiting for heart transplants. Smaller numbers of people needed lung, pancreas, or intestines transplants, or a combination of kidney/pancreas or heart/lung transplants.

Although people in need of donated kidneys and livers typically spend the longest time on the transplant waiting list, these are also the types of transplants that are performed most often. In 2015 surgeons performed 17,879 kidney transplants and 7,127 liver transplants. (See Figure 4.6.) By comparison, surgeons performed 2,804 heart and 2,057 lung transplants that year.

As Table 4.8 shows, the total number of organ donors fluctuated only slightly between 2007 and 2016, from a low of 14,010 in 2012 to a high of 15,949 in 2016. The total for 2011, 14,149, was the second lowest during this period. The number of living donors—almost all of whom donated kidneys in each year for which data were available—dropped during this period, from 6,315 in 2007 to 5,978 in 2016. The number of deceased donors increased from 8,085 in 2007 to 9,971 in 2016.

Among the 9,971 deceased donors in 2016, the most common causes of death were anoxia (lack of oxygen; 4,027 deaths), stroke or aneurysm (2,829), and head trauma (2,783). (See Table 4.9.) The number of donors whose deaths were caused by stroke decreased slightly between 2007 and 2016, whereas the number of donors who died from anoxia grew significantly during this

FIGURE 4.4

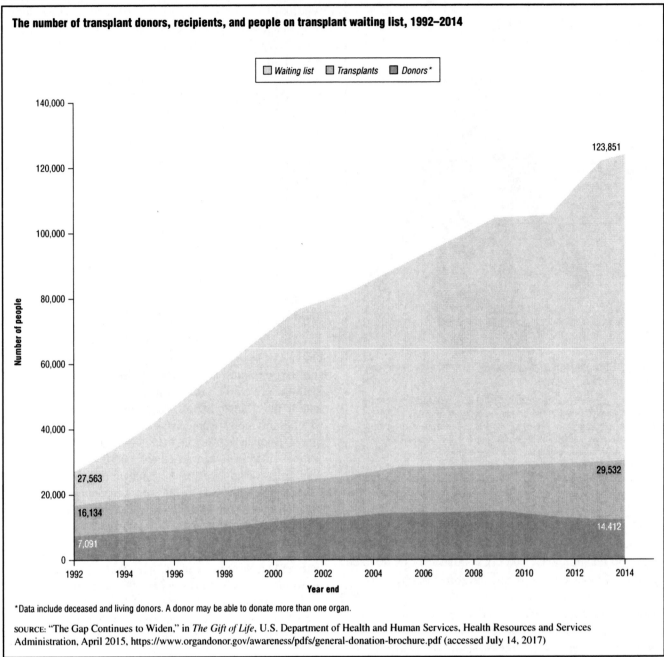

The number of transplant donors, recipients, and people on transplant waiting list, 1992–2014

Waiting list Transplants Donors*

*Data include deceased and living donors. A donor may be able to donate more than one organ.

SOURCE: "The Gap Continues to Widen," in *The Gift of Life*, U.S. Department of Health and Human Services, Health Resources and Services Administration, April 2015, https://www.organdonor.gov/awareness/pdfs/general-donation-brochure.pdf (accessed July 14, 2017)

period. In contrast, the number of donors who died from head trauma remained relatively consistent during this span. Many anoxia deaths are likely caused by drowning or by heart attacks in which the victims were revived after a lack of circulation or respiration had caused brain death. Motor vehicle accidents, gunshot wounds, and falls or blows to the head are common causes of fatal head trauma. Strokes and aneurysms can occur for a variety of reasons. People who die as a result of these causes frequently experience brain death although much of the body remains functional, making them good prospects for organ donation.

In spite of the tremendous good that deceased organ donors do for those in need of transplants, the fact that these deaths often occur by accident or are otherwise unforeseen makes the decision to donate organs a difficult one. As with determinations about other end-of-life issues, grieving family members often find the added decision making a burden for which they are unprepared. Therefore, it is vitally important for those adults who know they want to donate organs to make their wishes known.

The Uniform Anatomical Gift Act of 1968 established a person's right to sign a donor card indicating a desire to donate organs or tissue after death. (See Figure 4.7.) People who wish to be donors can complete a donor card and, provided they carry it at all times, health care professionals will consult it in the event of

FIGURE 4.5

Transplant wait list, by race and ethnicity, September 2016

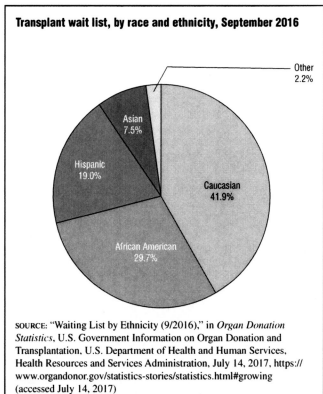

SOURCE: "Waiting List by Ethnicity (9/2016)," in *Organ Donation Statistics*, U.S. Government Information on Organ Donation and Transplantation, U.S. Department of Health and Human Services, Health Resources and Services Administration, July 14, 2017, https://www.organdonor.gov/statistics-stories/statistics.html#growing (accessed July 14, 2017)

TABLE 4.7

Transplant candidates on waiting list for organs, by organ needed, July 2017

All*	117,232
Kidney	97,132
Pancreas	907
Kidney/pancreas	1,709
Liver	14,301
Intestine	261
Heart	3,954
Lung	1,367
Heart/lung	38

*All candidates will be less than the sum due to candidates waiting for multiple organs.

SOURCE: "Waiting List Candidates as of Today 3:58 p.m.," in *Data*, U.S. Department of Health and Human Services, Health Resources and Services Administration, Organ Procurement and Transplantation Network, July 14, 2017, http://optn.transplant.hrsa.gov/data/ (accessed July 14, 2017)

unforeseen death. Alternatively, the wish to be a donor can be indicated on a driver's license or in a living will, or prospective donors may sign up for their state's registry online at http://www.organdonor.gov/becomingdonor/stateregistries.html. Prospective donors should inform their family and physician of their decision. At the time of death, hospitals always ask for the family's consent, even if a donor has already indicated his or her wish to donate organs. Should the family refuse, doctors will not take the organs, regardless of the deceased's wish.

HOSPICE CARE

The modern hospice movement developed in response to the need to provide humane care to terminally ill patients, while at the same time lending support to their families. The British physician Cicely Saunders (1918–2005) is considered to be the founder of the modern hospice movement—first in England in 1967 and later in Canada and the United States. The soothing, calming care provided by hospice workers is called palliative care, and it aims to relieve patients' pain and the accompanying symptoms of terminal illness, while providing comfort to patients and their families.

Hospice may refer to a place—a freestanding facility or designated floor in a hospital or nursing home—or to a program such as hospice home care, in which a team of health care professionals helps the dying patient and family at home. Hospice teams may involve physicians, nurses, social workers, pastoral counselors, and trained volunteers. In the United States hospice care generally begins when a terminally ill individual has been given a prognosis of six months or less to live.

Hospice workers consider the patient and family to be the "unit of care" and focus their efforts on attending to emotional, psychological, and spiritual needs as well as to physical comfort and well-being. With hospice care, as a patient nears death, medical details move to the background as personal details move to the foreground to avoid providing care that is not wanted by the patient, even if some clinical benefit might be expected.

The Population Served

According to the NHPCO, in *NHPCO's Facts and Figures: Hospice Care in America, 2015 Edition* (September 2015, https://www.nhpco.org/sites/default/files/public/Statistics_Research/2015_Facts_Figures.pdf), an estimated 1.6 million to 1.7 million Americans received hospice care in 2014. This included those who died in hospice care, those who began receiving care in 2013 and were still receiving care in 2014, and those who left hospice care prior to death. The number of hospice patients nationally has been steadily increasing since 2010, when 1.4 million people were served by hospice providers. Much of this growth in the hospice population has corresponded with increasing use of Medicare's hospice coverage provisions.

The NHPCO indicates that females accounted for more than half (53.7%) of hospice patients in 2014. More than eight out of 10 (83.9%) hospice patients were aged 65 years and older. Pediatric and young adult hospice patients under the age of 34 years accounted for less than 1% of the total hospice population, and adults aged 35 to 64 years accounted for 15.3% of the total. Cancer was the most common primary diagnosis among hospice patients, 36.6% of whom had some form of the disease. Dementia

FIGURE 4.6

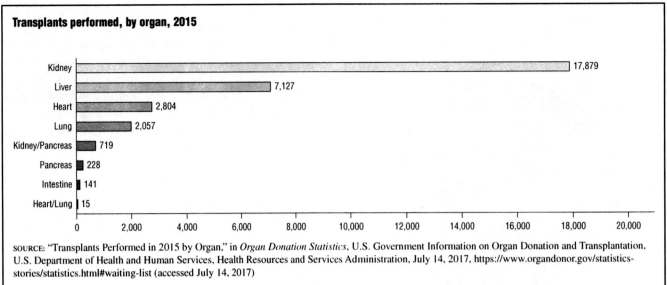

Transplants performed, by organ, 2015

SOURCE: "Transplants Performed in 2015 by Organ," in *Organ Donation Statistics*, U.S. Government Information on Organ Donation and Transplantation, U.S. Department of Health and Human Services, Health Resources and Services Administration, July 14, 2017, https://www.organdonor.gov/statistics-stories/statistics.html#waiting-list (accessed July 14, 2017)

was the primary diagnosis of 14.8% of patients, heart disease the primary diagnosis of 14.7%, and lung disease the primary diagnosis of 9.3%. A range of other conditions accounted for smaller proportions of hospice patients, while 1.9% had an unspecified debility.

A majority (58.9%) of hospice patients who died in 2014 did so in their place of residence, according to the NHPCO. For 35.7% of deceased hospice patients, that place of residence was a private home; for 14.5%, it was a nursing home; and for 8.7%, it was a residential facility other than a nursing home. Another 41.1% of hospice patients who died in 2014 passed away somewhere other than their home: 31.8% in a hospice inpatient facility and 9.3% in an acute care hospital setting.

In "Change in End-of-Life Care for Medicare Beneficiaries: Site of Death, Place of Care, and Health Care Transitions in 2000, 2005, and 2009" (*Journal of the American Medical Association*, vol. 309, no. 5, February 6, 2013), a comprehensive study of the shift toward increased utilization of hospice care (and of other early 21st-century changes in end-of-life care), J. M. Teno et al. find that although hospice use rapidly increased during the first decade of the 21st century, fully 28.4% of Medicare beneficiaries who died in hospice care in 2009 received such care for three days or less. Moreover, in 40% of these cases the shift to hospice care only occurred after a stay in a hospital's intensive care unit. This finding suggests that many people who might benefit from hospice care's focus on quality of life were not obtaining those benefits. Instead, many people appeared to be using hospice care as a last resort, once all medical interventions had been tried, rather than as a means of improving the end-of-life experience.

TABLE 4.8

Organ donors by donor type, 2007–16

[Based on OPTN data as of July 13, 2017]

		All donor types	Deceased donor	Living donor
2016	**All donors**	**15,949**	**9,971**	**5,978**
	Kidney	14,748	9,116	5,632
	Liver	8,497	8,152	345
	Heart	3,239	3,238	1
	Pancreas	1,344	1,344	0
	Lung	2,294	2,294	0
	Intestine	155	155	0
2015	**All donors**	**15,072**	**9,079**	**5,993**
	Kidney	13,881	8,250	5,631
	Liver	7,776	7,416	360
	Heart	2,854	2,854	0
	Pancreas	1,292	1,292	0
	Lung	2,018	2,018	0
	Intestine	158	156	2
2014	**All donors**	**14,417**	**8,596**	**5,821**
	Kidney	13,303	7,763	5,540
	Liver	7,344	7,064	280
	Heart	2,724	2,724	0
	Pancreas	1,273	1,273	0
	Lung	1,880	1,880	0
	Intestine	147	146	1
2013	**All donors**	**14,259**	**8,268**	**5,991**
	Kidney	13,283	7,547	5,736
	Liver	7,026	6,774	252
	Heart	2,582	2,582	0
	Pancreas	1,377	1,376	1
	Lung	1,898	1,896	2
	Intestine	122	121	1
2012	**All donors**	**14,010**	**8,143**	**5,867**
	Kidney	13,040	7,421	5,619
	Liver	6,876	6,630	246
	Heart	2,451	2,451	0
	Pancreas	1,451	1,451	0
	Lung	1,710	1,708	2
	Intestine	114	114	0
2011	**All donors**	**14,149**	**8,126**	**6,023**
	Kidney	13,207	7,434	5,773
	Liver	6,931	6,684	247
	Heart	2,380	2,380	0
	Pancreas	1,562	1,562	0
	Lung	1,758	1,756	2
	Intestine	136	135	1
2010	**All donors**	**14,504**	**7,943**	**6,561**
	Kidney	13,519	7,241	6,278
	Liver	6,893	6,611	282
	Heart	2,406	2,406	0
	Pancreas	1,660	1,660	0
	Lung	1,697	1,697	0
	Intestine	160	159	1
2009	**All donors**	**14,632**	**8,022**	**6,610**
	Kidney	13,636	7,248	6,388
	Liver	6,958	6,739	219
	Heart	2,281	2,281	0
	Pancreas	1,740	1,740	0
	Lung	1,569	1,568	1
	Intestine	189	187	2
2008	**All donors**	**14,207**	**7,989**	**6,218**
	Kidney	13,156	7,188	5,968
	Liver	7,000	6,751	249
	Heart	2,222	2,222	0
	Pancreas	1,830	1,829	1
	Lung	1,388	1,388	0
	Intestine	197	197	0

TABLE 4.8

Organ donors by donor type, 2007–16 [CONTINUED]

[Based on OPTN data as of July 13, 2017]

		All donor types	Deceased donor	Living donor
2007	**All donors**	**14,400**	**8,085**	**6,315**
	Kidney	13,283	7,240	6,043
	Liver	7,202	6,936	266
	Heart	2,286	2,286	0
	Pancreas	1,924	1,924	0
	Lung	1,388	1,382	6
	Intestine	206	205	1
2009	**All donors**	**14,632**	**8,022**	**6,610**
	Kidney	13,636	7,248	6,388
	Liver	6,958	6,739	219
	Heart	2,281	2,281	0
	Pancreas	1,740	1,740	0
	Lung	1,569	1,568	1
	Intestine	189	187	2
2008	**All donors**	**14,207**	**7,989**	**6,218**
	Kidney	13,156	7,188	5,968
	Liver	7,000	6,751	249
	Heart	2,222	2,222	0
	Pancreas	1,830	1,829	1
	Lung	1,388	1,388	0
	Intestine	197	197	0
2007	**All donors**	**14,400**	**8,085**	**6,315**
	Kidney	13,283	7,240	6,043
	Liver	7,202	6,936	266
	Hear	2,286	2,286	0
	Pancreas	1,924	1,924	0
	Lung	1,388	1,382	6
	Intestine	206	205	1

OPTN = Organ Procurement and Transplantation Network

SOURCE: Adapted from "Donors Recovered in the U.S. by Donor Type [Donors Recovered : January 1, 1988–June 30, 2017. Based on OPTN data as of July 13, 2017]," in *National Data*, U.S. Department of Health and Human Services, Health Resources and Services Administration, Organ Procurement and Transplantation Network, July 15, 2017, https://optn.transplant.hrsa.gov/data/view-data-reports/national-data/ (accessed July 15, 2017)

TABLE 4.9

Deceased organ donors by cause of death, 2007–16

[Based on OPTN data as of July 13, 2017]

	All causes	Not reported	Anoxia	Cerebro vascular/stroke	Head trauma	Central nervous system tumor	Not collected prior to 4/1/94	Other specify
2016	9,971	0	4,027	2,829	2,783	32	0	300
2015	9,079	0	3,426	2,673	2,711	34	0	235
2014	8,596	0	2,900	2,781	2,648	35	0	232
2013	8,268	0	2,599	2,760	2,682	37	0	190
2012	8,143	0	2,436	2,833	2,628	41	0	205
2011	8,126	0	2,278	2,932	2,685	41	0	190
2010	7,943	0	1,942	3,049	2,720	35	0	197
2009	8,022	0	1,893	3,178	2,671	43	0	237
2008	7,989	0	1,732	3,206	2,793	42	0	216
2007	8,085	0	1,489	3,308	3,026	46	0	216

OPTN = Organ Procurement and Transplantation Network

SOURCE: Adapted from "Deceased Donors Recovered in the U.S. by Cause of Death [Donors Recovered: January 1, 1988–June 30, 2017. Based on OPTN data as of July 13, 2017]," in *National Data*, U.S. Department of Health and Human Services, Health Resources and Services Administration, Organ Procurement and Transplantation Network, July 15, 2017, https://optn.transplant.hrsa.gov/data/view-data-reports/national-data/# (accessed July 15, 2017)

FIGURE 4.7

Organ/tissue donor card

Donate Life

Organ/Tissue Donor Card

I wish to donate my organs and tissues. I wish to give:

☐ any needed organs and tissues ☐ only the following organs and tissues:

____

Donor Signature ____________________ Date ________

Witness ____________________________

Witness ____________________________

SOURCE: Organ/Tissue Donor Card, U.S. Department of Health and Human Services, undated

CHAPTER 5
OLDER ADULTS

THE LONGEVITY REVOLUTION

The increase in life expectancy brought about by the combination of improved sanitation, medical advances, and reduced mortality rates for infants and children has fundamentally changed the nature of U.S. society. As Table 5.1 shows, the average life expectancy for all U.S. residents increased dramatically between 1900 and 1950 and continued on its pronounced upward trajectory through 2014; life expectancy in the United States then saw a slight decline between 2014 and 2015. A society in which most people expect to live to the age of 47.3 (the average U.S. life expectancy in 1900) is necessarily different from a society in which most people can expect to live to the age of 78.8 (the average U.S. life expectancy in 2015). As is noted in Chapter 1, adults aged 65 years and older constituted 13% of the total U.S. population in 2010 (up from 4% in 1900) and were projected to account for 24% of Americans in 2060.

The full implications of this "longevity revolution," as the aging of the U.S. population is sometimes called, have only begun to be understood. Although the personal benefits of a long life may be obvious, many older people struggle to redefine their goals and hopes once their working lives draw to a close and their children are grown. Other older adults welcome these changes and report higher levels of life satisfaction in their later years than at any other time of life. As more middle-aged adults find themselves caring for their aged parents for longer periods, changes in family and social life are likely. Adults who must be able to afford care both for children and for parents may be forced to extend their own careers into old age or to make other changes in household finances and family structures. As businesses and social institutions respond to the needs and desires of an older population, daily life in U.S. cities and towns will undoubtedly change.

The longevity revolution has many possible implications for the U.S. economy as well. Some economists predict a sustained economic slowdown as the population of working-age adults shrinks relative to the population as a whole. Likewise, in the absence of reform or a reallocation of resources, many economists and government officials expect the burgeoning of the elderly population to strain the public benefit programs that together provide a safety net for those aged 65 years and older. Programs such as Social Security, which provides those aged 65 years and older with pensions, and Medicare, which provides older people with universal health care coverage, are funded through contributions from working-age people. With a smaller working-age population attempting to support a greatly expanded population of retirees, there are widespread concerns about how these programs will continue to be funded.

Additionally, end-of-life controversies such as those addressed throughout this book are directly related to the social and political effects of the longevity revolution. How the country's institutions—from churches and medical facilities to the courts and government—respond to the many dilemmas raised at the end of life in the 21st century will undoubtedly be determined in large part by the needs and desires of an increasingly influential population of older Americans.

CHARACTERISTICS OF AGING AMERICANS

Although the population of Americans aged 65 years and older has been growing steadily since the early 20th century, an unprecedented acceleration in this group's rate of growth began in 2011, when the first baby boomers began turning 65. The Federal Interagency Forum on Aging-Related Statistics notes in *Older Americans 2016: Key Indicators of Well-Being* (August 2016, https://aging stats.gov/docs/LatestReport/Older-Americans-2016-Key-Indicators-of-WellBeing.pdf) that the number of older Americans is projected to expand dramatically between

TABLE 5.1

Life expectancy at birth, at age 65, and at age 75, by sex, race, and Hispanic origin, selected years 1900–2015

[Data are based on death certificates]

Specified age and year	All races Both sexes	Male	Female	White Both sexes	Male	Female	Black or African American[a] Both sexes	Male	Female
At birth				Life expectancy, in years					
1900[b, c]	47.3	46.3	48.3	47.6	46.6	48.7	33.0	32.5	33.5
1950[c]	68.2	65.6	71.1	69.1	66.5	72.2	60.8	59.1	62.9
1960[c]	69.7	66.6	73.1	70.6	67.4	74.1	63.6	61.1	66.3
1970	70.8	67.1	74.7	71.7	68.0	75.6	64.1	60.0	68.3
1975	72.6	68.8	76.6	73.4	69.5	77.3	66.8	62.4	71.3
1980	73.7	70.0	77.4	74.4	70.7	78.1	68.1	63.8	72.5
1990	75.4	71.8	78.8	76.1	72.7	79.4	69.1	64.5	73.6
1995	75.8	72.5	78.9	76.5	73.4	79.6	69.6	65.2	73.9
2000	76.8	74.1	79.3	77.3	74.7	79.9	71.8	68.2	75.1
2001	77.0	74.3	79.5	77.5	74.9	80.0	72.0	68.5	75.3
2002	77.0	74.4	79.6	77.5	74.9	80.1	72.2	68.7	75.4
2003	77.2	74.5	79.7	77.7	75.1	80.2	72.4	68.9	75.7
2004	77.6	75.0	80.1	78.1	75.5	80.5	72.9	69.4	76.1
2005	77.6	75.0	80.1	78.0	75.5	80.5	73.0	69.5	76.2
2006	77.8	75.2	80.3	78.3	75.8	80.7	73.4	69.9	76.7
2007	78.1	75.5	80.6	78.5	76.0	80.9	73.8	70.3	77.0
2008	78.2	75.6	80.6	78.5	76.1	80.9	74.3	70.9	77.3
2009	78.5	76.0	80.9	78.8	76.4	81.2	74.7	71.4	77.7
2010	78.7	76.2	81.0	78.9	76.5	81.3	75.1	71.8	78.0
2011	78.7	76.3	81.1	79.0	76.6	81.3	75.3	72.2	78.2
2012	78.8	76.4	81.2	79.1	76.7	81.4	75.5	72.3	78.4
2013[d]	78.8	76.4	81.2	79.0	76.7	81.4	75.5	72.3	78.4
2014[d]	78.9	76.5	81.3	79.1	76.7	81.4	75.6	72.5	78.5
2015[d]	78.8	76.3	81.2	79.0	76.6	81.3	75.5	72.2	78.5
At 65 years									
1950[c]	13.9	12.8	15.0	14.1	12.8	15.1	13.9	12.9	14.9
1960[c]	14.3	12.8	15.8	14.4	12.9	15.9	13.9	12.7	15.1
1970	15.2	13.1	17.0	15.2	13.1	17.1	14.2	12.5	15.7
1975	16.1	13.8	18.1	16.1	13.8	18.2	15.0	13.1	16.7
1980	16.4	14.1	18.3	16.5	14.2	18.4	15.1	13.0	16.8
1990	17.2	15.1	18.9	17.3	15.2	19.1	15.4	13.2	17.2
1995	17.4	15.6	18.9	17.6	15.7	19.1	15.6	13.6	17.1
2000	17.6	16.0	19.0	17.7	16.1	19.1	16.1	14.1	17.5
2001	17.9	16.2	19.2	18.0	16.3	19.3	16.2	14.2	17.7
2002	17.9	16.3	19.2	18.0	16.4	19.3	16.3	14.4	17.8
2003	18.1	16.5	19.3	18.2	16.6	19.4	16.5	14.5	18.0
2004	18.4	16.9	19.6	18.5	17.0	19.7	16.8	14.9	18.3
2005	18.4	16.9	19.6	18.5	17.0	19.7	16.9	15.0	18.3
2006	18.7	17.2	19.9	18.7	17.3	19.9	17.2	15.2	18.6
2007	18.8	17.4	20.0	18.9	17.4	20.1	17.3	15.4	18.8
2008	18.8	17.4	20.0	18.9	17.5	20.0	17.5	15.5	18.9
2009	19.1	17.7	20.3	19.2	17.7	20.3	17.8	15.9	19.2
2010	19.1	17.7	20.3	19.2	17.8	20.3	17.8	15.9	19.3
2011	19.2	17.8	20.3	19.2	17.8	20.3	18.0	16.2	19.4
2012	19.3	17.9	20.5	19.3	18.0	20.4	18.1	16.2	19.5
2013[d]	19.3	17.9	20.5	19.3	18.0	20.5	18.1	16.2	19.5
2014[d]	19.4	18.0	20.6	19.4	18.0	20.6	18.2	16.4	19.7
2015[d]	19.4	18.0	20.6	19.4	18.0	20.5	18.2	16.4	19.7
At 75 years									
1980	10.4	8.8	11.5	10.4	8.8	11.5	9.7	8.3	10.7
1990	10.9	9.4	12.0	11.0	9.4	12.0	10.2	8.6	11.2
1995	11.0	9.7	11.9	11.1	9.7	12.0	10.2	8.8	11.1
2000	11.0	9.8	11.8	11.0	9.8	11.9	10.4	9.0	11.3
2001	11.2	9.9	12.0	11.2	10.0	12.1	10.5	9.0	11.5
2002	11.2	10.0	12.0	11.2	10.0	12.1	10.5	9.1	11.5
2003	11.3	10.1	12.1	11.3	10.2	12.1	10.7	9.2	11.6
2004	11.5	10.4	12.4	11.6	10.4	12.4	10.9	9.4	11.8
2005	11.5	10.4	12.3	11.5	10.4	12.3	10.9	9.4	11.7
2006	11.7	10.6	12.5	11.7	10.6	12.5	11.1	9.6	12.0
2007	11.9	10.7	12.6	11.9	10.8	12.6	11.2	9.8	12.1
2008	11.8	10.7	12.6	11.8	10.7	12.6	11.3	9.8	12.2
2009	12.1	11.0	12.9	12.1	11.0	12.9	11.6	10.2	12.5
2010	12.1	11.0	12.9	12.1	11.0	12.8	11.6	10.2	12.5
2011	12.1	11.1	12.9	12.1	11.0	12.8	11.7	10.4	12.5
2012	12.2	11.2	12.9	12.1	11.1	12.9	11.8	10.4	12.7
2013[d]	12.2	11.2	12.9	12.1	11.1	12.9	11.8	10.4	12.7
2014[d]	12.3	11.2	13.1	12.2	11.2	13.0	11.9	10.6	12.8
2015[d]	12.3	11.2	13.0	12.2	11.2	13.0	11.9	10.6	12.8

TABLE 5.1

Life expectancy at birth, at age 65, and at age 75, by sex, race, and Hispanic origin, selected years 1900–2015 [CONTINUED]

[Data are based on death certificates]

Specified age and year	White, not Hispanic			Black, not Hispanic			Hispanic[e]		
	Both sexes	Male	Female	Both sexes	Male	Female	Both sexes	Male	Female
At birth					Life expectancy, in years				
2006	78.2	75.7	80.6	73.1	69.5	76.4	80.3	77.5	82.9
2007	78.4	75.9	80.8	73.5	69.9	76.7	80.7	77.8	83.2
2008	78.4	76.0	80.7	73.9	70.5	77.0	80.8	78.0	83.3
2009	78.7	76.3	81.0	74.4	71.0	77.4	81.1	78.4	83.5
2010	78.8	76.4	81.1	74.7	71.5	77.7	81.7	78.8	84.3
2011	78.7	76.4	81.1	75.0	71.8	77.8	81.8	79.2	84.2
2012	78.9	76.5	81.2	75.1	71.9	78.1	81.9	79.3	84.3
2013[d,f]	78.8	76.5	81.2	75.1	71.9	78.1	81.9	79.2	84.2
2014[d,f]	78.9	76.5	81.2	75.3	72.1	78.2	82.0	79.4	84.4
2015[d,f]	78.7	76.3	81.1	75.1	71.8	78.1	82.0	79.3	84.3
At 65 years									
2006	18.7	17.2	19.9	17.1	15.1	18.5	20.2	18.5	21.5
2007	18.8	17.4	20.0	17.2	15.3	18.7	20.5	18.7	21.7
2008	18.8	17.4	20.0	17.4	15.4	18.8	20.4	18.7	21.6
2009	19.1	17.7	20.3	17.7	15.8	19.1	20.7	19.0	21.9
2010	19.1	17.7	20.3	17.7	15.8	19.1	21.2	19.2	22.6
2011	19.1	17.8	20.3	17.9	16.1	19.2	21.2	19.5	22.5
2012	19.3	17.9	20.4	18.0	16.1	19.4	21.0	19.5	22.1
2013[d,f]	19.3	17.9	20.4	18.0	16.1	19.4	21.3	19.5	22.5
2014[d,f]	19.3	18.0	20.5	18.1	16.3	19.5	21.5	19.7	22.8
2015[d,f]	19.3	18.0	20.5	18.1	16.2	19.6	21.4	19.7	22.7
At 75 years									
2006	11.7	10.6	12.5	11.1	9.6	12.0	13.0	11.7	13.7
2007	11.8	10.7	12.6	11.2	9.7	12.1	13.1	11.8	13.8
2008	11.8	10.7	12.6	11.3	9.8	12.2	13.0	11.7	13.8
2009	12.0	11.0	12.8	11.6	10.1	12.4	13.3	12.0	14.1
2010	12.0	11.0	12.8	11.6	10.1	12.5	13.7	12.2	14.7
2011	12.0	11.0	12.8	11.7	10.4	12.5	13.7	12.4	14.5
2012	12.1	11.1	12.9	11.7	10.4	12.6	13.5	12.3	14.2
2013[d,f]	12.1	11.1	12.9	11.7	10.3	12.6	13.7	12.4	14.5
2014[d,f]	12.2	11.2	13.0	11.9	10.5	12.7	13.9	12.6	14.8
2015[d,f]	12.2	11.2	12.9	11.8	10.5	12.7	13.9	12.7	14.7

[a]Data shown for 1900–1960 are for the nonwhite population. Data for 1970 onwards are for the black or African American population only.

[b]Death registration area only. The death registration area increased from 10 states and the District of Columbia (D.C.) in 1900 to the coterminous United States in 1933.

[c]Includes deaths of persons who were not residents of the 50 states and D.C.

[d]Life expectancy estimates for 2013 are based on final Medicare data. Life expectancy estimates for 2014 and 2015 are based on preliminary Medicare data.

[e]Hispanic origin was added to the U.S. standard death certificate in 1989 and was adopted by every state in 1997. Life expectancies for the Hispanic populaf adjusted for underreporting on the death certificate of Hispanic ethnicity, but are not adjusted to account for the potential effects of return migration. To addr effects of age misstatement at the oldest ages, the probability of death for Hispanic persons older than 80 years is estimated as a function of non-Hispanic white mortality with the use of the Brass relational logit model.

[f]Tables by Hispanic origin are adjusted for race and Hispanic origin misclassification with classification ratios. Life expectancy estimates for 2010–2015 use tl classification ratios. See "Notes" section below.

Notes: Populations for computing life expectancy for 1991–1999 are 1990-based postcensal estimates of the U.S. resident population. Starting with *Health, United States, 2012*, populations for computing life expectancy for 2001–2009 were based on revised intercensal population estimates of the U.S. resident population. Populations for computing life expectancy for 2010 were based on 2010 census counts. Life expectancy for 2011 and beyond was computed using 2010-based postcensal estimates. In 1997, life table methodology was revised to construct complete life tables by single years of age that extend to age 100. (Anderson RN. Method for constructing complete annual U.S. life tables. NCHS. Vital Health Stat 2(129). 1999.) Previously, abridged life tables were constructed for 5-year age groups ending with 85 years and over. In 2000, the life table methodology was revised. The revised methodology is similar to that developed for the 1999–2001 decennial life tables. In 2008, the life table methodology was further refined. Estimates for 2001 and onwards were revised based on the methodology used in the 2008 life table report. Life expectancy for 2001–2015, except as noted in footnote d, was calculated using data from Medicare to supplement vital statistics and census data. Starting with *Health, United States, 2016*, life expectancy for 2010–2015 were revised to take into account updated race and Hispanic origin classification ratios. Starting with 2003 data, some states allowed the reporting of more than one race on the death certificate. The multiple-race data for these states were bridged to the single-race categories of the 1977 Office of Management and Budget standards, for comparability with other states. The race groups, white and black include persons of Hispanic and non-Hispanic origin. Persons of Hispanic origin may be of any race. Some data were revised and differ from previous editions of Health, United States.

SOURCE: "Table 15. Life Expectancy at Birth, at Age 65, and at Age 75, by Sex, Race, and Hispanic Origin: United States, Selected Years 1900–2015," in *Health, United States, 2016: With Chartbook on Long-term Trends in Health*, Centers for Disease Control and Prevention, National Center for Health Statistics, 2017, https://www.cdc.gov/nchs/-data/hus/hus16.pdf (accessed July 16, 2017)

2014 and 2030. After 2030, this group's rate of growth is expected to slow slightly. However, although the absolute number of older Americans will continue growing, the proportion of 65-and-older adults relative to the population as a whole is expected to remain steady at just over 20% through the middle of the 21st century.

The Oldest-Old

The "oldest-old" subset of the population (those aged 85 years and older) grew even more rapidly than the 65-and-older population between 1970 and 2010. According to the Federal Interagency Forum on Aging-Related Statistics, in *Older Americans 2016*, although the 65-and-older population doubled between 1970 and 2014, growing from 20.1 million to 46.2 million, the 85-and-older population quadrupled, growing from 1.5 million in 1970 to 6.2 million in 2014. The 65-and-older population is expected to double again between 2014 and 2060, when it will reach 98.2 million, whereas the 85-and-older population is expected to triple by 2060, growing to 19.7 million.

The population of centenarians (people who are aged 100 years old and older) has also increased rapidly since the late 20th century. In *A Profile of Older Americans: 2016* (March 2017, https://www.giaging.org/documents/A_Profile_of_Older_Americans__2016.pdf), the U.S. Department of Health and Human Services' Administration on Aging indicates that the centenarian population increased 139% between 1980 to 2015, from 32,194 to 76,974.

Although medical advances and lifestyle choices can explain increases in longevity in the aggregate, centenarians represent a special case within the larger story of the longevity revolution. The most comprehensive study of centenarians ever undertaken, the long-running New England Centenarian Study (http://www.bumc.bu.edu/centenarian/), which began in 1995 and was ongoing as of September 2017, involves research into the genetic makeup and lifestyles of approximately 1,600 centenarians, including more than 100 supercentenarians (people who are aged 110 years and older). The researchers have found that people who live more than 100 years are typically characterized by very specific genetic patterns not shared by those who die at younger ages. Nevertheless, the researchers have also found evidence suggesting that lifestyle may play a role in activating or suppressing certain genetic components of extreme longevity. Centenarians are united by their ability to escape, delay, or survive the chronic conditions that are the primary causes of death for most people who reach old age. Among the study's population of centenarians, 15% have been classified as "escapers," people who have no evidence of serious disease at all; 43% have been classified as "delayers," people who succumb to chronic conditions like most other elderly people but who do not exhibit symptoms prior to the age of 80; and 42% have been classified as "survivors," people who had serious diseases prior to the age of 80 but were able to recover their health.

Geographic Distribution

The aging of the U.S. population has not occurred at the same rate in all parts of the country. Figure 5.1 shows the variation in the 65-and-older population as a proportion of total population in each state as of 2015. People aged 65 years and older represented between 15% and 16.5% of the total population in 22 states. In addition, elderly Americans aged 65 years and older accounted for between 17% and 19.4% in seven states: Delaware, Florida, Maine, Montana,

Pennsylvania, Vermont, and West Virginia. In 20 states, the elderly population represented between 11.5% and 14.7% of the total population. The youngest states were Utah and Alaska, where between 9.9% and 10.3% of the population was aged 65 years and older.

In terms of absolute numbers, however, the elderly population tended to be largest in the states with the largest overall populations, although some of these states were not among those with the highest percentages of elderly residents. According to the Administration on Aging, in *A Profile of Older Americans*, more than half (54%) of all people aged 65 years and older lived in 10 states in 2015: California, Florida, Illinois, Michigan, New Jersey, New York, North Carolina, Ohio, Pennsylvania, and Texas.

Demographic Characteristics

Besides growing larger, the older population in the United States is growing more diverse, which is a reflection of the increased diversity in the population at large. This trend is expected to accelerate considerably in the 21st century. In 2014, 78% of 65-and-older adults were non-Hispanic white, 9% were non-Hispanic African American, 8% were Hispanic, and 4% were non-Hispanic Asian American. (See Figure 5.2.) By 2060 the 65-and-older population is expected to be 55% non-Hispanic white, 22% Hispanic, 12% non-Hispanic African American, and 9% non-Hispanic Asian American.

The marital status and living arrangements of the 65-and-older population vary significantly by sex. In 2016, 70% of men aged 65 years and older were married, compared with only 45% of elderly women, although roughly equal percentages of women and men were divorced or separated (16% of women and 13% of men) or single or never married (5% of both women and men). (See Figure 5.3.) There are two primary reasons for this disparity: women live longer than men, on average, and therefore are more likely to survive their husbands; and men are more likely than women to remarry after divorce or the death of a spouse. In 2016, 34% of 65-and-older women were widows, compared with only 12% of 65-and-older men. Accordingly, older women were much more likely than older men to live alone. Whereas 20% of older men lived alone in 2012, 35% of older women did. (See Figure 5.4.)

Besides growing and becoming more diverse, the older population has become steadily more educated since the start of the 21st century. In 1965 only 23.5% of 65-and-older adults had a high school diploma and only 5% had a bachelor's degree or higher. (See Figure 5.5.) By 2015, 84.3% of 65-and-older adults had at least a high school diploma and 26.7% had a bachelor's degree or higher.

FIGURE 5.1

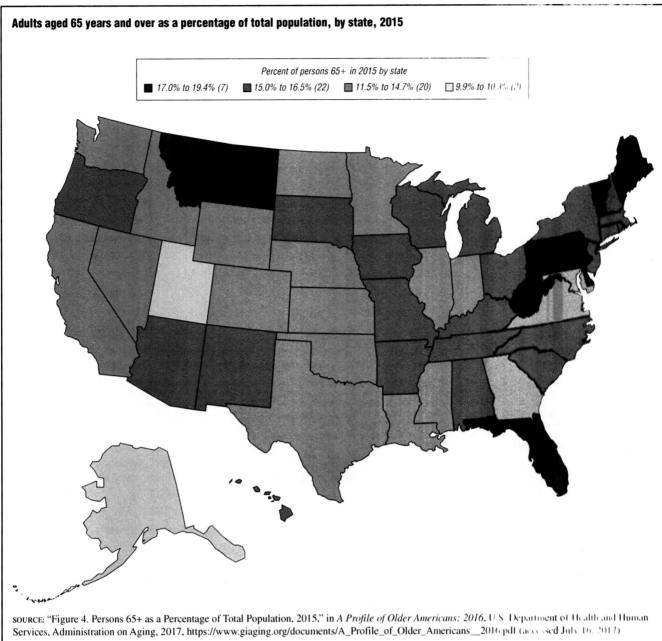

Adults aged 65 years and over as a percentage of total population, by state, 2015

Percent of persons 65+ in 2015 by state

■ 17.0% to 19.4% (7)   ■ 15.0% to 16.5% (22)   ■ 11.5% to 14.7% (20)   □ 9.9% to 10.9% (2)

SOURCE: "Figure 4. Persons 65+ as a Percentage of Total Population, 2015," in *A Profile of Older Americans: 2016*, U.S. Department of Health and Human Services, Administration on Aging, 2017, https://www.giaging.org/documents/A_Profile_of_Older_Americans__2016.pdf (accessed July 16, 2017)

Education levels are positively correlated with income levels and standard of living, and indeed, as Figure 5.6 shows, the period between 1974 and 2014 saw the older population's income distribution shift. In 1974, 14.6% of Americans aged 65 years and older lived below the federal poverty line, and another 34.6% were considered low income (i.e., their income represented between 100% and 199% of the poverty line). By 2014 only 10% of older people lived below the poverty line, and 22.5% were in the low-income group. The proportion of older Americans in the middle-income group (200% to 399% of poverty) remained relatively steady over this period, falling slightly from 32.6% to 31.1%, while the proportion of older Americans in the high-income group (400% of poverty or higher) doubled, rising from 18.2% to 36.4%.

Since the 1960s, Social Security has been the most important source of income for 65-and-older individuals and couples. In 2014 Social Security accounted for nearly half (49%) of per capita family income for all Americans aged 65 years and older. (See Figure 5.7.) This proportion varied according to an older American's overall family income level. Among elderly Americans in the lowest quintile (lowest fifth) of per capita income, Social Security accounted for more than two-thirds (67%) of household income. This percentage rose slightly for Americans aged 65 years and older living in the second-lowest quintile (second fifth) of per capita income, for whom nearly three-quarters (72%) of household income was derived from Social Security benefits. By contrast, for Americans aged 65 years and older in the top quintile

FIGURE 5.2

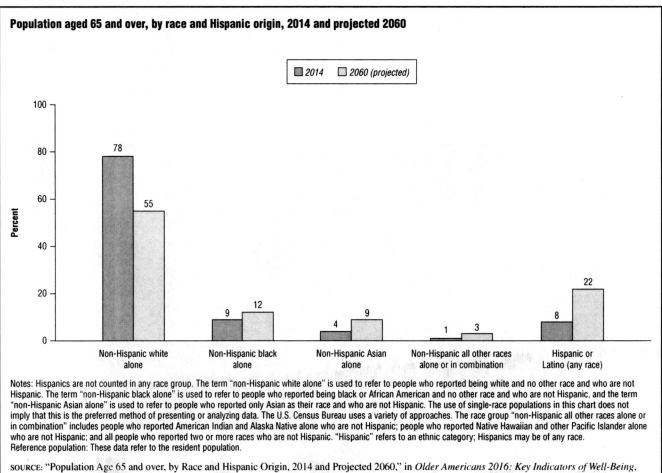

Population aged 65 and over, by race and Hispanic origin, 2014 and projected 2060

Notes: Hispanics are not counted in any race group. The term "non-Hispanic white alone" is used to refer to people who reported being white and no other race and who are not Hispanic. The term "non-Hispanic black alone" is used to refer to people who reported being black or African American and no other race and who are not Hispanic, and the term "non-Hispanic Asian alone" is used to refer to people who reported only Asian as their race and who are not Hispanic. The use of single-race populations in this chart does not imply that this is the preferred method of presenting or analyzing data. The U.S. Census Bureau uses a variety of approaches. The race group "non-Hispanic all other races alone or in combination" includes people who reported American Indian and Alaska Native alone who are not Hispanic; people who reported Native Hawaiian and other Pacific Islander alone who are not Hispanic; and all people who reported two or more races who are not Hispanic. "Hispanic" refers to an ethnic category; Hispanics may be of any race. Reference population: These data refer to the resident population.

SOURCE: "Population Age 65 and over, by Race and Hispanic Origin, 2014 and Projected 2060," in *Older Americans 2016: Key Indicators of Well-Being*, Federal Interagency Forum on Aging Related Statistics, 2016, https://agingstats.gov/docs/LatestReport/Older-Americans-2016-Key-Indicators-of-WellBeing.pdf (accessed July 16, 2017)

(highest fifth) of per capita income, Social Security represented only 18% of total household income in 2014.

HEALTH AND MORBIDITY AMONG OLDER ADULTS

Heart disease has historically been the leading cause of death for the 65-and-older population in the United States, and it remained so in the early 21st century. However, the rate of death from heart disease among older people has declined dramatically, from 2,547 deaths per 100,000 people in 1981 to 1,062 deaths per 100,000 people in 2014—a decrease of 58.3%. (See Figure 5.8.) Cancer remained the second-leading cause of death for older Americans during these decades, at 915 deaths per 100,000 in 2014, only 13.4% lower than the 1981 rate of 1,056. Between 1981 and 2014 the death rate from stroke fell even further than that of heart disease, from 624 to 247, a decrease of 60.4%. The death rate from influenza and pneumonia also fell significantly during this period, from 207 to 97. By contrast, older Americans in 2014 were more likely than their counterparts in 1981 to die from chronic lower respiratory diseases,

diabetes, and Alzheimer's disease. Among these causes of death, the rate for Alzheimer's had risen by far the most, from 6 per 100,000 in 1981 to 200 per 100,000 in 2014. This is in large part because the risk of being diagnosed with Alzheimer's rises with age. As more people live longer into old age, the prevalence of Alzheimer's inevitably increases, and there is no cure for the disease.

Significant proportions of the elderly population were living with chronic conditions as of 2013–14, with significant variations by sex evident in certain conditions. (See Figure 5.9.) Older men were substantially more likely to have heart disease, cancer, and diabetes than were older women; and older women were considerably more likely to have arthritis and slightly more likely to have hypertension (high blood pressure). Smaller numbers of both men and women reported having had a stroke, asthma, or chronic bronchitis or emphysema, and disparities by sex were less pronounced for these conditions.

According to the Federal Interagency Forum on Aging-Related Statistics, in *Older Americans 2016*, nearly eight out of 10 (78%) elderly adults reported being in good to excellent health in 2012–14. (See Figure 5.10.) There were significant differences in reported health status by race and Hispanic origin, however: whereas 80%

FIGURE 5.3

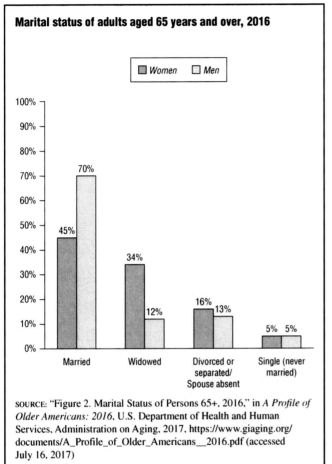

Marital status of adults aged 65 years and over, 2016

SOURCE: "Figure 2. Marital Status of Persons 65+, 2016," in *A Profile of Older Americans: 2016*, U.S. Department of Health and Human Services, Administration on Aging, 2017, https://www.giaging.org/documents/A_Profile_of_Older_Americans__2016.pdf (accessed July 16, 2017)

of non-Hispanic whites aged 65 years and older reported being in good to excellent health, only 66% of Hispanics and 65% non-Hispanic African Americans assessed their own health as good to excellent. Similar disparities occurred across all subgroups of the elderly population, with non-Hispanic whites being significantly more likely than their non-Hispanic African American and Hispanic counterparts to characterize their health as good to excellent between the ages of 65 and 74 years, 75 and 84 years, and over the age of 85 years.

As Figure 5.11 shows, more than one-third (35%) of people aged 65 and older lived with some type of disability in 2015. Nearly a quarter (23%) of Americans in this age demographic had ambulatory difficulty (moving from place to place), which was the most common problem among elderly adults. More than one-sixth of Americans aged 65 years and older either had trouble with their hearing (15%) or with living independently (15%) in 2015, while 9% struggled with cognitive difficulties, 8% had disabilities that made it difficult to take care of themselves, and 7% suffered from vision problems.

The near-universality of health and wellness challenges among the elderly is the primary reason for the existence of Medicare, the subsidized health insurance coverage that is universally available to U.S. citizens and permanent residents aged 65 years and older. Indeed, elderly Americans were far less likely to be uninsured in 2015 than those under the age of 65. As Table 5.2 shows, there were 47.5 million Americans aged 65 years and older in 2015; of these, 506,000 (1.1%) were not covered by some form of health insurance. By contrast, of the 271.3 million Americans aged 64 years and

FIGURE 5.4

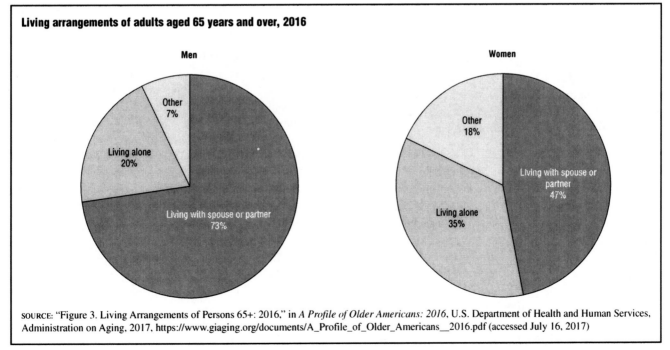

Living arrangements of adults aged 65 years and over, 2016

SOURCE: "Figure 3. Living Arrangements of Persons 65+: 2016," in *A Profile of Older Americans: 2016*, U.S. Department of Health and Human Services, Administration on Aging, 2017, https://www.giaging.org/documents/A_Profile_of_Older_Americans__2016.pdf (accessed July 16, 2017)

FIGURE 5.5

Educational attainment of the population aged 65 and over, selected years 1965–2015

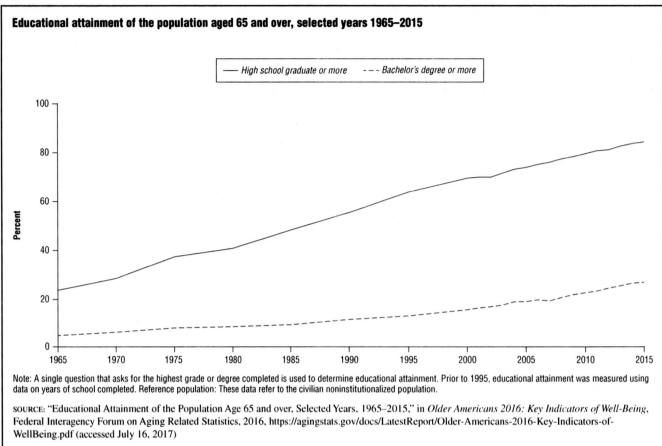

Note: A single question that asks for the highest grade or degree completed is used to determine educational attainment. Prior to 1995, educational attainment was measured using data on years of school completed. Reference population: These data refer to the civilian noninstitutionalized population.

SOURCE: "Educational Attainment of the Population Age 65 and over, Selected Years, 1965–2015," in *Older Americans 2016: Key Indicators of Well-Being*, Federal Interagency Forum on Aging Related Statistics, 2016, https://agingstats.gov/docs/LatestReport/Older-Americans-2016-Key-Indicators-of-WellBeing.pdf (accessed July 16, 2017)

younger that year, 28.5 million (10.5%) did not have health coverage. Among all age groups, the elderly were by far the most likely to be insured, and the reason for this was the comprehensiveness of coverage under Medicare. As Figure 5.12 shows, 93% of those aged 65 years and older had health coverage through Medicare in 2015. Some older Americans had other forms of coverage that supplanted or supplemented Medicare, including either employer-based or directly purchased individual private coverage (which 52% of older people had), Medicaid (a federal program that provides health coverage to impoverished children and adults of all ages; 7%), or coverage based on military service (7%). Medicare is thus a primary source of funding for end-of-life care.

As is discussed in Chapter 1, in the 20th and 21st centuries it is more common for people to die in hospitals or other institutional settings than in the home, as was the norm through the 19th century. End-of-life care often takes one of two forms: aggressive treatment intended to prolong life, which is commonly carried out in the intensive care units (ICUs) or critical care units (CCUs) of hospitals; and palliative and emotional support that focuses on quality of life, which is commonly carried out by hospice care providers either in the home or in hospice centers. Many elderly people receive both types of care at the end of life, and Medicare covers both. As

Figure 5.13 shows, 42.6% of Medicare recipients who died in 2009 used hospice care in the final month of life. This represents a dramatic increase since 1999, when only 19.2% of those who received end-of-life care through Medicare were in hospice care. By contrast, the proportion of Medicare recipients who received ICU or CCU care at the end of life was steadier throughout this period, rising from 22% in 1999 to 27.1% in 2009.

Hospitals remain the most common site of death for the elderly in the early 21st century, as in the late 20th century, but elderly people are becoming, on average, more likely to end their life outside of hospitals, perhaps in response to the broader cultural shift that emphasizes palliative care and quality of life. (See Figure 5.14.) Nearly one-third (32.4%) of 65-and-older deaths occurred in hospitals in 2009, compared with 48.7% in 1989. Meanwhile, the proportion of 65-and-older deaths that occurred in nursing homes or other long-term-care facilities (26.7%) had risen slightly since 1989 (from 21.3%), and the proportion of 65-and-older deaths that occurred in the home (24.3%) had risen more significantly (from 14.9%).

GERIATRICS

Geriatrics, the medical subspecialty that is concerned with the prevention and treatment of diseases in the

FIGURE 5.6

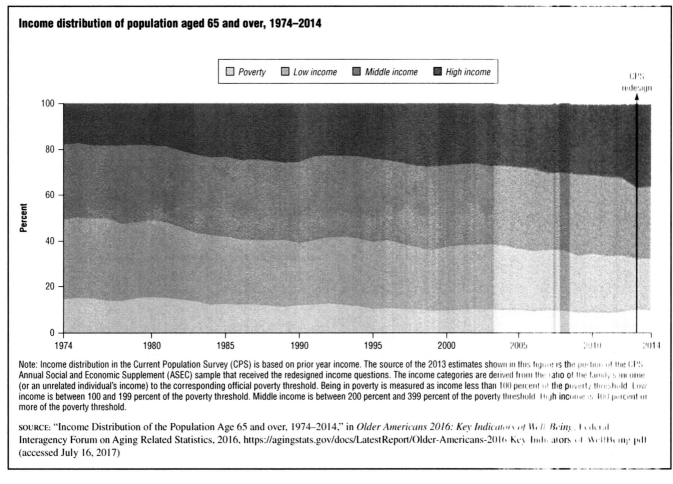

Income distribution of population aged 65 and over, 1974–2014

☐ Poverty ☐ Low income ■ Middle income ■ High income

CPS redesign

Note: Income distribution in the Current Population Survey (CPS) is based on prior year income. The source of the 2013 estimates shown in this figure is the portion of the CPS Annual Social and Economic Supplement (ASEC) sample that received the redesigned income questions. The income categories are derived from the ratio of the family's income (or an unrelated individual's income) to the corresponding official poverty threshold. Being in poverty is measured as income less than 100 percent of the poverty threshold. Low income is between 100 and 199 percent of the poverty threshold. Middle income is between 200 percent and 399 percent of the poverty threshold. High income is 400 percent or more of the poverty threshold.

SOURCE: "Income Distribution of the Population Age 65 and over, 1974–2014," in *Older Americans 2016: Key Indicators of Well-Being*, Federal Interagency Forum on Aging Related Statistics, 2016, https://agingstats.gov/docs/LatestReport/Older-Americans-2016-Key-Indicators-of-WellBeing.pdf (accessed July 16, 2017)

elderly, has evolved alongside the public-health advances that have extended life expectancy in the developed world. Geriatricians are physicians trained in internal medicine or family practice who obtain additional training and certification in the diagnosis and treatment of older adults. Geriatricians rely on the findings of researchers and gerontologists (nonphysician professionals who conduct scientific studies of aging and older adults) to help older adults maintain function and independence.

Gerontology was unheard of before the 19th century, when most people died at an early age. Those who reached old age accepted their deteriorating health as a part of aging. The field of research was born during the early 20th century, when scientists began investigating the pathological changes that accompany the aging process. The Association of American Medical Colleges has responded to the need for geriatric care by developing minimum geriatrics-specific competencies. The competencies establish performance benchmarks for medical school graduates who will care for geriatric patients when they are first-year residents. The competencies are organized under eight general areas: medication management; cognitive and behavioral disorders; self-care capacity; falls, balance, and gait disorders; health

care planning and promotion; atypical presentation of disease; palliative care (care that relieves the pain but does not cure the illness); and hospital care for elders.

Shortage of Geriatricians

According to the American Geriatrics Society (AGS), in the fact sheet "The Demand for Geriatric Care and the Evident Shortage of Geriatrics Healthcare Providers" (March 2013, http://www.americangeriatrics.org/files/documents/Adv_Resources/demand_for_geriatric_care.pdf), there are far fewer trained geriatricians than are necessary to meet the needs of a rapidly aging U.S. population. As of 2013, there were 7,500 geriatricians in the United States, each of which can care for approximately 700 elderly adults. This was enough geriatricians to serve approximately 5.3 million elderly patients, whereas there were closer to 12 million patients in need of geriatricians. As the elderly population continues to grow, the need for more geriatricians will only escalate. The AGS estimates that around 30,000 geriatricians will be needed by 2030, when the last of the baby boomers reach retirement age. To meet this demand, approximately 1,200 new geriatricians would have to be trained every year for the next 20 years.

FIGURE 5.7

Percentage distribution of per capita family income among persons aged 65 and older, by income quintile and source of income, 2014

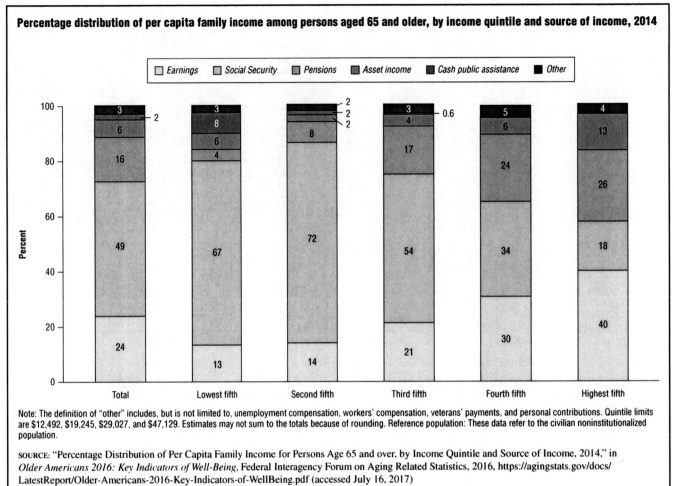

Note: The definition of "other" includes, but is not limited to, unemployment compensation, workers' compensation, veterans' payments, and personal contributions. Quintile limits are $12,492, $19,245, $29,027, and $47,129. Estimates may not sum to the totals because of rounding. Reference population: These data refer to the civilian noninstitutionalized population.

SOURCE: "Percentage Distribution of Per Capita Family Income for Persons Age 65 and over, by Income Quintile and Source of Income, 2014," in *Older Americans 2016: Key Indicators of Well-Being*, Federal Interagency Forum on Aging Related Statistics, 2016, https://agingstats.gov/docs/LatestReport/Older-Americans-2016-Key-Indicators-of-WellBeing.pdf (accessed July 16, 2017)

This is unlikely to happen based on present medical school trends. The AGS reports that in 2010 only 75 residents in internal medicine or family medicine nationwide entered fellowship programs associated with geriatric medicine, down from 112 in 2005. Geriatric medicine, like the practice of internal and general medicine more generally, is one of the lowest paying of all medical and surgical specialties. The high cost of medical school and the large student loans that graduates must repay once they become licensed physicians are believed to be primary factors in steering medical students away from geriatrics and into more lucrative specialties.

The lack of geriatric expertise extends beyond the ranks of general physicians. According to the AGS, less than 1% of registered nurses, pharmacists, and physician assistants have geriatric training, and only 2.6% of advanced practice registered nurses (nurses with specialized postgraduate training) have geriatric training. Additionally, there are only around 1,600 geriatric psychiatrists in the United States, only 3% of psychologists have practices devoted primarily to older adults, and only 4% of social workers emphasize geriatric issues.

These shortages are expected to result in significant failures to deliver the health care that older Americans will need in the coming decades.

FIGURE 5.8

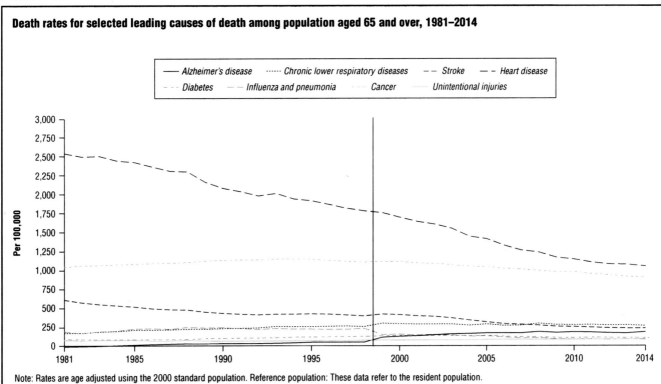

Death rates for selected leading causes of death among population aged 65 and over, 1981–2014

Legend: Alzheimer's disease · Chronic lower respiratory diseases · Stroke · Heart disease · Diabetes · Influenza and pneumonia · Cancer · Unintentional injuries

Note: Rates are age adjusted using the 2000 standard population. Reference population: These data refer to the resident population.

SOURCE: "Death Rates among People Age 65 and over, by Selected Leading Causes of Death, 1981–2014," in *Older Americans 2016: Key Indicators of Well-Being*, Federal Interagency Forum on Aging Related Statistics, 2016, https://agingstats.gov/docs/LatestReport/Older-Americans-2016-Key-Indicators-of-WellBeing.pdf (accessed July 16, 2017)

FIGURE 5.9

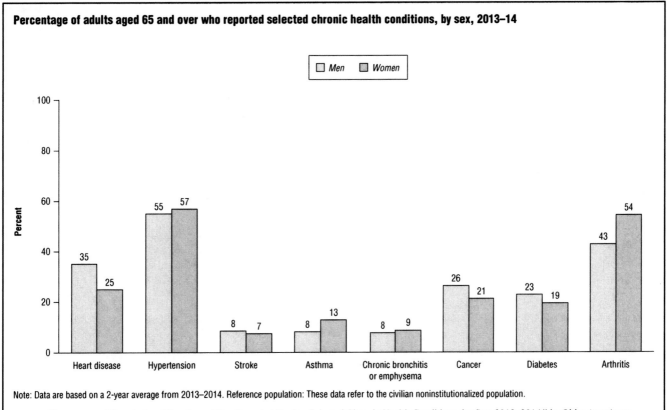

Percentage of adults aged 65 and over who reported selected chronic health conditions, by sex, 2013–14

Note: Data are based on a 2-year average from 2013–2014. Reference population: These data refer to the civilian noninstitutionalized population.

SOURCE: "Percentage of People Age 65 and over Who Reported Having Selected Chronic Health Conditions, by Sex, 2013–2014," in *Older Americans 2016: Key Indicators of Well-Being*, Federal Interagency Forum on Aging Related Statistics, 2016, https://agingstats.gov/docs/LatestReport/Older-Americans-2016-Key-Indicators-of-WellBeing.pdf (accessed July 16, 2017)

FIGURE 5.10

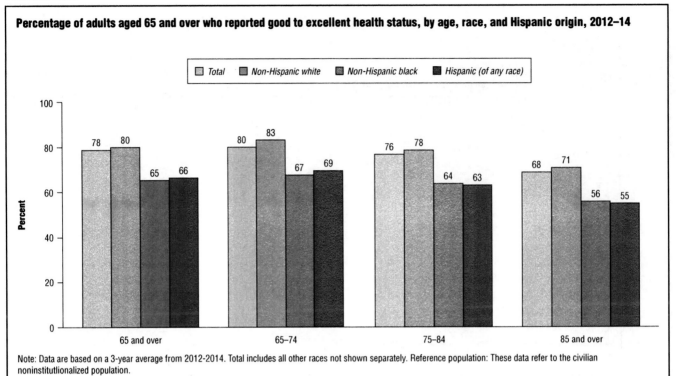

Percentage of adults aged 65 and over who reported good to excellent health status, by age, race, and Hispanic origin, 2012–14

Note: Data are based on a 3-year average from 2012-2014. Total includes all other races not shown separately. Reference population: These data refer to the civilian noninstitutlionalized population.

SOURCE: "Percentage of People Age 65 and over with Respondent-Assessed Good to Excellent Health Status, by Age Group and Race and Hispanic Origin, 2012–2014," in *Older Americans 2016: Key Indicators of Well-Being*, Federal Interagency Forum on Aging Related Statistics, 2016, https://agingstats .gov/docs/LatestReport/Older-Americans-2016-Key-Indicators-of-WellBeing.pdf (accessed July 16, 2017)

FIGURE 5.11

Percentage of adults aged 65 and over with a disability, 2015

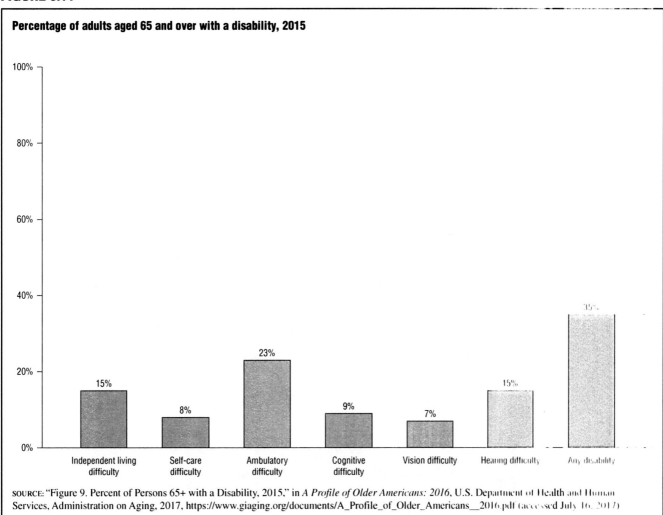

SOURCE: "Figure 9. Percent of Persons 65+ with a Disability, 2015," in *A Profile of Older Americans: 2016*, U.S. Department of Health and Human Services, Administration on Aging, 2017, https://www.giaging.org/documents/A_Profile_of_Older_Americans__2016.pdf (accessed July 16, 2017)

TABLE 5.2

Number of people with different types of health insurance coverage, by age, 2014 and 2015

[Numbers in thousands. Population as of March of the following year.]

Characteristic	Total		Any health insurance			Private health insurance[b]			Government health insurance[c]			Uninsured[d]		
	2014 Number	2015 Number	2014 Number	2015 Number	Change (2015 less 2014)[a]	2014 Number	2015 Number	Change (2015 less 2014)[a]	2014 Number	2015 Number	Change (2015 less 2014)[a]	2014 Number	2015 Number	Change (2015 less 2014)[a]
Total	316,168	318,868	283,200	289,903	6,702	208,600	214,238	5,639	115,470	118,395	2,924	32,968	28,966	-4,002
Age														
Under age 65	270,174	271,322	237,835	242,862	5,027	184,311	189,467	5,157	72,420	73,786	1,366	32,339	28,460	-3,879
Under age 18	73,920	74,062	69,448	70,196	748	44,832	46,138	1,306	31,878	31,853	-26	4,472	3,866	-606
Under age 19[e]	78,119	78,182	73,260	74,024	763	47,687	48,959	1,271	33,265	33,320	54	4,858	4,158	-700
Aged 18 to 64	196,254	197,260	168,387	172,666	4,279	139,479	143,330	3,851	40,541	41,933	1,392	27,867	24,594	-3,273
Aged 19 to 64	192,055	193,140	164,575	168,838	4,263	136,623	140,509	3,886	39,155	40,466	1,312	27,481	24,302	-3,178
Aged 19 to 25[f]	30,508	30,475	25,296	26,060	764	20,585	21,288	703	6,735	7,019	283	5,212	4,414	-798
Aged 26 to 34	38,415	38,960	31,425	32,622	1,197	25,807	27,098	1,290	7,812	7,814	2	6,990	6,337	-653
Aged 35 to 44	39,919	40,005	33,755	34,517	761	28,551	29,099	548	7,246	7,737	491	6,163	5,489	-675
Aged 45 to 64	83,213	83,701	74,098	75,639	1,540	61,680	63,025	1,345	17,360	17,896	536	9,115	8,062	-1,053
Aged 65 and older	45,994	47,547	45,365	47,041	1,676	24,289	24,771	482	43,051	44,609	1,558	629	506	-123

[a]Details may not sum to totals because of rounding.
[b]Private health insurance includes coverage provided through an employer or union, coverage purchased directly by an individual from an insurance company, or coverage through someone outside the household.
[c]Government health insurance coverage includes Medicaid, Medicare, TRICARE (the military health plan serving uniformed service members), CHAMPVA (Civilian Health and Medical Program of the Department of Veterans Affairs), and care provided by the Department of Veterans Affairs and the military.
[d]Individuals are considered to be uninsured if they do not have health insurance coverage for the entire calendar year.
[e]Children under the age of 19 are eligible for Medicaid/CHIP. (Children's Health Insurance Program).
[f]This age is of special interest because of the Affordable Care Act's dependent coverage provision. Individuals aged 19 to 25 may be eligible to be a dependent on a parent's health insurance plan.
Note: The estimates by type of coverage are not mutually exclusive; people can be covered by more than one type of health insurance during the year.

SOURCE: Jessica C. Barnett and Marina S. Vornovitsky, "Table A-2. Number of People by Type of Health Insurance Coverage by Age: 2014 and 2015," in *Health Insurance Coverage in the United States: 2015,* U.S. Census Bureau, September 2016, https://www.census.gov/content/dam/Census/library/publications/2016/demo/p60–257.pdf (accessed July 17, 2017)

FIGURE 5.12

Percentage of adults aged 65 and over with health insurance coverage, 2015

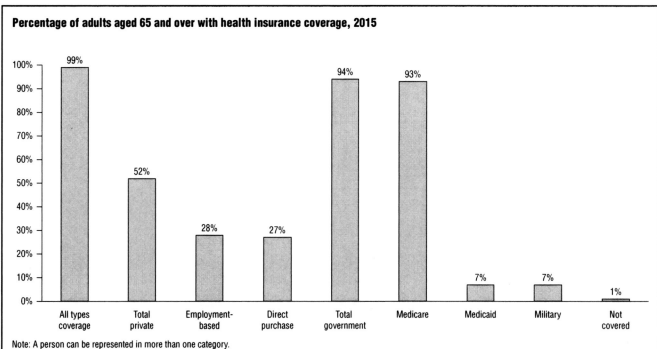

Note: A person can be represented in more than one category.

SOURCE: "Figure 8. Percentage of Persons 65+ by Type of Health Insurance Coverage, 2015," in *A Profile of Older Americans: 2016*, U.S. Department of Health and Human Services, Administration on Aging, 2017, https://www.giaging.org/documents/A_Profile_of_Older_Americans__2016.pdf (accessed July 16, 2017)

FIGURE 5.13

Percentage of Medicare participants 65 and over who used hospice or intensive care unit/coronary care unit services in last 30 days of life, 1999–2009

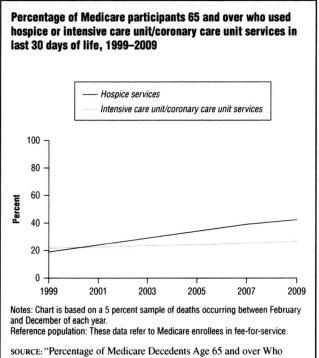

Notes: Chart is based on a 5 percent sample of deaths occurring between February and December of each year.
Reference population: These data refer to Medicare enrollees in fee-for-service.

SOURCE: "Percentage of Medicare Decedents Age 65 and over Who Used Hospice or Intensive Care Unit/Coronary Care Unit Services in Their Last 30 Days of Life, for Selected Years 1999–2009," in *Older Americans 2012: Key Indicators of Well-Being*, Federal Interagency Forum on Aging Related Statistics, 2012, https://agingstats.gov/docs/PastReports/2012/OA2012.pdf (accessed July 17, 2017)

FIGURE 5.14

Percentage distribution of deaths among adults 65 and over, by place of death, 1989–2009

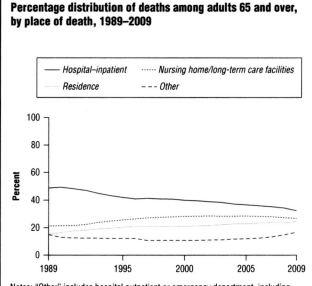

Notes: "Other" includes hospital outpatient or emergency department, including dead on arrival, inpatient hospice facilities, and all other places and unknown. Beginning in 2003, the term "long-term care facility" was added to the nursing home check box on the death certificate.
Reference population: These data refer to the resident population.

SOURCE: "Percent Distribution of Decedents Age 65 and over by Place of Death, 1989–2009," in *Older Americans 2012: Key Indicators of Well-Being*, Federal Interagency Forum on Aging Related Statistics, 2012, https://agingstats.gov/docs/PastReports/2012/OA2012.pdf (accessed July 17, 2017)

CHAPTER 6
INFANT AND CHILD DEATH

What greater pain could mortals have than this: To see their children dead before their eyes?

—Euripides

End-of-life issues are wrenching by definition, but those involving children have the potential to be particularly devastating. Parents who find themselves responsible for making decisions about how to handle their children's illnesses come into conflict with some of their most basic instincts, and unconditional love for a child can complicate rather than solve the dilemmas that arise in relation to the continuation of life support or other treatments. The parental need to protect one's child may be absolute, but what does protection mean in the case of a terminally ill child? Does protection translate into an infinite prolongation of life, even if this means exposing the child to unnecessary suffering? Or does protection translate into allowing the child to find relief from an agonizing existence even if the result is death?

Impossible as these decisions may seem, parents must regularly make them. In a best-case scenario, parents faced with such a terrible dilemma are aided by sensitive physicians and mental-health professionals, and they are able to make decisions with which they can eventually come to terms. Other cases present additional complications. What if the ailing child is an adolescent who refuses further treatment for a terminal illness? Whose wishes matter more: the suffering adolescent's, or the parent's?

This chapter focuses on infant and child death, the conditions that often cause mortality at young ages, and medical decision making for seriously ill children.

INFANT MORTALITY RATES AND CAUSES

Marian F. MacDorman and T. J. Mathews of the National Center for Health Statistics (NCHS) indicate in *Recent Trends in Infant Mortality in the United States* (October 2008, http://www.cdc.gov/nchs/data/databriefs/db09.pdf) that between 1900 and 2000 the U.S. infant

mortality rate declined dramatically. In 1900 the infant mortality rate was approximately 100 deaths per 1,000 live births, whereas in 2000 it was 6.9 deaths per 1,000 live births. Between 2000 and 2007 the infant mortality rate appeared to have stopped decreasing, but between 2007 and 2015 it resumed a downward trend. (See Figure 6.1.)

This improvement in the prospects for infants, which is common to all countries of the developed world, represents one of the most significant medical accomplishments in history. The same advances that prolonged life expectancies generally—especially those relating to sanitation, infectious diseases, antibiotics, and vaccination—played a major role in the early declines in infant mortality. Since 1960 advances in neonatology (the medical subspecialty that is concerned with the care of newborns) have been the primary drivers of the continued improvement in outcomes for newborn infants. Infants born prematurely or with low birth weights, who were once likely to die, now can survive life-threatening conditions because of the development of neonatal intensive care units, technologies, and treatments.

Babies are more likely to die in the neonatal period (the first 28 days of life) than in the postneonatal period (28 days to 11 months of age). (See Figure 6.1.) The NCHS states in *Health, United States, 2016: With Chartbook on Long-Term Trends in Health* (2017, https://www.cdc.gov/nchs/data/hus/hus16.pdf) that there were 3.93 neonatal deaths per 1,000 births in 2015. This figure was double that of the postneonatal mortality rate of 1.96 deaths per 1,000 births that same year.

U.S. Rates Compared with Those of Other Countries

Although infant mortality rates in the United States had reached historic lows by the early 21st century, they were considerably higher than rates in other wealthy countries. Table 6.1 shows the infant mortality rates for 1960–2013 for most of the member countries of the Organisation for Economic Co-operation and Development (OECD).

FIGURE 6.1

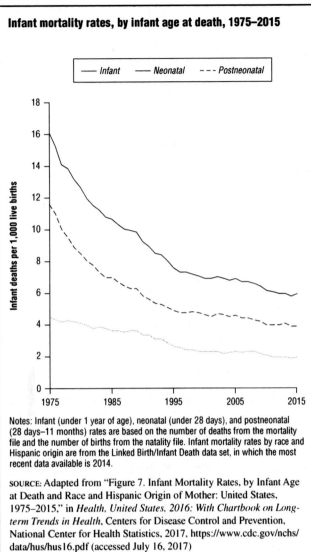

Infant mortality rates, by infant age at death, 1975–2015

— Infant   — Neonatal   - - - Postneonatal

Notes: Infant (under 1 year of age), neonatal (under 28 days), and postneonatal (28 days–11 months) rates are based on the number of deaths from the mortality file and the number of births from the natality file. Infant mortality rates by race and Hispanic origin are from the Linked Birth/Infant Death data set, in which the most recent data available is 2014.

SOURCE: Adapted from "Figure 7. Infant Mortality Rates, by Infant Age at Death and Race and Hispanic Origin of Mother: United States, 1975–2015," in *Health, United States, 2016: With Chartbook on Long-term Trends in Health,* Centers for Disease Control and Prevention, National Center for Health Statistics, 2017, https://www.cdc.gov/nchs/data/hus/hus16.pdf (accessed July 16, 2017)

The OECD is a group that promotes international economic and social well-being. It consists of most of the world's richest countries as well as a number of emerging countries. The United States has by far the largest economy of any OECD member country, but its 2013 infant mortality rate was surpassed by only those of Chile, Mexico, and Turkey, placing it 24th among the 27 countries for which data were available. (No 2013 data were available for Canada, France, or New Zealand, so the numerical rankings in this table reach only 27. Canada's infant mortality rate was, however, known to be lower than that of the United States during this time.)

Moreover, between 1960 and 2013 the U.S. infant mortality rate fell more slowly than the rates of comparably developed countries: its 1960 rate of 26 infant deaths per 1,000 live births translated into a ranking of 11th among the 27 countries for which data were available that year. Countries with comparable rates in 1960, such as Canada (27.3), France (27.7), the Slovak Republic (28.6),

and Ireland (29.3), all reduced their infant mortality rates more substantially over the subsequent five decades than did the United States. The U.S. rate was more than double that of all countries ranked one through seven in 2013 (because numerous countries had identical rates, there were eight countries in this group), and it was more than triple that of Finland, the country with the lowest infant mortality rate in the world that year (1.8 infant deaths per 1,000 births).

Some researchers have suggested that differences in the way countries classify live births explain some of the disparity between infant mortality rates in the United States and rates in the rest of the developed world. Specifically, some European countries use gestational weight, age, or both in their definitions of what constitutes a live birth, classifying the deaths of babies who do not surpass these limits as stillbirths rather than as infant deaths. Because the United States considers all babies born alive to be live births, it would necessarily have a higher infant mortality rate than a country that does not consider all such deaths to be infant deaths.

Since 1993, however, most developed countries have used the same definition as the United States, which is the definition recommended by the World Health Organization. The handful of countries that continue to classify some instances of infant mortality as stillbirths (the Czech Republic, France, Ireland, the Netherlands, and Poland) are not sufficient to skew the international data on their own. In *The U.S. Infant Mortality Rate: International Comparisons, Underlying Factors, and Federal Programs* (April 4, 2012, https://www.fas.org/sgp/crs/misc/R41378.pdf), Elayne J. Heisler of the Congressional Research Service notes that statisticians at the NCHS have concluded that, for the high U.S. rates to be explained by differences in the reporting of live births, all European countries "would have to misreport one-third of their infant deaths, which these researchers conclude is unlikely."

According to Heisler, NCHS researchers have shown that the high infant mortality rate in the United States is largely explained by its high rate of infant mortality due to short gestational age (prematurity) and low birth weight. The usual length of human pregnancy is 40 weeks, and infants born before 37 weeks of pregnancy are considered to be premature. A premature infant does not have fully formed organ systems. If the premature infant is born with a birth weight that is comparable to a full-term baby and has organ systems only slightly underdeveloped, the chances of survival are great. Conversely, premature infants of very low birth weight are susceptible to many risks and are less likely to survive. If they survive, they may suffer from intellectual disability and other abnormalities of the nervous system. A severe medical condition called respiratory distress syndrome

TABLE 6.1

Infant mortality rates and rankings for Organisation for Economic Co-operation and Development countries, selected years 1960–2013

[Data are based on reporting by OECD countries]

Country[b]	1960	1970	1980	1990	2000	2010	2012	2013	International rankings[a] 1960	International rankings[a] 2013
					Infant[c] deaths per 1,000 live birth					
Australia	20.2	17.9	10.7	8.2	5.2	4.1	3.3	3.6	5	16
Austria	37.5	25.9	14.3	7.8	4.8	3.9	3.2	3.1	19	10
Belgium	31.4	21.1	12.1	8.0	4.8	3.6	3.8	3.5	17	13
Canada	27.3	18.8	10.4	6.8	5.3	5.0	4.8	NA	12	NA
Chile	120.3	79.3	33.0	16.0	8.9	7.4	7.4	7.0	27	25
Czech Republic[d]	20.0	20.2	16.9	10.8	4.1	2.7	2.6	2.5	4	4
Denmark	21.5	14.2	8.4	7.5	5.3	3.4	3.4	3.5	8	13
Finland	21.0	13.2	7.6	5.6	3.8	2.3	2.4	1.8	6	1
France	27.7	18.2	10.0	7.3	4.5	3.6	3.5	NA	13	NA
Germany[e]	35.0	22.5	12.4	7.0	4.4	3.4	3.3	3.3	18	12
Greece	40.1	29.6	17.9	9.7	5.9	3.8	2.9	3.7	20	17
Hungary	47.6	35.9	23.2	14.8	9.2	5.3	4.9	5.0	23	22
Ireland	29.3	19.5	11.1	8.2	6.2	3.6	3.5	3.5	15	13
Israel[f]	NA	24.2	15.6	9.9	5.5	3.7	3.6	3.1	NA	10
Italy	43.9	29.6	14.6	8.1	4.3	3.0	2.9	2.9	22	7
Japan	30.7	13.1	7.5	4.6	3.2	2.3	2.2	2.1	16	2
Korea	NA	45.0	NA	NA	NA	3.2	2.9	3.0	NA	9
Mexico	92.3	NA	52.6	32.5	20.8	14.1	13.3	13.0	26	27
Netherlands	16.5	12.7	8.6	7.1	5.1	3.8	3.7	3.8	2	18
New Zealand	22.6	16.7	13.0	8.4	6.3	5.5	4.7	NA	10	NA
Norway	16.0	11.3	8.1	6.9	3.8	2.8	2.5	2.4	1	3
Poland	56.1	36.4	25.4	19.4	8.1	5.0	4.6	4.6	24	21
Portugal	77.5	55.5	24.3	10.9	5.5	2.5	3.4	2.9	25	7
Slovak Republic[d]	28.6	25.7	20.9	12.0	8.6	5.7	5.8	5.5	14	23
Spain	43.7	28.1	12.3[g]	7.6	4.4	3.2	3.1	2.7	21	5
Sweden	16.6	11.0	6.9	6.0	3.4	2.5	2.6	2.7	3	5
Switzerland	21.1	15.1	9.1	6.8	4.9	3.8	3.6	3.9	7	19
Turkey	NA	NA	NA	NA	28.4	12.0	11.6	10.8	NA	26
United Kingdom	22.5	18.5	12.1	7.9	5.6	4.2	4.0	3.9	9	19
United States	26.0	20.0	12.6	9.2	6.9	6.1	6.0	6.0	11	24

NA = data not available. OECD = Organisation for Economic Co-operation and Development.

[a]Rankings are from lowest to highest infant mortality rates (IMR). Countries with the same IMR receive the same rank. The country with the next highest IMR is assigned the rank it would have received had the lower-ranked countries not been tied, i.e., skip a rank. The latest year's international rankings are based on 2013 data because that is the most current data year for which most countries have reported their final data to OECD. Countries without an estimate in the OECD database are omitted from ranking. Relative rankings for individual countries may be affected if not all countries have reported data to OECD.

[b]Refers to countries, territories, cities, or geographic areas with at least 2.5 million population in 2000 (United Nations, Department of Economic and Social Affairs, Population Division. World Urbanization Prospects: The 2014 Revision, Volume I: Comprehensive Tables. ST/ESA/SER.A/379. 2015) and with complete counts of live births and infant deaths according to the United Nations Demographic Yearbook.

[c]The infant mortality rate is defined as the number of deaths of children under one year of age, expressed per 1,000 live births. Some of the international variation in infant mortality rates is due to variations among countries in registering practices for premature infants.

[d]In 1993, Czechoslovakia was divided into two nations, the Czech Republic and Slovakia. Data for years prior to 1993 are from the Czech and Slovak regions of Czechoslovakia.

[e]Until 1990, estimates refer to the Federal Republic of Germany; from 1995 onward data refer to Germany after reunification.

[f]Statistical data for Israel are supplied by, and under the responsibility of, the relevant Israeli authorities. The use of such data by the OECD is without prejudice to the status of the Golan Heights, East Jerusalem, and Israeli settlements in the West Bank under the terms of international law.

[g]Break in series.

Notes: Some rates for selected countries and selected years were revised and differ from previous editions of *Health, United States*.

SOURCE: "Table 13. Infant Mortality Rates and International Rankings: Organisation for Economic Co-operation and Development (OECD) Countries, Selected Years 1960–2013," in *Health, United States, 2016: With Chartbook on Long-term Trends in Health*, Centers for Disease Control and Prevention, National Center for Health Statistics, 2017, https://www.cdc.gov/nchs/data/hus/hus16.pdf (accessed July 16, 2017)

also commonly affects premature infants born before 35 weeks of pregnancy. In respiratory distress syndrome, immature lungs do not function properly, which may lead to infant death within hours after birth. Intensive care for such infants includes the use of a mechanical ventilator to facilitate breathing. Premature infants also commonly have immature gastrointestinal systems, which preclude them from taking in nourishment properly. Unable to suck and swallow, they must be fed through a stomach tube.

In the United States, as in the rest of the developed world, birth defects—which are officially classified as congenital malformations, deformations, and chromosomal abnormalities—account for more cases of infant mortality than any other cause. In the United States, however, the number of infant deaths caused by disorders related to prematurity and low birth weight is nearly as high as the number due to birth defects. As Table 6.2 shows, birth defects accounted for 4,778 infant deaths in 2013 and short gestation and low birth weight led to death in 4,213 cases. Maternal complications of pregnancy caused 1,597 infant deaths, sudden infant death syndrome caused 1,561 infant deaths, and accidents caused 1,150 infant deaths. Although the U.S. rate of

TABLE 6.2

Infant deaths and mortality rates for the five leading causes of infant death, by race and Hispanic origin of mother, 2013

[Rates per 100,000 live births in specified group]

Cause of death	All races			Non-Hispanic white			Non-Hispanic black			American Indian or Alaska Native			Asian or Pacific Islander[a]		
	Rank	Number	Rate	Rank	Number	Rate	Rank	Number	Rate	Rank	Number	Rate	Rank	Number	Rate
All causes	g	23,446	596.3	g	10,766	505.6	g	6,488	1,111.3	g	350	761.0	g	1,082	407.3
Congenital malformations, deformations and chromosomal abnormalities	1	4,778	121.5	1	2,443	114.7	2	827	141.6	1	71	154.4	1	236	88.8
Disorders related to short gestation and low birth weight, not elsewhere classified	2	4,213	107.1	2	1,585	74.4	1	1,522	260.7	2	44	95.7	2	193	72.6
Newborn affected by maternal complications of pregnancy	3	1,597	40.6	4	635	29.8	3	505	86.5	5	19	f	3	97	36.5
Sudden infant death syndrome	4	1,561	39.7	3	854	40.1	4	428	73.3	3	36	78.3	5	38	14.3
Accidents (unintentional injuries)	5	1,150	29.2	5	583	27.4	5	371	63.5	4	22	47.8	9	18	f

Cause of death	Total Hispanic[b]			Mexican[c]			Puerto Rican[d]			Central and South American[e]		
	Rank	Number	Rate	Rank	Number	Rate	Rank	Number	Rate	Rank	Number	Rate
All causes	g	4,507	500.2	g	2,672	490.1	g	405	593.0	g	565	430.3
Congenital malformations, deformations and chromosomal abnormalities	1	1,166	129.4	1	754	138.3	2	66	96.6	1	158	120.3
Disorders related to short gestation and low birth weight, not elsewhere classified	2	794	88.1	2	446	81.8	1	90	131.8	2	106	80.7
Newborn affected by maternal complications of pregnancy	3	298	33.1	3	178	32.6	3	33	48.3	3	40	30.5
Sudden infant death syndrome	4	195	21.6	4	123	22.6	6	13	f	7	11	f
Accidents (unintentional injuries)	6	151	16.8	6	88	16.1	4	24	35.1	10	10	f

[a]Newborn affected by complications of placenta, cord and membranes was the fourth leading cause of death, with 43 deaths and a rate of 16.2.
[b]Newborn affected by complications of placenta, cord and membranes was the fifth leading cause of death, with 168 deaths and a rate of 18.6.
[c]Newborn affected by complications of placenta, cord and membranes was the fifth leading cause of death, with 100 deaths and a rate of 18.3.
[d]Newborn affected by complications of placenta, cord and membranes was the fifth leading cause of death, with 15 deaths.
[e]Newborn affected by complications of placenta, cord and membranes was the fourth leading cause of death, with 24 deaths and a rate of 18.3. Bacterial sepsis of newborn (P36) was the fifth leading cause of death, with 20 deaths and a rate of 15.2.
[f]Figure does not meet standards of reliability or precision; based on fewer than 20 deaths in the numerator.
[g]Category not applicable.
Note: Reliable cause-specific infant mortality rates cannot be computed for Cuban infants because of the small number of infant deaths (57). Race and Hispanic origin are reported separately on birth certificates. Race categories are consistent with the 1977 Office of Management and Budget standards. Persons of Hispanic origin may be of any race. In this table, Hispanic women are classified only by place of origin; non-Hispanic women are classified by race.

SOURCE: T.J. Mathews, Marian F. MacDorman, and Marie E. Thoma, "Table 5. Infant Deaths and Mortality Rates for the Five Leading Causes of Infant Death, by Race and Hispanic Origin of Mother: United States, 2013 Linked File," in "Infant Mortality Statistics from the 2013 Period Linked Birth/Infant Death Data Set," *National Vital Statistics Reports*, vol. 64, no. 9, August 6, 2015, https://www.cdc.gov/nchs/data/nvsr/nvsr64/nvsr64_09.pdf (accessed July 17, 2017)

infant mortality due to birth defects is similar to that of other developed countries, it has a far higher rate of low birth weight and short gestational age births. Heisler reports that "the U.S. [infant mortality rate] would be 3.9 if the United States had the same rate of low birth-weight and short gestational age births as Sweden."

The prevalence of low birth weight and short gestational age births is, in turn, linked to disparities among different racial and ethnic groups in the United States. African American and Native American infants are exposed, in the aggregate, to inequalities in medical care and other social resources. They have long been considerably more likely to die during the first year after birth than have babies of other races and ethnicities. As Table 6.3 shows, the infant mortality rate for African American mothers stood at 19.2 per 1,000 live births in 1983, and that of Native American or Alaskan Native mothers stood at 15.2. By comparison, the rate for Hispanic mothers was 9.5, the rate for non-Hispanic white mothers was 9.3, and the rate for Asian or Pacific Islander mothers was

8.3. Since the 1980s, infant mortality rates have fallen faster for both African American and Native American or Alaskan Native mothers than for the other groups. By 1995 the African American infant mortality rate was 14.6, and the Native American or Alaskan Native rate was 9. Thereafter, the rate for Native American or Alaskan Native mothers fluctuated, remaining significantly higher than that for Hispanic, non-Hispanic white, and Asian or Pacific Islander mothers. The rate for African American mothers continued to drop, but it remained more than double that of Hispanic, non-Hispanic white, and Asian American mothers throughout the early years of the 21st century. As shown in Figure 6.2, the infant mortality rate in 2014 was lowest among Asian or Pacific Islanders, with 3.68 infant deaths per 1,000 live births, followed by non-Hispanic whites (4.89 per 1,000 live births), Hispanics (5.01), Native American and Alaskan Natives (7.66), and African Americans (10.93).

As Table 6.2 shows, birth defects were the leading cause of infant death among non-Hispanic whites,

TABLE 6.3

Infant, neonatal, and postneonatal mortality rates, by race and Hispanic origin of mother, selected years 1983–2014

[Data are based on linked birth and death certificates for infants and fetal death records]

Maternal race and Hispanic origin	1983[a]	1985[a]	1990[a]	1995[b]	2000[b]	2005[b]	2010[b]	2013[b]	2014[b]
				Infant[c] deaths per 1,000 live births					
All mothers	10.9	10.4	8.9	7.6	6.9	6.9	6.1	6.0	5.8
White	9.3	8.9	7.3	6.3	5.7	5.7	5.2	5.1	4.9
Black or African American	19.2	18.6	16.9	14.6	13.5	13.3	11.2	10.8	10.7
American Indian or Alaska Native	15.2	13.1	13.1	9.0	8.3	8.1	8.3	7.6	7.6
Asian or Pacific Islander[d]	8.3	7.8	6.6	5.3	4.9	4.9	4.3	4.1	3.9
Hispanic or Latina[e,f]	9.5	8.8	7.5	6.3	5.6	5.6	5.3	5.0	5.0
Mexican	9.1	8.5	7.2	6.0	5.4	5.5	5.1	4.9	4.8
Puerto Rican	12.9	11.2	9.9	8.9	8.2	8.3	7.1	5.9	7.2
Cuban	7.5	8.5	7.2	5.3	4.6	4.4	3.8	3.0	3.9
Central and South American	8.5	8.0	6.8	5.5	4.6	4.7	4.4	4.3	4.3
Other and unknown Hispanic or Latina	10.6	9.5	8.0	7.4	6.9	6.4	6.1	5.9	5.4
Not Hispanic or Latina:[f]									
White	9.2	8.6	7.2	6.3	5.7	5.8	5.2	5.1	4.9
Black or African American	19.1	18.3	16.9	14.7	13.6	13.6	11.5	11.1	10.9
				Neonatal[c] deaths per 1,000 live births					
All mothers	7.1	6.8	5.7	4.9	4.6	4.5	4.0	4.0	3.9
White	6.1	5.8	4.6	4.1	3.8	3.8	3.5	3.4	3.3
Black or African American	12.5	12.3	11.1	9.6	9.1	8.9	7.3	7.3	7.3
American Indian or Alaska Native	7.5	6.1	6.1	4.0	4.4	4.0	4.3	4.1	4.1
Asian or Pacific Islander[d]	5.2	4.8	3.9	3.4	3.4	3.4	3.0	3.0	2.8
Hispanic or Latina[e,f]	6.2	5.7	4.8	4.1	3.8	3.9	3.6	3.6	3.5
Mexican	5.9	5.4	4.5	3.9	3.6	3.8	3.5	3.5	3.5
Puerto Rican	8.7	7.6	6.9	6.1[i]	5.8	5.9	4.8	4.2	5.0
Cuban	5.0[i]	6.2	5.3	3.6[i]	3.2[i]	3.1[i]	2.9[i]	2.3[i]	2.6
Central and South American	5.8	5.6	4.4	3.7	3.3	3.2	3.0	3.1	3.1
Other and unknown Hispanic or Latina	6.4	5.6	5.0	4.8	4.6	4.3	4.0	4.0	3.7
Not Hispanic or Latina:[f]									
White	5.9	5.6	4.5	4.0	3.8	3.7	3.4	3.3	3.2
Black or African American	12.0	11.9	11.0	9.6	9.2	9.1	7.5	7.5	7.4
				Postneonatal[c] deaths per 1,000 live births					
All mothers	3.8	3.6	3.2	2.6	2.3	2.3	2.1	1.9	1.9
White	3.2	3.1	2.7	2.2	1.9	2.0	1.8	1.6	1.6
Black or African American	6.7	6.3	5.9	5.0	4.3	4.3	3.9	3.5	3.4
American Indian or Alaska Native	7.7	7.0	7.0	5.1	3.9	4.0	4.0	3.5	3.5
Asian or Pacific Islander[d]	3.1	2.9	2.7	1.9	1.4	1.5	1.3	1.1	1.0
Hispanic or Latina[e,f]	3.3	3.2	2.7	2.1	1.8	1.8	1.7	1.5	1.5
Mexican	3.2	3.2	2.7	2.1	1.8	1.7	1.6	1.4	1.4
Puerto Rican	4.2	3.5	3.0	2.8	2.4	2.4	2.3	1.7	2.2
Cuban	2.5[i]	2.3[i]	1.9[i]	1.7[i]	*	1.4[i]	*	*	1.3[i]
Central and South American	2.6	2.4	2.4	1.9	1.4	1.5	1.4	1.2	1.1
Other and unknown Hispanic or Latina	4.2	3.9	3.0	2.6	2.3	2.1	2.1	1.9	1.7
Not Hispanic or Latina:[f]									
White	3.2	3.0	2.7	2.2	1.9	2.1	1.8	1.7	1.7
Black or African American	7.0	6.4	5.9	5.0	4.4	4.5	4.0	3.7	3.5
				Fetal[g,h,i] deaths per 1,000 live births plus fetal deaths					
All mothers	NA	NA	NA	7.0	6.6	6.2	6.0	6.0	6.0
Hispanic or Latina[e]	NA	NA	NA	NA	5.8	5.4	5.2	5.2	5.1
Not Hispanic or Latina:									
White	NA	NA	NA	NA	5.3	4.8	4.8	4.9	4.9
Black or African American	NA	NA	NA	NA	12.0	11.1	10.8	10.5	10.7
				Late fetal[g,h,i] deaths per 1,000 live births plus late fetal deaths					
All mothers	NA	NA	NA	3.6	3.3	3.0	3.0	3.0	2.8
Hispanic or Latina[e]	NA	NA	NA	NA	3.1	2.8	2.6	2.7	2.5
Not Hispanic or Latina:									
White	NA	NA	NA	NA	2.8	2.4	2.5	2.6	2.4
Black or African American	NA	NA	NA	NA	5.2	4.8	4.7	4.7	4.6
				Perinatal[g,h,k] deaths per 1,000 live births plus late fetal deaths					
All mothers	NA	NA	NA	7.6	7.0	6.6	6.2	6.2	6.0
Hispanic or Latina[e]	NA	NA	NA	NA	6.1	5.9	5.5	5.6	5.4
Not Hispanic or Latina:									
White	NA	NA	NA	NA	5.7	5.4	5.1	5.3	5.0
Black or African American	NA	NA	NA	NA	12.6	12.2	10.6	10.7	10.6

Hispanics, Native Americans or Alaskan Natives, and Asian or Pacific Islanders in 2013. Disorders related to short gestation and low birth weight were the leading cause of infant death among African Americans. Short gestation and low birth weight caused the deaths of 1,522 African American babies that year, whereas birth

TABLE 6.3

Infant, neonatal, and postneonatal mortality rates, by race and Hispanic origin of mother, selected years 1983–2014 [CONTINUED]

NA = data not available.
[a]Rates based on unweighted birth cohort data.
[b]Rates based on a period file using weighted data.
[c]Infant (under 1 year of age), neonatal (under 28 days), and postneonatal (28 days-11 months).
[d]Estimates are not available for Asian or Pacific Islander subgroups because not all states have adopted the 2003 revision of the U.S. Standard Certificate of Live Birth.
[e]Persons of Hispanic origin may be of any race.
[f]Prior to 1995, data are shown only for states with an Hispanic-origin item on their birth certificates.
[g]Rates for 1999–2004 (shown in spreadsheet version) exclude data from Oklahoma, which did not report Hispanic origin on the fetal death report in those years,
[h]Starting with 2014 data, the obstetric estimate of gestation at delivery replaced the gestational age measure based on the date of the last normal menses, which was used for prior years. For more information on the impact of this change.
[i]Number of fetal deaths of 20 weeks or more gestation per 1,000 live births plus fetal deaths.
[j]Number of fetal deaths of 28 weeks or more gestation (late fetal deaths) per 1,000 live births plus late fetal deaths.
[k]Number of late fetal deaths plus infant deaths within 7 days of birth per 1,000 live births plus late fetal deaths.
[l]Estimates are considered unreliable. Rates preceded by an asterisk are based on fewer than 50 deaths in the numerator. Rates not shown are based on fewer than 20 deaths in the numerator.
Note: The race groups, white, black, American Indian or Alaska Native, and Asian or Pacific Islander include persons of Hispanic and non-Hispanic origina. Starting with 2003 data, some states reported multiple-race data. The multiple-race data for these states were bridged to the single-race categories of the 1977 Office of Management and Budget standards.

SOURCE: "Table 10. Infant, Neonatal, Postneonatal, Fetal, and Perinatal Mortality Rates, by Detailed Race and Hispanic Origin of Mother: United States, Selected Years 1983–2014," in *Health, United States, 2016: With Chartbook on Long-term Trends in Health*, Centers for Disease Control and Prevention, National Center for Health Statistics, 2017, https://www.cdc.gov/nchs/data/hus/husl6.pdf (accessed July 16, 2017)

FIGURE 6.2

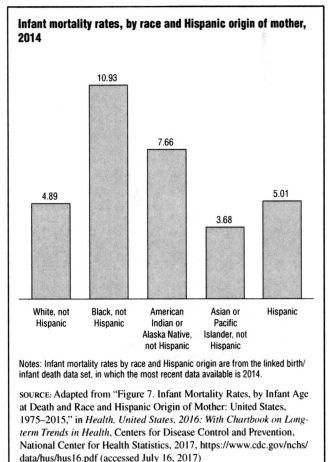

Infant mortality rates, by race and Hispanic origin of mother, 2014

Notes: Infant mortality rates by race and Hispanic origin are from the linked birth/infant death data set, in which the most recent data available is 2014.

SOURCE: Adapted from "Figure 7. Infant Mortality Rates, by Infant Age at Death and Race and Hispanic Origin of Mother: United States, 1975–2015," in *Health, United States, 2016: With Chartbook on Long-term Trends in Health*, Centers for Disease Control and Prevention, National Center for Health Statistics, 2017, https://www.cdc.gov/nchs/data/hus/hus16.pdf (accessed July 16, 2017)

defects led to death in 827 cases. The African American infant mortality rate associated with short gestation and low birth weight in 2013, 260.7 per 100,000 live births, was three-and-a-half times greater than that for non-Hispanic whites (74.4) and nearly three times greater than that for Hispanics (88.1).

These infant deaths are to a substantial degree preventable, given access to high-quality prenatal care. The Office of Minority Health of the U.S. Department of Health and Human Services (HHS) reports in "Infant Mortality and African Americans" (September 3, 2015, https://minorityhealth.hhs.gov/omh/browse.aspx?lvl=4& lvlid=23) that between 2009 and 2011 non-Hispanic African American mothers were almost as likely as non-Hispanic white mothers to receive prenatal care at the stage in their pregnancy when they desired care: 79.5% of African American mothers received prenatal care that year, compared with 87.5% of white mothers. Nevertheless, there can be wide variations in the quality and consistency of prenatal care. Adequate care should start during the first trimester of pregnancy, and the Office of Minority Health notes that as of 2008 (the most recent year for which data were available as of September 2017), African American mothers were 2.3 times more likely than non-Hispanic whites to receive prenatal care either not at all or beginning in the third trimester of pregnancy.

The Causes of Low Birth Weight and Prematurity

As Figure 6.3 shows, the prevalence of preterm births in the United States (births that occurred before 37 completed weeks of gestation) increased markedly between 1990 and 2006. In 1990, 10.6% of infants were born preterm. By 2006, 12.8% of all infants were born preterm, an increase of more than 20%. Over the same period, the percentage of infants born very preterm (less than 32 weeks of gestation) rose from 1.92 to 2.04, a 6% increase. Since 2006 the prevalence of preterm and very preterm births has generally declined. In 2015, 9.63% of infants were born preterm and 1.59% of infants were born very preterm. (See Table 6.4.) These rates remained elevated relative to rates during the 1980s and 1990s,

FIGURE 6.3

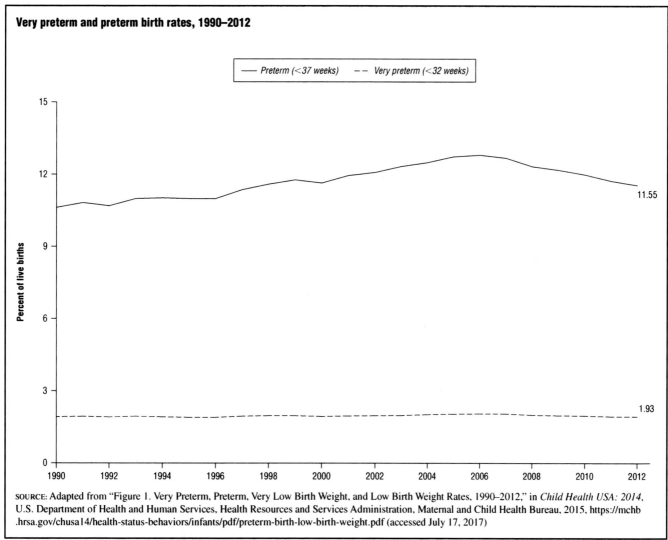

Very preterm and preterm birth rates, 1990–2012

Legend: —— Preterm (<37 weeks)   – – Very preterm (<32 weeks)

11.55

1.93

SOURCE: Adapted from "Figure 1. Very Preterm, Preterm, Very Low Birth Weight, and Low Birth Weight Rates, 1990–2012," in *Child Health USA: 2014*, U.S. Department of Health and Human Services, Health Resources and Services Administration, Maternal and Child Health Bureau, 2015, https://mchb .hrsa.gov/chusa14/health-status-behaviors/infants/pdf/preterm-birth-low-birth-weight.pdf (accessed July 17, 2017)

however, and the preterm birth rate did increase some-what from 2014 to 2015.

Low birth weight rates have followed a pattern similar to that for preterm births, which is understandable given that premature babies typically weigh less than full-term babies. Among all races, the low birth weight (less than 5 pounds, 8 ounces [2,500 g]) and very low birth weight (less than 3 pounds, 4 ounces [1,500 g]) rates both rose steadily from 1990 to 2006. (See Table 6.4.) Subsequently, these rates gradually declined, although the low birth weight rate did see a slight increase between 2012 and 2015.

In "Births: Final Data for 2015" (*National Vital Statistics Reports*, vol. 66, no. 1, January 5, 2017), Joyce A. Martin et al. of the NCHS state that one reason for the rise in births prior to 39 weeks may have been an increase in the rates of delivery via cesarean section (delivery of a fetus by surgical incision through the abdominal wall and uterus) between 1996 and 2009. The subsequent decline in such births from 2009 to 2015 may be partly linked to efforts by medical professionals and other experts to dissuade people from delivering via cesarean section except in cases when it is medically necessary.

Another reason for the rise in low birth weight and preterm babies may be the dramatic rise in the multiple-birth rate between the 1980s and 2005. Twins, triplets, and higher-order multiple births are more likely to be born prematurely than are single infants; and even when they are born closer to full term, they are more likely to weigh less than single infants. Between 1980 and 2015 the multiple-birth rate for all races and ethnicities rose dramatically, from 19.3 per 1,000 live births to 34.5 per 1,000. (See Table 6.5.) The 2015 multiple-birth rate was highest among African American mothers, at 40.4 per 1,000 live births, followed closely by non-Hispanic white mothers (37.3 per 1,000 live births). The multiple-birth rate for Hispanic mothers was much lower throughout this period, although it also saw a considerable increase, from 18.4 in 1990 to 25.1 in 2015.

Preterm delivery and low birth weight rates are clearly correlated with maternal age. As Table 6.6 shows,

TABLE 6.4

Very preterm and preterm births, and very low birthweight and low birthweight births, by race and Hispanic origin of mother, 1989–2015

Year	Very preterm[a] All races[c]	Non-Hispanic White[d]	Non-Hispanic Black[d]	Hispanic[e]	Preterm[b] All races[c]	Non-Hispanic White[d]	Non-Hispanic Black[d]	Hispanic[e]
				Percent				
2015	1.59	1.27	3.09	1.44	9.63	8.88	13.41	9.14
2014	1.60	1.29	3.08	1.45	9.57	8.91	13.23	9.03
2013	1.62	1.31	3.16	1.44	9.62	8.94	13.25	9.08
2012	1.63	1.32	3.19	1.45	9.76	9.13	13.48	9.09
2011	1.64	1.33	3.20	1.42	9.81	9.21	13.54	9.02
2010	1.65	1.36	3.20	1.41	9.98	9.41	13.81	9.09
2009	1.65	1.35	3.28	1.41	10.07	9.50	14.05	9.12
2008	1.67	1.37	3.26	1.43	10.36	9.81	14.38	9.38
2007	1.71	1.39	3.48	1.46	10.44	9.90	14.71	9.35

Year	Very low birthweight[f] All races[c]	Non-Hispanic White[d]	Non-Hispanic Black[d]	Hispanic[e]	Low birthweight[g] All races[c]	Non-Hispanic White[d]	Non-Hispanic Black[d]	Hispanic[e]
				Percent				
2015	1.40	1.09	2.89	1.23	8.07	6.93	13.35	7.21
2014	1.40	1.10	2.87	1.23	8.00	6.96	13.17	7.05
2013	1.41	1.11	2.90	1.21	8.02	6.98	13.08	7.09
2012	1.42	1.13	2.94	1.22	7.99	6.97	13.18	6.97
2011	1.44	1.14	2.99	1.20	8.10	7.09	13.33	7.02
2010	1.45	1.16	2.98	1.20	8.15	7.14	13.53	6.97
2009	1.45	1.16	3.06	1.19	8.16	7.19	13.61	6.94
2008	1.46	1.18	3.01	1.20	8.18	7.22	13.71	6.96
2007	1.49	1.19	3.20	1.21	8.22	7.28	13.90	6.93
2006	1.49	1.20	3.15	1.19	8.26	7.32	13.97	6.99
2005	1.49	1.21	3.27	1.20	8.19	7.29	14.02	6.88
2004	1.48	1.20	3.15	1.20	8.08	7.20	13.74	6.79
2003	1.45	1.18	3.12	1.16	7.93	7.04	13.55	6.69
2002	1.46	1.17	3.15	1.17	7.82	6.91	13.39	6.55
2001	1.44	1.17	3.08	1.14	7.68	6.76	13.07	6.47
2000	1.43	1.14	3.10	1.14	7.57	6.60	13.13	6.41
1999	1.45	1.15	3.18	1.14	7.62	6.64	13.23	6.38
1998	1.45	1.15	3.11	1.15	7.57	6.55	13.17	6.44
1997	1.42	1.12	3.05	1.13	7.51	6.47	13.11	6.42
1996	1.37	1.08	3.02	1.12	7.39	6.36	13.12	6.28
1995	1.35	1.04	2.98	1.11	7.32	6.20	13.21	6.29
1994	1.33	1.01	2.99	1.08	7.28	6.06	13.34	6.25
1993	1.33	1.00	2.99	1.06	7.22	5.92	13.43	6.24
1992[h]	1.29	0.94	2.97	1.04	7.08	5.73	13.40	6.10
1991[h]	1.29	0.94	2.97	1.02	7.12	5.72	13.62	6.15
1990[i]	1.27	0.93	2.93	1.03	6.97	5.61	13.32	6.06
1989[j]	1.28	0.93	2.97	1.05	7.05	5.62	13.61	6.18

[a]Births of less than 32 completed weeks of gestation based on the obstetric estimate of gestation.
[b]Births of less than 37 completed weeks of gestation based on the obstetric estimate of gestation.
[c]Includes races other than white and black and origin not stated.
[d]Race and Hispanic origin are reported separately on birth certificates. Persons of Hispanic origin may be of any race. Race categories are consistent with 1977 Office of Management and Budget standards. Forty-nine states and the District of Columbia reported multiple-race data for 2015 that were bridged to single-race categories for comparability with other states. Multiple-race reporting areas vary for 2003–2015.
[e]Includes all persons of Hispanic origin of any race.
[f]Less than 1,500 grams.
[g]Less than 2,500 grams.
[h]Data by Hispanic origin exclude New Hampshire, which did not report Hispanic origin.
[i]Data by Hispanic origin exclude New Hampshire and Oklahoma, which did not report Hispanic origin.
[j]Data by Hispanic origin exclude New Hampshire, Oklahoma, and Louisiana, which did not report Hispanic origin.

SOURCE: Joyce A. Martin et al., "Table 24. Very Preterm and Preterm Births: United States, 2007–2015, and Very Low Birthweight and Low Birthweight Births, by Race and Hispanic Origin of Mother: United States, 1989–2015," in "Births: Final Data for 2015," *National Vital Statistics Reports*, vol. 66, no. 1, January 5, 2017, https://www.cdc.gov/nchs/data/nvsr/nvsr66/nvsr66_01.pdf (accessed July 17, 2017)

in 2015 mothers aged 20 to 34 years had the lowest rates of preterm delivery and low birth weight. Mothers aged 45 to 54 years had the highest rates for both measures, followed by those aged 14 years and younger. This was true of mothers across racial and ethnic categories, with the exception of African Americans. African American mothers aged 30 years and older had higher preterm birth rates than mothers aged 14 years and younger. The average age at which women begin to have children has significantly increased since the late 20th century, and it has become much more common for women aged 40 years and older to give birth, thanks to advancements in

TABLE 6.5

Twin, triplet, and higher-order multiple births, by race and Hispanic origin of mother, 1980–2015

Year and race and Hispanic origin of mother	Total births	Twin births	Triplet and higher-order births	Multiple birth rate[a]	Twin birth rate[b]	Triplet and higher-order birth rate[c]
All races[d]						
2015	3,978,497	133,155	4,123	34.5	33.5	103.6
2014	3,988,076	135,336	4,526	35.1	33.9	113.5
2013	3,932,181	132,324	4,700	34.8	33.7	119.5
2012	3,952,841	131,024	4,919	34.4	33.1	124.4
2011	3,953,590	131,269	5,417	34.6	33.2	137.0
2010	3,999,386	132,562	5,503	34.5	33.1	137.6
2009	4,130,665	137,217	6,340	34.8	33.2	153.5
2008	4,247,694	138,660	6,268	34.1	32.6	147.6
2007	4,316,233	138,961	6,427	33.7	32.2	148.9
2006	4,265,555	137,085	6,540	33.7	32.1	153.3
2005	4,138,349	133,122	6,694	33.8	32.2	161.8
2004	4,112,052	132,219	7,275	33.9	32.2	176.9
2003	4,089,950	128,665	7,663	33.3	31.5	187.4
2002	4,021,726	125,134	7,401	33.0	31.1	184.0
2001	4,025,933	121,246	7,471	32.0	30.1	185.6
2000	4,058,814	118,916	7,325	31.1	29.3	180.5
1999	3,959,417	114,307	7,321	30.7	28.9	184.9
1998	3,941,553	110,670	7,625	30.0	28.1	193.5
1997	3,880,894	104,137	6,737	28.6	26.8	173.6
1996	3,891,494	100,750	5,939	27.4	25.9	152.6
1995	3,899,589	96,736	4,973	26.1	24.8	127.5
1994	3,952,767	97,064	4,594	25.7	24.6	116.2
1993	4,000,240	96,445	4,168	25.2	24.1	104.2
1992	4,065,014	95,372	3,883	24.4	23.5	95.5
1991	4,110,907	94,779	3,346	23.9	23.1	81.4
1990	4,158,212	93,865	3,028	23.3	22.6	72.8
1989	4,040,958	90,118	2,798	23.0	22.3	69.2
1988	3,909,510	85,315	2,385	22.4	21.8	61.0
1987	3,809,394	81,778	2,139	22.0	21.5	56.2
1986	3,756,547	79,485	1,814	21.6	21.2	48.3
1985	3,760,561	77,102	1,925	21.0	20.5	51.2
1984	3,669,141	72,949	1,653	20.3	19.9	45.1
1983	3,638,933	72,287	1,575	20.3	19.9	43.3
1982	3,680,537	71,631	1,484	19.9	19.5	40.3
1981	3,629,238	70,049	1,385	19.7	19.3	38.2
1980	3,612,258	68,339	1,337	19.3	18.9	37.0
Non-Hispanic white[e]						
2015	2,130,279	76,848	2,617	37.3	36.1	122.8
2014	2,149,302	78,788	3,028	38.1	36.7	140.9
2013	2,129,196	78,072	3,134	38.1	36.7	147.2
2012	2,134,044	78,449	3,264	38.3	36.8	152.9
2011	2,146,566	78,638	3,670	38.3	36.6	171.0
2010	2,162,406	79,728	3,842	38.6	36.9	177.7
2009	2,212,552	81,954	4,457	39.1	37.0	201.4
2008	2,267,817	82,903	4,493	38.5	36.6	198.1
2007	2,310,333	83,632	4,559	38.2	36.2	197.3
2006	2,308,640	83,108	4,805	38.1	36.0	208.1
2005	2,279,768	82,223	4,966	38.2	36.1	217.8
2004	2,296,683	83,346	5,590	38.7	36.3	243.4
2003	2,321,904	81,691	5,922	37.7	35.2	255.0
2002	2,298,156	79,949	5,754	37.3	34.8	250.4
2001	2,326,578	77,882	5,894	36.0	33.5	253.3
2000	2,362,968	76,018	5,821	34.6	32.2	246.3
1999	2,346,450	73,964	5,909	34.0	31.5	251.8
1998	2,362,462	71,270	6,206	32.8	30.2	262.8
1997	2,333,363	67,191	5,386	31.1	28.8	230.8
1996	2,358,989	65,523	4,885	29.8	27.8	207.1
1995	2,382,638	62,370	4,050	27.9	26.2	170.0
1994	2,438,855	62,476	3,721	27.1	25.6	152.6
1993	2,472,031	61,525	3,360	26.2	24.9	135.9
1992[f]	2,527,207	60,640	3,115	25.2	24.0	123.3
1991[f]	2,589,878	60,904	2,612	24.5	23.5	100.9
1990[g]	2,626,500	60,210	2,358	23.8	22.9	89.8

fertility treatments. Additionally, some fertility treatments increase rates of prematurity and low birth weight because they are more likely to result in multiple births. However, women aged 20 to 34 years accounted for the overwhelming majority of both preterm and low birth weight babies in 2015. Thus, the prevalence of prematurity and low birth weight in the United States cannot be fully explained by trends in maternal age.

TABLE 6.5

Twin, triplet, and higher-order multiple births, by race and Hispanic origin of mother, 1980–2015 [CONTINUED]

Year and race and Hispanic origin of mother	Total births	Twin births	Triplet and higher-order births	Multiple birth rate[a]	Twin birth rate[b]	Triplet and higher-order birth rate[c]
Non-Hispanic black[e]						
2015	589,047	23,204	615	40.4	39.4	104.4
2014	588,891	23,546	528	40.9	40.0	89.7
2013	583,834	22,346	623	39.3	38.3	106.7
2012	583,489	21,545	629	38.0	36.9	107.8
2011	582,345	21,681	634	38.3	37.2	108.9
2010	589,808	21,804	574	37.9	37.0	97.3
2009	609,584	23,159	644	39.0	38.0	105.6
2008	623,029	22,924	569	37.7	36.8	91.3
2007	627,191	23,101	612	37.8	36.8	97.6
2006	617,247	22,702	580	37.7	36.8	94.0
2005	583,759	21,254	616	37.5	36.4	105.5
2004	578,772	20,605	577	36.6	35.6	99.7
2003	576,033	20,010	631	35.8	34.7	109.5
2002	578,335	20,064	591	35.7	34.7	102.2
2001	589,917	19,974	531	34.8	33.9	90.0
2000	604,346	20,173	506	34.2	33.4	83.7
1999	588,981	18,920	561	33.1	32.1	95.2
1998	593,127	18,589	518	32.2	31.3	87.3
1997	581,431	17,472	523	30.9	30.0	90.0
1996	578,099	16,873	425	29.9	29.2	73.5
1995	587,781	16,622	340	28.9	28.3	57.8
1994	619,198	17,934	357	29.5	29.0	57.7
1993	641,273	18,115	314	28.7	28.2	49.0
1992[f]	657,450	18,294	346	28.4	27.8	52.6
1991[f]	666,758	18,243	367	27.9	27.4	55.0
1990[g]	661,701	17,646	306	27.1	26.7	46.2
Hispanic[h]						
2015	924,048	22,593	611	25.1	24.5	66.1
2014	914,065	22,051	588	24.8	24.1	64.3
2013	901,033	21,511	643	24.6	23.9	71.4
2012	907,677	20,505	636	23.3	22.6	70.1
2011	918,129	21,236	723	23.9	23.1	78.7
2010	945,180	21,359	721	23.4	22.6	76.3
2009	999,548	22,481	835	23.3	22.5	83.5
2008	1,041,239	23,266	834	23.1	22.3	80.1
2007	1,062,779	23,405	857	22.8	22.0	80.6
2006	1,039,077	22,698	787	22.6	21.8	75.7
2005	985,505	21,723	761	22.8	22.0	77.2
2004	946,349	20,351	723	22.3	21.5	76.4
2003	912,329	19,472	784	22.2	21.3	85.9
2002	876,642	18,128	737	21.5	20.7	84.1
2001	851,851	17,257	710	21.1	20.3	83.3
2000	815,868	16,470	659	21.0	20.2	80.8
1999	764,339	15,388	583	20.9	20.1	76.3
1998	734,661	15,015	553	21.2	20.4	75.3
1997	709,767	13,821	516	20.2	19.5	72.7
1996	701,339	13,014	409	19.1	18.6	58.3
1995	679,768	12,685	355	19.2	18.7	52.2
1994	665,026	12,206	348	18.9	18.4	52.3
1993	654,418	12,294	321	19.3	18.8	49.1
1992[f]	643,271	11,932	239	18.9	18.5	37.2
1991[f]	623,085	11,356	235	18.6	18.2	37.7
1990[g]	595,073	10,713	235	18.4	18.0	39.5

[a]Number of live births in all multiple deliveries per 1,000 live births.
[b]Number of live births in twin deliveries per 1,000 live births.
[c]Number of live births in triplet and other higher-order deliveries per 100,000 live births.
[d]Includes races other than white and black and origin not stated.
[e]Race and Hispanic origin are reported separately on birth certificates. Persons of Hispanic origin may be of any race. Race categories are consistent with 1977 Office of Management and Budget standards. Forty-nine states and the District of Columbia reported multiple-race data for 2015 that were bridged to single-race categories for comparability with other states. Multiple-race reporting areas vary for 2003–2015.
[f]Excludes data for New Hampshire, which did not report Hispanic origin.
[g]Excludes data for New Hampshire and Oklahoma, which did not report Hispanic origin.
[h]Includes all persons of Hispanic origin of any race.

SOURCE: Joyce A. Martin et al., "Table 27. Twin, Triplet, and Higher-Order Multiple Births, by Race and Hispanic Origin of Mother, United States: 1980–2015," in "Births: Final Data for 2015," *National Vital Statistics Reports*, vol. 66, no. 1, January 5, 2017, https://www.cdc.gov/nchs/data/nvsr/nvsr66/nvsr66_01.pdf (accessed July 17, 2017)

TABLE 6.6

Preterm and low birthweight births, by age and race and Hispanic origin of mother, 2015

Age and race and Hispanic origin of mother	Preterm[a]										Low birthweight[b]						
	Percent			Number				Percent			Number			
	Total	Early[c]	Late[d]	Total	Early[c]	Late[d]	Unknown	Total	Very[e]	Moderately[f]	Total	Very[e]	Moderately[f]	Unknown
All races[g]														
All ages	9.63	2.76	6.87	382,786	109,660	273,126	2,926	8.07	1.40	6.67	320,869	55,592	265,277	3,621
Under 15	13.78	5.75	8.04	343	143	200	11	12.57	3.32	9.25	314	83	231	2
15–19	9.91	3.05	6.86	22,735	6,989	15,746	243	9.48	1.64	7.84	21,756	3,765	17,991	163
15	10.58	3.32	7.27	801	251	550	20	9.84	2.03	7.81	746	154	592	8
16	10.53	3.45	7.08	1,938	635	1,303	33	10.20	1.89	8.30	1,878	349	1,529	10
17	9.94	3.06	6.89	3,493	1,074	2,419	37	9.58	1.66	7.92	3,368	583	2,785	19
18	9.95	3.12	6.82	6,310	1,982	4,328	60	9.62	1.74	7.88	6,103	1,104	4,999	47
19	9.71	2.90	6.81	10,193	3,047	7,146	93	9.21	1.50	7.71	9,661	1,575	8,086	79
20–24	9.28	2.68	6.59	78,833	22,812	56,021	710	8.38	1.42	6.96	71,177	12,039	59,138	711
25–29	8.92	2.51	6.41	102,751	28,932	73,819	901	7.45	1.28	6.17	85,776	14,754	71,022	1,090
30–34	9.35	2.63	6.72	102,345	28,785	73,560	637	7.49	1.30	6.19	81,925	14,184	67,741	1,017
35–39	11.07	3.18	7.89	58,419	16,801	41,618	328	8.74	1.57	7.17	46,092	8,273	37,819	507
40–44	13.68	4.05	9.63	15,288	4,530	10,758	91	10.80	1.97	8.83	12,068	2,203	9,865	122
45–54	23.23	7.49	15.74	2,072	668	1,404	5	19.75	3.26	16.49	1,761	291	1,470	9
Non-Hispanic white[h]														
All ages	8.88	2.34	6.54	189,146	49,817	139,329	1,196	6.93	1.09	5.84	147,479	23,118	124,361	1,828
Under 15	13.25	4.99	8.26	77	29	48	1	10.15	3.61	6.54	59	21	38	1
15–19	9.56	2.85	6.72	8,677	2,583	6,094	83	8.45	1.42	7.02	7,668	1,292	6,376	59
15	10.63	3.48	7.15	226	74	152	8	7.97	2.48	5.48	170	53	117	1
16	10.22	3.30	6.91	597	193	404	11	9.06	1.62	7.43	530	95	435	3
17	9.79	3.06	6.72	1,214	380	834	12	8.72	1.60	7.12	1,082	198	884	7
18	9.86	2.96	6.90	2,504	752	1,752	18	8.82	1.50	7.32	2,241	381	1,860	14
19	9.20	2.63	6.56	4,136	1,184	2,952	34	8.11	1.26	6.85	3,645	565	3,080	34
20–24	8.66	2.28	6.38	34,551	9,094	25,457	281	7.17	1.11	6.06	28,612	4,437	24,175	301
25–29	8.28	2.14	6.14	53,155	13,723	39,432	361	6.44	1.00	5.44	41,317	6,387	34,930	575
30–34	8.58	2.24	6.35	55,480	14,453	41,027	289	6.48	1.01	5.47	41,862	6,504	35,358	571
35–39	10.03	2.65	7.39	29,173	7,694	21,479	147	7.51	1.20	6.31	21,833	3,492	18,341	262
40–44	12.75	3.50	9.25	7,012	1,924	5,088	32	9.62	1.55	8.07	5,290	855	4,435	54
45–54	21.93	6.81	15.12	1,021	317	704	2	18.01	2.79	15.22	838	130	708	5
Non-Hispanic black[h]														
All ages	13.41	4.83	8.58	78,911	28,438	50,473	451	13.35	2.89	10.45	78,514	17,013	61,501	728
Under 15	15.26	6.44	8.82	128	54	74	6	16.59	3.79	12.80	140	32	108	1
15–19	12.05	4.30	7.75	6,020	2,147	3,873	71	13.63	2.58	11.05	6,813	1,289	5,524	64
15	12.46	4.20	8.26	258	87	171	8	12.92	2.51	10.41	268	52	216	5
16	12.22	4.71	7.51	547	211	336	9	14.08	2.77	11.32	631	124	507	6
17	12.13	3.82	8.30	945	298	647	10	13.60	2.13	11.47	1,060	166	894	9
18	11.77	4.50	7.27	1,593	609	984	16	13.71	2.73	10.99	1,856	369	1,487	19
19	12.12	4.26	7.85	2,677	942	1,735	28	13.57	2.62	10.95	2,998	578	2,420	25
20–24	12.38	4.36	8.02	21,722	7,653	14,069	135	13.20	2.63	10.57	23,144	4,614	18,530	217
25–29	12.91	4.66	8.25	21,396	7,726	13,670	111	12.77	2.80	9.97	21,162	4,645	16,517	193
30–34	14.08	5.11	8.97	16,880	6,122	10,758	78	13.09	3.08	10.01	15,683	3,690	11,993	151

TABLE 6.6

Preterm and low birthweight births, by age and race and Hispanic origin of mother, 2015 [CONTINUED]

Age and race and Hispanic origin of mother	Preterm[a] Percent Total	Early[c]	Late[d]	Preterm Number Total	Early[c]	Late[d]	Unknown	Low birthweight[b] Percent Total	Very[e]	Moderately[f]	Low birthweight Number Total	Very[e]	Moderately[f]	Unknown
Non-Hispanic black[h]														
35–39	16.17	6.01	10.16	9,835	3,653	6,182	32	14.59	3.53	11.06	8,870	2,145	6,725	83
40–44	17.99	6.64	11.35	2,622	968	1,654	18	16.47	3.70	12.78	2,401	539	1,862	17
45–54	24.84	9.27	15.56	308	115	193	—	24.31	4.77	19.55	301	59	242	2
Hispanic[i]														
All ages	9.14	2.52	6.62	84,418	23,266	61,152	601	7.21	1.23	5.98	66,623	11,361	55,262	427
Under 15	12.82	5.39	7.43	126	53	73	3	10.65	1.48	7.33	105	24	81	—
15–19	8.89	2.47	6.42	7,137	1,986	5,151	74	8.07	1.29	6.78	6,484	1,037	5,447	25
15	9.17	2.64	6.53	285	82	203	3	8.81	1.48	7.33	274	46	228	1
16	9.88	2.87	7.01	733	213	520	13	9.04	1.57	7.47	672	117	555	—
17	8.71	2.55	6.16	1,187	347	840	11	8.06	1.39	6.67	1,099	189	910	2
18	8.91	2.42	6.50	1,981	537	1,444	25	8.05	1.39	6.66	1,790	309	1,481	11
19	8.70	2.38	6.32	2,951	807	2,144	22	7.81	1.11	6.70	2,649	376	2,273	11
20–24	8.07	2.17	5.91	19,062	5,118	13,944	165	6.86	1.06	5.79	16,191	2,505	13,686	94
25–29	8.35	2.22	6.13	21,370	5,693	15,677	165	6.54	1.10	5.44	16,740	2,807	13,933	118
30–34	9.49	2.65	6.84	19,887	5,551	14,336	121	7.02	1.27	5.75	14,719	2,666	12,053	106
35–39	11.41	3.28	8.13	12,775	3,670	9,105	60	8.42	1.55	6.87	9,427	1,736	7,691	66
40–44	13.65	4.00	9.65	3,699	1,083	2,616	13	9.85	1.97	7.88	2,670	534	2,136	18
45–54	23.83	7.37	16.46	362	112	250	—	18.89	3.42	15.47	287	52	235	—

[a]Less than 37 completed weeks of gestation based on the obstetric estimate.
[b]Less than 2,500 grams.
[c]Less than 34 completed weeks of gestation based on the obstetric estimate.
[d]34–36 completed weeks of gestation based on the obstetric estimate.
[e]Less than 1,500 grams.
[f]1,500–2,499 grams.
[g]Includes races other than white and black and origin not stated.
[h]Race and Hispanic origin are reported separately on birth certificates. Persons of Hispanic origin may be of any race. Race categories are consistent with 1977 Office of Management and Budget standards. Forty-nine states and the District of Columbia reported multiple-race data for 2015 that were bridged to single-race categories for comparability with other states.
[i]Includes all persons of Hispanic origin of any race.
—Quantity zero.

SOURCE: Joyce A. Martin et al., "Table 25. Preterm and Low Birthweight Births, by Age and Race and Hispanic Origin of Mother: United States, 2015," in "Births: Final Data for 2015," *National Vital Statistics Reports,* vol. 66, no. 1, January 5, 2017, https://www.cdc.gov/nchs/data/nvsr/nvsr66/nvsr66_01.pdf (accessed July 17, 2017)

Other factors that commonly result in prematurity and low birth weight include poor maternal nutrition, drug and alcohol use, smoking, and sexually transmitted infections.

Birth Defects and End-of-Life Issues

The Centers for Disease Control and Prevention (CDC) reports in "Birth Defects: Data and Statistics" (October 11, 2016 https://www.cdc.gov/ncbddd/birth defects/data.html) that one out of every 33 babies born in the United States each year has a birth defect. The CDC notes that babies born with birth defects are more likely to have poor health and long-term disabilities than babies born without birth defects. Babies born with birth defects typically account for around 20% of total infant mortality.

Two of the more serious birth defects are anencephaly (absence of the majority of the brain) and spina bifida (incomplete development of the back and spine). Anencephaly and spina bifida are classified as neural tube defects because they result from the failure of the neural tube (the embryo's precursor to the central nervous system) to develop properly during early pregnancy. Down syndrome is a condition in which babies are born with an extra copy of chromosome 21 in their cells. It results in anatomical and developmental problems along with cognitive deficits. Down syndrome children may be born with birth defects that are fatal, including defects of the heart, lungs, and gastrointestinal tract. Many Down syndrome children, however, live well into their 50s and beyond.

Some birth defects are genetic in nature. For example, Tay-Sachs disease, a fatal condition that progressively destroys brain and spinal cord cells, primarily affects children of Eastern European Jewish ancestry as a result of inherited genetic irregularities. Down syndrome is also genetically transmitted, although it is not specific to any particular genetic subgroup. Other birth defects result from environmental factors such as maternal drug use or infections during pregnancy. The specific causes of many birth defects are unknown, but scientists theorize that a combination of genetic and environmental factors may explain numerous conditions. Most birth defects cannot be prevented. Exceptions include those caused by maternal alcohol and drug consumption during pregnancy. Additionally, prenatal consumption of folic acid, a B vitamin, can help prevent neural tube defects.

Racial and ethnic variations in birth defects are not well understood, although differences in the prevalence of individual conditions have been observed. As Table 6.7 shows, non-Hispanic African American mothers and Native American/Alaskan Native mothers are more likely than Hispanic mothers and non-Hispanic Asian American mothers to have babies with trisomy 18 (a chromosomal

TABLE 6.7

The prevalence of birth defects by race and ethnicity

	Much higher occurrence[a]	Much lower occurrence[b]
Non-Hispanic American Indian/Alaskan Native	Encephalocele Anotia/Microtia Cleft lip with or without cleft palate Upper limb deficiency Lower limb deficiency Any limb deficiency Trisomy 18	Hypospadias
Non-Hispanic Asian		Spina bifida without anencephaly Truncus arteriosus Aortic valve stenosis Hypoplastic left heart syndrome Coarctation of the aorta Esophageal atresia Pyloric stenosis Hypospadias Gastroschisis Omphalocele
Non-Hispanic Black	Encephalocele Trisomy 18	Aortic valve stenosis Cleft lip with or without cleft palate Pyloric stenosis Gastroschisis
Hispanic	Anencephaly Encephalocele Anotia/Microtia	Hypospadias

[a]These conditions were found to have statistically significantly higher occurrences in the noted races and ethnicities compared to non-Hispanic white
[b]These conditions were found to have statistically significantly lower occurrences in the noted races and ethnicities compared to non-Hispanic white
Note: Even though programs try to collect information on all occurrences, some birth defects might not be captured by programs if the outcome is not a live birth. This could underestimate the occurrences of some birth defects.

SOURCE: "Differences in Birth Defect Occurrence by Race/Ethnicity," in *Birth Defects: Data & Statistics*, Centers for Disease Control and Prevention, September 21, 2016, https://www.cdc.gov/ncbddd/birthdefects/data.html (accessed July 17, 2017) defect that is frequently fatal), while Hispanic mothers are more likely to have babies with anencephaly. Native American/Alaskan Native mothers are more likely than mothers from any other race or ethnicity to have babies with cleft lips or limb deficiencies.

NEURAL TUBE DEFECTS: ANENCEPHALY AND SPINA BIFIDA. The two most common neural tube defects, and therefore the ones that raise the most questions regarding end-of-life care, are anencephaly and spina bifida. Anencephalic infants die before birth (in utero or stillborn) or shortly thereafter. Medical advances have not meaningfully increased the chances for survival of these infants. Spina bifida was once a death sentence for most babies. However, with the advent of antibiotics and advanced surgical techniques, some newborns with spina bifida can now be saved.

According to T. J. Mathews, in *Trends in Spina Bifida and Anencephalus in the United States, 1991–2006* (April 2009, http://www.cdc.gov/nchs/data/hestat/spine_anen/spine_anen.pdf), the most recent comprehensive report on this topic as of April 2017, the incidence of anencephaly (also known as anencephalus) decreased significantly from 18.38 cases per 100,000 live births in 1991 to 11.21 cases per 100,000 live births in 2006. (See Figure 6.4 and Table 6.8.) The largest drop during this period was between 1991 and 1992. Between 1993 and 2001 the general trend was downward. Between 2001 and 2003 the rate increased from 9.42 cases per 100,000 live births to 11.14 cases per 100,000 live births. Between 2003 and 2006 the anencephaly rate was relatively stable. The rate in 2006 was 11.21 cases per 100,000 live births.

Mathews notes that spina bifida rates increased from 22.84 cases per 100,000 live births in 1992 to 27.98 cases per 100,000 live births in 1995, but that after 1995 the rates declined to 17.96 cases per 100,000 live births in 2005 and 17.99 cases per 100,000 live births in 2006—the lowest spina bifida rates ever reported. (See Figure 6.5 and Table 6.9.) The CDC attributes some of the success in reducing spina bifida rates to the preventive use of folic acid during pregnancy. Women who receive adequate prenatal care are generally directed to ingest prenatal vitamins that contain folic acid. Additionally, in 1992 the U.S. Food and Drug Administration issued a directive mandating that, by 1998, cereal manufacturers add folic acid to their enriched cereal grain products.

Issues related to brain death and organ donation sometimes arise in cases of anencephaly. One case that gained national attention was that of Theresa Ann Campo in 1992. Before their daughter's birth, Theresa's parents discovered through prenatal testing that their baby would be born without a fully developed brain. They decided to carry the fetus to term and donate her organs for transplantation. When baby Theresa was born, her parents asked for her to be declared brain dead. Theresa's brain stem, however, was still functioning, so the court ruled against the parents' request. When Theresa died 10 days

FIGURE 6.4

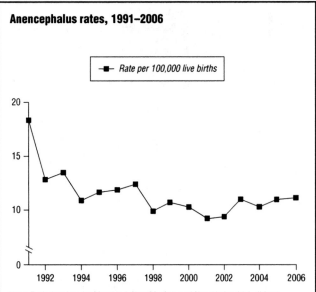

Anencephalus rates, 1991–2006

Note: Excludes data for Maryland, New Mexico, and New York, which did not require reporting for anencephalus for some years.

SOURCE: Adapted from T. J. Mathews, "Figure 2. Anencephalus Rates, 1991–2006," in *Trends in Spina Bifida and Anencephalus in the United States, 1991–2006*, Health E-Stats, Centers for Disease Control and Prevention, National Center for Health Statistics, April 2009, https://www.cdc.gov/nchs/data/hestat/spine_anen/spine_anen.pdf (accessed July 17, 2017)

TABLE 6.8

Number of live births, anencephalus cases, and anencephalus rates, 1991–2006

	Anencephalus cases	Total live births	Rate
2006	436	3,890,949	11.21
2005	432	3,887,109	11.11
2004	401	3,860,720	10.39
2003	441	3,715,577	11.14
2002	348	3,645,770	9.55
2001	343	3,640,555	9.42
2000	376	3,640,376	10.33
1999	382	3,533,565	10.81
1998	349	3,519,240	9.92
1997	434	3,469,667	12.51
1996	416	3,478,723	11.96
1995	408	3,484,539	11.71
1994	387	3,527,482	10.97
1993	481	3,562,723	13.50
1992	457	3,572,890	12.79
1991	655	3,564,453	18.38

Note: Excludes data for Maryland, New Mexico, and New York, which did not require reporting for anencephalus for some years.

SOURCE: Adapted from T. J. Mathews, "Table 2. Number of Live Births with Anencephalus and Rates per 100,000 Live Births: United States, 1991–2006," in *Trends in Spina Bifida and Anencephalus in the United States, 1991–2006*, Health E-Stats, Centers for Disease Control and Prevention, National Center for Health Statistics, April 2009, https://www.cdc.gov/nchs/data/hestat/spine_anen/spine_anen.pdf (accessed July 17, 2017)

FIGURE 6.5

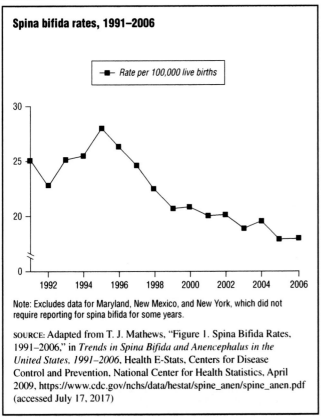

Spina bifida rates, 1991–2006

Note: Excludes data for Maryland, New Mexico, and New York, which did not require reporting for spina bifida for some years.

SOURCE: Adapted from T. J. Mathews, "Figure 1. Spina Bifida Rates, 1991–2006," in *Trends in Spina Bifida and Anencephalus in the United States, 1991–2006*, Health E-Stats, Centers for Disease Control and Prevention, National Center for Health Statistics, April 2009, https://www.cdc.gov/nchs/data/hestat/spine_anen/spine_anen.pdf (accessed July 17, 2017)

TABLE 6.9

Number of live births, spina bifida cases, and spina bifida rates, 1991–2006

	Spina bifida cases	Total live births	Rate
2006	700	3,890,949	17.99
2005	698	3,887,109	17.96
2004	755	3,860,720	19.56
2003	702	3,715,577	18.89
2002	734	3,645,770	20.13
2001	730	3,640,555	20.05
2000	759	3,640,376	20.85
1999	732	3,533,565	20.72
1998	790	3,519,240	22.45
1997	857	3,469,667	24.70
1996	917	3,478,723	26.36
1995	975	3,484,539	27.98
1994	900	3,527,482	25.51
1993	896	3,562,723	25.15
1992	816	3,572,890	22.84
1991	887	3,564,453	24.88

Note: Excludes data for Maryland, New Mexico, and New York, which did not require reporting for spina bifida for some years.

SOURCE: Adapted from T. J . Mathews, "Table 1. Number of Live Births with Spina Bifida and Rates per 100,000 Live Births: United States, 1991–2006," in *Trends in Spina Bifida and Anencephalus in the United States, 1991–2006*, Health E-Stats, Centers for Disease Control and Prevention, National Center for Health Statistics, April 2009, https://www.cdc.gov/nchs/data/hestat/spine_anen/spine_anen.pdf (accessed July 17, 2017)

later, her organs were not usable for transplant because they had deteriorated as a result of oxygen deprivation.

Some physicians and ethicists argue that even if anencephalic babies have a brain stem, they should be considered brain dead. Lacking a functioning higher brain, these babies can feel nothing and have no consciousness. Others fear that declaring anencephalic babies dead could be the start of a slippery slope that might eventually include babies with other birth defects in the same category. Other people are concerned that anencephalic babies may be kept alive for the purpose of harvesting their organs for transplant at a later date.

CHILD MORTALITY

In the United States, children under the age of one are a much greater risk of death than older children are. As Table 6.10 shows, the 2014 death rate for infants in the United States was 588 deaths per 100,000 people. The death rate for children aged one to four years, 24 deaths per 100,000, was nearly 25 times less than that of infants. The death rate of children aged five to nine years, 11.5 deaths per 100,000, was more than 50 times less than that of infants. Only past age 55 did the average U.S. resident have a greater statistical probability of dying than the average infant.

Child mortality is thus much rarer than infant mortality in the United States. This is true in other developed countries as well. This phenomenon is unusual. Researchers believe that for most of human history people were more likely to die as children than as infants, and they were roughly as likely to die between the age of one and the onset of adolescence as they were to survive to adolescence. In a paper considering the role that child mortality played in human evolution, "Is Child Death the Crucible of Human Evolution?" (*Journal of Social, Evolutionary, and Cultural Psychology*, vol. 2, no. 4, December 2008), Tony Volk and Jeremy Atkinson provide a survey of scholarly estimates of the child mortality rates in various ancient and medieval societies. Evidence suggests, for example, that in ancient Rome (200 BC–AD 200) the infant mortality rate was approximately 30% (i.e., 30% of children did not survive their first year of life), while the child mortality rate was 50% (only half of children made it to adolescence). Volk and Atkinson find that evidence points to similar rates of infant and child mortality in 14th-century Japan, 17th-century France and Sweden, and 17th- and 18th-century China. They also find similar rates of infant (23%) and child (46%) mortality among hunter-gatherers in the modern age, who live without access to advanced medicine or sanitation.

Infant and child mortality rates began to decline during the mid-19th century, as improvements in sanitation, nutrition, and medical practices. Through the early 20th century, the death of children, although much rarer in the developed world than in ancient and medieval

TABLE 6.10

Deaths and death rates, by age and sex, 2014

Age (years)	All races			Age (years)	All races		
	Both sexes	Male	Female		Both sexes	Male	Female
	Number				Rate		
All ages	2,626,418	1,328,241	1,298,177	All ages[a]	823.7	846.4	801.7
Under 1 year	23,215	12,886	10,329	Under 1 year[b]	588.0	638.6	535.0
1–4	3,830	2,172	1,658	1–4	24.0	26.7	21.3
5–9	2,357	1,357	1,000	5–9	11.5	13.0	10.0
10–14	2,893	1,771	1,122	10–14	14.0	16.8	11.1
15–19	9,586	6,828	2,758	15–19	45.5	63.3	26.8
20–24	19,205	14,289	4,916	20–24	83.8	121.7	44.0
25–29	21,925	15,619	6,306	25–29	99.7	139.9	58.2
30–34	25,252	17,078	8,174	30–34	117.3	158.0	76.3
35–39	29,325	18,500	10,825	35–39	147.2	186.1	108.4
40–44	41,671	25,193	16,478	40–44	202.4	246.5	158.9
45–49	65,016	39,281	25,735	45–49	311.3	379.6	244.2
50–54	110,901	67,096	43,805	50–54	491.3	605.7	381.1
55–59	157,170	95,992	61,178	55–59	730.6	919.1	552.8
60–64	191,638	116,206	75,432	60–64	1,032.2	1,308.9	778.6
65–69	222,834	129,802	93,032	65–69	1,454.0	1,790.6	1,151.9
70–74	248,707	138,846	109,861	70–74	2,246.1	2,722.5	1,839.3
75–79	282,072	149,259	132,813	75–79	3,560.5	4,250.5	3,011.1
80–84	342,432	167,171	175,261	80–84	5,944.6	7,018.6	5,187.5
85 and over	826,226	308,785	517,441	85 and over	13,407.9	14,642.2	12,765.7
Not stated	163	110	53				

[a]Figures for age not stated are included in "All ages" but are not distributed among age groups.
[b]Death rates for "Under 1 year" (based on population estimates) differ from infant mortality rates (based on live births).
Notes: Rates per 100,000 population in specified group. Populations used for computing death rates are postcensal estimates based on the 2010 census estimated as of July 1, 2014. Data for specified races other than white and black should be interpreted with caution because of inconsistencies between reporting race on death certificates and on censuses and surveys.

SOURCE: Adapted from Kenneth D. Kochanek et al., "Table 3. Number of Deaths and Death Rates, by Age, Race, and Sex: United States, 2014," in "Deaths: Final Data for 2014," *National Vital Statistics Reports*, vol. 65, no. 4, June 30, 2016, https://www.cdc.gov/nchs/data/nvsr/nvsr65/nvsr65_04.pdf (accessed July 14, 2017)

times, remained tragically commonplace. In *Child Mortality in the United States, 1935–2007: Large Racial and Socioeconomic Disparities Have Persisted over Time* (2010), Gopal K. Singh of the HHS reports that between 1900 and 1902, 90.2% of U.S. children who made it to their first birthday survived to age 15. He goes on to state that, in 1907, the mortality rate for U.S. children aged one to four years was 1,418.8 deaths per 100,000 people, and the rate for children aged five to 14 years was 307.5.

Table 6.11 shows that there were precipitous declines in child mortality rates between 1980 and 2014. Although declines were comparably dramatic for both white and African American children, African American children had a substantially higher likelihood of dying at all points throughout this period. In 2014, the mortality rate for non-Hispanic white children aged one to four years was 22.6 per 100,000 live births. For African American children in this age range, the mortality rate was 37.1 per 100,000 live births. Native Americans in this age range also had an exceptionally high mortality rate of 30.8 per 100,000 live births in 2014. For children aged five to 14 years in 2014, African Americans had the highest mortality rate, at 17.9 per 100,000 live births. Whites had the second-highest mortality rate in this age range, 12.1 per 100,000 live births, but this was nevertheless below the overall average for mortality in this group: 12.8 per 100,000.

In recent times, accidents have consistently been the leading cause of death for children in the United States. Melonie Heron reports in "Deaths: Leading Causes for 2014" (*National Vital Statistics Reports*, vol. 65, no. 5, June 30, 2016) that among the 6,187 deaths of U.S. residents aged one to nine years in 2014, 1,946, or 31.5%, were the result of accidents. (See Figure 6.6.) Other major causes of death in this age group were cancer (12.2% of deaths), birth defects (9.6%), and homicide (7.9%). Accidents accounted for an even greater percentage of deaths among children and young adults aged 10 to 24 years. As Heron notes, of the 31,684 deaths reported in this age group in 2014, 12,547 (39.6%) were accident related. Other leading causes of death among children and young adults aged 10 to 24 years included suicide (17.4% of deaths), homicide (13.7%), and cancer (6.3%).

CARING FOR TERMINALLY ILL INFANTS AND CHILDREN

In "Pediatric End-of-Life Issues and Palliative Care" (*Clinical Pediatric Emergency Medicine*, vol. 8, no. 3, September 2007), Kelly Nicole Michelson and David M. Steinhorn report that as of 2007 more than 56% of the annual average of 55,000 pediatric deaths (including both

TABLE 6.11

Child death rates, by race and Hispanic origin, selected years 1980—2014

	1980	1985	1990	1995	2000	2005	2006	2007	2008	2009	2010	2011	2012	2013	2014
Ages 1–4	**63.9**	**51.8**	**46.8**	**40.6**	**32.4**	**29.9**	**29.1**	**29.4**	**29.3**	**27.4**	**26.5**	**26.3**	**26.3**	**25.5**	**24.0**
Race and Hispanic origin															
Non-Hispanic white	—	45.3	37.6	33.9	28.5	26.7	25.6	26.3	27.0	25.0	24.7	24.1	29.9	23.7	22.6
Black	97.6	80.7	76.8	70.3	49.9	43.5	45.3	44.4	42.4	39.8	38.1	38.3	37.3	37.1	37.1
Hispanicª	—	46.1	43.5	36.7	29.6	28.7	26.5	26.3	25.9	24.7	22.7	23.5	21.8	20.8	18.7
Asian/Pacific Islander	43.2	40.1	38.6	25.4	21.6	18.0	18.6	20.6	18.0	16.1	17.9	11.6	15.5	18.8	13.4
American Indianᵇ	—	—	—	—	42.4	40.6	36.8	36.2	35.2	27.4	29.4	22.0	28.5	33.6	30.8
Ages 5–14	**30.6**	**26.5**	**24.0**	**22.5**	**18.0**	**16.3**	**15.2**	**15.2**	**13.9**	**13.8**	**12.9**	**13.2**	**12.6**	**13.0**	**12.8**
Race and Hispanic origin															
Non-Hispanic white	—	23.1	21.5	20.1	17.1	15.3	14.1	14.3	13.2	12.4	12.6	12.8	11.8	12.6	12.1
Black	39.0	35.5	34.4	33.4	24.2	22.8	20.7	20.3	19.3	19.5	17.1	17.6	17.7	17.2	17.9
Hispanicª	—	19.3	20.0	20.5	15.7	13.5	13.9	13.7	11.6	12.9	10.2	11.0	11.1	10.8	11.2
Asian/Pacific Islander	24.2	20.8	16.9	16.8	12.3	12.4	10.3	10.2	9.7	10.5	8.2	8.5	8.1	10.0	8.2
American Indianᵇ	—	—	—	—	19.0	17.2	13.9	14.0	13.9	15.9	14.4	12.7	13.3	11.5	11.7

ªPersons of Hispanic origin may be of any race.
ᵇAmerican Indians include Alaska Natives.

SOURCE: Adapted from "Appendix 1. Infant, Child, and Teen Death Rates (per 100,000 Population): Selected Years, 1980–2014," in *Infant, Child, and Teen Mortality: Indicators of Child Well-Being*, Child Trends DataBank, November 2016, https://www.childtrends.org/wp-content/uploads/2016/11/63_Child_Mortality.pdf (accessed July 18, 2017)

FIGURE 6.6

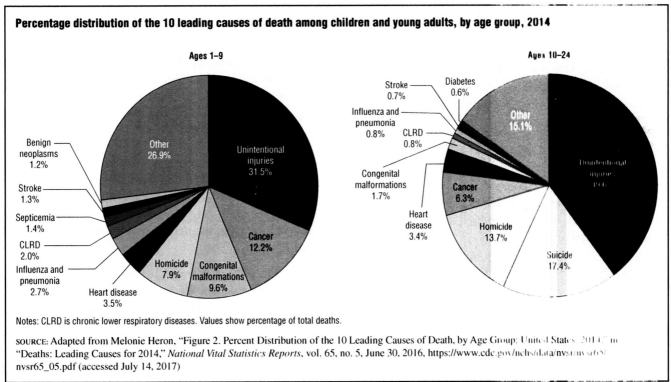

Percentage distribution of the 10 leading causes of death among children and young adults, by age group, 2014

Notes: CLRD is chronic lower respiratory diseases. Values show percentage of total deaths.

SOURCE: Adapted from Melonie Heron, "Figure 2. Percent Distribution of the 10 Leading Causes of Death, by Age Group: United States, 2014," in "Deaths: Leading Causes for 2014," *National Vital Statistics Reports*, vol. 65, no. 5, June 30, 2016, https://www.cdc.gov/nchs/data/nvsr/nvsr65/nvsr65_05.pdf (accessed July 14, 2017)

infant deaths and the deaths of children and young people up to the age of 19 years) occurred in hospitals. Almost all of these hospital deaths occurred in pediatric or neonatal intensive care units; a small minority occurred in emergency departments. Whereas end-of-life care for adults is often focused on chronic conditions, especially heart disease and cancer, palliative care for children must address a wider array of concerns, on average. Michelson

and Steinhorn note that this was evident in the statistics for one hospital, where approximately one-third of pediatric deaths were associated with cardiac events or conditions; around 40% were split roughly evenly between the diagnostic categories of neonatal-specific diagnoses, birth defects, and infectious conditions; 10% were due to cancer; and 6% were due to trauma (major injuries caused by an external source).

In spite of the significant differences in the distribution of conditions, palliative care for children follows much the same template as palliative care for adults. In "WHO Definition of Palliative Care" (2017, http://www.who.int/cancer/palliative/definition/en/), the World Health Organization's definition of palliative care for children is consistent with its definition of palliative care for adults, but with different emphases:

- Palliative care for children is the active total care of the child's body, mind and spirit, and also involves giving support to the family.

- It begins when illness is diagnosed, and continues regardless of whether or not a child receives treatment directed at the disease.

- Health providers must evaluate and alleviate a child's physical, psychological, and social distress.

- Effective palliative care requires a broad multidisciplinary approach that includes the family and makes use of available community resources; it can be successfully implemented even if resources are limited.

- It can be provided in tertiary care facilities, in community-health centres and even in children's homes.

Parents play a major role in shaping end-of-life care for children. Although it is part of the caregiver's job to assess and respond to the needs of the patient's family members, parents must also be clear about their feelings, preferences, and concerns if caregivers are to provide the best possible care for the dying child.

Perhaps surprisingly, effective palliative care for children includes an emphasis on including the patient in discussions of care, including honest discussions about death. Michelson and Steinhorn reference studies suggesting that, difficult as it is for parents and caregivers to talk about death with dying children, parents typically do not regret doing so. Parents who do not speak with their dying children about death do, however, typically come to regret this approach. The American Society of Clinical Oncology notes in "Caring for a Terminally Ill Child: A Guide for Parents" (November 2015, http://www.cancer.net/coping/end-life-care/caring-terminally-ill-child-guide-parents) that most children with advanced terminal illnesses are aware, either consciously or subconsciously, that they are dying. Even older children and adolescents who understand death fully may have large areas of uncertainty in their thinking, and the uncertainty can increase their levels of fear and anxiety. Health care professionals recommend that parents allow children to voice their own fears and concerns thoroughly, so that discussions can be shaped according to the understanding and needs of each child. Parents are advised to speak clearly and directly, rather than obscuring the nature of death by using euphemisms. Sometimes, additionally, children feel that they need "permission" to die, because they are worried about their parents' and family members' well-being.

The relief of pain and discomfort is, as with adults, a primary concern of pediatric palliative caregivers. Pain is, of course, a highly subjective experience, and even with adults, its management varies from patient to patient and requires great sensitivity to the individual and his or her needs. With children, the complexity of pain management is further complicated by different experiences of pain depending on the child's developmental stage.

Another major focus of palliative care in both children and adults involves addressing patients' social, psychological, and spiritual concerns. As with pain management, a caregiver's job in this realm is highly dependent on the child's stage of development. Infants and children up to the preschool level, for example, typically have little or no understanding of death. Often, then, the process of addressing mental and emotional needs involves acts of physical soothing, such as caressing or holding the child. Older children and adolescents typically understand death more fully, and they often benefit from being allowed to assume control whenever possible, such as by being included in medical discussions about their conditions and treatment options.

Children's inner needs may also be addressed outside of the medical setting, for example, by taking a vacation with parents, by being encouraged to continue engaging in "normal" activities for as long as possible, and by having the chance to say good-bye to friends, teachers, and other important people. Dealing sensitively with spiritual concerns and allowing for the comfort that religion or other forms of belief can provide is also part of the palliative caregiver's job. When parents communicate their religious beliefs to caregivers, these beliefs can be included in the overall process of making the child comfortable.

In cases where terminally ill children are expected to live less than six months and are no longer receiving treatment, palliative care gives way to hospice care. Hospice services, while similar to palliative care, often focus on increasing the comfort of the child and family in the home. Some families, however, find more comfort in the hospital setting as the end of life approaches. Hospice caregivers can typically accommodate families in either setting, provided that parents communicate their needs to the child's health care team.

MEDICAL DECISION MAKING FOR INFANTS

Before the 1980s U.S. courts were supportive of biological parents making decisions regarding the medical care of their newborns. Parents often made these decisions in consultation with pediatricians. Beginning in the

1980s medical advancements allowed for the survival of infants who would have not had a chance for survival before that time. Parents' and physicians' decisions became more challenging and complex.

The modern history of federal and state laws pertaining to the medical care of infants dates to 1982, when the Baby Doe regulations were issued. These regulations created a standard of medical care for infants: the possibility of future handicaps in a child should play no role in his or her medical treatment decisions.

The Baby Doe Rules

In April 1982 an infant with Down syndrome was born at Bloomington Hospital in Indiana. The infant also had esophageal atresia, an obstruction in the esophagus that prevents the passage of food from the mouth to the stomach. Following their obstetrician's recommendation, the parents decided to forgo surgery to repair the baby's esophagus. The baby would be kept pain-free with medication and allowed to die. The hospital, however, disagreed with the parents' decision and took the matter to the county court. The judge ruled that the parents had the legal right to their decision, which was based on a valid medical recommendation. The Indiana Supreme Court refused to hear the appeal. Before the county prosecutor could present the case to the U.S. Supreme Court, the six-day-old baby died.

The public outcry following the death of "Baby Doe" (the infant's court-designated name) brought immediate reaction from the administration of President Ronald Reagan (1911–2004). The HHS informed all hospitals receiving federal funding that discrimination against handicapped newborns would violate section 504 of the Rehabilitation Act of 1973. This section (nondiscrimination under federal grants and programs) states: "No otherwise qualified individual with a disability in the United States … shall, solely by reason of her or his disability, be excluded from participation in, be denied the benefits of, or be subjected to discrimination under any program, service or activity receiving Federal financial assistance."

Furthermore, all hospitals receiving federal aid were required to post signs that read: "Discriminatory failure to feed and care for handicapped infants in this facility is prohibited by Federal law." The signs listed a toll-free hotline for anonymous reports of failure to comply.

Although government investigators (called Baby Doe squads) were summoned to many hospitals to verify claims of mistreatment (the hotline had 500 calls in its first three weeks alone), no violation of the law could be found. On the contrary, the investigators found doctors resuscitating babies who were beyond treatment because they feared legal actions. Finally, a group led by the American Academy of Pediatrics filed suit in March 1983 to have the Baby Doe rules overturned because they believed them to be harsh, unreasonably intrusive, and not necessarily in the best interests of the child. After various legal battles, in 1986 the U.S. Supreme Court ruled that the HHS did not have the authority to require such regulations and invalidated them.

Child Abuse Amendments and Their Legacy

As the Baby Doe regulations were being fought in the courts, President Reagan signed the Child Abuse Amendments (CAA) of 1984. The CAA extended and improved the provisions of the Child Abuse Prevention and Treatment Act (1974) and the Child Abuse Prevention and Treatment and Adoption Reform Act of 1978. The CAA established that states' child protection services systems would respond to complaints of medical neglect of children, including instances of withholding medically indicated treatment from disabled infants with life-threatening conditions. It noted that parents were the ones to make medical decisions for their disabled infants based on the advice of their physicians. These laws have been amended many times over the years, most recently by the Keeping Children and Families Safe Act of 2003, without voiding the states' and parents' responsibilities to disabled infants.

Born-Alive Infants Protection Act

The Born-Alive Infants Protection Act (BAIPA) was signed by President George W. Bush (1946–) in August 2002. The purpose of the law was to ensure that all infants born alive, whether developmentally able to survive long term or not, were given legal protection as people under federal law. The law did not prohibit or require medical care for newly born infants who were below a certain weight or developmental age, nor did it address gestational age. David Boyle et al. of the American Academy of Pediatrics Neonatal Resuscitation Program Steering Committee supported this point of view in "Born-Alive Infants Protection Act of 2001, Public Law No. 107-207" (*Pediatrics*, vol. 111, no. 3, March 1, 2003), stating that the law:

Should not in any way affect the approach that physicians currently follow with respect to the extremely premature infant…. At the time of delivery, and regardless of the circumstances of the delivery, the medical condition and prognosis of the newly born infant should be assessed. At that point decisions about withholding or discontinuing medical treatment that is considered futile may be considered by the medical care providers in conjunction with the parents acting in the best interest of their child. Those newly born infants who are deemed appropriate to not resuscitate or to have medical support withdrawn should be treated with dignity and respect, and provided with "comfort care" measures.

By 2005, however, the opinion that the BAIPA should not affect physicians' approach to their care of premature infants was questioned. In "Baby Doe Redux? The Department of Health and Human Services and the Born-Alive Infants Protection Act of 2002: A Cautionary Note on Normative Neonatal Practice" (*Pediatrics*, vol. 116, no. 4, October 1, 2005), Sadath A. Sayeed of the University of California, San Francisco, notes that in 2005 the HHS announced that it would investigate circumstances in which medical care had been withheld from any born-alive infant. The agency also suggested, as with the Baby Doe regulations, that individuals in health care facilities should report any infractions of the law that they might notice.

Sayeed criticizes the law's "all-encompassing definition of born alive," reporting that it includes any fetus "'at any stage of development … regardless of whether the expulsion or extraction occurs as a result of natural or induced labor, cesarean section, or induced abortion,' and it makes no reference to standards of care or best interests, nor does it specifically protect a parent's decision-making authority. Under the law's strict logic, an 18-week miscarried fetus with a detectable heart beat after delivery is entitled to the full protections of the law as determined by 'any Act of Congress, or any ruling, regulation, or interpretation of the various administrative bureaus and agencies.'"

In "Resuscitation of Likely Nonviable Newborns: Would Neonatology Practices in California Change if the Born-Alive Infants Protection Act Were Enforced?" (*Pediatrics*, vol. 123, no. 4, April 2009), J. Colin Partridge et al. of the University of California, San Francisco, address the effects of the BAIPA. The researchers note that in 2005 they conducted a survey of neonatologists in active practice in California. More than half of the respondents had neither heard of the BAIPA nor its enforcement guidelines. The physicians admitted rarely assessing the medical condition and prognosis of any fetus less than 23 weeks of gestation; 23 weeks of gestation appears to be the threshold for a fetus to have a chance of survival outside of the womb. Only 6% of the responding neonatologists thought the law should be enforced. Partridge et al. conclude that "until outcomes for infants of <24 weeks' gestation improve, legislation that changes resuscitation practices for extreme prematurity seems an unjustifiable restriction of physician practice and parental rights."

MEDICAL DECISION MAKING FOR CHILDREN

Under U.S. law, children under the age of 18 years cannot provide legally binding consent regarding their health care. Parents or guardians legally provide that consent, and, in most situations, physicians and the courts give parents wide latitude in the medical decisions they make for their children.

Religious Beliefs and Medical Treatment

Some parents refuse medical treatment for their children because of religious reasons. When such refusal is likely to result in death or undue suffering for a child, the government may step in. Although the U.S. Constitution prohibits government interference with religious practices and guarantees freedom of religion, the government concurrently has a responsibility to safeguard the health and well-being of its citizens.

Bruce Patsner of the University of Houston Law Center explains in "Faith versus Medicine: When a Parent Refuses a Child's Medical Care" (June 2009, http://www.law .uh.edu/Healthlaw/perspectives/2009/(BP)%20Faith.pdf) that the power of the government to intervene in the medical affairs of its citizens has limits, which are partly based on whether the intervention meets a "public health justification" criterion. For example, Patsner notes that the government's responsibility to protect the public health is the basis on which the government can implement mandatory vaccination programs. In cases that do not threaten public health, Patsner suggests that state family laws, rather than federal laws, should provide the standards for parental decision making. Nonetheless, Patsner explains, "while parents may be entitled to believe whatever they want to believe from a religious point of view, denials of life-saving medical care to their children quickly cross over from mere belief into conduct, and this is not protected to the same degree. Put another way, parents are generally not allowed to sacrifice the lives of their children whose health interests they are supposed to protect before the children are legally old enough to be able to make their own decisions."

WISCONSIN COURT CASE. In 2009 two cases came to state courts that tested governmental limits to intervene in the medical decisions for a minor child when the parents refused medical treatment. The first case concerned 11-year-old Kara Neumann, who died in March 2008 from diabetic ketoacidosis, a complication of her undiagnosed and untreated type 1 diabetes. In "Trials for Parents Who Chose Faith over Medicine" (NYTimes.com, January 20, 2009), Dirk Johnson reports that although Kara "had grown so weak that she could not walk or speak," her parents refused to obtain medical care for her and instead relied on prayer to heal her. About a month after her death, Jill Falstad, the state attorney of Marathon County, Wisconsin, filed charges against Kara's parents. Each was found guilty of second-degree reckless homicide in 2009 and sentenced to six months in prison along with 10 years of probation.

MINNESOTA COURT CASE. The second important 2009 court case involving parental decisions about a child's medical condition concerned 13-year-old Daniel Hauser, who had developed Hodgkin's lymphoma (a cancer of the immune system). Maura Lerner explains in "Sleepy Eye Parents, Teen Fight to Refuse Chemo" (StarTribune.com, May 7, 2009) that in January 2009 Hauser was diagnosed with the cancer and prescribed six rounds of chemotherapy and radiation. After undergoing the first round of chemotherapy to treat a tumor in his chest, Hauser became sick, as is common for chemotherapy patients. His parents responded by refusing any more treatments and chose instead to treat him themselves by changing his diet. Hauser and his parents belonged to the Nemenhah, a Native American religious organization that favors natural healing processes over medical intervention. They cited religious reasons for their decision.

James Olson, the attorney for Brown County, Minnesota, learned of Hauser's refusal and filed a petition against his parents, citing child neglect and endangerment. Olson asked the judge to order the boy into treatment for his highly curable cancer. Agreeing with the petition, the judge ordered the parents to have their son continue his chemotherapy and radiation treatments.

In May 2009 Hauser's mother took him to California to avoid the judge's order but returned a week later. Eventually, Hauser resumed treatments, and in November 2009 the judge closed the case after the court-ordered chemotherapy and radiation treatments put the cancer into remission.

End-of-Life Decisions for Adolescents

Although many laws concerning adolescents have changed since the mid-20th century, such as those allowing adolescents to seek medical treatment for reproductive health and birth control services without parental consent, most states have no laws for end-of-life decisions by adolescents. Caprice Knapp et al. indicate in "Adolescents with Life-Threatening Illnesses" (*American Journal of Hospice and Palliative Care*, vol. 27, no. 2, March 2010) that although U.S. laws do not consider adolescents under the age of 18 years to be competent to make their own health care decisions, health care practitioners often do. In a review of available studies, the researchers add, however, that practitioners from various medical fields differ on the question of how much to involve adolescents in life-altering decisions. For example, studies "suggest that adolescents do not have the capacity to make long-term decisions considering their stage of development," and that they are more likely than adults "to make decisions based on emotions rather than facts."

Conversely, behaviorists note that "a portfolio of evidence suggests that adolescents are capable of consenting to procedures and have the capacity to make decisions." Indeed, as Katharina M. Ruhe et al argue in "End-of-Life Decision Making in Pediatrics: Literature Review on Children's and Adolescents' Participation" (*AJOB Empirical Bioethics*, vol. 51, no. 1, January 2014), pediatricians view some level of patient involvement as crucial to making effective end-of-life decisions in cases involving terminally ill children and adolescents. According to Ruhe et al., the degree of patient participation depends on a range of individual and developmental factors. At the same time, Ruhe et al. note, the relationship between patient, parent, and physician must also be given careful consideration in determining a meaningful end-of-life decision.

CHAPTER 7
SUICIDE, EUTHANASIA, AND ASSISTED SUICIDE

SUICIDE

Suicide is a taboo subject for many people in the contemporary United States. Religious prohibitions against killing oneself, negative stereotypes about the mentally ill, and a general unwillingness to dwell on intractable emotional and physical pain may be among the factors that make suicide a topic to be avoided for most people. Nevertheless, suicide is a common occurrence in the United States, as in other countries, and it is in the interest of public health to be able to consider the phenomenon clearly.

As Table 4.1 in Chapter 4 shows, suicide was the 10th-leading cause of death nationally in 2014, accounting for 42,826 deaths. The age-adjusted rate of death by suicide, at 13 per 100,000 people in 2014, was consistent with historic rates of suicide. The age-adjusted rate of death by suicide has fluctuated within a fairly narrow range since 1950, from 13.2 in 1950 to 10.4 in 2000. (See Table 7.1.) In general, then, the likelihood that a person of any age in the United States will commit suicide has been consistent since the beginning of the post–World War II period.

Demographic Variations in the Suicide Rate

Although the overall rate of suicide in the United States has been relatively steady since 1950, there have been sizable variations by demographic subgroups, and the suicide rates for different age groups have changed noticeably over time.

At all points between 1950 and 2015, U.S. males have been roughly four times as likely as females to commit suicide. (See Table 7.1.) The age-adjusted suicide rate for males was 21.2 deaths per 100,000 population in 1950 and 21.1 in 2015, and the age-adjusted suicide rate for females was 5.6 in 1950 and 6 in 2015. According to the Centers for Disease Control and Prevention (CDC), in "Suicide: Facts at a Glance" (2015, https://www.cdc.gov/violenceprevention/pdf/suicide-data

sheet-a.pdf), males accounted for 77.9% of all suicides in 2013, but females were more likely to have considered suicide than males. Females are the most likely to commit suicide by poisoning, the method used in 34.8% of female suicides in 2013, whereas men are the most likely to commit suicide by firearm, the method used in 56.9% of male suicides that year.

Table 7.2 shows the numbers of deaths and the death rates not only for suicide but also for other types of deaths stemming from external injuries, such as accidents and homicides, classified according to the mechanism of death. In 2014 the suicide rate was 13.4 deaths per 100,000 population, compared with 62.6 deaths per 100,000 from all injuries that year. The number of suicides, at 42,826, was more than two and a half times greater than the number of homicides (15,872). Of particular note is the fact that, of the 33,594 firearm deaths in the United States that year, 21,386 (63.7%) were suicides, compared with 11,008 homicides (32.8%).

Many analysts suggest that the ease of obtaining firearms in the United States contributes significantly to the suicide rate. Whereas other methods of committing suicide, such as poisoning (which accounted for 6,808 suicides in 2014) and suffocation (11,407) are not always successful and in general take longer to complete, the use of a firearm minimizes the gap between the impulse and the act of suicide, and it is almost always fatal. (See Table 7.2.) Other observers note, however, that suicide rates in the United States are not disproportionately high compared with developed countries where firearms are less readily available.

Suicide rates have historically been higher for older people than for younger people, but the increase in rates as men age has typically been larger than the increase for women as they age. (See Table 7.1.) Moreover, the trend for women reverses past age 65, so that the oldest women

TABLE 7.1

Death rates for suicide, by sex, race, Hispanic origin, and age, selected years 1950–2015

[Data are based on death certificates]

Sex, race, Hispanic origin, and age	1950[a, b]	1960[a, b]	1970[b]	1980[b]	1990[b]	2000[c]	2010[c]	2014[c]	2015[c]
All persons				Deaths per 100,000 resident population					
All ages, age-adjusted[d]	13.2	12.5	13.1	12.2	12.5	10.4	12.1	13.0	13.3
All ages, crude	11.4	10.6	11.6	11.9	12.4	10.4	12.4	13.4	13.7
Under 1 year	CNA	CNA	CNA	CNA	CNA	CNA	CNA	CNA	CNA
1–4 years	CNA	CNA	CNA	CNA	CNA	CNA	CNA	CNA	CNA
5–14 years	0.2	0.3	0.3	0.4	0.8	0.7	0.7	1.0	1.0
15–24 years	4.5	5.2	8.8	12.3	13.2	10.2	10.5	11.6	12.5
15–19 years	2.7	3.6	5.9	8.5	11.1	8.0	7.5	8.7	9.8
20–24 years	6.2	7.1	12.2	16.1	15.1	12.5	13.6	14.2	15.1
25–44 years	11.6	12.2	15.4	15.6	15.2	13.4	15.0	15.8	16.4
25–34 years	9.1	10.0	14.1	16.0	15.2	12.0	14.0	15.1	15.7
35–44 years	14.3	14.2	16.9	15.4	15.3	14.5	16.0	16.6	17.1
45–64 years	23.5	22.0	20.6	15.9	15.3	13.5	18.6	19.5	19.6
45–54 years	20.9	20.7	20.0	15.9	14.8	14.4	19.6	20.2	20.3
55–64 years	26.8	23.7	21.4	15.9	16.0	12.1	17.5	18.8	18.9
65 years and over	30.0	24.5	20.8	17.6	20.5	15.2	14.9	16.7	16.6
65–74 years	29.6	23.0	20.8	16.9	17.9	12.5	13.7	15.6	15.2
75–84 years	31.1	27.9	21.2	19.1	24.9	17.6	15.7	17.5	17.9
85 years and over	28.8	26.0	19.0	19.2	22.2	19.6	17.6	19.3	19.4
Male									
All ages, age-adjusted[d]	21.2	20.0	19.8	19.9	21.5	17.7	19.8	20.7	21.1
All ages, crude	17.8	16.5	16.8	18.6	20.4	17.1	19.9	21.1	21.5
Under 1 year	CNA	CNA	CNA	CNA	CNA	CNA	CNA	CNA	CNA
1–4 years	CNA	CNA	CNA	CNA	CNA	CNA	CNA	CNA	CNA
5–14 years	0.3	0.4	0.5	0.6	1.1	1.2	0.9	1.3	1.2
15–24 years	6.5	8.2	13.5	20.2	22.0	17.1	16.9	18.2	19.4
15–19 years	3.5	5.6	8.8	13.8	18.1	13.0	11.7	13.0	14.2
20–24 years	9.3	11.5	19.3	26.8	25.7	21.4	22.2	22.9	24.2
25–44 years	17.2	17.9	20.9	24.0	24.4	21.3	23.6	24.4	25.2
25–34 years	13.4	14.7	19.8	25.0	24.8	19.6	22.5	23.8	24.7
35–44 years	21.3	21.0	22.1	22.5	23.9	22.8	24.6	25.0	25.9
45–64 years	37.1	34.4	30.0	23.7	24.3	21.3	29.2	29.7	29.5
45–54 years	32.0	31.6	27.9	22.9	23.2	22.4	30.4	30.0	30.1
55–64 years	43.6	38.1	32.7	24.5	25.7	19.4	27.7	29.4	28.9
65 years and over	52.8	44.0	38.4	35.0	41.6	31.1	29.0	31.4	31.0
65–74 years	50.5	39.6	36.0	30.4	32.2	22.7	23.9	26.6	26.2
75–84 years	58.3	52.5	42.8	42.3	56.1	38.6	32.3	34.9	35.2
85 years and over	58.3	57.4	42.4	50.6	65.9	57.5	47.3	49.9	48.2
Female									
All ages, age-adjusted[d]	5.6	5.6	7.4	5.7	4.8	4.0	5.0	5.8	6.0
All ages, crude	5.1	4.9	6.6	5.5	4.8	4.0	5.2	6.0	6.2
Under 1 year	CNA	CNA	CNA	CNA	CNA	CNA	CNA	CNA	CNA
1–4 years	CNA	CNA	CNA	CNA	CNA	CNA	CNA	CNA	CNA
5–14 years	0.1	0.1	0.2	0.2	0.4	0.3	0.4	0.7	0.8
15–24 years	2.6	2.2	4.2	4.3	3.9	3.0	3.9	4.6	5.3
15–19 years	1.8	1.6	2.9	3.0	3.7	2.7	3.1	4.2	5.1
20–24 years	3.3	2.9	5.7	5.5	4.1	3.2	4.7	5.0	5.5
25–44 years	6.2	6.6	10.2	7.7	6.2	5.4	6.4	7.2	7.5
25–34 years	4.9	5.5	8.6	7.1	5.6	4.3	5.3	6.3	6.6
35–44 years	7.5	7.7	11.9	8.5	6.8	6.4	7.5	8.2	8.4
45–64 years	9.9	10.2	12.0	8.9	7.1	6.2	8.6	9.8	10.2
45–54 years	9.9	10.2	12.6	9.4	6.9	6.7	9.0	10.7	10.7
55–64 years	9.9	10.2	11.4	8.4	7.3	5.4	8.0	8.9	9.7
65 years and over	9.4	8.4	8.1	6.1	6.4	4.0	4.2	5.0	5.1
65–74 years	10.1	8.4	9.0	6.5	6.7	4.0	4.8	5.9	5.7
75–84 years	8.1	8.9	7.0	5.5	6.3	4.0	3.7	4.3	4.6
85 years and over	8.2	6.0	5.9	5.5	5.4	4.2	3.3	3.4	4.2
White male[e]									
All ages, age-adjusted[d]	22.3	21.1	20.8	20.9	22.8	19.1	22.0	23.3	23.6
All ages, crude	19.0	17.6	18.0	19.9	22.0	18.8	22.6	24.2	24.6
15–24 years	6.6	8.6	13.9	21.4	23.2	17.9	18.3	19.9	20.9
25–44 years	17.9	18.5	21.5	24.6	25.4	22.9	26.2	27.5	28.6
45–64 years	39.3	36.5	31.9	25.0	26.0	23.2	33.0	34.0	33.8
65 years and over	55.8	46.7	41.1	37.2	44.2	33.3	31.7	34.7	34.3
65–74 years	53.2	42.0	38.7	32.5	34.2	24.3	26.3	29.5	29.1
75–84 years	61.9	55.7	45.5	45.5	60.2	41.1	34.9	38.3	38.6
85 years and over	61.9	61.3	45.8	52.8	70.3	61.6	50.8	54.4	52.5

TABLE 7.1

Death rates for suicide, by sex, race, Hispanic origin, and age, selected years 1950–2015 [CONTINUED]

[Data are based on death certificates]

Sex, race, Hispanic origin, and age	1950[a,b]	1960[a,b]	1970[b]	1980[b]	1990[b]	2000[c]	2010	2014	2015[c]
Black or African American male[e]					Deaths per 100,000 resident population				
All ages, age-adjusted[d]	7.5	8.4	10.0	11.4	12.8	10.0	9.1	9.5	9.6
All ages, crude	6.3	6.4	8.0	10.3	12.0	9.4	8.7	9.2	9.4
15–24 years	4.9	4.1	10.5	12.3	15.1	14.2	11.1	12.0	12.9
25–44 years	9.8	12.6	16.1	19.2	19.6	14.3	14.5	14.4	14.8
45–64 years	12.7	13.0	12.4	11.8	13.1	9.9	9.5	9.9	9.7
65 years and over	9.0	9.9	8.7	11.4	14.9	11.5	8.3	8.9	8.6
65–74 years	10.0	11.3	8.7	11.1	14.7	11.1	7.6	7.7	7.3
75–84 years[f]	h	h	h	10.5	14.4	12.1	9.9	11.0	11.2
85 years and over	DNA	h	h	h	h	h		h	h
American Indian or Alaska Native male[e]									
All ages, age-adjusted[d]	DNA	DNA	DNA	19.3	20.1	16.0	15.5	16.4	18.8
All ages, crude	DNA	DNA	DNA	20.9	20.9	15.9	16.1	16.0	18.5
15–24 years	DNA	DNA	DNA	45.3	49.1	26.2	30.6	23.5	29.5
25–44 years	DNA	DNA	DNA	31.2	27.8	24.5	20.9	26.2	27.3
45–64 years	DNA	DNA	DNA	h	h	15.4	17.8	15.1	20.8
65 years and over	DNA	DNA					13.4		13.2
Asian or Pacific Islander male[e]									
All ages, age-adjusted[d]	DNA	DNA	DNA	10.7	9.6	8.6	9.5	8.9	9.1
All ages, crude	DNA	DNA	DNA	8.8	8.7	7.9	9.3	9.0	9.2
15–24 years	DNA	DNA	DNA	10.8	13.5	9.1	10.9	12.9	15.6
25–44 years	DNA	DNA	DNA	11.0	10.6	9.9	10.6	9.7	9.6
45–64 years	DNA	DNA	DNA	13.0	9.7	9.7	12.8	12.1	10.9
65 years and over	DNA	DNA	DNA	18.6	16.8	15.4	14.9	11.6	12.6
Hispanic or Latino male[e,g]									
All ages, age-adjusted	DNA	DNA	DNA	DNA	13.7	10.3	9.9	10.3	9.9
All ages, crud	DNA	DNA	DNA	DNA	11.4	8.4	8.5	9.2	9.0
15–24 years	DNA	DNA	DNA	DNA	14.7	10.9	10.7	11.6	12.8
25–44 years	DNA	DNA	DNA	DNA	16.2	11.2	11.2	12.6	12.2
45–64 years	DNA	DNA	DNA	DNA	16.1	12.0	12.9	12.4	11.4
65 years and over	DNA	DNA	DNA	DNA	23.4	19.5	15.7	15.9	14.5
White, not Hispanic or Latino male[g]									
All ages, age-adjusted[d]	DNA	DNA	DNA	DNA	23.5	20.2	24.2	25.9	26.6
All ages, crude	DNA	DNA	DNA	DNA	23.1	20.4	25.7	27.7	28.3
15–24 years	DNA	DNA	DNA	DNA	24.4	19.5	20.4	22.4	23.4
25–44 years	DNA	DNA	DNA	DNA	26.4	25.1	30.3	31.8	33.5
45–64 years	DNA	DNA	DNA	DNA	26.8	24.0	35.4	37.2	37.2
65 years and over	DNA	DNA	DNA	DNA	45.4	33.9	32.7	36.1	35.9
White female[e]									
All ages, age-adjusted[d]	6.0	5.9	7.9	6.1	5.2	4.3	5.6	6.6	6.9
All ages, crud	5.5	5.3	7.1	5.9	5.3	4.4	5.9	6.9	7.2
15–24 years	2.7	2.3	4.2	4.6	4.2	3.1	4.2	5.0	5.6
25–44 years	6.6	7.0	11.0	8.1	6.6	6.0	7.3	8.4	8.7
45–64 years	10.6	10.9	13.0	9.6	7.7	6.9	9.9	11.5	11.9
65 years and over	9.9	8.8	8.5	6.4	6.8	4.3	4.5	5.5	5.6
Black or African American female[e]									
All ages, age-adjusted[d]	1.8	2.0	2.9	2.4	2.4	1.8	1.8	2.1	2.0
All ages, crude	1.5	1.6	2.6	2.2	2.3	1.7	1.8	2.1	2.1
15–24 years	1.8	*	3.8	2.3	2.3	2.2	2.0	2.6	3.6
25–44 years	2.3	3.0	4.8	4.3	3.8	2.6	2.8	2.9	2.7
45–64 years	2.7	3.1	2.9	2.5	2.9	2.1	2.1	2.7	2.6
65 years and over	*	*	2.6	*	1.9	1.3		1.3	0.9

are among the least likely to commit suicide, whereas the oldest men are the most likely to commit suicide.

Specifically, boys and men aged 15 to 24 years had a suicide rate of 19.4 deaths per 100,000 population in 2015, men aged 25 to 44 years had a suicide rate of 25.2, men aged 45 to 64 years had a suicide rate of 29.5, and men aged 65 years and older had a suicide rate of 31. (See Table 7.1.) By contrast, the suicide rate for girls and women aged 15 to 24 years was 5.3 deaths per 100,000 population, the rate for women aged 25 to 44 years was 7.5, the rate for women aged 45 to 64 years was 10.2, and the rate for women over the age of 65 years was 5.1. Among men, those aged 85 years and older had the highest suicide rate of any age-based subgroup (48.2 deaths per 100,000 population), whereas women aged

TABLE 7.1

Death rates for suicide, by sex, race, Hispanic origin, and age, selected years 1950–2015 [CONTINUED]

[Data are based on death certificates]

Sex, race, Hispanic origin, and age	1950[a, b]	1960[a, b]	1970[b]	1980[b]	1990[b]	2000[c]	2010[c]	2014[c]	2015[c]
American Indian or Alaska Native female[e]				Deaths per 100,000 resident population					
All ages, age-adjusted[d]	DNA	DNA	DNA	4.7	3.6	3.8	6.1	5.5	6.5
All ages, crude	DNA	DNA	DNA	4.7	3.7	4.0	5.9	5.6	6.6
15–24 years	DNA	DNA	DNA	[h]	[h]	[h]	10.4	9.6	11.7
25–44 years	DNA	DNA	DNA	10.7	[h]	7.2	7.4	9.7	8.8
45–64 years	DNA	DNA	DNA	[h]	[h]	[h]	6.2	[h]	6.9
65 years and over	DNA	DNA	DNA	[h]	[h]	[h]	[h]	[h]	[h]
Asian or Pacific Islander female[e]									
All ages, age-adjusted[d]	DNA	DNA	DNA	5.5	4.1	2.8	3.4	3.4	4.0
All ages, crude	DNA	DNA	DNA	4.7	3.4	2.7	3.4	3.5	4.1
15–24 years	DNA	DNA	DNA	[h]	3.9	2.7	3.5	4.1	4.9
25–44 years	DNA	DNA	DNA	5.4	3.8	3.3	4.1	4.0	4.5
45–64 years	DNA	DNA	DNA	7.9	5.0	3.2	4.7	4.2	5.2
65 years and over	DNA	DNA	DNA	[h]	8.5	5.2	4.3	5.2	5.2
Hispanic or Latina female[e, g]									
All ages, age-adjusted[d]	DNA	DNA	DNA	DNA	2.3	1.7	2.1	2.5	2.6
All ages, crude	DNA	DNA	DNA	DNA	2.2	1.5	2.0	2.4	2.6
15–24 years	DNA	DNA	DNA	DNA	3.1	2.0	3.1	3.4	3.9
25–44 years	DNA	DNA	DNA	DNA	3.1	2.1	2.4	3.0	3.2
45–64 years	DNA	DNA	DNA	DNA	2.5	2.5	2.8	3.5	3.8
65 years and over	DNA	DNA	DNA	DNA	[h]	[h]	2.2	2.1	1.9
White, not Hispanic or Latina female[f]									
All ages, age-adjusted[d]	DNA	DNA	DNA	DNA	5.4	4.7	6.2	7.5	7.8
All ages, crude	DNA	DNA	DNA	DNA	5.6	4.9	6.7	7.9	8.3
15–24 years	DNA	DNA	DNA	DNA	4.3	3.3	4.4	5.4	6.1
25–44 years	DNA	DNA	DNA	DNA	7.0	6.7	8.6	9.8	10.3
45–64 years	DNA	DNA	DNA	DNA	8.0	7.3	10.7	12.6	13.1
65 years and over	DNA	DNA	DNA	DNA	7.0	4.4	4.7	5.8	6.0

CNA = category not applicable

DNA = data not available

[a]Includes deaths of persons who were not residents of the 50 states and the District of Columbia (D.C.).

[b]Underlying cause of death was coded according to the 6th Revision of the *International Classification of Diseases* (ICD) in 1950, 7th Revision in 1960, 8th Revision in 1970, and 9th Revision in 1980–1998.

[c]Starting with 1999 data, cause of death is coded according to ICD—10.

[d]Age-adjusted rates are calculated using the year 2000 standard population. Prior to 2001, age-adjusted rates were calculated using standard million proportions based on rounded population numbers. Starting with 2001 data, unrounded population numbers are used to calculate age-adjusted rates.

[e]The race groups, white, black, Asian and Pacific Islander, and American Indian or Alaska Native, include persons of Hispanic and non-Hispanic origin. Persons of Hispanic origin may be of any race. Death rates for Hispanic, American Indian or Alaska Native, and Asian or Pacific Islander persons should be interpreted with caution because of inconsistencies in reporting Hispanic origin or race on the death certificate (death rate numerators) compared with population figures (death rate denominators). The net effect of misclassification is an underestimation of deaths and death rates for races other than white and black.

[f]In 1950, rate is for the age group 75 years and over.

[g]Prior to 1997, data from states that did not report Hispanic origin on the death certifcate were excluded.

[h]Rates based on fewer than 20 deaths are considered unreliable and are not shown.

Notes: Starting with *Health, United States,* 2003, rates for 1991–1999 were revised using intercensal population estimates based on the 1990 and 2000 censuses. For 2000, population estimates are bridged-race April 1 census counts. Starting with *Health, United States, 2012,* rates for 2001–2009 were revised using intercensal population estimates based on the 2000 and 2010 censuses. For 2010, population estimates are bridged-race April 1 census counts. Rates for 2011 and beyond were computed using 2010-based postcensal estimates. Figures for 2001 include September 11-related deaths for which death certificates were filed as of October 24, 2002. Age groups were selected to minimize the presentation of unstable age-specific death rates based on small numbers of deaths and for consistency among comparison groups. Starting with 2003 data, some states began to collect information on more than one race on the death certificate, according to 1997 Office of Management and Budget (OMB) standards. The multiple-race data for these states were bridged to the single-race categories of the 1977 OMB standards, for comparability with other states. Some data have been revised and differ from previous editions of *Health, United States.*

SOURCE: "Table 30. Death Rates for Suicide, by Sex, Race, Hispanic Origin, and Age: United States, Selected Years 1950–2015," in *Health, United States, 2016: With Chartbook on Long-term Trends in Health,* Centers for Disease Control and Prevention, National Center for Health Statistics, 2017, https://www.cdc.gov/nchs/data/hus/hus16.pdf (accessed July 16, 2017)

85 years and older had one of the lowest suicide rates of any subgroup (4.2 deaths per 100,000 population).

Although older men have significantly higher suicide rates than younger men, in general older people are less likely to commit suicide in the 21st century than in earlier decades. (See Table 7.1.) The suicide rate for men and women aged 65 years and older decreased by nearly half between 1950 and 2015, falling from 30 deaths per 100,000 population to 16.6, and the suicide rate for men and women aged 45 to 64 years fell from 23.5 to 19.6. Meanwhile, the suicide rate for teenagers and young adults aged 15 to 24 years has nearly tripled, from 4.5 in 1950 to 12.5 in 2015, and the rate for adults aged 25 to 44 years has risen from 11.6 in 1950 to 16.4 in 2015.

TABLE 7.2

Number of deaths and death rates, by mechanism and intent of death, 2014

Mechanism and intent of death (based on ICD–10)	Number	Rate	Age-adjusted rate
All injury	199,752	62.6	60.1
Unintentional	135,928	42.6	40.5
Suicide	42,826	13.4	13.0
Homicide	15,872	5.0	5.1
Undetermined	4,597	1.4	1.4
Legal intervention/war	529	0.2	0.2
Cut/pierce	2,609	0.8	0.8
Unintentional	109	0.0	0.0
Suicide	740	0.2	0.2
Homicide	1,740	0.5	0.6
Undetermined	20	0.0	0.0
Legal intervention/war	QZ	*	*
Drowning	3,995	1.3	1.2
Unintentional	3,406	1.1	1.1
Suicide	372	0.1	0.1
Homicide	32	0.0	0.0
Undetermined	185	0.1	0.1
Fall	33,018	10.4	9.1
Unintentional	31,959	10.0	8.8
Suicide	994	0.3	0.3
Homicide	4	*	*
Undetermined	61	0.0	0.0
Fire/hot object or substance	3,196	1.0	0.9
Unintentional	2,772	0.9	0.8
Suicide	180	0.1	0.0
Homicide	89	0.0	0.0
Undetermined	155	0.0	0.0
Legal intervention/war	QZ	*	*
Fire/flame	3,122	1.0	0.9
Unintentional	2,701	0.8	0.8
Suicide	180	0.1	0.0
Homicide	86	0.0	0.0
Undetermined	155	0.0	0.0
Hot object/substance	74	0.0	0.0
Unintentional	71	0.0	0.0
Suicide	QZ	*	*
Homicide	3	*	*
Undetermined	QZ	*	*
Firearm	33,594	10.5	10.3
Unintentional	461	0.1	0.1
Suicide	21,386	6.7	6.4
Homicide	11,008	3.5	3.5
Undetermined	275	0.1	0.1
Legal intervention/war	464	0.1	0.2
Machinery	605	0.2	0.2
All transport	37,444	11.7	11.4
Unintentional	37,195	11.7	11.3
Suicide	177	0.1	0.1
Homicide	56	0.0	0.0
Undetermined	16	*	*
Legal intervention/war	QZ	*	*
Motor vehicle traffic	33,736	10.6	10.3
Occupant	8,098	2.5	2.5
Motorcyclist	4,036	1.3	1.2
Pedal cyclist	623	0.2	0.2
Pedestrian	5,226	1.6	1.6
Other	9	*	*
Unspecified	15,744	4.9	4.8

As Table 7.1 further shows, suicide rates vary significantly by race and ethnicity. Age-adjusted rates in 2015, as in previous decades, were highest for non-Hispanic white males (23.6 deaths per 100,000 population) and Native American males (18.8). Asian or Pacific Islander males (9.1), African American males (9.6), and Hispanic males (9.9) were considerably less likely to commit suicide. Likewise, non-Hispanic white females (6.9) and Native American females (6.5) were more likely to commit suicide than their African American (2), Hispanic (2.6), and Asian or Pacific Islander (4) counterparts.

Cross-Cultural and Historical Attitudes toward Suicide

Attitudes about suicide, like rates of suicide, vary significantly across and within cultures. Although cultural influences are notoriously difficult to isolate in

TABLE 7.2

Number of deaths and death rates, by mechanism and intent of death, 2014 [CONTINUED]

Mechanism and intent of death (based on ICD–10)	Number	Rate	Age-adjusted rate
Pedal cyclist, other	279	0.1	0.1
Pedestrian, other	1,032	0.3	0.3
Other land transport	1,591	0.5	0.5
Unintentional	1,342	0.4	0.4
Suicide	177	0.1	0.1
Homicide	56	0.0	0.0
Undetermined	16	*	*
Other transport	806	0.3	0.3
Unintentional	806	0.3	0.3
Homicide	QZ	*	*
Legal intervention/war	QZ	*	*
Natural/environmental	1,625	0.5	0.5
Overexertion	9	*	*
Poisoning	51,966	16.3	16.2
Unintentional	42,032	13.2	13.1
Suicide	6,808	2.1	2.0
Homicide	100	0.0	0.0
Undetermined	3,026	0.9	0.9
Legal intervention/war	QZ	*	*
Struck by or against	1,022	0.3	0.3
Unintentional	908	0.3	0.3
Suicide	1	*	*
Homicide	111	0.0	0.0
Undetermined	2	*	*
Legal intervention/war	QZ	*	*
Suffocation	18,646	5.8	5.7
Unintentional	6,580	2.1	1.9
Suicide	11,407	3.6	3.6
Homicide	520	0.2	0.2
Undetermined	139	0.0	0.0
Other specified, classifiable	2,097	0.7	0.6
Unintentional	1,323	0.4	0.4
Suicide	517	0.2	0.2
Homicide	203	0.1	0.1
Undetermined	19	*	*
Legal intervention/war	35	0.0	0.0
Other specified, not elsewhere classified	1,888	0.6	0.6
Unintentional	1,096	0.3	0.3
Suicide	165	0.1	0.1
Homicide	424	0.1	0.1
Undetermined	175	0.1	0.1
Legal intervention/war	28	0.0	0.0
Unspecified	8,038	2.5	2.3
Unintentional	5,848	1.8	1.6
Suicide	79	0.0	0.0
Homicide	1,585	0.5	0.5
Undetermined	524	0.2	0.1
Legal intervention/war	2	*	*

ICD–10 = International Classification of Diseases, Tenth Revision

QZ = quantity zero

*Figure does not meet standards of reliability or precision.

Notes: Totals for selected causes of death differ from those shown in other tables that utilize standard mortality tabulation lists. Rates are per 100,000 population; age-adjusted rates are per 100,000 U.S. standard population. Populations used for computing death rates are postcensal estimates based on the 2010 census estimated as of July 1, 2014. 0.0 quantity is more than zero but less than 0.05.

SOURCE: Kenneth D. Kochanek et al., "Table 18. Number of Deaths, Death Rates, and Age-Adjusted Death Rates for Injury Deaths, by Mechanism and Intent of Death: United States, 2014," in "Deaths: Final Data for 2014," *National Vital Statistics Reports*, vol. 65, no. 4, June 30, 2016, https://www.cdc.gov/nchs/data/nvsr/nvsr65/nvsr65_04.pdf (accessed July 16, 2017)

scientific studies, a large body of literature exists testifying to the different ways that cultures and religions throughout history have understood the act of ending one's own life.

In ancient Greece, the suicides of those who had decided that their life was no longer useful were considered acceptable and even rational acts, and there was no prohibition on their seeking help from others in the carrying out of their wishes. Similarly, ancient Romans who dishonored themselves or their families were expected to commit suicide to maintain their dignity and, frequently, the family property. Early Christians were quick to embrace martyrdom as a guarantee of eternal salvation, but during the fourth century St. Augustine of Hippo (354–430) discouraged the practice. He and later theologians were concerned that many Christians who were suffering in this world would see suicide as a reasonable and legitimate way to depart to a better place in the hereafter. The view of the Christian theologian St. Thomas Aquinas (c. 1225–1274) is reflected in *Catechism of the Catholic Church* (2017, http://www.vatican.va/archive/ccc_css/archive/catechism/ccc_toc.htm), which states that "suicide contradicts the natural inclination of the human being to preserve and perpetuate his life [and] is contrary to love for the living God."

Islam and Judaism also condemn the taking of one's own life. By contrast, Buddhist monks and nuns have been known to commit suicide by self-immolation (burning themselves alive) as a form of social protest. In a ritual called *suttee*, which is now outlawed, widows in India showed devotion to their deceased husbands by being cremated with them, sometimes throwing themselves on the funeral pyres, although it was not always voluntary. Widowers (men whose wives had died) did not follow this custom.

The Japanese people have traditionally associated a certain idealism with suicide. During the 12th century samurai warriors practiced voluntary *seppuku* (ritual self-disembowelment) to avoid dishonor at the hands of their enemies. Some samurai committed this form of slow suicide to atone for wrongdoing or to express devotion to a superior who had died. As recently as 1970 the novelist Kimitake Hiraoka (1925–1970) publicly committed *seppuku*. During World War II (1939–1945) Japanese kamikaze pilots inflicted serious casualties by purposely crashing their planes into enemy ships, killing themselves along with enemy troops.

Quasi-religious reasons sometimes motivate mass suicide. In 1978 more than 900 members of a group known as the People's Temple killed themselves in Jonestown, Guyana. In 1997 a group called Heaven's Gate committed mass suicide in California. The devastating September 11, 2001, terrorist attacks against the United States were the result of a suicidal plot enacted by a religious extremist group. Suicide bombings in other parts of the world have also been attributed to extremist groups that have twisted or misinterpreted the fundamental tenets of Islam to further their political objectives.

CONTEMPORARY ATTITUDES TOWARD SUICIDE. In *In More Religious Countries, Lower Suicide Rates* (July 3, 2008, http://www.gallup.com/poll/108625/More-Religious-Countries-Lower-Suicide-Rates.aspx), Brett Pelham and Zsolt Nyiri of Gallup, Inc., indicate that in 2008 the United States' suicide rate of 11.05 deaths per 100,000 population was near the median (the middle value; half are lower and half are higher) suicide rate when compared with other countries of the world. The United States also fell near the median level of scores on the Gallup Religiosity Index, which is a measure of the importance of religion in people's lives. Pelham and Nyiri determine that the suicide rates of

countries worldwide tend to rise and fall with their level of religiosity: those having a higher level of religiosity (a higher score) often have a lower suicide rate. Conversely, those having a lower level of religiosity (a lower score) typically have a higher suicide rate. The religiosity score for the United States on the Gallup Religiosity Index was 61 and the suicide rate was 11.05 deaths per 100,000 population in 2008. In comparison, the religiosity score for Kuwait was 83 and the suicide rate was 1.95 deaths per 100,000 population, and the religiosity score for Russia was 28 and the suicide rate was 36.15 deaths per 100,000 population.

Sascha O. Becker and Ludger Woessmann show in *Knocking on Heaven's Door? Protestantism and Suicide* (June 10, 2011, http://www2.warwick.ac.uk/fac/soc/economics/research/workingpapers/2011/twerp_966.pdf) that suicide rates are higher in countries that are mainly Protestant than in countries that are mainly Catholic. The researchers compare data from the Prussian countries during the 19th century and more recent data from the Organisation for Economic Co-operation and Development. The data clearly show that in all circumstances, more people committed suicide in Protestant countries than in Catholic countries. Becker and Woessmann suggest that "sociological and theological differences between Protestants and Catholics make suicide more likely among the former group."

In *Views on End-of-Life Medical Treatments* (November 21, 2013, http://assets.pewresearch.org/wp-content/uploads/sites/11/2013/11/end-of-life-survey-report-full-pdf.pdf), the Pew Research Center reports that a growing percentage of Americans believes that individuals have a moral right to kill themselves in certain circumstances. In 2013 nearly six out of 10 (62%) U.S. adults expressed a belief in an individual's right to end his or her life if that person "is suffering great pain with no hope of improvement," and 56% supported the individual's right to die if she or he "has an incurable disease." By contrast, in 1990 support for the right to suicide in cases involving great pain with no hope of improvement stood at 55%, and support for the right to suicide in cases involving incurable disease stood at 49%. Growing minorities of U.S. adults also supported an individual's right to suicide if he or she is "ready to die [because] living has become a burden" (38% of Americans, up from 27% in 1990) or if he or she "is an extremely heavy burden on his or her family" (32% of Americans, up from 29% in 1990).

Suicide among Teenagers and Young Adults

The suicide rate among young people aged 15 to 24 years nearly tripled between 1950 and 1990, from 4.5 suicides per 100,000 population to 13.2. (See Table 7.1.) Between 1990 and 2015 the teen and young adult suicide rate fell slightly, while remaining well above mid-20th-century levels. This increase in the youth suicide rate was historically unprecedented. Prior to the 1950s, suicide rates had always been observed to increase with age, in keeping with common assumptions about why a person might choose to end his or her life. Older people, faced with declining health and a shrinking sense of possibility, might be said to turn to suicide for reasons that can be rationally supported. By contrast, young people have a great deal of life and possibility ahead of them, and they cannot claim to know what they might make of their future. Accordingly, self-harm is not considered a rational decision for a teenager or young adult.

The reasons for the dramatic rise in the suicide rates for those aged 15 to 24 years have not been firmly established, partly because suicide in general resists sociological and scientific analysis. Kimberly A. Van Orden et al. explain in "The Interpersonal Theory of Suicide" (*Psychological Review*, vol. 117, no. 2, April 2010) that suicide is difficult to study because, although effective research requires large sample sizes, the number of people who commit or attempt suicide is low relative to the overall population. Additionally, suicidal people generally cannot be included in clinical study groups because of researchers' concerns about safety, and people who succeed in committing suicide are not, obviously, available for study after the fact. Finally, Van Orden et al. suggest that the study of suicide has been held back by a relative absence of comprehensive theories about the phenomenon.

One influential, if not universally accepted, explanation for the rise in youth suicide in the late 20th century is that of the economists David M. Cutler, Edward L. Glaeser, and Karen E. Norberg in "Explaining the Rise in Youth Suicide" (Jonathan Gruber, ed., *Risky Behavior among Youths: An Economic Analysis*, 2001). Cutler, Glaeser, and Norberg suggest that young people use suicide to attract attention from others because they have few other forms of power, and they find evidence that suicide functions virally among peer groups, elevating the overall numbers of suicide attempts among teens and young adults. In attempting to isolate the societal changes that may have triggered the sustained rise in teen suicides, the authors suggest that the most important variable is the rise of young people living in homes with a divorced parent. Although they do not discount the fact that this variable interacts with other variables, such as racial and ethnic background, access to firearms, and income, they maintain that no single factor influences the suicide rate among young people more powerfully than the divorce rate.

As with other age groups, male teens and young adults are far more likely to commit suicide than female teens and young adults. As Table 7.1 shows, the suicide rate for males aged 15 to 24 years was 19.4 per 100,000 people in 2015, compared with 5.3 for females aged 15 to 24 years. According to the CDC, in "Suicide among Youth" (August 1, 2013, https://www.cdc.gov/health communication/toolstemplates/entertainmented/tips/suicide youth.html), males account for 81% of all suicide deaths among young people aged 10 to 24 years.

However, the public-health concerns relating to suicide among young people go beyond deaths. Far more teens attempt suicide than successfully commit suicide. According to Cutler, Glaeser, and Norberg, for every teen who commits suicide, 400 other teens attempt suicide, 100 require medical treatment for their suicide attempts, and 30 are hospitalized in the aftermath of their suicide attempts. Moreover, the demographic characteristics of those teens and young adults who die from suicide differ considerably from the characteristics of those who attempt suicide but do not ultimately die.

Whereas young males are more likely to commit suicide, young females are more likely to consider and attempt it. As Table 7.3 shows, 17.7% of high school students reported seriously considering suicide in 2015, down from 19% in 2001 and 29% in 1991. More females (23.4%) than males (12.2%) seriously considered suicide in 2015, and the rates were highest among girls in the ninth and 10th grades. Among males, non-Hispanic African Americans (11%) were less likely than non-Hispanic whites (11.5%) or Hispanics (12.4%) to have seriously considered suicide. Among females, Hispanics (25.6%) were more likely than either non-Hispanic whites (22.8%) or non-Hispanic African Americans (18.7%) to have seriously considered self-harm.

Similar patterns applied to those high school students who attempted suicide in 2015. (See Table 7.4.) More female (11.6%) than male (5.5%) high school students attempted suicide, and girls in the ninth (15.1%) and 10th (13%) grades were the most likely age group to have attempted suicide. Among female students, Hispanics (15.1%) were far more likely to have attempted suicide than non-Hispanic African Americans (10.2%) and non-Hispanic whites (9.8%). Similarly, among male students Hispanics (7.6%) were slightly more likely than non-Hispanic African Americans (7.2%) and non-Hispanic whites (3.7%) to have attempted suicide. Among those suicide attempts that required medical treatment, there was more convergence between female and male numbers, but the numbers were still higher among females (3.7%) than males (1.9%). Likewise, Hispanic females (4.5%) and females in the ninth (4.7%) and 10th (3.9%) grades were significantly more likely than other subgroups to have made a suicide attempt that necessitated medical treatment.

Hispanic high school students' increased likelihood of considering and attempting suicide is not well understood, but analysts have offered possible explanations for the phenomenon. As Jane Delgado, the president and chief executive officer of the National Alliance for Hispanic Health, tells Hope Gillette in "Attempted Suicide, Suicidal Fantasies More Common in Hispanic Teens"

TABLE 7.3

Percentage of students in grades 9–12 who seriously considered suicide, by sex, grade level, race, and Hispanic origin, 1991, 2001, 2013, and 2015

[Data are based on a national sample of high school students, grades 9–12]

Sex, grade level, race, and Hispanic origin	Seriously considered suicide*			
	1991	2001	2013	2015
Total	**29.0**	**19.0**	**17.0**	**17.7**
Male				
Total	**20.8**	**14.2**	**11.6**	**12.2**
9th grade	17.6	14.7	9.9	10.7
10th grade	19.5	13.8	11.3	10.8
11th grade	25.3	14.1	14.0	13.3
12th grade	20.7	13.7	11.0	14.0
Not Hispanic or Latino:				
White	21.7	14.9	11.4	11.5
Black or African American	13.3	9.2	10.2	11.0
Hispanic or Latino	18.0	12.2	11.5	12.4
Female	37.2	23.6	22.4	23.4
Total	**40.3**	**26.2**	**24.6**	**26.5**
9th grade	39.7	24.1	23.4	25.7
10th grade	38.4	23.6	22.3	22.1
11th grade	30.7	18.9	18.7	18.6
12th grade	38.6	24.2	21.1	22.8
Not Hispanic or Latina:	29.4	17.2	18.6	18.7
White	34.6	26.5	26.0	25.6
Black or African American				
Hispanic or Latina				

*During the past 12 months.

Notes: Only youths attending school participated in the survey. The Youth Risk Behavior Survey (YRBS) is conducted biennially. Persons of Hispanic origin may be of any race. Not all questions were asked for all years. All available and comparable data are presented as shown.

SOURCE: Adapted from "Table 52. Health Risk Behaviors among Students in Grades 9–12, by Sex, Grade Level, Race, and Hispanic Origin: United States, Selected Years 1991–2015," in *Health, United States, 2016: With Chartbook on Long-term Trends in Health*, Centers for Disease Control and Prevention, National Center for Health Statistics, 2017, https://www.cdc.gov/nchs/data/hus/hus16.pdf (accessed July 16, 2017)

TABLE 7.4

Percentage of high school students who attempted suicide and whose suicide attempt resulted in the need for medical attention, by sex, race/ethnicity, and grade, 2015

Category	Attempted suicide			Suicide attempt treated by a doctor or nurse		
	Female	Male	Total	Female	Male	Total
	%	%	%	%	%	%
Race/Ethnicity						
White*	9.8	3.7	6.8	3.4	0.9	2.1
Black*	10.2	7.2	8.9	3.6	4.0	3.8
Hispanic	15.1	7.6	11.3	4.5	2.9	3.7
Grade						
9	15.1	5.1	9.9	4.7	1.9	3.2
10	13.0	5.7	9.4	3.9	2.2	3.1
11	10.2	5.8	8.0	3.4	2.0	2.6
12	7.2	5.2	6.2	2.3	1.4	1.9
Total	11.6	5.5	8.6	3.7	1.9	2.8

*Non-Hispanic.

Note: Refers to high school students who attempted suicide one or more times during the 12 months before the survey.

SOURCE: Adapted from "Table 27. Percentage of High School Students Who Attempted Suicide and Whose Suicide Attempt Resulted in an Injury, Poisoning, or Overdose That Had to Be Treated by a Doctor or Nurse, by Sex, Race/Ethnicity, and Grade—United States, Youth Risk Behavior Survey, 2015," in "Youth Risk Behavior Surveillance—United States, 2015," *Morbidity and Mortality Weekly Report*, vol. 65, no. 6, June 10, 2016, https://www.cdc.gov/healthyyouth/data/yrbs/pdf/2015/ss6506_updated.pdf (accessed July 20, 2017)

(VOXXI.com, January 29, 2013), the higher rates of suicidal thinking and attempted suicide are concentrated among a particular subset of Hispanic girls: first-generation immigrants who were born in the United States. Delgado

TABLE 7.5

Percentage of high school students who attempted suicide and whose suicide attempt resulted in the need for medical attention, by sex and selected sites in the United States, 2015

Site	Attempted suicide			Suicide attempt treated by a doctor or nurse		
	Female	Male	Total	Female	Male	Total
	%	%	%	%	%	%
State surveys						
Alabama	13.0	8.7	11.2	4.8	3.3	4.3
Alaska	11.0	10.4	10.7	4.0	3.0	3.5
Arizona	12.6	6.2	9.6	3.7	1.5	2.7
Arkansas	13.8	10.2	12.1	4.6	4.4	4.5
California	11.8	4.7	8.2	2.8	1.0	1.9
Connecticut	8.7	6.6	7.9	—N/A	—	—
Delaware	10.2	4.8	7.6	2.4	2.1	2.3
Florida	9.6	5.2	7.6	2.8	1.9	2.5
Hawaii	11.0	9.3	10.5	3.1	3.5	3.4
Idaho	14.0	5.8	9.8	4.4	1.7	3.1
Illinois	9.5	9.8	9.8	2.9	5.7	4.3
Indiana	10.9	8.7	9.9	4.4	3.3	3.9
Kentucky	12.9	5.7	9.4	5.3	2.5	3.9
Maine	11.2	8.4	9.9	—	—	—
Maryland	—	—	—	—	—	—
Massachusetts	8.2	5.4	7.0	2.9	2.5	2.8
Michigan	11.1	7.1	9.2	3.0	2.4	2.7
Mississippi	13.4	11.2	12.7	5.5	5.9	5.7
Missouri	10.3	9.2	9.8	3.2	3.1	3.2
Montana	11.5	6.3	8.9	4.0	2.4	3.1
Nebraska	9.4	7.7	8.9	3.0	3.5	3.3
Nevada	13.1	8.0	10.7	3.2	2.3	2.8
New Hampshire	8.9	4.6	6.8	3.5	1.5	2.5
New Mexico	12.4	6.4	9.4	3.8	2.5	3.2
New York	9.9	9.3	9.9	4.2	4.4	4.4
North Carolina	—	—	—	8.8	9.6	9.3
North Dakota	9.6	9.3	9.4	—	—	—
Oklahoma	10.2	4.5	7.4	2.4	1.6	2.0
Pennsylvania	9.6	5.3	7.5	3.0	2.2	2.6
Rhode Island	12.5	8.3	10.5	4.4	3.8	4.1
South Carolina	12.6	9.4	11.0	3.5	3.3	3.4
South Dakota	10.0	6.8	8.4	4.2	3.2	3.8
Tennessee	12.5	7.3	9.9	4.2	3.3	3.8
Vermont	8.0	3.7	5.9	2.6	1.2	2.0
Virginia	8.7	4.6	6.7	2.4	1.3	1.9
West Virginia	11.3	8.5	9.9	3.7	2.6	3.2
Wyoming	14.7	7.7	11.1	4.5	3.7	4.1
Median	11.0	7.3	9.6	3.7	2.6	3.2
Large urban school district surveys						
Baltimore, MD	16.2	20.5	18.7	4.9	9.4	7.3
Boston, MA	8.2	7.9	8.1	2.4	2.4	2.4
Broward County, FL	11.8	6.2	9.3	4.3	2.6	3.5
Cleveland, OH	22.6	17.7	20.7	—	—	—
DeKalb County, GA	11.2	8.6	9.9	4.1	5.1	4.6
Detroit, MI	15.1	16.4	16.0	6.4	8.4	7.4
District of Columbia	13.7	11.1	12.7	4.8	4.9	5.0
Duval County, FL	18.9	17.9	18.9	—	—	—
Ft. Worth, TX	11.8	3.9	7.8	3.9	1.7	2.9
Houston, TX	14.1	11.2	13.0	5.2	3.9	4.6
Los Angeles, CA	10.1	6.5	8.4	2.2	2.1	2.1
Miami-Dade County, FL	7.4	5.6	6.4	2.2	1.9	2.1

observes, "Adolescence is the transition from childhood to adulthood and while we know that is a difficult time for most young people, it is even more difficult when a person has to negotiate the cultural norms of their family with those of the larger society."

Youth suicide is, additionally, more prevalent in rural areas than in urban areas. Cutler, Glaeser, and Norberg point out that, although the period corresponding with the rise in teen suicide rates (1950 to 1990) was characterized by increasing poverty and crime in inner cities, the states that saw the largest increases in youth suicides were Idaho, Montana, New Mexico, South Dakota, and Wyoming. Meanwhile, a number of states whose populations were highly concentrated in troubled inner cities during that time—Delaware, Massachusetts, New Jersey, and New York—saw the smallest increases in the teen suicide rate. Similarly, the proportion of high school students who reported attempting suicide in 2015 was highest in a number of states that were largely rural. (See Table 7.5.)

TABLE 7.5

Percentage of high school students who attempted suicide and whose suicide attempt resulted in the need for medical attention, by sex and selected sites in the United States, 2015 [CONTINUED]

Site	Attempted suicide			Suicide attempt treated by a doctor or nurse		
	Female	Male	Total	Female	Male	Total
	%	%	%	%	%	%
New York City, NY	10.1	6.2	8.3	2.9	2.6	2.8
Oakland, CA	12.8	9.8	11.3	2.8	3.9	3.4
Orange County, FL	12.1	6.1	9.1	4.5	2.2	3.4
Palm Beach County, FL	11.1	8.1	10.1	4.2	3.0	3.7
Philadelphia, PA	12.6	8.8	11.0	3.8	3.3	3.6
San Diego, CA	11.0	6.9	8.9	2.2	1.7	1.9
San Francisco, CA	11.3	7.8	9.8	4.3	3.7	4.3
Median	11.8	8.1	9.9	4.1	3.0	3.5

N/A = not available

Note: Refers to high school students who attempted suicide one ore more times during the 12 months before the survey.

SOURCE: Adapted from "Table 28. Percentage of High School Students Who Attempted Suicide and Whose Suicide Attempt Resulted in an Injury, Poisoning, or Overdose That Had to Be Treated by a Doctor or Nurse, by Sex—Selected U.S. Sites, Youth Risk Behavior Survey, 2015," *Youth Risk Behavior Surveillance—United States, 2015, Morbidity and Mortality Weekly Report*, vol. 65, no. 6, June 10, 2016, https://www.cdc.gov/healthyyouth/data/yrbs/pdf/2015/ss6506_updated.pdf (accessed July 20, 2017)

The states with the largest proportion of students who attempted suicide that year were Mississippi (12.7%), Arkansas (12.1%), Alabama (11.2%), Wyoming (11.1%), South Carolina (11%), Alaska (10.7%), Nevada (10.7%), Hawaii (10.5%), and Rhode Island (10.5%).

SUICIDE AMONG LESBIAN, GAY, BISEXUAL, AND TRANSGENDER ADOLESCENTS. Another possible reason for the elevated rate of suicide attempts and deaths among young people is that a significant number of teens find themselves, as newly sexual beings, struggling to come to terms with same-sex attraction. Although the 21st century has witnessed a rapid increase in the levels of public acceptance of lesbian, gay, bisexual, and transgender (LGBT) people, mainstream attitudes have not changed at the same rate in all parts of the United States. Additionally, even for adolescents in more obviously tolerant cities and towns, self-acceptance, peer-group acceptance, and parental acceptance can represent forbidding obstacles.

The CDC notes in "Lesbian, Gay, Bisexual and Transgender Health: LGBT Youth" (June 21, 2017, https://www.cdc.gov/lgbthealth/youth.htm) that a 2015 survey of LGBT high school students found that 34% had been physically bullied at school, 28% had been victims of electronic bullying, 18% had experienced physical dating violence, and 10% had been threatened or injured with a weapon at school. Furthermore, 12% of LGBT students reported having skipped school at least once in the previous month due to safety concerns. By contrast, 5% of heterosexual students reported missing school during the past 30 days out of fear for their safety. The CDC also notes that studies find that, compared with LGBT teens whose parents support and accept them, LGBT teens who experience high levels of rejection from their parents are significantly more likely, as young adults, to suffer from depression, to use illegal drugs, to engage in unprotected sex, and to attempt suicide.

Because mortality data generally do not include information about sexual orientation, it is unclear what proportion of teen suicides might be related to sexuality. However, according to the Suicide Prevention Resource Center, in *Suicide Risk and Prevention for Lesbian, Gay, Bisexual, and Transgender Youth* (2008, http://www.sprc.org/sites/sprc.org/files/library/SPRC_LGBT_Youth.pdf), research indicates that gay and lesbian young people aged 15 to 24 years are between one and a half to three times more likely than their straight counterparts to consider suicide and are one and a half to seven times more likely to attempt suicide.

EUTHANASIA AND PHYSICIAN-ASSISTED SUICIDE

The word *euthanasia*, which is derived from a Greek word meaning "good death," is commonly used to describe situations in which a terminally ill person requests assistance in ending his or her life to prevent further pain and suffering. The term *euthanasia*, however, has also been used to refer to the practice of killing people without their consent, supposedly for reasons of helping them or improving society. This latter form of the practice is linked in the public imagination with the Nazi regime of Adolf Hitler (1889–1945). The Nazis' version of euthanasia was a bizarre interpretation of an idea espoused by two German professors, the psychiatrist Alfred Hoche (1865–1943) and the jurist Karl Binding (1841–1920), in their 1920 book *Die Freigabe der Vernichtung lebensunwerten Lebens* (*The Permission to Destroy Life Unworthy of Life*). While initially maintaining that it was ethical for physicians to assist in the deaths of those who requested an end to their suffering, the authors later argued that it was also permissible to end the lives of the intellectually disabled and the mentally ill. Besides targeting the intellectually disabled and mentally ill, the Nazi euthanasia program attempted to wipe out the entire Jewish people, along with other peoples it considered undesirable. Some contemporary opponents of euthanasia fear that a society that allows the practice will embark on a slippery slope leading in the direction of a euthanasia program such as the Nazis'.

In reality, euthanasia has been an accepted part of many societies throughout history, without having led to any such programs of involuntary euthanasia. As mentioned at the outset of this chapter, in ancient Greece and Rome, suicide in cases when the individual had become a burden to himself, his family, or his society was considered a rational act. Moreover, the contemporary movement to legalize euthanasia is strongly rooted in humanist thinking, which prioritizes the autonomy of the individual. Although still unacceptable to many religious traditions that emphasize God's authority to determine matters of life and death, euthanasia is generally motivated by compassion for suffering and ideas maintaining that true liberty includes the freedom to determine the time and manner of one's own death.

The modern euthanasia movement began in England, with the 1935 founding of the Voluntary Euthanasia Society, whose membership included well-known figures such as the playwright George Bernard Shaw (1856–1950), the philosopher Bertrand Russell (1872–1970), and the novelist H. G. Wells (1866–1946). In 1936 the House of Lords (the house of the English Parliament historically composed of aristocratic landowners, officials from the Church of England, and others appointed by the monarch) defeated a bill that would have permitted euthanasia in cases of terminal illness. Nonetheless, it was common knowledge that physicians of the era practiced euthanasia. That same year it was rumored that King George V (1865–1936), who had been seriously ill for several years, was "relieved of his sufferings" by his physician, with the approval of his wife, Queen Mary (1867–1953).

Some people call the act of forgoing medical treatment in the knowledge that death will result as passive euthanasia. This action is relatively uncontroversial and even permitted by many religious traditions, because it is the underlying illness that causes death by running its natural course. Terminally ill individuals in the United States have a right to refuse medical treatment, as do those who are sick but not terminally ill.

Much more controversial in the United States and other parts of the developed world is the practice of active euthanasia, also commonly referred to as physician-assisted suicide. Currently legal (in different forms) in Belgium, Luxembourg, the Netherlands, and Switzerland as well as in the U.S. states of California, Colorado, Oregon, Washington, and Vermont (along with the District of Columbia), physician-assisted suicide typically involves the hastening of death through the administration of lethal drugs, as requested by the patient or another competent individual who represents the patient's wishes.

DIFFERING VIEWPOINTS ON THE RIGHT TO DIE
Federal Law

The U.S. Constitution does not guarantee the right to choose to die. However, the U.S. Supreme Court recognizes that Americans have a fundamental right to privacy, or what is sometimes called the "right to be left alone." Although the right to privacy is not explicitly mentioned in the Constitution, the Supreme Court has interpreted several amendments as encompassing this right. For example, in *Roe v. Wade* (410 U.S. 113 [1973]), the court ruled that the 14th Amendment protects the right to privacy against state action, specifically a woman's right to abortion. Another example is the landmark Karen Ann Quinlan case, which was based on right-to-privacy rulings by the U.S. Supreme Court. In *In re Quinlan* (70 N.J. 10, 355 A.2d 647 [1976]), the New Jersey Supreme Court held that the right to privacy included the right to refuse unwanted medical treatment and, as a consequence, the right to die (see Chapter 9).

Public Opinion

In "When Is Physician Assisted Suicide or Euthanasia Acceptable?" (*Journal of Medical Ethics*, vol. 29, no. 6, December 2003), Stéphanie Frileux et al. examine the opinion of the general public on euthanasia and physician-assisted suicide. The researchers define these terms as follows: "In physician assisted suicide, the physician provides the patient with the means to end his or her own life. In euthanasia, the physician deliberately and directly intervenes to end the patient's life; this is sometimes called 'active euthanasia' to distinguish it from withholding or withdrawing treatment needed to sustain life." Their study posed the questions: "Should a terminally ill patient be allowed to die? Should the medical profession have the option of helping such a patient to die?" Frileux et al. find that acceptability of euthanasia and physician-assisted suicide by the general public appears to depend on four factors: the level of patient suffering, the extent to which the patient requested death, the age of the patient, and the degree of curability of the illness.

Meanwhile, Andrew Dugan of Gallup finds that Americans' expressed views on the subject of physician-assisted suicide vary only slightly depending on how pollsters word their questions. In *In U.S., Support up for Doctor-Assisted Suicide* (May 27, 2015, http://www.gallup.com/poll/183425/support-doctor-assisted-suicide.aspx), Dugan reports that, based on polling conducted in May 2015, 70% of Americans expressed support for euthanasia in cases of terminal illness when it is described as allowing physicians to "end the patient's life by some painless means." (See Figure 7.1.) When the

FIGURE 7.1

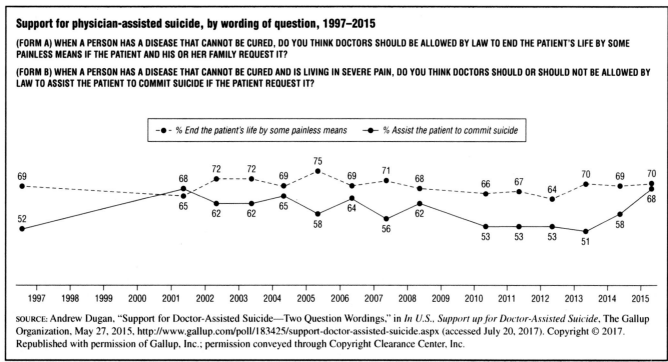

Support for physician-assisted suicide, by wording of question, 1997–2015

(FORM A) WHEN A PERSON HAS A DISEASE THAT CANNOT BE CURED, DO YOU THINK DOCTORS SHOULD BE ALLOWED BY LAW TO END THE PATIENT'S LIFE BY SOME PAINLESS MEANS IF THE PATIENT AND HIS OR HER FAMILY REQUEST IT?

(FORM B) WHEN A PERSON HAS A DISEASE THAT CANNOT BE CURED AND IS LIVING IN SEVERE PAIN, DO YOU THINK DOCTORS SHOULD OR SHOULD NOT BE ALLOWED BY LAW TO ASSIST THE PATIENT TO COMMIT SUICIDE IF THE PATIENT REQUEST IT?

SOURCE: Andrew Dugan, "Support for Doctor-Assisted Suicide—Two Question Wordings," in *In U.S., Support up for Doctor-Assisted Suicide*, The Gallup Organization, May 27, 2015, http://www.gallup.com/poll/183425/support-doctor-assisted-suicide.aspx (accessed July 20, 2017). Copyright © 2017. Republished with permission of Gallup, Inc.; permission conveyed through Copyright Clearance Center, Inc.

FIGURE 7.2

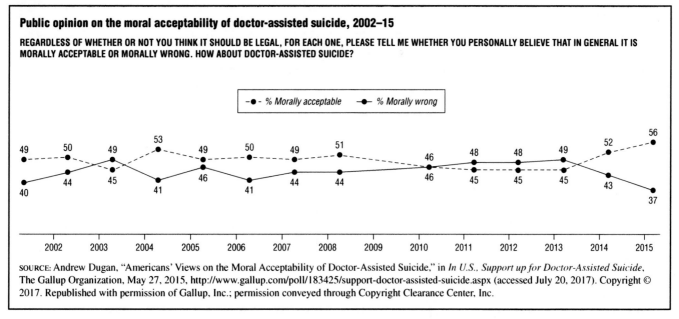

Public opinion on the moral acceptability of doctor-assisted suicide, 2002–15

REGARDLESS OF WHETHER OR NOT YOU THINK IT SHOULD BE LEGAL, FOR EACH ONE, PLEASE TELL ME WHETHER YOU PERSONALLY BELIEVE THAT IN GENERAL IT IS MORALLY ACCEPTABLE OR MORALLY WRONG. HOW ABOUT DOCTOR-ASSISTED SUICIDE?

SOURCE: Andrew Dugan, "Americans' Views on the Moral Acceptability of Doctor-Assisted Suicide," in *In U.S., Support up for Doctor-Assisted Suicide*, The Gallup Organization, May 27, 2015, http://www.gallup.com/poll/183425/support-doctor-assisted-suicide.aspx (accessed July 20, 2017). Copyright © 2017. Republished with permission of Gallup, Inc.; permission conveyed through Copyright Clearance Center, Inc.

practice is described as assisting a patient to "commit suicide," 68% of Americans supported it.

Previous Gallup polls, however, revealed a much wider discrepancy in how people responded to the wording of each question. For example, in 2013, 70% of Americans expressed support for allowing physicians to "end the patient's life by some painless means," whereas only 51% supported allowing physicians to help patients "commit suicide." (See Figure 7.1.) Dugan indicates that Gallup's polling using the "suicide" version of the

question dates back to 1996 and that the 2013 levels of support for allowing the practice, 51%, were very similar to levels of support in 1996. Support stood at 52% in 1996 and then climbed steadily to 68% in 2001, before falling to 53% in 2010. As Figure 7.2 shows, 56% of Americans believed assisted suicide was morally acceptable in 2015, while only 37% felt it was morally unacceptable. Dugan also reports that political affiliation is a factor in determining support for physician-assisted suicide. In 2015 Independents (80%) were the most likely to express support for doctor-assisted

TABLE 7.6

Support for physician-assisted "suicide," by age group and political party affiliation, 2014 and 2015

WHEN A PERSON HAS A DISEASE THAT CANNOT BE CURED AND IS LIVING IN SEVERE PAIN, DO YOU THINK DOCTORS SHOULD OR SHOULD NOT BE ALLOWED BY LAW TO ASSIST THE PATIENT TO COMMIT SUICIDE IF THE PATIENT REQUESTS IT?

[% Yes, should be allowed]

	May 2014	May 2015	Change
	%	%	pct. pts.
18 to 34 years old	62	81	+19
35 to 54 years old	57	65	+8
55 and older	56	61	+5
Republicans	51	61	+10
Independents	64	80	+16
Democrats	59	72	+13

SOURCE: Andrew Dugan, "Support for Doctor-Assisted 'Suicide,' by Year," in *In U.S., Support up for Doctor-Assisted Suicide*, The Gallup Organization, May 27, 2015, http://www.gallup.com/poll/183425/support-doctor-assisted-suicide.aspx (accessed July 20, 2017). Copyright © 2017. Republished with permission of Gallup, Inc.; permission conveyed through Copyright Clearance Center, Inc.

suicide, followed by Democrats (72%) and Republicans (61%). (See Table 7.6.)

The Medical Profession

Joris Gielen et al. interviewed 14 physicians and 13 nurses working in palliative care programs to determine what they thought about palliative sedation in end-of-life care and reported their findings in "The Attitudes of Indian Palliative-Care Nurses and Physicians to Pain Control and Palliative Sedation" (*Indian Journal of Palliative Care*, vol. 17, no. 1, January–April 2011). The health care providers all thought that palliative care painkillers were fine to administer, provided that they were titrated (gradually increased to achieve efficacy with the least amount of side effects) to the patient's pain. They thought that such light sedation was useful but disagreed whether deep sedation was acceptable.

In general, physician-assisted suicide is seen as being at odds with the work of doctors and nurses. In 2012 the American College of Physicians officially opposed physician-assisted suicide, reaffirming its statements of opposition from 2001 and 2005. The organization's formal position statement on this topic was published in the sixth edition of *Ethics Manual* (2012, https://www.acponline.org/clinical-information/ethics-and-professionalism/acp-ethics-manual-sixth-edition/acp-ethics-manual-sixth-edition). The statement reads:

> The College does not support legalization of physician-assisted suicide or euthanasia. After much consideration, the College concluded that making physician-assisted suicide legal raised serious ethical, clinical, and social concerns and that the practice might undermine patient trust; distract from reform in end-of-life care; and be used in vulnerable patients, including those

who are poor, are disabled, or are unable to speak for themselves or minority groups who have experienced discrimination. The major emphasis of the College and its members, including those who lawfully participate in the practice, should be ensuring that all persons can count on good care through to the end of life, with prevention or relief of suffering insofar as possible, an unwavering commitment to human dignity and relief of pain and other symptoms, and support for family and friends. Physicians and patients must continue to search together for answers to the problems posed by the difficulties of living with serious illness before death, neither violating the physician's personal and professional values, nor abandoning the patient to struggle alone.

The American Medical Association (AMA) updated its position statements on euthanasia and physician-assisted suicide in the 2016 edition of *AMA Code of Medical Ethics* (2017, https://www.ama-assn.org/delivering-care/ama-code-medical-ethics). AMA policies regarding both issues appear in "Chapter 5: Opinions on Caring for Patients at the End of Life," in which the association states, "Euthanasia is fundamentally incompatible with the physician's role as healer, would be difficult or impossible to control, and would pose serious societal risks. Euthanasia could readily be extended to incompetent patients and other vulnerable populations." The AMA further warns that "the involvement of physicians in euthanasia heightens the significance of its ethical prohibition. The physician who performs euthanasia assumes unique responsibility for the act of ending the patient's life." The AMA distinguishes between euthanasia, in which the physician takes an active role in the patient's death, and physician-assisted suicide. The association opposes physician-assisted suicide with language identical to that in its policy statement against euthanasia, while adding that rather than "engaging in assisted suicide, physicians must aggressively respond to the needs of patients at the end of life."

In April 2013 the American Nurses Association released the position statement *Euthanasia, Assisted Suicide, and Aid in Dying* (http://www.nursingworld.org/euthanasiaanddying), updating its 1994 statement that prohibited the practices. The statement reads: "The American Nurses Association (ANA) prohibits nurses' participation in assisted suicide and euthanasia because these acts are in direct violation of *Code of Ethics for Nurses with Interpretive Statements* (ANA, 2001 ...), the ethical traditions and goals of the profession, and its covenant with society. Nurses have an obligation to provide humane, comprehensive, and compassionate care that respects the rights of patients but upholds the standards of the profession in the presence of chronic, debilitating illness and at end-of-life."

LEGAL PHYSICIAN-ASSISTED SUICIDE IN THE UNITED STATES

As of September 2017, California, Colorado, Oregon, Washington, and Vermont were the only U.S. states (along with the District of Columbia) that allowed physician-assisted suicide. In Montana, physician-assisted suicide has been in legal limbo since 2009, when the state supreme court ruled that the practice was legal under Montana law. The state legislature has not, however, formally created laws that allow and regulate the practice. In all five states that currently allow physician-assisted suicide, the option is available only to patients who have been given a prognosis of six months or less to live.

Oregon was the first state to legalize assisted suicide or, as the state and many advocates for the practice call it, "death with dignity." The Oregon Death with Dignity Act (DWDA) was passed in 1994 but was held up by legal challenges until 1997, when it was officially enacted. Oregon created strict limits and procedures for the practice of assisted suicide, intending to address concerns about physicians' roles in the process and about overuse of the procedure. Terminally ill Oregonians with six months or less to live are allowed to request prescriptions for lethal doses of drugs. They then must take the drugs on their own, without the help of a physician. Physicians who write prescriptions for life-ending medication must file paperwork with the state within seven days of doing so. In some cases, psychiatric evaluation is required. Thus, the approval of individual prescriptions is subject to medical review and monitored by the state. Physicians may not take an active role in the actual death, ensuring that the motivation for the act comes from the patient. As part of the Oregon law, detailed data are collected on those who request life-ending medication, and the state issues annual reports that describe the extent of its reach and the characteristics of participating patients. These annual data releases indicate that since the law's implementation very few people have actually used it to end their suffering and that it has been used only in the sorts of cases for which it was intended.

The constitutionality of Oregon's law was ultimately decided by the U.S. Supreme Court in 2006, as described in further detail below. Following the Supreme Court's decision that Oregon was acting within its authority in implementing the practice of assisted suicide, voters in the neighboring state of Washington passed their own Death with Dignity Act, modeled closely on Oregon's, in 2008. Facing no serious legal challenges, Washington's law went into effect the following year. Vermont followed suit in 2013, again naming its own law the Death with Dignity Act and using the well-regarded Oregon template. As in Washington, the act met with no serious legal challenges and was implemented soon after being signed by the governor in mid-2013. California and Colorado enacted legislation that allows assisted suicide in 2016, while the District of Columbia followed in 2017.

Conflict with Federal Law

As mentioned earlier, Oregon's DWDA was kept on hold due to legal challenges for three years after voters

passed it in 1994, and in November 1997 a ballot measure to repeal the law was put before voters statewide. Oregonians voted to defeat the measure.

Immediately after this voter reaffirmation of the DWDA, the U.S. Drug Enforcement Administration (DEA) warned Oregon doctors that they could be arrested or have their medical license revoked for prescribing lethal doses of drugs. The DEA administrator Thomas A. Constantine (1938–2015), who was under pressure from some members of Congress, stated that prescribing a drug for suicide would be a violation of the Controlled Substances Act (CSA) of 1970 because assisted suicide was not a "legitimate medical purpose." Janet Reno (1938–2016), the U.S. attorney general, overruled Constantine in 1998 and decided that that portion of the CSA would not apply to states that legalize assisted suicide. Those opposed to the practice observed that Reno's ruling was inconsistent with other rulings, citing the government's opposite ruling in states that have legalized marijuana for medical use. (Reno maintained that the prescription of marijuana was still illegal, regardless of its medicinal value.)

In response to the DEA decision, Congress moved toward the passage of the Pain Relief Promotion Act. This law would promote the use of federally controlled drugs for the purpose of palliative care but would prevent their use for euthanasia and assisted suicide. In 2000 the U.S. House of Representatives passed the bill, but the U.S. Senate did not. The act never became law.

On November 6, 2001, John D. Ashcroft (1942–), who succeeded Reno as the U.S. attorney general, overturned Reno's 1998 ruling that prohibited the DEA from acting against physicians who administer drugs under the DWDA. Ashcroft said that taking the life of terminally ill patients was not a "legitimate medical purpose" for federally controlled drugs. The Oregon Medical Association and the Washington State Medical Association opposed Ashcroft's ruling. Even physicians who were opposed to assisted suicide expressed concern that the ruling might compromise patient care and that any DEA investigation might discourage physicians from prescribing pain medication to patients in need.

The state of Oregon disagreed so vehemently with Ashcroft's interpretation of the CSA that on November 7, 2001, the attorney general of Oregon filed suit, claiming that Ashcroft was acting unconstitutionally. A November 8, 2001, restraining order allowed the DWDA to remain in effect while the case was tried.

On April 17, 2002, in *State of Oregon and Peter A. Rasmussen et al. v. John Ashcroft* (Civil No. 01-1647-JO), Judge Robert E. Jones (1927–) of the U.S. District Court for the District of Oregon ruled in favor of the DWDA. His decision read, in part

State statutes, state medical boards, and state regulations control the practice of medicine. The CSA was never intended, and the [U.S. Department of Justice] and DEA were never authorized, to establish a national medical practice or act as a national medical board. To allow an attorney general—an appointed executive whose tenure depends entirely on whatever administration occupies the White House—to determine the legitimacy of a particular medical practice without a specific congressional grant of such authority would be unprecedented and extraordinary.... Without doubt there is tremendous disagreement among highly respected medical practitioners as to whether assisted suicide or hastened death is a legitimate medical practice, but opponents have been heard and, absent a specific prohibitive federal statute, the Oregon voters have made the legal, albeit controversial, decision that such a practice is legitimate in this sovereign state.

The U.S. Department of Justice appealed the ruling to the U.S. Court of Appeals for the Ninth Circuit in San Francisco. On May 26, 2004, the court stopped Ashcroft's attempts to override the Oregon law. The divided three-judge panel ruled that Ashcroft overstepped his authority when he declared that physicians who prescribe lethal drug doses are in violation of the CSA and when he instructed the DEA to prosecute the physicians. In addition, the court noted that Ashcroft's interpretation of the CSA violated Congress's intent.

The administration of George W. Bush (1946–) appealed the case to the U.S. Supreme Court, and in February 2005 the high court agreed to hear the DWDA challenge. On January 17, 2006, the court ruled in favor of Oregon in *Gonzales v. Oregon* (546 U.S. 243), holding that the CSA "does not allow the Attorney General to prohibit doctors from prescribing regulated drugs for use in physician-assisted suicide under state law permitting the procedure." Justice Anthony M. Kennedy (1936–), writing for the majority, stated that the U.S. attorney general did not have the power to override the Oregon physician-assisted suicide law. Kennedy also added that it should not be the attorney general who determines what is a "legitimate medical purpose" for the administration of drugs, because the job description for the attorney general does not include making health and medical policy.

DWDA Patients and Their Characteristics

Oregon, Washington, and Vermont each collect and release data about those who request prescriptions and die under the auspices of their death with dignity laws. Oregon's data, as mentioned earlier, have been instrumental in establishing that its DWDA has functioned as designed and not been subject to abuse or unforeseen problems. Washington's 2009 through 2015 data releases have in general reinforced this picture of how such a law functions in practice. As of September 2017, Vermont had not yet released an official DWDA report. However, the Death with Dignity National Center notes in

"Vermont: Current Status" (https://www.deathwithdignity.org/states/vermont/) that as of April 2017, 49 Vermontians had received medications through the state's assisted suicide law. California, Colorado, and the District of Columbia had published no DWDA data as of September 2017.

OREGON. Between 1998, when Oregon's DWDA was implemented, and 2016 prescriptions for life-ending medication were written for 1,749 people, 1,127 of whom are known to have died from ingesting these medications. (See Figure 7.3.) The number of prescriptions as well as the number of deaths rose steadily between 1998 and 2015, before falling slightly in 2016.

In 2016, 204 Oregonians (out of a population of approximately 4.1 million) requested a prescription to end their life, and 133 of these patients' deaths were confirmed as being caused by the prescription. (See Figure 7.3 and Figure 7.4.) The gap between the number of prescriptions and the number of deaths accounts for several subsets of patients: those who have not taken their prescription by year's end but who go on to do so in the following year; those who choose not to take their life-ending medication and die of other causes; and those who die but whose paperwork has not been received by the state or is incomplete at the time of the data release. Figure 7.4 summarizes the outcomes for those patients who received medication under the DWDA in 2016, including those who received medication in previous years and those who did not take the medication they were prescribed in 2016.

The median age for those 133 Oregonians who died from ingesting life-ending medication in 2016 was 73, slightly higher than the median age of 71 over the life of the DWDA's implementation. (See Table 7.7.) So far, men (51.6%) and women (48.4%) have been almost equally likely to use life-ending prescriptions under the terms of the DWDA. Among racial and ethnic groups, use of DWDA prescriptions has been confined almost exclusively to white Oregonians, who account for 1,083 (96.5%) of the total 1,127 deaths under the program between 1998 and 2016. (Non-Hispanic whites accounted for 76.4% of Oregon's total population in 2016.) DWDA participants in 2016 tended to be well educated relative to the population at large. Nearly 79% had either attended (28.8%) or graduated from (50%) college, while 17.4% had earned a high school diploma; only 3.8% had less than a high school diploma.

As Table 7.7 shows, almost all DWDA participants (88.7% in 2016 and 90.2% since 1998) were in hospice care prior to requesting life-ending medication. (Hospice care generally begins when a patient's remaining life expectancy is six months or less.) The overwhelming majority of DWDA participants had cancer (78.9% in 2016 and 77.4% since 1998).

FIGURE 7.3

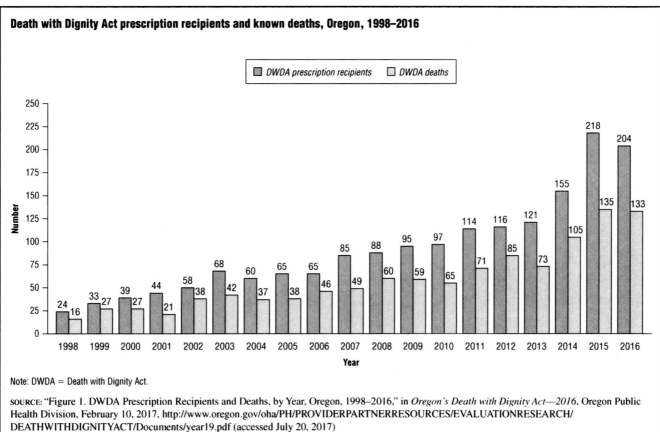

Death with Dignity Act prescription recipients and known deaths, Oregon, 1998–2016

Note: DWDA = Death with Dignity Act.

SOURCE: "Figure 1. DWDA Prescription Recipients and Deaths, by Year, Oregon, 1998–2016," in *Oregon's Death with Dignity Act—2016*, Oregon Public Health Division, February 10, 2017, http://www.oregon.gov/oha/PH/PROVIDERPARTNERRESOURCES/EVALUATIONRESEARCH/ DEATHWITHDIGNITYACT/Documents/year19.pdf (accessed July 20, 2017)

FIGURE 7.4

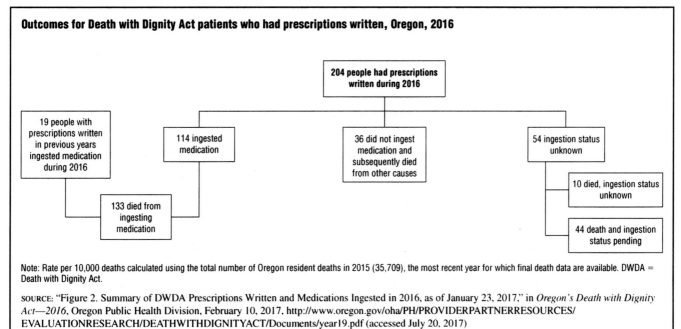

Outcomes for Death with Dignity Act patients who had prescriptions written, Oregon, 2016

Note: Rate per 10,000 deaths calculated using the total number of Oregon resident deaths in 2015 (35,709), the most recent year for which final death data are available. DWDA = Death with Dignity Act.

SOURCE: "Figure 2. Summary of DWDA Prescriptions Written and Medications Ingested in 2016, as of January 23, 2017," in *Oregon's Death with Dignity Act—2016*, Oregon Public Health Division, February 10, 2017, http://www.oregon.gov/oha/PH/PROVIDERPARTNERRESOURCES/ EVALUATIONRESEARCH/DEATHWITHDIGNITYACT/Documents/year19.pdf (accessed July 20, 2017)

Almost all Oregonians who have died under the terms of the DWDA informed their families of their decision (89.5% in 2016 and 93% since 1998) and died at home (88.6% in 2016 and 93.4% since 1998). (See Table 7.7.) Almost all 2016 DWDA patients cited the loss of autonomy (89.5%) and the decreasing ability to engage in activities that make life enjoyable (89.5%) as their reasons for choosing to end their life. Two-thirds

TABLE 7.7

Characteristics and end-of-life care of Death with Dignity Act patients who ingested lethal medication and have died, Oregon, 1998–2016

Characteristics	2016 (population = 133) Population (%)*	1998–2015 (population = 994) Population (%)*	Total (population = 1,127) Population (%)*
Sex			
Male (%)	72 (54.1)	510 (51.3)	582 (51.6)
Female (%)	61 (45.9)	484 (48.7)	545 (48.4)
Age			
18–34 (%)	1 (0.8)	8 (0.8)	9 (0.8)
35–44 (%)	1 (0.8)	23 (2.3)	24 (2.1)
45–54 (%)	6 (4.5)	64 (6.4)	70 (6.2)
55–64 (%)	18 (13.5)	206 (20.7)	224 (19.9)
65–74 (%)	52 (39.1)	289 (29.1)	341 (30.3)
75–84 (%)	31 (23.3)	259 (26.1)	290 (25.7)
85+ (%)	24 (18.0)	145 (14.6)	169 (15.0)
Median years (range)	73 (32–97)	71 (25–102)	71 (25–102)
Race			
White (%)	127 (96.2)	956 (96.6)	1,083 (96.5)
African American (%)	0 (0.0)	1 (0.1)	1 (0.1)
American Indian (%)	0 (0.0)	2 (0.2)	2 (0.2)
Asian (%)	2 (1.5)	13 (1.3)	15 (1.3)
Pacific Islander (%)	0 (0.0)	1 (0.1)	1 (0.1)
Other (%)	0 (0.0)	3 (0.3)	3 (0.3)
Two or more races (%)	1 (0.8)	4 (0.4)	5 (0.4)
Hispanic (%)	2 (1.5)	10 (1.0)	12 (1.1)
Unknown	1	4	5
Marital status			
Married (including registered domestic partner) (%)	62 (47.0)	449 (45.4)	511 (45.5)
Widowed (%)	26 (19.7)	232 (23.4)	258 (23.0)
Never married (%)	8 (6.1)	78 (7.9)	86 (7.7)
Divorced (%)	36 (27.3)	231 (23.3)	267 (23.8)
Unknown	1	4	5
Education			
Less than high school (%)	5 (3.8)	58 (5.9)	63 (5.6)
High school graduate (%)	23 (17.4)	218 (22.1)	241 (21.5)
Some college (%)	38 (28.8)	261 (26.4)	299 (26.7)
Baccalaureate or higher (%)	66 (50.0)	450 (45.6)	516 (46.1)
Unknown	1	7	8

*Unknowns are excluded when calculating percentages.
Note: DWDA = Death with Dignity Act.

SOURCE: "Table 1. Characteristics and End-of-Life Care of 1,127 DWDA Patients Who Have Died from Ingesting a Lethal Dose of Medication as of January 23, 2016, by Year, Oregon, 1998–2016," in *Oregon's Death with Dignity Act—2016*, Oregon Public Health Division, February 10, 2017, http://www.oregon.gov/oha/PH/PROVIDERPARTNERRESOURCES/EVALUATIONRESEARCH/DEATHWITHDIGNITYACT/Documents/year19.pdf (accessed July 20, 2017)

(65.4%) cited loss of dignity, and nearly half (48.9%) cited the feeling of being a burden on family, friends, and/or caregivers. Loss of control over bodily functions (36.8%), pain (35.3%), and financial concerns (5.3%) were cited by a minority of participants.

WASHINGTON. Between 2009, when Washington's DWDA was implemented, and 2016 prescriptions for life-ending medication were written for 1,188 people in the state, and 1,166 are known to have died from ingesting these medications. (See Figure 7.5.) The number of prescriptions and the number of deaths rose in each year after the law's passage.

In 2016, 248 Washingtonians (out of a population of 7.3 million) requested a prescription to end their life, and 240 of these patients' deaths were confirmed as being caused by the prescription. (See Figure 7.5 and Figure 7.6.)

The gap between the number of prescriptions and the number of deaths was smaller than in Oregon, but the reasons for the gap are similar. Figure 7.6 summarizes the outcomes for those patients who received medication under Washington's DWDA in 2016.

The demographic characteristics of those who ended their life under Washington's DWDA in 2016 are similar to those who did so in Oregon. Equal numbers of men and women died, and 93% of participants were aged 55 years and older. (See Table 7.8.) Participants were more likely to be white than in the state at large, and they were more likely to have some advanced education and to have graduated from college.

Of the 240 Washingtonians who died under the terms of the DWDA, 184 (77%) had cancer. (See Table 7.8.) Washington DWDA patients' top end-of-life concerns

FIGURE 7.5

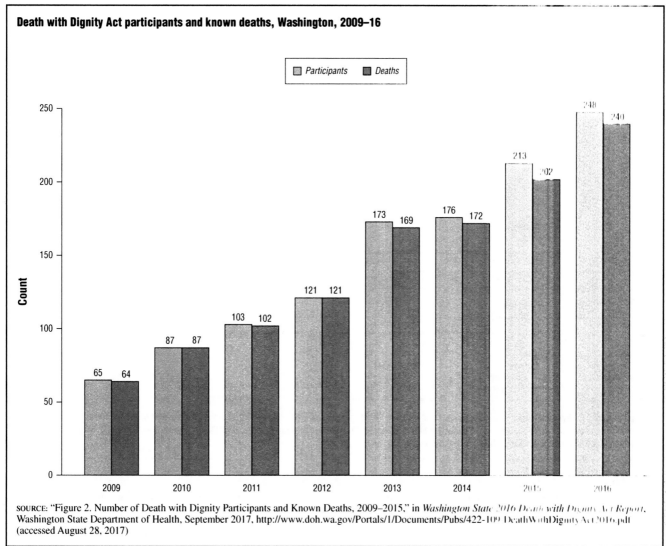

Death with Dignity Act participants and known deaths, Washington, 2009–16

SOURCE: "Figure 2. Number of Death with Dignity Participants and Known Deaths, 2009–2015," in *Washington State 2016 Death with Dignity Act Report*, Washington State Department of Health, September 2017, http://www.doh.wa.gov/Portals/1/Documents/Pubs/422-109 DeathWithDignity Act2016.pdf (accessed August 28, 2017)

were similar to those of their counterparts in Oregon: 87% cited the loss of autonomy as one of their reasons for choosing to end their life, and 84% cited the decreasing ability to engage in activities that make life enjoyable. (See Table 7.9.) The loss of dignity was a factor for 66% of patients, worries about burdening family, friends, and/or caregivers were a factor for 51%, and loss of control over bodily functions was a factor for 43%. Pain (41%) and financial concerns (8%) were, as in Oregon, much less often cited.

EUTHANASIA AND ASSISTED SUICIDE AROUND THE WORLD

Switzerland

Active euthanasia is illegal in Switzerland, but assisted suicide has been legal since 1940, provided that no selfish motive is involved. All assisted suicides in Switzerland must be videotaped and reported to the police. Following the patient's death, the police are contacted so that they can begin an investigation. If no selfish motive is established, the death is recorded and the case is closed.

The Swiss Academy of Medical Sciences has historically been opposed to physicians' involvement in assisted suicide, but a number of private groups of non-physicians have been established to provide accompaniment and assistance for those who choose to die in the country. The most prominent of these organizations are DIGNITAS and EXIT-Deutsche Schweiz, which also provide a range of end-of-life services and advocate on behalf of right-to-die and end-of-life issues.

Netherlands

Legal euthanasia in the Netherlands became gradually decriminalized between the 1970s and the early years of the new century. In 1971 a Dutch physician who helped her terminally ill 78-year-old mother die was found guilty of murder but sentenced extremely lightly, to a one-week suspended jail sentence and one-year probation. This sentence encouraged other physicians to

FIGURE 7.6

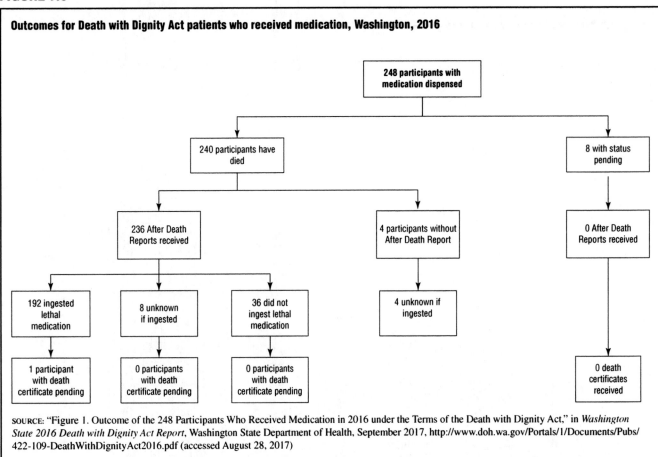

Outcomes for Death with Dignity Act patients who received medication, Washington, 2016

SOURCE: "Figure 1. Outcome of the 248 Participants Who Received Medication in 2016 under the Terms of the Death with Dignity Act," in *Washington State 2016 Death with Dignity Act Report*, Washington State Department of Health, September 2017, http://www.doh.wa.gov/Portals/1/Documents/Pubs/422-109-DeathWithDignityAct2016.pdf (accessed August 28, 2017)

come forward, admitting that they had also assisted in patients' suicides. Two years later the Royal Dutch Medical Association announced that, should a physician assist in the death of a terminally ill patient, it was up to the court to decide if the physician's action could be justified by "a conflict of duties." In 1984 the Dutch Supreme Court, ruling on a well-known 1982 case, found the physician involved not guilty of murder. Thereafter, each euthanasia case brought under prosecution was judged on its individual circumstances. Compliance with certain guidelines for performing euthanasia laid down by the Royal Dutch Medical Association and the Dutch courts in 1984 protected physicians from prosecution.

In April 2001 the Dutch Parliament systematized the practice of euthanasia, voting 46–28 in favor of the Termination of Life on Request and Assisted Suicide (Review Procedures) Act. Arguments in favor of the bill included public approval ratings of 90%. In May 2001 the results of a Dutch public opinion poll revealed that nearly half of respondents favored making lethal drugs available to older adults who no longer wanted to live.

Belgium

The Belgian Act on Euthanasia passed in 2002, following the passage of the 2001 law in the Netherlands.

The Belgian law applies to competent adults who have an incurable illness that causes unbearable, constant suffering and to patients in a persistent vegetative state who made their wishes known within the previous five years in front of two witnesses. It allows someone to terminate the life of another at his or her "voluntary, well-considered, and repeated" request, but does not allow physician-assisted suicide. All acts of euthanasia must be reported. Belgium also offers all patients in the country free medication for pain relief to ensure that people do not choose to end their life because they cannot afford to alleviate their suffering.

Luxembourg

In February 2008 the Parliament of the Grand Duchy of Luxembourg passed a bill that decriminalized euthanasia. However, Henri Guillaume (1955–), the grand duke of Luxembourg, refused to sign the bill into law. In 2009 his power was curtailed by the parliament, and his signature is no longer required for bills to become law. In April of that year the bill that decriminalized euthanasia officially went into force.

United Kingdom and Canada

As of September 2017, the United Kingdom still prohibited the practice of any form of euthanasia

TABLE 7.8

Characteristics of Death with Dignity Act participants who have died, Washington, 2014–16

	2016		2015[a]		2014[a]	
	Number	**%**	**Number**	**%**	**Number**	**%**
Sex[b]						
Male	120	50	106	53	75	44
Female	119	50	93	47	97	56
Age (years)[b]						
18–44	6	3	5	2	7	4
45–54	12	5	12	6	10	6
55–64	53	22	38	19	33	19
65–74	59	25	63	31	53	31
75–84	67	28	42	21	40	23
85+	42	18	42	21	29	17
Range (min-max)	33–98		20–97		21–101	
Race and ethnicity[b]						
White	232	97	194	98	159	92
Other	7	3	5	2	12	7
Unknown	0	0	0	0	1	1
Marital status[b]						
Married	103	43	93	47	81	47
Widowed	47	20	41	20	34	20
Divorced	65	27	53	27	37	21
Domestic partner (state-registered)	2	1	0	0	18	10
Never married/single	17	7	12	6	1	1
Unknown	5	1	0	0	1	1
Education[b]						
Less than high school	10	4	8	4	4	2
High school graduate	65	27	42	21	37	22
Some college	84	35	55	27	42	24
Baccalaureate or higher	77	32	93	47	86	50
Unknown	3	1	1	1	3	2
Residence[c,d]						
West of the Cascades	224	94	191	95	161	95
East of the Cascades	15	6	11	5	9	5
Underlying illness[c]						
Cancer	184	77	146	72	129	76
Neuro-degenerative disease (including ALS[e])	18	8	17	8	21	13
Respiratory disease (including COPD[f])	18	8	11	6	4	2
Heart disease	14	6	18	9	10	6
Other illnesses	5	2	10	5	6	3
Insurance status[g]						
Private only	43	18	28	14	33	23
Medicare or Medicaid only	109	46	140	71	82	57
Combination of private & Medicare/Medicaid	40	17	20	10	18	13
None	1	<1	4	2	3	2
Unknown	16	6	5	3	7	5
Other (including VA and other insurance)	27	11				

Note:
[a]Updated data derived from the death certificate (sex, age, race/ethnicity, marital status, and education) is pending for 2015. Data have been updated for 3 of the 2014 participants with information received since the 2014 report was published. At time of publication, death certificate data are available for 172 of the 2014 participants.
[b]Data are collected from the death certificate. At time of publication, data are available for 239 of the 240 participants in 2016 who died.
[c]Data are collected from multiple documents (After Death Reporting Form, Attending Physician Compliance Form, and Death Certificate). At time of publication, data are available for 239 of the 240 participants in 2016 who died.
[d]Counties west of the Cascades include: Clallam, Clark, Cowlitz, Grays Harbor, Island, Jefferson, King, Kitsap, Lewis, Mason, Pacific, Pierce, San Juan, Skagit, Skamania, Snohomish, Thurston, Wahkiakum, and Whatcom. Counties east of the Cascades include: Adams, Asotin, Benton, Chelan, Columbia, Douglas, Ferry, Franklin, Garfield, Grant, Kittitas, Klickitat, Lincoln, Okanogan, Pend Oreille, Spokane, Stevens, Walla Walla, Whitman, and Yakima.
[e]Amyotrophic Lateral Sclerosis (ALS).
[f]Chronic Obstructive Pulmonary Disease (COPD).
[g]Data are collected from the After Death Reporting form. At the time of publication, data are available for 236 of the 240 participants in 2016 .

SOURCE: "Table 1. Characteristics of the Participants of the Death with Dignity Act Who Have Died," in *Washington State 2016 Death with Dignity Act Report*, Washington State Department of Health, September 2017, http://www.doh.wa.gov/Portals/1/Documents/Pubs/422-109-DeathWithDignityAct2016.pdf (accessed August 28, 2017)

or assisted suicide, although a large majority of citizens approved of allowing mentally competent people with terminal illnesses to end their life with medical assistance. Debate and legal actions related to right-to-die issues also suggested the possibility of change in the near future.

TABLE 7.9

End of life concerns of Death with Dignity Act participants who have died, Washington, 2014–16

End of life concerns[b, c]	2016 Number	2016 %	2015[a] Number	2015[a] %	2014[a] Number	2014[a] %
Losing autonomy	206	87	169	86	127	89
Less able to engage in activities making life enjoyable	199	84	170	86	135	94
Loss of dignity	156	66	135	69	113	79
Burden on family, friends/caregivers	120	51	105	52	85	59
Losing control of bodily functions	101	43	96	49	73	51
Inadequate pain control or concern about it	97	41	70	35	59	41
Financial implications of treatment	18	8	25	13	12	8

Notes:
[a]Data published in 2014 and 2015 reports.
[b]Data are collected from the After Death Reporting form. At the time of publication, data are available for 236 of the 240 participants in 2016 who died.
[c]Participants may have selected more than one end of life concern. Thus the totals are greater than 100 percent.

SOURCE: "Table 2. End of Life Concerns of Participants of the Death with Dignity Act Who Have Died," in *Washington State 2016 Death with Dignity Act Report*, Washington State Department of Health, September 2017, http://www.doh.wa.gov/Portals/1/Documents/Pubs/422-109-DeathWith DignityAct2016.pdf (accessed August 28, 2017)

Parts of the United Kingdom measurably eased their prohibitions on assisted suicide in 2010, when Keir Starmer (1962–), the director of public prosecutions for the country's Crown Prosecution Service (the legal office responsible for criminal prosecutions in England and Wales), announced new guidelines for the prosecution of those who assisted loved ones in ending their life. Although assisting in a suicide carried a possible prison sentence of 14 years in the United Kingdom, the new guidelines suggested that in cases meeting certain conditions—conditions that showed that the act was one of compassion carried out at the clear request of a person with an incurable illness or disability—loved ones who assisted in a suicide would not be prosecuted. Subsequent cases of assisted suicide, some of which occurred in England and Wales and some of which involved loved ones traveling with terminally ill people to commit suicide in Switzerland, have not typically resulted in prosecutions since 2010. Bonnie Gardner notes in "Support for Doctor-Assisted Suicide" (YouGov.co.uk, July 5, 2012) that public opinion polls conducted by YouGov found that in 2012, 69% of the United Kingdom population supported the legalization of assisted suicide in cases where the patient is terminally ill.

Euthanasia and assisted suicide became legal in Canada in February 2015, when the Canadian Supreme Court unanimously overturned the nation's ban on the practice. Although the previous prohibition on euthanasia and assisted suicide had been affirmed by a Supreme Court ruling in 1993, the country saw a reopening of the debate on this in 2011. In that year a daughter who accompanied her terminally ill 89-year-old mother to Switzerland to end her life and a woman suffering from advanced amyotrophic lateral sclerosis (ALS; a degenerative neurologic condition commonly known as Lou Gehrig's disease) filed suit in British Columbia, challenging the Canadian law that made assisted suicide illegal. Represented by the British Columbia Civil Liberties Association (BCCLA), the case made it to the British Columbia Supreme Court (the second-highest court at the provincial level). The court ruled in 2012 that the Criminal Code of Canada violated the rights of the terminally ill, and it granted the ALS patient the right to an assisted suicide. However, the federal government appealed the ruling, which was subsequently overturned by the British Columbia Court of Appeals. The ALS patient died in 2012 from her underlying illness, but the BCCLA appealed to the Canadian Supreme Court.

In January 2014 the high court agreed to hear the case. Adrian Morrow reports in "Majority of Canadians Approve of Assisted Suicide: Poll" (GlobeandMail.com, October 11, 2013) that approximately 70% of Canadians (with variations depending on the wording of the question) approved of legalizing assisted suicide in 2013. Two years later, in the landmark decision *Carter v. Canada (Attorney General)* (2015 SCC 5), the Supreme Court directed the Canadian government to pass legislation that legalized euthanasia and assisted suicide. After receiving a six-month extension, the government enacted Bill C-14, which allowed terminally ill adults over the age of 18 years to participate in euthanasia or assisted suicide with the approval of two health care professionals. In "Interim Update on Medical Assistance in Dying in Canada June 17 to December 31, 2016" (2017, https://www.canada.ca/en/health-canada/services/publications/health-system-services/medical-assistance-dying-interim-report-dec-2016.html), the Canadian government reports that during the first six months following the law's implementation, 507 Canadians had ended their life with medical assistance.

CHAPTER 8
ADVANCE CARE PLANNING

As patients in the United States have come to enjoy more autonomy in their medical decision making, as medical technologies for extending life indefinitely have become common, and as the number of elderly Americans has skyrocketed, advance planning for the medical care that one will receive at the end of life has become increasingly important. The likelihood that a given person might one day be chronically or terminally ill and unable to make decisions about his or her own medical treatments is much higher for people who are alive today than for people in prior generations. Other decisions that need to be made as the end of life approaches involve the circumstances in which patients would like to spend their final weeks and days in the event that an underlying illness has reached its terminal stages.

When a patient's own wishes about such matters are unknown, the responsibility for making decisions falls to loved ones. In many cases, this responsibility is an unwelcome and forbidding one, requiring sons and daughters, for example, to make choices that may or may not correspond with their parents' wishes. This may disrupt the loved ones' attempts to grieve appropriately, and it may add unnecessary guilt to their feelings of loss. Additionally, patients who are incapacitated as they approach the end of life may consign themselves to unnecessary suffering and a diminishment in the quality of their life if they have not made their wishes known in advance. For example, artificial nutrition and hydration (ANH) is believed to cause excess discomfort in those whose bodies are naturally shutting down. Likewise, medical procedures intended to prolong life but that result in only an additional week or month of life may cause so much pain and stress that the additional time may not seem worthwhile.

For those patients who do not want their life extended regardless of the cost to their comfort and quality of life, advance care planning is particularly crucial. In U.S. hospitals, illness is treated aggressively and life is prolonged

at all costs unless doctors and staff are given specific requests that indicate otherwise. In the absence of specific requests not to treat all illnesses aggressively, doctors are likely to keep even the oldest and sickest patients alive for as long as possible.

Advance care planning involves thinking through one's preferences about the end of life, ideally in consultation with medical professionals who can provide guidance about what the trajectory of a disease or chronic condition may look like. The most thorough plans for the end of life foresee the maximum number of possible scenarios in which a medical decision might be necessary. Advance directives are also dependent on the individual's religious and ethical beliefs. In thinking through end-of-life options, some people find it helpful to discuss their decisions with spiritual counselors, mental health professionals, and others.

Once an individual has come to conclusions about how medical decisions should be made on his or her behalf in the event of incapacitation, the resulting wishes must be clearly expressed in legal documents known as advance directives.

ADVANCE DIRECTIVES

Advance directives are legal documents that help protect patients' rights of self-determination (the right to make one's own medical decisions, including the right to accept or refuse treatment). These documents are a person's requests concerning health care should he or she be unable to communicate them when the need arises due to physical or mental disabilities. There are two primary types of advance directives: a living will and a durable power of attorney for health care.

A living will should not be confused with a last will and testament, which is a legal document that details how a deceased person's property is to be allocated after his or her death. A living will is, instead, a legal document that states a person's wishes for dealing with life-sustaining medical procedures and other issues associated with end-of-life care. It applies to decisions made while the individual is alive but unable to speak or reason clearly in the moment, due to his or her medical condition. Living wills commonly address the following issues: to what extent life-sustaining treatments and technologies such as ventilators, respirators, and dialysis machines will be used; whether or not cardiopulmonary resuscitation should be used if the heartbeat or breathing stops; whether and to what extent ANH will be supplied; and whether, following death, one's organs and tissues will be donated.

A durable power of attorney for health care (also called a health care proxy, durable power of attorney, medical power of attorney, or appointment of health care agent) is the other primary type of advance directive. It is a legal document in which one person gives another the legal authority to act or speak on his or her behalf should he or she become debilitated and not able to make decisions. While especially important in end-of-life care, a durable power of attorney for health care can also be useful to those who are not on the point of death but who are temporarily unable to make medical decisions for themselves. A physician determines when a patient is unable to make decisions, and at the point that the physician's determination has been made, the durable power of attorney for health care goes into effect.

The purposes of these two types of advance directives may seem to overlap because both are attempts to provide ways of making decisions on behalf of the patient once he or she is unable to do so. However, legal and medical professionals usually advise individuals to craft both forms of advance directive. A living will might cover all medical decisions that can be foreseen, but medical situations are inherently complicated, and as a situation changes, it may be necessary to have someone present to make decisions under the terms of a durable power of attorney for health care.

The Patient Self-Determination Act

In 1990 Congress enacted the Patient Self-Determination Act (PSDA) as part of the Omnibus Budget Reconciliation Act of 1990. This legislation was intended to "reinforce individuals' constitutional right to determine their final health care."

The PSDA took effect in December 1991. It requires most health care institutions to provide patients, on admission, with a summary of their health care decision-making rights and to ask them if they have an advance directive. Health care institutions must also inform the patient of the facility's policies with respect to honoring advance directives. The PSDA requires health care providers to educate their staff and the community about advance

directives. It also prohibits hospital personnel from discriminating against patients based on whether they have an advance directive, and patients are informed that having an advance directive is not a prerequisite to receiving medical care.

Advance Directives and State Law

All 50 states and the District of Columbia have laws that recognize the use of living wills and durable powers of attorney for health care, but the provisions of these laws vary from state to state. Charles P. Sabatino of the American Bar Association conducted an extensive literature review of health care advance planning and published his findings in "The Evolution of Health Care Advance Planning Law and Policy" (*Milbank Quarterly*, vol. 88, no. 2, June 2010). He indicates that in the 30 years since advance health care planning had been available as of 2010, laws from various states had evolved in a heterogeneous (diverse) manner but with important points of convergence. Sabatino notes that one convergent point is the movement from a "legal transactional approach" to a "communications approach." The latter is evolving into Physician Orders for Life-Sustaining Treatment (POLST), and the communications approach and its evolution toward POLST help translate patients' wishes and desires in end-of-life care into "visible and portable medical orders."

Because of the heterogeneity of state laws regarding advance directives, it is important for individuals to understand their own state's requirements prior to crafting an advance directive. Advance directives that meet one state's guidelines may not be honored by hospitals in another state. The National Hospice and Palliative Care Organization maintains a database of advance directive forms that meet the legal requirements of all U.S. states. Individuals can access the database at http://www.caring info.org/i4a/pages/index.cfm?pageid=3289.

Since the 1980s the Uniform Law Commission (also known as the National Conference of Commissioners on Uniform State Laws), a nonprofit group that advocates for consistency among the laws of individual states in the United States, has urged state legislatures to adopt uniform laws regarding patient autonomy, advance directives, and medical decision making. In 1993 the organization created a law called the Uniform Health-Care Decisions Act (http://www.uniformlaws.org/ActSummary .aspx?title=Health-Care%20Decisions%20Act), which was intended to serve as a model for state legislative bills. Endorsed by the American Bar Association and adopted by a number of states since first being introduced, the act remains one of the best standardized approaches to advance directives and other issues, in the opinion of many legal experts. The act includes a model advance directive, which is reprinted in Table 8.1.

TABLE 8.1

Advance health-care directive

Optional Form

The following form may, but need not, be used to create an advance health-care directive. The other sections of this [Act] govern the effect of this or any other writing used to create an advance health-care directive. An individual may complete or modify all or any part of the following form:

ADVANCE HEALTH-CARE DIRECTIVE

Explanation

You have the right to give instructions about your own health care. You also have the right to name someone else to make health-care decisions for you. This form lets you do either or both of these things. It also lets you express your wishes regarding donation of organs and the designation of your primary physician. If you use this form, you may complete or modify all or any part of it. You are free to use a different form.

Part 1 of this form is a power of attorney for health care. Part 1 lets you name another individual as agent to make health-care decisions for you if you become incapable of making your own decisions or if you want someone else to make those decisions for you now even though you are still capable. You may also name an alternate agent to act for you if your first choice is not willing, able, or reasonably available to make decisions for you. Unless related to you, your agent may not be an owner, operator, or employee of [a residential long-term health-care institution] at which you are receiving care.

Unless the form you sign limits the authority of your agent, your agent may make all health-care decisions for you. This form has a place for you to limit the authority of your agent. You need not limit the authority of your agent if you wish to rely on your agent for all health-care decisions that may have to be made. If you choose not to limit the authority of your agent, your agent will have the right to:

(a) consent or refuse consent to any care, treatment, service, or procedure to maintain, diagnose, or otherwise affect a physical or mental condition;
(b) select or discharge health-care providers and institution;
(c) approve or disapprove diagnostic tests, surgical procedures, programs of medication, and orders not to resuscitate; and
(d) direct the provision, withholding, or withdrawal of artificial nutrition and hydration and all other forms of health care.

Part 2 of this form lets you give specific instructions about any aspect of your health care. Choices are provided for you to express your wishes regarding the provision, withholding, or withdrawal of treatment to keep you alive, including the provision of artificial nutrition and hydration, as well as the provision of pain relief. Space is also provided for you to add to the choices you have made or for you to write out any additional wishes.

Part 3 of this form lets you express an intention to donate your bodily organs and tissues following your death.

Part 4 of this form lets you designate a physician to have primary responsibility for your health care.

After completing this form, sign and date the form at the end. It is recommended but not required that you request two other individuals to sign as witnesses. Give a copy of the signed and completed form to your physician, to any other health-care providers you may have, to any health-care institution at which you are receiving care, and to any health-care agents you have named. You should talk to the person you have named as agent to make sure that he or she understands your wishes and is willing to take the responsibility.

You have the right to revoke this advance health-care directive or replace this form at any time.

* * * * * * * * *

PART 1

POWER OF ATTORNEY FOR HEALTH CARE

1. DESIGNATION OF AGENT: I designate the following individual as my agent to make health-care decisions for me:

_____
(name of individual you choose as agent)

| (address) | (city) | (state) | (zip code) |

| (home phone) | (work phone) |

OPTIONAL: If I revoke my agent's authority or if my agent is not willing, able, or reasonably available to make a health-care decision for me, I designate as my first alternate agent:

_____
(name of individual you choose as first alternate agent)

| (address) | (city) | (state) | (zip code) |

| (home phone) | (work phone) |

OPTIONAL: If I revoke the authority of my agent and first alternate agent or if neither is willing, able, or reasonably available to make a health-care decision for me, I designate as my second alternate agent:

_____
(name of individual you choose as first alternate agent)

| (address) | (city) | (state) | (zip code) |

| (home phone) | (work phone) |

(Add additional sheets if needed.)

Another commonly used template for advance directives, called "Five Wishes," was developed in Florida by the nonprofit organization Aging with Dignity. The document probes legal and medical issues as well as spiritual and emotional ones. It even outlines small details, such as requests for favorite music to be played and poems to be read, and provides space for individuals to record their wishes for funeral arrangements. Free of legal and medical jargon, the "Five Wishes" form is comparatively easy to complete. As of September 2017, "Five Wishes"

TABLE 8.1

Advance health-care directive [CONTINUED]

2. AGENT'S AUTHORITY: My agent is authorized to make all health-care decisions for me, including decisions to provide, withhold, or withdraw artificial nutrition and hydration and other forms of health care to keep me alive, except as I state here:

_____

_____

_____

3. WHEN AGENT'S AUTHORITY BECOMES EFFECTIVE: My agent's authority becomes effective when my primary physician determines that I am unable to make my own health-care decisions unless I mark the following box. If I mark this box [ ], my agent's authority to make health-care decisions for me takes effect immediately.

4. AGENT'S OBLIGATION: My agent shall make health-care decisions for me in accordance with this power of attorney for health care, any instructions I give in Part 2 of this form, and my other wishes to the extent known to my agent. To the extent my wishes are unknown, my agent shall make health-care decisions for me in accordance with what my agent determines to be in my best interest. In determining my best interest, my agent shall consider my personal values to the extent known to my agent.

NOMINATION OF GUARDIAN: If a guardian of my person needs to be appointed for me by a court, I nominate the agent designated in this form. If that agent is not willing, able, or reasonably available to act as guardian, I nominate the alternate agents whom I have named, in the order designated.

PART 2
INSTRUCTIONS FOR HEALTH CARE

If you are satisfied to allow your agent to determine what is best for you in making end-of-life decisions, you need not fill out this part of the form. If you do fill out this part of the form, you may strike any wording you do not want.

6. END-OF-LIFE DECISIONS: I direct that my health-care providers and others involved in my care provide, withhold, or withdraw treatment in accordance with the choice I have marked below:

[   ] (a) Choice Not To Prolong Life
   I do not want my life to be prolonged if (i) I have an incurable and irreversible condition that will result in my death within a relatively short time, (ii) I become unconscious and, to a reasonable degree of medical certainty, I will not regain consciousness, or (iii) the likely risks and burdens of treatment would outweigh the expected benefits, OR

[   ] (b) Choice To Prolong Life
   I want my life to be prolonged as long as possible within the limits of generally accepted health-care standards.

7. ARTIFICIAL NUTRITION AND HYDRATION: Artificial nutrition and hydration must be provided, withheld, or withdrawn in accordance with the choice I have made in paragraph (6) unless I mark the following box. If I mark this box [   ], artificial nutrition and hydration must be provided regardless of my condition and regardless of the choice I have made in paragraph (6).

8. RELIEF FROM PAIN: Except as I state in the following space, I direct that treatment for alleviation of pain or discomfort be provided at all times, even if it hastens my death:

_____

_____

9. OTHER WISHES: (If you do not agree with any of the optional choices above and wish to write your own, or if you wish to add to the instructions you have given above, you may do so here.) I direct that:

_____

_____

(Add additional sheets if needed.)

PART 3
DONATION OF ORGANS AT DEATH (OPTIONAL)

10. Upon my death (mark applicable box)

[   ] (a) I give any needed organs, tissues, or parts, OR
[   ] (b) I give the following organs, tissues, or parts only

_____

[   ] (c) My gift is for the following purposes (strike any of the following you do not want)
      (i) Transplant
      (ii) Therapy
      (iii) Research
      (iv) Education

met living will or advance directive criteria in 42 states and the District of Columbia. It did not meet advance directive criteria in eight states: Alabama, Indiana, Kansas, New Hampshire, Ohio, Oregon, Texas, and Utah. Other forms were necessary in these states, although the "Five Wishes" document could still serve as a guide for family and physicians and could be attached to the state's required form. The "Five Wishes" form can be filled out online (or a blank form can be printed) at https://five wishesonline.agingwithdignity.org/.

TABLE 8.1

Advance health-care directive [CONTINUED]

PART 4
PRIMARY PHYSICIAN (OPTIONAL)

11. I designate the following physician as my primary physician:

_____
(name of physician)

_____
(address)   (city)   (state)   (zip code)

_____
(phone)

OPTIONAL: If the physician I have designated above is not willing, able, or reasonably available to act as my primary physician, I designate the following physician as my primary physician:

_____
(name of physician)

_____
(address)   (city)   (state)   (zip code)

_____
(phone)

* * * * * * * * * *

EFFECT OF COPY: A copy of this form has the same effect as the original.

12. SIGNATURES: Sign and date the form here:

_____   _____
(date)   (sign your name)

_____   _____
(address)   (print name)

_____
(city)   (state)

Optional SIGNATURES OF WITNESSES:

_____   _____
(First witness)   (Second witness)

_____   _____
(print name)   (print name)

_____   _____
(address)   (address)

_____   _____
(city)   (state)   (city)   (state)

_____   _____
(signature of witness)   (signature of witness)

_____   _____
(date)   (date)

SOURCE: "Advance Health-Care Directive," in *Patient Self-Determination Act: Providers Offer Information on Advance Directives but Effectiveness Uncertain*, U.S. General Accounting Office, August 1995, http://www.gao.gov/archive/1995/he95135.pdf (accessed July 20, 2017)

PRO-LIFE ALTERNATIVE TO LIVING WILLS. The National Right to Life Committee opposes active and passive euthanasia and seeks to define all life as equally worthy of preservation. In the interest of promoting its viewpoint, the organization offers an alternative to standard living wills. Called the "Will to Live" (http://www.nrlc.org/medethics/willtolive/), it does not consider ANH as forms of medical treatment but as basic necessities for the preservation of life.

In the Absence of a Durable Power of Attorney for Health Care

Physicians usually involve family members in medical decisions when the patient has not designated a proxy or surrogate in advance. Many states have surrogate consent laws for this purpose. Some have laws that designate the order in which family members may assume the role of surrogate decision maker. For example, the spouse may be the prime surrogate, followed by an adult child, then the patient's parent, and so on.

Most states specify a decision-making standard for surrogates: either a substituted judgment standard, a best interests standard, or a combination of the two. A substituted judgment standard requires the surrogate to do what the patient would do in the situation were the patient competent. A best interests standard requires the surrogate to weigh health care options for the patient and then decide what is in the patient's best interest.

The Importance of Communicating Wishes

The completion of an advance directive should be the start of an ongoing discussion among the individual, family members, and the family doctor about end-of-life health care. Discussions about one's advance directive do not have to be limited to treatment preferences and medical circumstances. Sometimes knowing things such as the patient's religious beliefs and values can be important for the proxy when speaking for the patient's interests. The Institute for Ethics at the University of New Mexico has devised a values history form (http://hscethics.unm.edu/common/pdf/values-history.pdf) to help people examine their attitudes about issues related to illness, health care, and dying. It may serve as a valuable tool to guide discussions between the patient and the proxy, as well as among family members.

When preparing an advance directive, it is vitally important for the family and proxy to have a thorough understanding of the patient's desires for end-of-life care. However, even when a patient has a living will calling for no "heroic measures," there is no guarantee that these instructions will be followed. Indeed, advance directives are not always widely accessible to providers, particularly in cases when a patient is being treated by more than one physician. Paula Span reports in "When Advance Directives Are Ignored" (NYTimes.com, June 24, 2014) that a survey conducted by the University of California, Los Angeles, found that of 800 elderly patients who had shared advance directives with their health care providers, fewer than half had these directives readily available in their medical records. According to Span, one possible solution to this issue could be the creation of online advance directive databases, which would be easily accessible to all providers and emergency medical technicians. Span notes that one such registry was established in Oregon in 2009; the POLST program proved highly effective in ensuring that patients received the treatment outlined in their advance directive.

Advance Directives and the Cost of End-of-Life Care

In "Regional Variation in the Association between Advance Directives and End-of-Life Medicare Expenditures" (*Journal of the American Medical Association*, vol. 306, no. 13, October 5, 2011), Lauren Hersch Nicholas et al. of the University of Michigan seek to determine if there is a connection between advance directives and Medicare costs for end-of-life care. The researchers find that there is a variability of Medicare costs nationally in end-of-life care and that there are some regions of the country in which end-of-life care costs much more than in other regions. These are the regions in which there appears to be a connection between end-of-life care costs and advance directives.

By using a variety of statistical methods, Nicholas et al. note that "advance directives are associated with important differences in treatment during the last six months of life for patients who live in areas of high medical expenditures but not in other regions." The researchers also indicate, "This suggests that the clinical effect of advance directives is critically dependent on the context in which a patient receives care. Advance directives may be especially important for ensuring treatment consistent with patients' preferences for those who prefer less aggressive treatment at the end of life but are patients in systems characterized by high intensity of treatment." What Nicholas et al. mean is that Medicare payments might go down in areas of the country in which high-intensity care is given at the end of life. Many people in their advance directives indicate whether they want certain high-intensity care.

The Prevalence of Advance Directives

The Centers for Disease Control and Prevention (CDC) notes in *Advance Care Planning: Ensuring Your Wishes Are Known and Honored If You Are Unable to Speak for Yourself* (2012, http://www.cdc.gov/aging/pdf/advanced-care-planning-critical-issue-brief.pdf) that polling organizations and other surveyors routinely find that most people would prefer to die at home rather than in a hospital, nursing home, or other facility. Nevertheless, a majority of people die in medical facilities each year. According to the CDC, only about one-third of adults have an advance directive. The prevalence of advance directives is low even among the severely or terminally ill, less than half of whom have legal documents in their medical files to guide their end-of-life treatment. The CDC further notes that even when patients have advance directives, their doctors are usually unaware of this fact.

There are a number of explanations for the low prevalence of advance directives in the United States. One of the leading explanations is that a lack of clarity surrounds the process for crafting an advance directive and communicating with a physician about it. The differences in state laws, together with the fact that the process varies from hospital to hospital and physician to physician, make it hard for patients to know the right way to communicate their end-of-life desires. Another key reason for the low utilization of advance directives is the more general unwillingness in American society to consider death honestly. The idea of thinking through the end of one's life and dwelling on circumstances in which one might be near death and unable to speak or make decisions is actively discouraged by some societal norms.

Many Americans also worry that prioritizing palliative care or otherwise expressing wishes about quality of life will come into conflict with doctors' commitment to saving their life. In reality, there is no conflict between the two priorities, as medical ethics demands that a shift from prolongation of life to quality of life would only occur after there was no hope for a meaningful prolongation of life. However, the areas of confusion and denial surrounding the end of life obscure this reality. As a result, most people approve of prioritizing quality of life and comfort in the abstract, but when faced with concrete scenarios that involve their own life, they are less certain.

The low prevalence of advance directives is, finally, partly a function of cultural attitudes. For example, African American and Hispanic patients are considerably less likely than white patients to have advance directives. (See Figure 8.1.) These groups are, accordingly, more likely to prioritize life-extending interventions, which are the norm in U.S. hospitals in the absence of advance directives.

In *Advance Directives: Information on Federal Oversight, Provider Implementation, and Prevalence* (April 2015, http://www.gao.gov/assets/670/669906.pdf), the U.S. Government Accountability Office (GAO) describes the prevalence of advance care planning in three populations whose need for advance care planning is generally seen to be more acute than that of other subgroups: people receiving home health care, people receiving hospice care, and people residing in nursing homes. Based on a survey of nursing home patients conducted in 2004 and surveys of home health care and hospice patients conducted in 2007, the GAO finds that 28% of home health care patients had advance directives. (See Figure 8.2.) Advance directives were more prevalent among residents of nursing homes (65%) and discharged hospice patients (88%; patients can be discharged from hospice either due to death or due to the determination that, contrary to previous diagnoses, they have more than six months to live).

These variations are logical, in the GAO's view, given that among the three populations, those receiving home health care can generally expect to live the longest and thus to put off making decisions about their end-of-life care. Residents of nursing homes have in many cases seen a progression of their diseases and conditions beyond the point at which they can be adequately cared for in the home, and hospice patients are typically in the final six months of life. In 2014 more than half (55%) of nursing home patients had advance directives. (See Figure 8.3.)

FIGURE 8.1

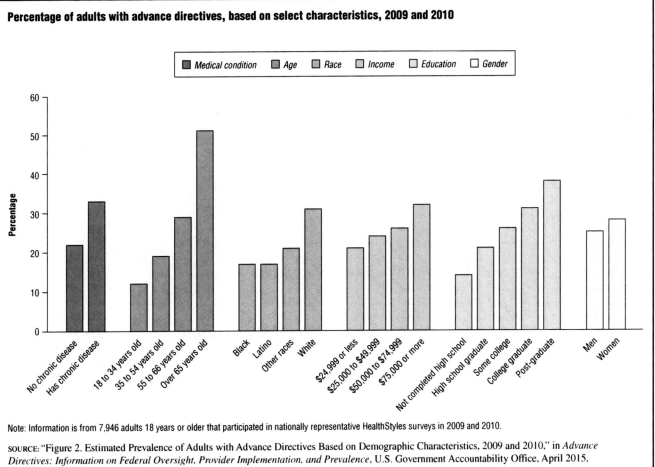

Percentage of adults with advance directives, based on select characteristics, 2009 and 2010

Note: Information is from 7,946 adults 18 years or older that participated in nationally representative HealthStyles surveys in 2009 and 2010.

SOURCE: "Figure 2. Estimated Prevalence of Adults with Advance Directives Based on Demographic Characteristics, 2009 and 2010," in *Advance Directives: Information on Federal Oversight, Provider Implementation, and Prevalence*, U.S. Government Accountability Office, April 2015, www.gao.gov/assets/670/669906.pdf (accessed July 20, 2017)

FIGURE 8.2

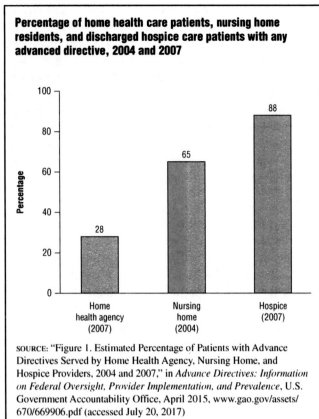

Percentage of home health care patients, nursing home residents, and discharged hospice care patients with any advanced directive, 2004 and 2007

SOURCE: "Figure 1. Estimated Percentage of Patients with Advance Directives Served by Home Health Agency, Nursing Home, and Hospice Providers, 2004 and 2007," in *Advance Directives: Information on Federal Oversight, Provider Implementation, and Prevalence*, U.S. Government Accountability Office, April 2015, www.gao.gov/assets/670/669906.pdf (accessed July 20, 2017)

As would be expected, the rates of advance directive prevalence varied by population. For example, those older than 65 years were more likely than any other age group to have an advance directive. (See Figure 8.1.) Income level and educational attainment also appeared to be significant factors in determining whether an individual had an advance directive. Patients with an annual income of $75,000 or more were more likely to have an advance directive than those earning less than $25,000 per year, while patients with a postgraduate degree were more likely to have an advance directive than patients without a high school diploma.

The most common type of advance directive among people receiving home health care, people residing in nursing homes, and people receiving hospice care is a do-not-resuscitate order, which is typically considered only one of several elements addressed by a living will. (See Figure 8.4.) The second most-common type of advance directive among the three populations surveyed was a living will. (See Figure 8.5.) A comparison of Figure 8.4 and Figure 8.5 shows that a much smaller percentage of nursing home residents and hospice patients had living wills than do-not-resuscitate orders, whereas home health care patients were more likely to have a living will than a do-not-resuscitate order.

FIGURE 8.3

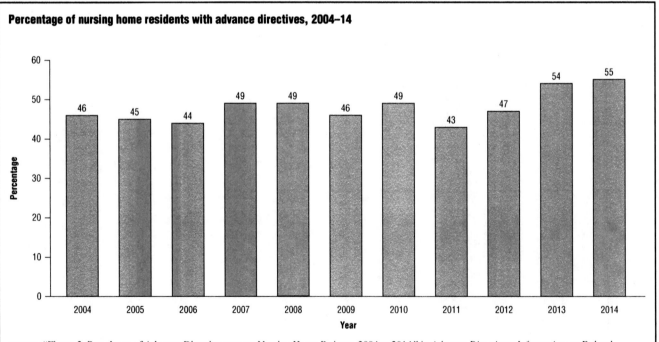

Percentage of nursing home residents with advance directives, 2004–14

SOURCE: "Figure 3. Prevalence of Advance Directives among Nursing Home Patients, 2004 to 2014," in *Advance Directives: Information on Federal Oversight, Provider Implementation, and Prevalence*, U.S. Government Accountability Office, April 2015, www.gao.gov/assets/670/669906.pdf (accessed July 20, 2017)

FIGURE 8.4

Percentage of home health care patients, nursing home residents, and discharged hospice care patients with a do not resuscitate order, by age, 2004 and 2007

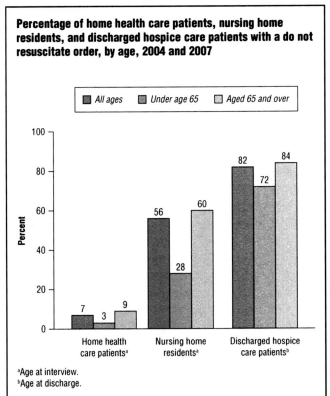

^aAge at interview.
^bAge at discharge.

SOURCE: Adrienne L. Jones, Abigail J. Moss, and Lauren D. Harris-Kojetin, "Figure 5. Percentage of Home Health Care Patients, Nursing Home Residents, and Discharged Hospice Care Patients with a Do Not Resuscitate Order, by Age: United States, 2004 and 2007," in "Use of Advance Directives in Long-term Care Populations," *NCHS Data Brief*, no. 54, Centers for Disease Control and Prevention, National Center for Health Care Statistics, January 2011, https://www.cdc.gov/nchs/data/databriefs/db54.pdf (accessed July 20, 2018)

FIGURE 8.5

Percentage of home health care patients, nursing home residents, and discharged hospice care patients with a living will, by age, 2004 and 2007

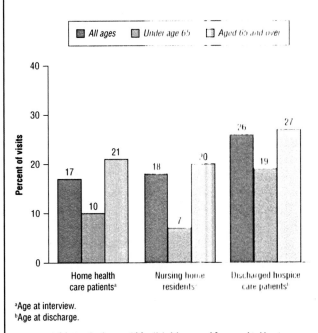

^aAge at interview.
^bAge at discharge.

SOURCE: Adrienne L. Jones, Abigail J. Moss, and Lauren D. Harris-Kojetin, "Figure 4. Percentage of Home Health Care Patients, Nursing Home Residents, and Discharged Hospice Care Patients with a Living Will, by Age: United States, 2004 and 2007," in "Use of Advance Directives in Long-term Care Populations," *NCHS Data Brief*, no. 54, Centers for Disease Control and Prevention, National Center for Health Care Statistics, January 2011, https://www.cdc.gov/nchs/data/databriefs/db54.pdf (accessed July 20, 2017)

CHAPTER 9
COURTS AND THE END OF LIFE

The Ad Hoc Committee of the Harvard Medical School's redefinition of death, in 1968, as brain death rather than the cessation of circulation and respiration, was an early attempt to clarify the new physiological and ethical issues raised by advances in medical technology. Such issues were not settled with the redefinition of death, however, as the foregoing chapters have made clear.

There are many patients near the end of life whose bodies cannot function but who are nevertheless not legally brain dead, and many of these people can be kept alive through artificial respiration and artificial nutrition and hydration (ANH) for months or even years. Debate frequently arises in cases when such patients can be kept alive but are in a permanent vegetative state (PVS) with no hope for recovery. Should they be kept alive for decades even though they will never be fully conscious again? Who is entitled to make such decisions?

Debate also arises in situations when patients are conscious but are able to remain alive only with the help of a ventilator and ANH. Should these people be allowed to end their own life? What role should doctors and hospitals play in these situations? What if these people are not mentally competent to make these decisions? Decisions about these and other complex life-and-death situations have frequently ended up in state and federal courts, and the resulting decisions have gradually accumulated into the evolving body of law that now governs end-of-life issues.

THE RIGHT TO PRIVACY: KAREN ANN QUINLAN

The landmark case of Karen Ann Quinlan (1954–1985) was the first to deal with the dilemma of withdrawing life-sustaining treatment from a patient who was not terminally ill but who was not really "alive." The decision to terminate life support, which was once a private matter between the patient's family and doctor, became an issue to be decided by the courts. The New

Jersey Supreme Court ruling on this case became the precedent for nearly all right-to-die cases nationwide.

In 1975, 21-year-old Karen Ann Quinlan suffered cardiopulmonary arrest after ingesting a combination of alcohol and drugs. She subsequently went into a PVS. Fred Plum (1924–2010), a world-renowned neurologist who had coined the term *persistent vegetative state*, described her as no longer having any cognitive function but retaining the capacity to maintain the vegetative parts of neurological function. She grimaced, made chewing movements, uttered sounds, and maintained a normal blood pressure, but she was entirely unaware of anyone or anything. The medical opinion was that Quinlan had some brain stem function, but that it could not support breathing. She had been on a respirator since her admission to the hospital.

Quinlan's parents asked that her respirator be removed and that she be allowed to die. Quinlan's doctor refused, claiming that his patient did not meet the Harvard Criteria for brain death. Joseph Quinlan (1925–1996), Quinlan's father, went to court to seek appointment as his daughter's guardian (because she was of legal age) and to gain the power to authorize "the discontinuance of all extraordinary medical procedures now allegedly sustaining Karen's vital processes." The court refused to grant him guardianship over his daughter and denied his petition to have Quinlan's respirator turned off.

First and Eighth Amendments
Are Irrelevant to the Case

Joseph Quinlan subsequently appealed to the New Jersey Supreme Court. He requested, as a parent, to have Quinlan's life support removed based on the U.S. Constitution's First Amendment (the right to religious freedom). In *In re Quinlan* (70 N.J. 10, 355 A.2d 647 [1976]), the court rejected his request. It also indicated that the Eighth Amendment (protection against cruel and unusual punishment) did not apply to Quinlan's case, explaining that this amendment applied to protection from excessive criminal punishment. The court considered Quinlan's cruel and unusual circumstances not punishment inflicted by the law or state, but the result of an "accident of fate and nature."

The Right to Privacy

However, the New Jersey Supreme Court stated that an individual's right to privacy was most relevant to the case. Although the Constitution does not expressly indicate a right to privacy, U.S. Supreme Court rulings in past cases had not only recognized this right but had also determined that some areas of the right to privacy are guaranteed by the Constitution. The New Jersey Supreme Court ruled that "Karen's right of privacy may be asserted in her behalf, in this respect, by her guardian and family under the particular circumstances presented by this record," and further noted, "We have no doubt ... that if Karen were herself miraculously lucid for an interval (not altering the existing prognosis of the condition to which she would soon return) and perceptive of her irreversible condition, she could effectively decide upon discontinuance of the life-support apparatus, even if it meant the prospect of natural death."

The State's Interest

Balanced against Quinlan's constitutional right to privacy was the state's interest in preserving life. Judge Richard J. Hughes (1909–1992) of the New Jersey Supreme Court noted that in many cases the court had ordered medical treatment continued because the minimal bodily invasion (usually blood transfusion) resulted in recovery. He indicated that in Quinlan's case bodily invasion was far greater than minimal, consisting of 24-hour nursing care, antibiotics, respirator, catheter, and feeding tube. Judge Hughes further noted, "We think that the State's interest ... weakens and the individual's right to privacy grows as the degree of bodily invasion increases and the prognosis dims. Ultimately there comes a point at which the individual's rights overcome the State's interest."

Prevailing Medical Standards and Practices

Quinlan's physicians had refused to remove the respirator because they did not want to violate the prevailing medical standards and practices. Although Quinlan's physicians assured the court that the possibility of lawsuits and criminal sanctions did not influence their decision in this specific case, the court believed that the threat of legal ramifications strongly influenced the existing medical standards and practices of health care providers.

The court also observed that life-prolongation advances had rendered the existing medical standards ambiguous, leaving doctors in a quandary. Moreover, modern devices used for prolonging life, such as respirators, had confused the issue of "ordinary" and "extraordinary" measures. Therefore, the court suggested that respirators could be considered "ordinary" care for a curable patient, but "extraordinary" care for irreversibly unconscious patients.

The court also suggested that hospitals should form ethics committees to assist physicians with difficult cases such as Quinlan's. These committees would be similar to a multi-judge panel exploring different solutions to an appeal. The committees would not only diffuse professional responsibility but would also eliminate any possibly unscrupulous motives of physicians or families. The justices considered the court's intervention on medical decisions an infringement on the physicians' field of competence.

The state had promised to prosecute anyone who terminated Quinlan's life support because such an act would constitute homicide. The New Jersey Supreme Court, however, rejected this consequence because the resulting death would be from natural causes.

After Quinlan's Respirator Was Removed

In March 1976 the New Jersey Supreme Court ruled that, if the hospital ethics committee agreed that Quinlan would not recover from irreversible coma, her respirator could be removed. Furthermore, all parties involved would be legally immune from criminal and civil prosecution. After Quinlan's respirator was removed, however, she continued to breathe on her own and remained in a PVS until she died of multiple infections in 1985.

Some people wondered why the Quinlans did not request permission to discontinue Karen's ANH. In *Karen Ann: The Quinlans Tell Their Story* (1977), the Quinlans explain that they had moral problems with depriving their daughter of food and antibiotics.

SUBSTITUTED JUDGMENT

Superintendent of Belchertown State School et al. v. Joseph Saikewicz

Joseph Saikewicz was a mentally incompetent resident of the Belchertown State School of the Massachusetts Department of Mental Health. In April 1976 Saikewicz was diagnosed with acute myeloblastic monocytic leukemia (cancer of the blood). He was 67 years old but had the mental age of about two years and eight months. The superintendent of the mental institution petitioned the court for a guardian ad litem (a temporary guardian for the duration of the trial). The court-appointed guardian recommended that it would be in the patient's best interests that he not undergo chemotherapy.

In May 1976 the probate judge ordered nontreatment of the disease based in part on findings of medical experts, who indicated that chemotherapy might produce remission of leukemia in 30% to 50% of the cases. If remission occurred, it would last between two and 13 months. Chemotherapy, however, would make Saikewicz suffer adverse side effects that he would not understand. Without chemotherapy, the patient might live for several weeks or months, but would die without the pain or discomfort associated with chemotherapy.

Saikewicz died on September 4, 1976, from pneumonia, a complication of the leukemia. Nevertheless, his case, *Superintendent of Belchertown State School et al. v. Joseph Saikewicz* (370 N.E.2d 417 [Mass. 1977]), was heard by the Massachusetts Supreme Court to establish a precedent on the question of substituted judgment (letting another entity, such as a court, ethics committee, surrogate, or guardian, determine what the patient would do in the situation were the patient competent).

The court agreed that extraordinary measures should not be used if the patient will not recover from the disease. The court also ruled that a person has a right to the preservation of his or her bodily integrity and can refuse medical invasion. The Massachusetts Supreme Court turned to *In re Quinlan* for support of its right of privacy argument.

THE RIGHTS OF AN INCOMPETENT PATIENT. Once the right to refuse treatment had been established, the court declared that everyone, including an incompetent person, has the right of choice. Referring to *Quinlan*, the court recommended that the patient not receive the treatment most people with leukemia would choose. (Unlike some later courts, the *Quinlan* court accepted the premise that a vegetative patient would not want to remain "alive.") The *Saikewicz* court believed that the "substituted judgment" standard would best preserve respect for the integrity and autonomy of the patient. In other words, the decision maker (in this case, the court) would put itself in Saikewicz's position and make the treatment decision the patient most likely would make were he competent. The court believed Saikewicz would have refused treatment.

In evaluating the role of the hospital and the guardian in the decision-making process, the *Saikewicz* court rejected the *Quinlan* court's recommendation that an ethics committee should be the source of the decision. The court instead concluded that the judicial branch of government was the proper venue.

Charles S. Soper, as Director of Newark Developmental Center et al. v. Dorothy Storar

John Storar, a 52-year-old intellectually and developmentally disabled man with a mental age of about 18 months, was diagnosed with terminal cancer in 1980. His mother, Dorothy Storar, petitioned the court to discontinue blood transfusions that were delaying her son's death, which would probably occur within three to six months.

At the time of the hearing, Storar required two units of blood about every one to two weeks. He found the transfusions disagreeable and had to be given a sedative before the procedure. He also had to be restrained during the transfusions. Storar's physician reported that after the transfusions, however, Storar had more energy and was able to resume most of his normal activities. Without the blood transfusions there would be insufficient oxygen in his blood, causing his heart to beat faster and his respiratory rate to increase, impeding normal activities.

The probate court granted Dorothy Storar the right to terminate the treatments, but the order was stayed and treatment continued pending an appeal to the New York Appellate Division (or appellate court). Storar died before the case, *Charles S. Soper, as Director of Newark Developmental Center et al. v. Dorothy Storar* (420 N.E.2d 64 [N.Y. 1981]), could be heard, rendering the decision moot, but because the issue was considered to be of public importance, the appellate court proceeded to hear the case.

The appellate court agreed with the probate court that a guardian can make medical decisions for an incompetent patient. Nevertheless, the parent/guardian "may not deprive a child of life-saving treatment." In this case there were two threats to Storar's life: the incurable cancer and the loss of blood that could be remedied with transfusions. Because the transfusions did not, in the eyes of the majority opinion written by Judge Sol Wachtler (1930–), cause much pain, the appellate court overturned the probate court's ruling.

Dissenting from this determination, Judge Hugh R. Jones (1914–2001) believed the treatments did not serve Storar's best interests. They did not relieve his pain and, in fact, caused him additional pain. Because the blood transfusions would not cure his cancer, they could be considered extraordinary treatments. Finally, Judge Jones reasoned that Storar's mother had cared for him for a long time and knew best how he felt, and therefore the court should respect her decision.

COMPETENT PATIENTS' WISHES
Michael J. Satz etc. v. Abe Perlmutter

Not all the cases of patients seeking to terminate life support concern incompetent people. Abe Perlmutter, aged 73, was suffering from amyotrophic lateral sclerosis (ALS; a degenerative neurologic condition commonly known as Lou Gehrig's disease). ALS is always fatal after prolonged physical degeneration, but it does not affect mental function.

Perlmutter's 1978 request to have his respirator removed was approved by the Circuit Court of Broward County, Florida. At a bedside hearing, the court questioned whether the patient truly understood the consequences of his request. Perlmutter told the judge that if the respirator were removed, "It can't be worse than what I'm going through now."

The state appealed the case before the Florida District Court of Appeals (appellate court), citing the state's duty to preserve life and to prevent the unlawful killing of a human being. The state also noted the hospital's and the doctors' fear of criminal prosecution and civil liability. In *Michael J. Satz, State Attorney for Broward County, Florida v. Abe Perlmutter* (362 So.2d, 160 [Fla. App. 1978]), the appellate court concluded that Perlmutter's right to refuse treatment overrode the state's interests and found in Perlmutter's favor.

THE STATE'S INTERESTS. An individual's right to refuse medical treatment is generally honored as long as it is consistent with the state's interests, which include:

- Interest in the preservation of life

- Need to protect innocent third parties

- Duty to prevent suicide

- Requirement that it help maintain the ethical integrity of medical practice

In the *Perlmutter* case, the Florida District Court of Appeals found that the preservation of life is an important goal, but not when the disease is incurable and causes the patient to suffer. The need to protect innocent third parties refers to cases in which a parent refuses treatment for him- or herself and a third party suffers, such as the abandonment of a minor child when the parent dies. Perlmutter's children were all adults and Perlmutter was not committing suicide. Were it not for the respirator, he would be dead; therefore, disconnecting it would not cause his death but would result in the disease running its natural course. Finally, the court turned to *Quinlan* and *Saikewicz* to support its finding that there are times when medical ethics dictates that a dying person needs comfort more than treatment. The court concluded:

> Abe Perlmutter should be allowed to make his choice to die with dignity. ... It is all very convenient to insist on continuing Mr. Perlmutter's life so that there can be no question of foul play, no resulting civil liability and no possible trespass on medical ethics. However, it is quite another matter to do so at the patient's sole expense and against his competent will, thus inflicting never-ending physical torture on his body until the inevitable, but artificially suspended, moment of death. Such a course of conduct invades the patient's constitutional right of privacy, removes his freedom of choice and invades his right to self-determination.

The state again appealed the case, this time to the Florida Supreme Court, which, in *Michael J. Satz etc. v. Abe Perlmutter* (379 So.2d 359 [Fla. 1980]), supported the decision by the Florida District Court of Appeals.

Shortly after this ruling, Perlmutter's respirator was disconnected, and he died of his disease on October 6, 1978.

THE SUBJECTIVE, LIMITED-OBJECTIVE, AND PURE-OBJECTIVE TESTS

In the Matter of Claire C. Conroy

Claire Conroy was an 84-year-old nursing-home patient suffering from "serious and irreversible mental and physical impairments with a limited life expectancy." In March 1984 her nephew (her guardian and only living relative) petitioned the Superior Court of Essex County, New Jersey, to remove her nasogastric feeding tube (a tube running from her nose into her stomach). Conroy's court-appointed guardian ad litem opposed the petition. The superior court approved the nephew's request, and the guardian ad litem appealed. Conroy died with the nasogastric tube in place while the appeal was pending. Nonetheless, the appellate court chose to hear the case *In the Matter of Claire C. Conroy* (486 A.2d 1209 [N.J. 1985]). The court reasoned that this was an important case and that its ruling could influence future cases with comparable circumstances.

Conroy suffered from heart disease, hypertension, and diabetes. She also had a gangrenous leg, bedsores, and an eye problem that required irrigation. She lacked bowel control, could not speak, and had a limited swallowing ability. In the appeals trial one medical expert testified that Conroy, although awake, was seriously demented. Another doctor testified that "although she was confused and unaware, 'she responds somehow.'"

Neither expert was sure if Conroy could feel pain, although she had moaned when subjected to painful stimuli. They agreed, however, that if the nasogastric tube were removed, Conroy would die a painful death.

Conroy's nephew testified that his aunt would never have wanted to be maintained in this manner. She feared doctors and had avoided them all her life. Because she was Roman Catholic, a priest was brought in to testify. In his judgment the removal of the tube would be ethical and moral even though her death might be painful.

The appeals court held that "the right to terminate life-sustaining treatment based on a guardian's judgment was limited to incurable and terminally ill patients who are brain dead, irreversibly comatose, or vegetative, and who would gain no medical benefit from continued treatment."

Furthermore, a guardian's decision did not apply to food withdrawal, which hastens death. The court deemed this active euthanasia, which it did not consider ethically permissible.

THE THREE TESTS. The court proposed three tests to determine if Conroy's feeding tube should have been removed. The subjective test served to clarify what Conroy would have decided about her tube feeding if she were able to do so. The court listed acceptable expressions of intent that should be considered by surrogates or by the court: spoken expressions, living wills, durable powers of attorney, oral directives, prior behavior, and religious beliefs.

If the court determines that patients in Conroy's circumstance have not explicitly expressed their wishes, two other "best interests" tests may be used: the limited-objective and the pure-objective tests. The limited-objective test permits discontinuing life-sustaining treatment if medical evidence shows that the patient would reject treatment that would only prolong suffering and that medication would not alleviate pain. Under this test, the court requires the additional evidence from the subjective test. The pure-objective test applies when there is no trustworthy evidence, or any evidence at all, to help guide a decision. The burden imposed on the patient's life by the treatment should outweigh whatever benefit would result from the treatment.

In January 1985 the court concluded that Conroy failed the tests. Her intentions, while perhaps clear enough to help support a limited-objective test (she had shown some evidence of a desire to reject treatment), were not strong enough for the subjective test (clear expressions of her intent). In addition, the information on her possible pain versus benefits of remaining alive was not sufficient for either the limited-objective test (her pain might outweigh her pleasure in life) or the pure-objective test (her pain would be so great it would be inhumane to continue treatment). Had Conroy survived the appellate court's decision, the court would have required her guardian to investigate these matters further before reaching a decision.

Justice Alan B. Handler (1931–), dissenting in part, disagreed with the majority's decision to measure Conroy's "best interests" in terms of the possible pain she could have been experiencing. First, in many cases pain can be controlled through medication. Second, pain levels cannot always be determined, as was shown in Conroy's case. Finally, not all patients decide based on pain. Some fear being dependent on others, especially when their bodily functions deteriorate; others value personal privacy and dignity.

CAN DOCTORS BE HELD LIABLE?
Barber v. Superior Court of the State of California

Historically, physicians have been free from prosecution for terminating life support. However, a precedent was set in 1983, when two doctors (Neil Barber and Robert Nejdl) were charged with murder and conspiracy to commit murder after agreeing to requests from a patient's family to discontinue life support.

Clarence Herbert suffered cardiorespiratory arrest following surgery. He was revived and placed on a respirator. Three days later his doctors diagnosed him as deeply comatose. The prognosis was that he would likely never recover. The family requested in writing that Herbert's respirator and other life-sustaining equipment be removed. The doctors complied, but Herbert continued to breathe on his own. After two days the family asked the doctors to remove the intravenous tubes that provided ANH. The request was honored. From that point until his death, Herbert received care that provided a clean and hygienic environment and allowed for the preservation of his dignity.

A superior court judge ruled that because the doctors' behavior intentionally shortened the patient's life, they had committed murder. However, the court of appeals found in *Barber v. Superior Court of the State of California* (195 Cal.Rptr. 484 [Cal.App. 2 Dist. 1983]) that a patient's right to refuse treatment, and a surrogate's right to refuse treatment for an incompetent, superseded any liability that could be attributed to the physicians.

In ruling that the physicians' compliance with the request of Herbert's family did not constitute murder, the court of appeals stated that "cessation of 'heroic' life support measures is not an affirmative act but rather a withdrawal or omission of further treatment." In addition, ANH also constituted a medical treatment.

WHAT ARE THE HOSPITAL'S RIGHTS?
Patricia E. Brophy v. New England Sinai Hospital

In 1983 Paul E. Brophy Sr. (1937–1986) suffered the rupture of an aneurysm (a part of an artery wall that weakens, causing it to balloon outward with blood) that left him in a PVS. He was neither brain dead nor terminal. He had been a fireman and an emergency medical technician and often expressed the opinion that he never wanted to be kept alive artificially.

Brophy's wife, Patricia Brophy, brought suit when physicians refused to remove or clamp a gastrostomy tube (g-tube) that supplied ANH to her husband. The Massachusetts Appeals Court ruled against Brophy, but in *Patricia E. Brophy v. New England Sinai Hospital* (497 N.E.2d 626 [Mass. 1986]) the Massachusetts Supreme Court allowed substituted judgment for a comatose patient who had previously made his intentions clear.

However, the Massachusetts Supreme Court did agree with the Massachusetts Appeals Court ruling that the hospital could not be forced to withhold food and water, which went against the hospital's ethical beliefs. Consequently, the Massachusetts Supreme Court ordered New England Sinai Hospital to facilitate Brophy's transfer to another facility or to his home, where his wife could carry out his wishes.

In October 1986 Brophy was moved to Emerson Hospital in Concord, Massachusetts. He died there on October 23 after eight days with no food. The official cause of death was pneumonia.

VITALIST DISSENSIONS. In *Brophy*, Justices Joseph Richard Nolan (1925–2013) and Neil L. Lynch (1930–2014) of the Massachusetts Supreme Court strongly disagreed with the majority opinion to allow withdrawal of ANH. Justice Nolan argued that food and water were not medical treatments that could be refused. In his view, food and water are basic human needs, and by permitting the removal of the g-tube, the court gave its stamp of approval to euthanasia and suicide.

Justice Lynch believed the Massachusetts Supreme Court majority had ignored what he considered to be valid findings by the Massachusetts Appeals Court, which found that Brophy's wishes, as expressed in his wife's substituted-judgment decision of withholding food and water, did not concern intrusive medical treatment. Rather, Brophy's decision, if he were competent to make it, was to knowingly terminate his life by declining food and water. This was suicide and the state was, therefore, condoning suicide.

In the Matter of Beverly Requena

Beverly Requena was a competent 55-year-old woman with ALS. She informed St. Clare's/Riverside Medical Center, a Roman Catholic hospital, that when she lost the ability to swallow, she would refuse artificial feeding. The hospital filed a suit to force Requena to leave the hospital, citing its policy against withholding food or fluids from a patient.

Requena was paralyzed from the neck down and was unable to make sounds, although she could form words with her lips. At the time of the hearing, she could not eat but could suck some nutrient liquids through a straw. Her abilities were quickly deteriorating, however.

The court did not question Requena's right to refuse nutrition, nor did the hospital question that right. That was a right that had been upheld in many previous cases. Nevertheless, reasserting its policy of refusing to participate in the withholding or withdrawal of ANH, the hospital offered to help transfer Requena to another facility that was willing to fulfill her wishes.

Requena did not want to transfer to another hospital. In the last 17 months, she had formed a relationship of trust in, and affection for, the staff. She also liked the familiar surroundings. The court found that being forced to leave would upset her emotionally and psychologically. The hospital staff was feeling stress as well. It was fond of Requena and did not want to see her die a presumably painful death from dehydration.

Judge Reginald Stanton (1933–2016) ruled in *In the Matter of Beverly Requena* (517 A.2d 869 [N.J.Super .A.D. 1986]) that Requena could not be removed from the hospital without her consent and that the hospital would have to comply with her wishes. He stressed the importance of preserving the personal worth, dignity, and integrity of the patient. The hospital may provide her information about her prognosis and treatment options, but Requena alone had the right to decide what was best for her. Following the ruling, the hospital honored Requena's request and stopped giving her artificial nutrition. She died in December 1987.

Bouvia v. Superior Court of Los Angeles County

In 1983, 26-year-old Elizabeth Bouvia, a mentally competent college-educated quadriplegic with cerebral palsy and painful arthritis, could neither support nor feed herself and required ANH to remain alive. Completely bedridden, Bouvia could not sit up, relied on other people for every need, was in significant pain, was unable to find any enjoyment, and could find no permanent place to live where her needs could be met. Citing the torment that her condition imposed on her, Bouvia wanted to cease being artificially fed and hydrated, and she wanted to be allowed to do so in a California public hospital so that doctors could manage her pain while she died.

The hospital refused Bouvia's request, and she continued to be fed through a nasogastric tube against her will as she pursued her cause in court. A Los Angeles County trial court upheld the hospital's refusal, denying Bouvia's request to be allowed to die in the hospital and mandating that she continue being force-fed rather than be allowed to refuse medical treatment "motivated not by a bona fide exercise of her right of privacy but by a desire to terminate her life." Bouvia's life expectancy, provided that she be fed either mechanically or by hand, was likely to exceed 15 years, and the court reasoned that the state's interest in preserving her life for such a substantial period outweighed Bouvia's right to determine her own fate.

Bouvia appealed the decision, and in *Bouvia v. Superior Court of Los Angeles County* (179 Cal. App. 3d 1127 [1986]) a California appeals court reversed the trial court's ruling. By the time of this second trial, Bouvia had attempted to live in a number of different housing settings and was currently residing in a second public hospital in Los Angeles County. The appellate judges reasoned that Bouvia was exercising the well-established right to refuse medical treatment, that her motives were not relevant, and that removal of the feeding tube would not constitute assisted suicide. The appeals court further argued that the trial court mistakenly emphasized the duration of time Bouvia could expect to live given continued medical intervention, while ignoring her concerns about the quality of her life during that time. The court ordered that the hospital remove Bouvia's feeding tube and prohibited doctors, nurses, and other hospital staff from replacing it or equipping her with any similar device.

Bouvia's feeding tube was removed. She lost weight and suffered from severe discomfort, but she reportedly found the process of starvation too painful to carry out, even with the help of medication. She began accepting ANH again, and she lived well beyond even the 15 years of life expectancy predicted at the time of her first court case. Nine years after first requesting the right to die, Bouvia told Beverly Beyette, in "The Reluctant Survivor: Nine Years after Helping Her Fight for the Right to Die, Elizabeth Bouvia's Lawyer and Confidante Killed Himself—Leaving Her Shaken and Living the Life She Dreaded" (LATimes.com, September 13, 1992), "I'm very bitter that in 1983 the decision was against me because in 1983 physically I was strong enough and was ready to go through (with starving herself)." As of 2017, although she avoided media attention, Bouvia was still believed to be alive.

WHAT ARE THE NURSING HOME'S RIGHTS?
In the Matter of Nancy Ellen Jobes

In 1980, 24-year-old Nancy Ellen Jobes was in a car accident. At the time, she was four-and-a-half months pregnant. Doctors who treated her determined that her fetus was dead. During the surgery to remove the fetus, Jobes suffered a loss of oxygen and blood flow to the brain. Never regaining consciousness, she was moved to the Lincoln Park Nursing Home several months later.

The nursing home provided nourishment to Jobes through a jejunostomy tube (j-tube) that was inserted into the jejunum (midsection) of her small intestine. Five years later Jobes's husband, John Jobes, asked the nursing home to stop his wife's artificial feeding. The nursing home refused, citing moral considerations.

The trial court appointed a guardian ad litem, who, after reviewing the case, filed in favor of John Jobes. The nursing home moved to appoint a life advocate (a person who would support retaining the feeding tube), which was turned down by the trial court. The New Jersey Supreme Court heard the case *In the Matter of Nancy Ellen Jobes* (529 A.2d 434 [N.J. 1987]).

DIFFERING INTERPRETATIONS OF PVS. Whether Jobes was in a PVS was hotly debated, which revealed how different medical interpretations of the same patient's condition can produce different conclusions. After John Jobes initiated the suit, his wife was transferred to Cornell Medical Center for four days of observation and testing. The neurologist Fred Plum (1924–2010) and his associate David Levy concluded, after extensive

examination and testing, that Jobes was indeed in a PVS and would never recover.

On the contrary, the neurologists Maurice Victor (1920–2001) and Allan H. Ropper testified for the nursing home. Having examined Jobes for about one-and-a-half hours, Victor reported that although the patient was severely brain damaged, he did not believe she was in a PVS. She had responded to his commands, such as to pick up her head or to stick out her tongue. However, he could not back up his testimony with any written record of his examination.

Ropper had also examined Jobes for about an hour and a half. He testified that some of the patient's motions, such as lifting an arm off the bed, excluded her from his definition of PVS. (His definition of PVS differed from Plum's in that it excluded patients who made reflexive responses to outside stimuli, a definition that would have also excluded Quinlan.) Testimony from the nurses who had cared for Jobes over the past years was also contradictory, with some asserting she smiled or responded to their care and others saying they saw no cognitive responses.

The New Jersey Supreme Court concluded that the neurological experts, especially Plum and Levy, "offered sufficiently clear and convincing evidence to support the trial court's finding that Mrs. Jobes is in an irreversible vegetative state." However, the court could find no "clear and convincing" evidence that Jobes, if she were competent, would want the j-tube removed. Jobes's family and friends, including her minister, had testified that in general conversation she had mentioned that she would not want to be kept alive with artificial life-support measures. The court did not accept these past remarks as clear evidence of the patient's intent.

With no clear and convincing evidence of Jobes's beliefs about artificial feeding, the New Jersey Supreme Court turned to *In re Quinlan* for guidance. The court stated, "Our review of these cases and medical authorities confirms our conclusion that we should continue to defer, as we did in *Quinlan*, to family members' substituted judgments about medical treatment for irreversibly vegetative patients who did not clearly express their medical preferences while they were competent. Those decisions are best made by the family because the family is best able to decide what the patient would want."

THE NURSING HOME'S RESPONSIBILITY. The New Jersey Supreme Court reversed the trial court decision that had allowed the nursing home to refuse to participate in the withdrawal of the feeding tube. The court noted, "Mrs. Jobes' family had no reason to believe that they were surrendering the right to choose among medical alternatives when they placed her in the nursing home." The court pointed out that it was not until 1985, five years after Jobes's admission to the Lincoln Park Nursing Home, and only after her family requested the removal of her feeding tube, that her family learned of the nursing home's policy. The court ordered the nursing home to comply with the family's request. Jobes died in August 1987 after the court ruling allowed her husband to have the feeding tube removed.

Justice Daniel J. O'Hern (1930–2009) dissented on both issues. He claimed that not all families may be as loving as Jobes's. He was concerned for other individuals whose families might not be so caring but who would still have the authority to order the withdrawal of life-sustaining treatments. He also disagreed with the order given the nursing home to comply with the family's request to discontinue Jobes's feeding. "I believe a proper balance could be obtained by adhering to the procedure adopted in *In re Quinlan* … that would have allowed the nonconsenting physician not to participate in the life-terminating process."

CLEAR AND CONVINCING EVIDENCE

Throughout the history of right-to-die cases, there has been considerable debate about how to determine a patient's wishes. How clearly must a patient have expressed his or her wishes before becoming incompetent? Does a parent or other family member best represent the patient? Are casual conversations sufficient to reveal intentions, or must there be written instructions?

In the Matter of Philip K. Eichner, on Behalf of Joseph C. Fox v. Denis Dillon, as District Attorney of Nassau County

Eighty-three-year-old Joseph C. Fox went into a PVS after a hernia operation. He was a member of the Society of Mary, a Roman Catholic religious order. The local director of the society, Philip K. Eichner, filed suit, asking for permission to have Fox's respirator removed.

In *In the Matter of Philip K. Eichner, on Behalf of Joseph C. Fox v. Denis Dillon, as District Attorney of Nassau County* (420 N.E.2d 64 [N.Y. 1981]), the court reasoned that "the highest burden of proof beyond a reasonable doubt should be required when granting the relief that may result in the patient's death." The need for high standards "forbids relief whenever the evidence is loose, equivocal, or contradictory." Fox, however, had discussed his feelings in the context of formal religious conversations. Only two months before his final hospitalization, he had stated that he did not want his life prolonged if his condition became hopeless. The court argued, "These were obviously solemn pronouncements and not casual remarks made at some social gathering, nor can it be said that he was too young to realize or feel the consequences of his statements." Following the ruling,

Fox's respirator was removed, and he died from congestive heart failure on January 24, 1980.

Fox's case was the first where the reported attitudes of an incompetent patient were accepted as "clear and convincing."

In the Matter of Westchester County Medical Center, on Behalf of Mary O'Connor

Not all patients express their attitudes about the use of life-sustaining treatments in serious religious discussions as did Fox. Nonetheless, courts have accepted evidence of "best interests" or "substituted judgments" in allowing the termination of life-sustaining treatments.

In 1985 Mary O'Connor had a stroke that rendered her mentally and physically incompetent. More than two years later she suffered a second major stroke, after which she had additional disabilities and difficulty swallowing. O'Connor's two daughters moved her to a long-term geriatric facility that was associated with the Westchester County Medical Center. During her hospital admission, her daughters submitted a signed statement to be added to her medical records. The document stated that O'Connor had indicated in many conversations that "no artificial life support be started or maintained in order to continue to sustain her life."

In June 1988, when O'Connor's condition deteriorated, she was admitted to Westchester County Medical Center. Because she was unable to swallow, her physician prescribed a nasogastric tube. The daughters objected to the procedure, citing their mother's expressed wish. The hospital petitioned the court for permission to provide artificial feeding, without which O'Connor would starve to death within seven to 10 days. The lower court found in favor of O'Connor's daughters. The hospital subsequently brought the case *In the Matter of Westchester County Medical Center, on Behalf of Mary O'Connor* (531 N.E.2d 607 [N.Y. 1988]) before the New York Court of Appeals.

O'Connor's physician testified that she was not in a coma. Although he anticipated that O'Connor's awareness might improve in the future, he believed she would never regain the mental ability to understand complex matters. This included the issue of her medical condition and treatment. The physician further indicated that, if his patient were allowed to starve to death, she would experience pain and "extreme, intense discomfort."

A neurologist testifying for the daughters reported that O'Connor's brain damage would keep her from experiencing pain. If she did have pain in the process of starving to death, she could be given medication. The doctor admitted, however, that he could not be "medically certain" because he had never had a patient die under the same circumstances.

The New York Court of Appeals majority concluded that although family and friends testified that O'Connor "felt that nature should take its course and not use further artificial means" and that it is "monstrous" to keep someone alive by "machinery," these expressions did not constitute clear and convincing evidence of her present desire to die. Also, she had never specifically discussed the issue of ANH. Nor had she ever expressed her wish to refuse artificial medical treatment should such refusal result in a painful death.

The court further noted that O'Connor's statements about refusing artificial treatments had generally been made in situations involving terminal illness, specifically cancer: her husband, two of her brothers, her stepmother, and a close friend had all died of cancer. Speaking for the court of appeals majority, Judge Wachtler stressed that O'Connor was not terminally ill, was conscious, and could interact with others, albeit minimally. Her main problem was that she could not eat on her own, and her physician could help her with that. Writing for the majority, Judge Wachtler stated, "Every person has a right to life, and no one should be denied essential medical care unless the evidence clearly and convincingly shows that the patient intended to decline the treatment under some particular circumstances. ... This is a demanding standard, the most rigorous burden of proof in civil cases. It is appropriate here because if an error occurs it should be made on the side of life."

THIS IS TOO RESTRICTIVE. Judge Richard D. Simons (1927–) of the New York Court of Appeals differed from the majority in his opinion of O'Connor's condition. O'Connor's "conversations" were actually limited to saying her name and words such as "okay," "all right," and "yes." Neither the hospital doctor nor the neurologist who testified for her daughters could say for certain that she understood their questions. The court majority mentioned the patient squeezing her doctor's hand in response to some questions, but failed to add that she did not respond to most questions.

Although O'Connor was not terminally ill, her severe mental and physical injuries (should nature take its course) would result in her death. Judge Simons believed the artificial feeding would not cure or improve her deteriorating condition.

Judge Wachtler noted that O'Connor had talked about refusing artificial treatment in the aftermath of the deaths of loved ones from cancer. He claimed this had no bearing on her present condition, which was not terminal. Judge Simons pointed out that O'Connor had worked for 20 years in a hospital emergency room and pathology laboratory. She was no casual observer of death, and her "remarks" about not wanting artificial treatment for herself carried a lot of weight. Her expressed wishes to her daughters, who were nurses and coworkers in the same

hospital, could not be considered "casual," as the majority observed. Judge Simons stated, "Judges, the persons least qualified by training, experience or affinity to reject the patient's instructions, have overridden Mrs. O'Connor's wishes, negated her long-held values on life and death, and imposed on her and her family their ideas of what her best interests require." O'Connor died 10 months later with the feeding tube still in place.

Daniel Gindes suggests in "Judicial Postponement of Death Recognition: The Tragic Case of Mary O'Connor" (*American Journal of Law and Medicine*, vol. 15, nos. 2–3, 1989) that the court made an error in its judgment. He concludes by stating that "artificial hydration and nutrition is not 'food.' It is a desperate treatment best used as a transition from acute crisis to normal functioning. This miraculous technology, misused, harms the very patients medicine purports to help. One can argue that the 'sanctity of life' is more offended by warehousing bodies, than by cessation of treatment. Incompetent patients, who have suffered structural damage to necessary nerve centers, do not get better. Feeding tubes cannot regenerate this fragile tissue. Perhaps one day doctors will be able to make people like Mary O'Connor well. Until then, they should leave them alone."

THE CASE OF NANCY BETH CRUZAN

Although *O'Connor* set a rigorous standard of proof for the state of New York, *Cruzan* was the first right-to-die case to be heard by the U.S. Supreme Court. It confirmed the legality of such strict standards for the entire country.

Nancy Beth Cruzan, by Co-guardians, Lester L. Cruzan Jr. and Joyce Cruzan v. Robert Harmon

In January 1983, 25-year-old Nancy Beth Cruzan (1957–1990) lost control of her car. A state trooper found her lying face down in a ditch. She was in cardiac and respiratory arrest. Paramedics were able to revive her, but a neurosurgeon indicated that she had "a probable cerebral contusion compounded by significant anoxia." The final diagnosis estimated that she had suffered anoxia (deprivation of oxygen) for 12 to 14 minutes. After six minutes of oxygen deprivation, the brain generally suffers permanent damage.

Doctors surgically implanted a feeding tube about a month after the accident, following the consent of her husband. Within a year of the accident, however, Cruzan's husband had their marriage dissolved. In January 1986 Cruzan became a ward of the state of Missouri.

Medical experts diagnosed Cruzan to be in a PVS and indicated that she was capable of living another 30 years. Cruzan's parents, Joyce and Lester Cruzan Jr., believed that their daughter would not want to live in a PVS sustained by a feeding tube and asked the hospital to remove the tube; hospital employees refused to do so. Because Cruzan was an adult, her parents had no legal standing in the courts, so they became the legal guardians of their daughter. They petitioned a Missouri trial court to have the feeding tube removed. The court gave Cruzan's parents the right to terminate ANH. However, the state and the court-appointed guardian ad litem appealed to the Missouri Supreme Court. Although the guardian ad litem believed it was in Cruzan's best interests to have the artificial feeding tube removed, he considered it his duty as her attorney to take the case to the state supreme court because it was a case of first impression (without a precedent) in the state of Missouri.

THE RIGHT TO PRIVACY. In *Nancy Beth Cruzan, by Co-guardians, Lester L. Cruzan Jr. and Joyce Cruzan v. Robert Harmon* (760 S.W.2d 408 [Mo.banc 1988]), the Missouri Supreme Court stressed that the state constitution did not expressly provide for the right of privacy, which would support an individual's right to refuse medical treatment. Although the U.S. Supreme Court had recognized the right of privacy in cases such as *Griswold v. Connecticut* (381 U.S. 479 [1965]) and *Roe v. Wade* (410 U.S. 113 [1973]), this right did not extend to the withdrawal of food and water. In fact, the U.S. Supreme Court, in *Roe v. Wade*, stressed that it "has refused to recognize an unlimited right of this kind in the past."

THE STATE'S INTEREST IN LIFE. In Cruzan's case the Missouri Supreme Court majority confirmed that the state's interest in life encompassed the sanctity of life and the prolongation of life. The state's interest in the prolongation of life was especially valid in Cruzan's case. She was not terminally ill and, based on medical evidence, would "continue a life of relatively normal duration if allowed basic sustenance." Furthermore, the state was not interested in the quality of life. The court was mindful that its decision would apply not only to Cruzan but also to others and feared treading a slippery slope. "Were [the] quality of life at issue, persons with all manner of handicaps might find the state seeking to terminate their lives. Instead, the state's interest is in life; that interest is unqualified."

THE GUARDIANS' RIGHTS. The Missouri Supreme Court ruled that Cruzan had no constitutional right to die and that there was no clear and convincing evidence that she would not wish to continue her vegetative existence. The majority further found that her parents, or guardians, had no right to exercise substituted judgment on their daughter's behalf. The court concluded, "We find no principled legal basis which permits the co-guardians in this case to choose the death of their ward. In the absence of such a legal basis for that decision and in the face of this State's strongly stated policy in favor of life, we choose to err on the side of life, respecting the rights of incompetent persons who may wish to live despite a severely diminished quality of life."

Therefore, the Missouri Supreme Court reversed the judgment of the Missouri trial court that had allowed discontinuance of Cruzan's artificial feeding.

THE STATE DOES NOT HAVE AN OVERRIDING INTEREST. In his dissent, Judge Charles B. Blackmar (1922–2007) indicated that the state should not be involved in cases such as Cruzan's. He was not convinced that the state had spoken better for Cruzan's interests than did her parents. He also questioned the state's interest in life in the context of espousing capital punishment, which clearly establishes the "proposition that some lives are not worth preserving."

Judge Blackmar did not share the majority's opinion that yielding to the guardians' request would lead to the mass euthanasia of handicapped people whose conditions did not come close to Cruzan's. He stressed that a court ruling is precedent only for the facts of that specific case. Besides, one of the purposes of courts is to protect incompetent people against abuse. He claimed, "The principal opinion attempts to establish absolutes, but does so at the expense of human factors. In so doing it unnecessarily subjects Nancy and those close to her to continuous torture which no family should be forced to endure."

"ERRONEOUS DECLARATION OF LAW." Judge Andrew J. Higgins (1921–2011), also dissenting, mainly disagreed with the majority's premise that the more than 50 precedent-setting cases from 16 other states were based on an "erroneous declaration of law." Yet, he noted that all the cases cited by the majority upheld an individual's right to refuse life-sustaining treatment, either personally or through the substituted judgment of a guardian. He could not understand the majority's contradiction of its own argument.

Cruzan v. Director, Missouri Department of Health

Cruzan's father appealed the Missouri Supreme Court's decision, and in December 1989 the U.S. Supreme Court heard arguments in *Cruzan v. Director, Missouri Department of Health* (497 U.S. 261 [1990]). This was the first time the right-to-die issue had been brought before the U.S. Supreme Court, which chose not to rule on whether Cruzan's parents could have her feeding tube removed. Instead, it considered whether the U.S. Constitution prohibited the state of Missouri from requiring clear and convincing evidence that an incompetent person desires withdrawal of life-sustaining treatment. In a 5–4 decision the court held that the Constitution did not prohibit the state of Missouri from requiring convincing evidence that an incompetent person wants life-sustaining treatment withdrawn.

Chief Justice William H. Rehnquist (1924–2005) wrote the opinion, with Justices Byron R. White (1917–2002), Sandra Day O'Connor (1930–), Antonin Scalia (1936–2016), and Anthony M. Kennedy (1936–) joining. The court majority believed that the Missouri Supreme Court's rigorous requirement of clear and convincing evidence that Cruzan had refused termination of life-sustaining treatment was justified. An erroneous decision not to withdraw the patient's feeding tube meant that the patient would continue to be sustained artificially. Possible medical advances or new evidence of the patient's intent could correct the error. An erroneous decision to terminate the artificial feeding could not be corrected, because the result of that decision (death) is irrevocable. The chief justice concluded, "No doubt is engendered by anything in this record but that Nancy Cruzan's mother and father are loving and caring parents. If the State were required by the United States Constitution to repose a right of 'substituted judgment' with anyone, the Cruzans would surely qualify. But we do not think the Due Process Clause requires the State to repose judgment on these matters with anyone but the patient herself." The due process clause of the 14th Amendment indicates that no state shall "deprive any person of life, liberty, or property, without due process of law."

STATE INTEREST SHOULD NOT OUTWEIGH THE FREE- DOM OF CHOICE. Dissenting, Justice William J. Brennan Jr. (1906–1997) pointed out that the state of Missouri's general interest in the preservation of Cruzan's life in no way outweighed her freedom of choice (in this case the choice to refuse medical treatment). He stated, "The regulation of constitutionally protected decisions . . . must be predicated on legitimate state concerns other than disagreement with the choice the individual has made. . . . Otherwise, the interest in liberty protected by the Due Process Clause would be a nullity."

Justice Brennan believed the state of Missouri had imposed an uneven burden of proof. The state would accept only clear and convincing evidence that the patient had made explicit statements refusing ANH. It did not, however, require any proof that she had made specific statements desiring continuance of such treatment. Hence, it could not be said that the state had accurately determined Cruzan's wishes.

Justice Brennan disagreed that it is better to err on the side of life than death. He argued that, to the patient, erring from either side is "irrevocable." He explained, "An erroneous decision to terminate artificial nutrition and hydration, to be sure, will lead to failure of that last remnant of physiological life, the brain stem, and result in complete brain death. An erroneous decision not to terminate life-support, however, robs a patient of the very qualities protected by the right to avoid unwanted medical treatment. His own degraded existence is perpetuated; his family's suffering is protracted; the memory he leaves behind becomes more and more distorted."

STATE USES NANCY CRUZAN FOR "SYMBOLIC EFFECT." In a separate dissenting opinion, Justice John Paul Stevens (1920–) believed the state of Missouri was using Cruzan for the "symbolic effect" of defining life. The state sought to equate Cruzan's physical existence with life. Justice Stevens, however, pointed out that life is more than physiological functions. In fact, life connotes a person's experiences that make up his or her whole history, as well as "the practical manifestation of the human spirit."

Justice Stevens viewed the state's refusal to let Cruzan's guardians terminate her artificial feeding as ignoring their daughter's interests, and therefore, was "unconscionable":

Insofar as Nancy Cruzan has an interest in being remembered for how she lived rather than how she died, the damage done to those memories by the prolongation of her death is irreversible. Insofar as Nancy Cruzan has an interest in the cessation of any pain, the continuation of her pain is irreversible. Insofar as Nancy Cruzan has an interest in a closure to her life consistent with her own beliefs rather than those of the Missouri legislature, the State's imposition of its contrary view is irreversible. To deny the importance of these consequences is in effect to deny that Nancy Cruzan has interests at all, and thereby to deny her personhood in the name of preserving the sanctity of her life.

***CRUZAN* CASE FINALLY RESOLVED.** On December 14, 1990, nearly eight years after Cruzan's car accident, a Missouri circuit court ruled that new evidence presented by three more friends constituted clear and convincing evidence that she would not want to continue existing in a PVS. The court allowed the removal of her artificial feeding. Within two hours of the ruling, Cruzan's doctor removed the tube. Cruzan's family kept a 24-hour vigil with her, until she died on December 26, 1990. Cruzan's family, however, believed she had left them many years earlier.

THE TERRI SCHIAVO CASE

Like Cruzan, the case of Terri Schiavo (1963–2005) involved a young woman in a PVS and the question of whether her ANH could be discontinued.

In 1990 Schiavo suffered a loss of potassium in her body due to an eating disorder. This physiological imbalance caused her heart to stop beating, which deprived her brain of oxygen and resulted in a coma. She underwent surgery to implant a stimulator in her brain, an experimental treatment. The brain stimulator implant appeared to be a success, and the young woman appeared to be slowly emerging from her coma.

Nonetheless, even though Schiavo was continually provided with appropriate stimulation to recover, she remained in a PVS years later. Her husband, Michael Schiavo, believing that she would never recover and saying that his wife did not want to be kept alive by artificial means, petitioned a Florida court to remove her feeding tube. Her parents, however, believed that she could feel, understand, and respond. They opposed the idea of removing the feeding tube.

In 2000 a Florida trial court determined that Schiavo did not wish to be kept alive by artificial means based on her clear and direct statement to that effect to her husband. However, Schiavo's parents appealed the ruling, based on their belief that their daughter responded to their voices and could improve with therapy. They also contested the assertion that their daughter did not want to be kept alive by artificial means. Schiavo had left no living will to clarify her position, but under Florida's Health Care Advance Directives Law, a patient's spouse was second in line to decide about whether life support should be suspended (after a previously appointed guardian), adult children were third, and parents were fourth.

Constitutional Breach?

By October 2003 Schiavo's parents had exhausted their appeals, and the Florida appellate courts upheld the ruling of the trial court. At that time, a Florida judge ruled that removal of the tube take place. Schiavo's parents, however, requested that the Florida governor Jeb Bush (1953–) intervene. In response, the Florida legislature developed House Bill 35-E (Terri's Law) and passed this bill on October 21, 2003. The law gave Governor Bush the authority to order Schiavo's feeding tube reinserted, and he did that by issuing Executive Order No. 03-201 that same day, six days after the feeding tube had been removed.

Legal experts noted that the Florida legislature, in passing Terri's Law, appeared to have taken judicial powers away from the judicial branch of the Florida government and had given them to the executive branch. If this were the case, then the law was unconstitutional under article 2, section 3 of the Florida constitution, which states, "No person belonging to one branch shall exercise any powers appertaining to either of the other branches unless expressly provided herein." Thus, Michael Schiavo challenged the law's constitutionality in the Pinellas County Circuit Court. Governor Bush requested that the Pinellas County Circuit Court judge dismiss Schiavo's lawsuit arguing against Terri's Law. On April 30, 2004, Judge Charles A. Davis Jr. (1948–) rejected the governor's technical challenges, thereby denying the governor's motion to dismiss. In May 2004 the law that allowed Governor Bush to intervene in the case was ruled unconstitutional by a Florida appeals court.

Continued Appeals

Schiavo's parents then appealed the case to the Florida Supreme Court, which heard the case in September 2004. The court upheld the ruling of the lower court, with the seven justices ruling unanimously and writing that Terri's Law was "an unconstitutional encroachment on the power that has been reserved for the independent judiciary." Nonetheless, Schiavo's parents continued their legal fight to keep her alive, so a stay on the tube's removal was put in place while their appeals were pending. In October 2004 Governor Bush asked the Florida Supreme Court to reconsider its decision. The court refused the request.

Attorneys for the Florida governor then asked the U.S. Supreme Court to hear the Schiavo case. The Supreme Court rejected the request, essentially affirming the lower court rulings that the governor had no legal right to intervene in the matter. In February 2005 a Florida judge ruled that Michael Schiavo could remove his wife's feeding tube in March of that year. On March 18, 2005, the tube was removed. Days later, in an unprecedented action, the U.S. House of Representatives and the U.S. Senate approved legislation, which was quickly signed by President George W. Bush (1946–), that granted Terri Schiavo's parents the right to sue in federal court. In effect, this legislation allowed the court to intervene in the case and restore Terri's feeding tube. Nonetheless, when Schiavo's parents appealed to the court, a federal judge refused to order the feeding tube reinserted. They then filed an appeal with the U.S. Supreme Court. Once again, the high court refused to hear the case.

The Effect of the Schiavo Situation on End-of-Life Decision Making

Terri Schiavo died on March 31, 2005. Her death and the events leading up to her death resulted in an intense debate among Americans over end-of-life decisions and brought new attention to the question of who should make the decision to stop life support.

Timothy Williams reports in "Schiavo's Brain Was Severely Deteriorated, Autopsy Says" (NYTimes.com, June 15, 2005) that the medical examiners who conducted Schiavo's autopsy found her brain "severely 'atrophied,'" weighing half the normal size, and noted that "no amount of therapy or treatment would have regenerated the massive loss of neurons." An autopsy cannot definitively establish a PVS, but the Schiavo findings were seen as "consistent" with a PVS.

THE CONSTITUTIONALITY OF ASSISTED SUICIDE

Washington v. Glucksberg

In January 1994 four doctors from Washington State, three terminally ill patients, and the organization

Compassion in Dying filed a suit in the U.S. District Court for the Western District of Washington. The plaintiffs sought to have the Washington Revised Code 9A.36.060(1) (1994) declared unconstitutional. This law states, "A person is guilty of promoting a suicide attempt when he knowingly causes or aids another person to attempt suicide."

The plaintiffs argued that under the equal protection clause of the 14th Amendment mentally competent terminally ill adults have the right to a physician's assistance in determining the time and manner of their death. In *Compassion in Dying v. Washington* (850 F. Supp. 1454 [W.D. Wash. 1994]), the district court agreed, stating that the Washington Revised Code violated the equal protection clause's provision that "all persons similarly situated should be treated alike."

In its decision, the district court relied on *Planned Parenthood of Southeastern Pennsylvania v. Casey* (505 U.S. 833 [1992]; a reaffirmation of *Roe v. Wade*'s holding of the right to abortion) and *Cruzan v. Director, Missouri Department of Health* (the right to refuse unwanted life-sustaining treatment). The court found Washington's statute against assisted suicide "unconstitutional because it places an undue burden on the exercise of a protected Fourteenth Amendment liberty interest."

In *Compassion in Dying v. State of Washington* (49 F. 3d 586 [1995]), a panel (three or more judges but not the full court) of the U.S. Court of Appeals for the Ninth Circuit reversed the district court's decision, stressing that in more than 200 years of U.S. history no court had ever recognized the right to assisted suicide. However, in *Compassion in Dying v. State of Washington* (79 F. 3d 790 [1996]), the court of appeals reheard the case en banc (by the full court), reversed the panel's decision, and affirmed the district court's ruling.

The en banc court of appeals did not mention the equal protection clause violation as indicated by the district court. Nevertheless, it referred to *Casey* and *Cruzan*, adding that the U.S. Constitution recognizes the right to die. Quoting from *Casey*, Judge Stephen R. Reinhardt (1931–) wrote, "Like the decision of whether or not to have an abortion, the decision how and when to die is one of 'the most intimate and personal choices a person may make in a lifetime, … central to personal dignity and autonomy.'"

THE U.S. SUPREME COURT DECIDES. The state of Washington and its attorney general appealed the case *Washington v. Glucksberg* (521 U.S. 702 [1997]) to the U.S. Supreme Court. Instead of addressing the plaintiffs' initial question of whether mentally competent terminally ill adults have the right to physician-assisted suicide, Chief Justice Rehnquist reframed the issue by focusing on "whether Washington's prohibition against

'caus[ing]' or 'aid[ing]' a suicide offends the Fourteenth Amendment to the United States Constitution."

Chief Justice Rehnquist recalled the more than 700 years of Anglo American common-law tradition disapproving of suicide and assisted suicide. He added that assisted suicide is considered to be a crime in almost every state, with no exceptions granted to mentally competent terminally ill adults.

PREVIOUS SUBSTANTIVE DUE-PROCESS CASES. The plaintiffs argued that in previous substantive due-process cases, such as *Cruzan*, the U.S. Supreme Court had acknowledged the principle of self-autonomy by ruling "that competent, dying persons have the right to direct the removal of life sustaining medical treatment and thus hasten death." Chief Justice Rehnquist claimed that, although committing suicide with another's help is just as personal as refusing life-sustaining treatment, it is not similar to refusing unwanted medical treatment. In fact, according to the chief justice, the *Cruzan* court specifically stressed that most states ban assisted suicide.

STATE'S INTEREST. The court pointed out that the state of Washington's interest in preserving human life includes the entire spectrum of that life, from birth to death, regardless of a person's physical or mental condition. The court agreed with the state that allowing assisted suicide might imperil the lives of vulnerable populations such as the poor, the elderly, and the disabled. The state included the terminally ill in this group.

Furthermore, the court agreed with the state of Washington that legalizing physician-assisted suicide would eventually lead to voluntary and involuntary euthanasia. Because a health care proxy's decision is legally accepted as an incompetent patient's decision, what if the patient cannot self-administer the lethal medication? In such a case a physician or a family member would have to administer the drug, thus committing euthanasia.

The court unanimously ruled that:

[The Washington Revised] Code … does not violate the Fourteenth Amendment, either on its face or "as applied to competent, terminally ill adults who wish to hasten their deaths by obtaining medication prescribed by their doctors."

Throughout the Nation, Americans are engaged in an earnest and profound debate about the morality, legality, and practicality of physician assisted suicide. Our holding permits this debate to continue, as it should in a democratic society. The decision of the en banc Court of Appeals is reversed, and the case is remanded [sent back] for further proceedings consistent with this opinion.

PROVISION OF PALLIATIVE CARE. Concurring, Justices O'Connor and Stephen G. Breyer (1938–) wrote that "dying patients in Washington and New York can obtain palliative care [care that relieves pain, but does not cure the illness], even when doing so would hasten their deaths." Hence, the justices did not see the need to address a dying person's constitutional right to obtain relief from pain. Justice O'Connor believed the court was justified in banning assisted suicide for two reasons, "The difficulty in defining terminal illness and the risk that a dying patient's request for assistance in ending his or her life might not be truly voluntary."

Vacco, Attorney General of New York et al. v. Quill et al.

REFUSING LIFE-SUSTAINING TREATMENT IS ESSENTIALLY THE SAME AS ASSISTED SUICIDE. In 1994 three New York physicians and three terminally ill patients sued the New York attorney general. In *Quill v. Koppell* (870 F. Supp. 78 [S.D.N.Y. 1994]), they claimed before the U.S. District Court for the Southern District of New York that New York violated the equal protection clause by prohibiting physician-assisted suicide. The state permits a competent patient to refuse life-sustaining treatment, but not to obtain physician-assisted suicide. The plaintiffs claimed that these are "essentially the same thing." The court disagreed, stating that withdrawing life support to let nature run its course differs from intentionally using lethal drugs to cause death.

The plaintiffs brought their case *Quill v. Vacco* (80 F. 3d 716 [1996]) to the U.S. Court of Appeals for the Second Circuit, which reversed the district court's ruling. The court of appeals found that the New York statute does not treat equally all competent terminally ill patients wishing to hasten their death. The court stated, "The ending of life by [the withdrawal of life-support systems] is nothing more nor less than assisted suicide."

REFUSING LIFE-SUSTAINING TREATMENT DIFFERS FROM ASSISTED SUICIDE. New York's attorney general appealed the case to the U.S. Supreme Court. In *Vacco, Attorney General of New York v. Quill* (521 U.S. 793 [1997]), the court distinguished between withdrawing life-sustaining medical treatment and assisted suicide. The court contended that when a patient refuses life support, he or she dies because the disease has run its natural course. By contrast, if a patient self-administers lethal drugs, death results from that medication.

The court also distinguished between the physician's role in both scenarios. A physician who complies with a patient's request to withdraw life support does so to honor a patient's wish because the treatment no longer benefits the patient. Likewise, when a physician prescribes painkilling drugs, the needed drug dosage might hasten death, although the physician's only intent is to ease pain. However, when a physician assists in suicide, his or her prime intention is to hasten death. Therefore, the court reversed the ruling made by the Court of Appeals for the Second Circuit.

Gonzales v. Oregon

In their *Quill* opinions, Justices Stevens and David H. Souter (1939–) let it be known that they thought there might be legal grounds for permitting physician-assisted suicide in certain cases. Oregon legislators had by that time already passed the Oregon Death with Dignity Act, and the act survived a number of challenges in state court. Voters reaffirmed the act via a 1997 referendum, and the act was implemented in 1998. In late 2001 the U.S. attorney general John D. Ashcroft (1942–) took aim at the Oregon law, reversing a decision made by his predecessor, Janet Reno (1938–2016), and asserting that the Controlled Substances Act of 1970 could be used against Oregon physicians who helped patients commit suicide by prescribing lethal drugs. The U.S. Drug Enforcement Administration could thereby revoke the prescription-writing privileges of any Oregon physician who prescribed drugs commonly used for assisted suicide, and those physicians would be subject to criminal prosecution. In response, the state of Oregon filed in November 2001 a lawsuit against Ashcroft's decision, claiming that he was acting unconstitutionally.

In April 2002, in *State of Oregon and Peter A. Rasmussen et al. v. John Ashcroft* (Civil No. 01-1647-JO), Judge Robert E. Jones (1927–) of the U.S. District Court for the District of Oregon ruled in favor of the Oregon Death with Dignity Act. The U.S. Department of Justice appealed the ruling to the U.S. Court of Appeals for the Ninth Circuit. In May 2004 the court of appeals upheld the Oregon Death with Dignity Act. The decision, by a divided three-judge panel, said the Department of Justice did not have the power to punish physicians for prescribing medication for the purpose of assisted suicide. The majority opinion stated that Ashcroft overstepped his authority in trying to block enforcement of Oregon's law.

In February 2005 the U.S. Supreme Court agreed to hear the Bush administration's challenge of Oregon's physician-assisted suicide law. On January 17, 2006, the court let stand in *Gonzales v. Oregon* (546 U.S. 243) Oregon's physician-assisted suicide law. The high court held that the Controlled Substances Act "does not allow the Attorney General to prohibit doctors from prescribing regulated drugs for use in physician-assisted suicide under state law permitting the procedure." Writing for the majority, Justice Kennedy explained that both Ashcroft and Alberto R. Gonzales (1955–), who succeeded Ashcroft as the U.S. attorney general, did not have the power to override the Oregon physician-assisted suicide law. Furthermore, Justice Kennedy added that the attorney general does not have the authority to make health and medical policy.

Baxter v. Montana

Physician-assisted suicide technically became legal in the state of Montana in 2009 via a court case rather than a legislative act, as in the other five states (California, Colorado Oregon, Vermont, and Washington) and the District of Columbia allowing the practice. The Montana court case was originally initiated at the district level by Robert Baxter, a 76-year-old Montana truck driver with terminal cancer. Four physicians and the organization Compassion & Choices joined Baxter in the case *Baxter v. State of Montana* (Case No. ADV-2007-787). Baxter had been battling leukemia for more than a decade and wished to end his life with prescribed medication. On December 5, 2008, Judge Dorothy McCarter ruled that the Montana constitution protected a mentally competent terminally ill patient's right to die with the help of medication prescribed by a physician. The ruling, which Baxter never heard, came the same day he died of his underlying disease.

The state of Montana appealed the ruling to the Montana Supreme Court in *Baxter v. State of Montana* (DA 09-0051 [2009 MT 449]). On December 31, 2009, the high court ruled 5–2 that physician-assisted suicide was not criminalized by either the Montana constitution or public policy. Although the court ruling protected physicians from prosecution in physician-assisted suicide, it did not declare that physician-assisted suicide is a right allowed to Montana residents. The high court left that debate to be settled in the state legislature.

OTHER HIGH-PROFILE CASES

Besides the many precedent-setting cases discussed in this chapter, there have been several high-profile cases centering on end-of-life and right-to-die issues that do not set legal precedent. Often, these cases make their way into the media based on the poignancy of the situations or the advocacy of individuals or organizations who believe the cases support right-to-die or pro-life stances.

For example, in December 2013, Jahi McMath, a 13-year-old girl who was in an Oakland, California, hospital undergoing a tonsillectomy, suffered cardiac arrest while on the operating table and was declared brain dead. McMath's family members were devout Christians, however, and they insisted that she was still alive as long as her heart was beating. Thus, the family pressed for the right to have McMath remain on a ventilator and receive ANH despite the fact that she was dead according to California law. McMath was kept on life support during the weeks-long court case before a judge finally ruled, in early January 2014, that the hospital could not be required to keep her alive by artificial means. The family ultimately won the right to keep McMath on life support while she was transported from the hospital to an undisclosed facility, where her body was being kept alive as of September 2017.

The McMath case neither raised new legal issues nor involved any controversial interpretation of existing issues. Instead, it created a media sensation in which McMath's family's claims that the young girl was still alive were frequently repeated uncritically by newscasters and journalists, and in which comparisons were drawn to cases such as that of Terri Schiavo. Schiavo, however, had not been brain dead but in a PVS, a condition raising very different and more contentious legal and ethical issues. Bioethicists lamented the media coverage of the McMath case, noting that it wrongly obscured the relevant ethical and legal issues. "The ability to get clear about brain death has been a real obstacle," Arthur Caplan, a bioethicist at New York University's Langone Medical Center, told Lee Romney in "Jahi McMath Case Muddies an Already Agonizing Subject" (LATimes.com, January 6, 2014). "This hasn't helped at all."

CHAPTER 10
THE COST OF HEALTH CARE

Advances in health care have revolutionized life in the developed world, eradicating or controlling once-fatal diseases, making infant and child mortality a rarity rather than a nearly universal occurrence, and extending average life spans dramatically. The elderly population in wealthy countries has accordingly grown, both in raw numerical terms and as a share of total population.

Although the health advances that have led to increased life expectancies represent one of humankind's greatest achievements, it is an achievement that has given rise to many new problems. In the United States, one of the largest unsolved problems relating to end-of-life care (and to health care in general), is cost. An aging population is a population with an ever-expanding need for medical care, and new technological and pharmaceutical advances are expensive, more so in the United States than in any other country.

THE HIGH COST OF HEALTH CARE
IN THE UNITED STATES

Most developed countries other than the United States manage their health care systems for the benefit of the public rather than as an ordinary part of the market economy. The United States, by contrast, has a predominantly private and market-based health care system, in which health care companies and caregivers are allowed to price their goods and services according to their interests as for-profit businesses or nonprofit foundations tasked with maximizing their efficiency. In the United States most people pay for their health care with private insurance policies that they obtain through their employers (who typically share costs with employees) or on their own, although a substantial proportion receive care subsidized through government programs. In other developed countries the government typically provides a base level of free or subsidized health care coverage to the entire population. Although other countries' systems may offer much of the same technology and pharmaceuticals as in the United States, and although their physicians and nurses receive the same level of training, their governments are able to exert greater influence on the market for health care and keep prices down. In the United States, by contrast, the government exerts less downward pressure on the price of health care.

Many advocates for the market-based health care system maintain that high health costs in the United States are a function not of insufficient government participation in the system but of insufficiently free markets. In this view, one main problem with the U.S. system is that consumers, accustomed to paying only part of the fees for the medical goods and services they obtain (while employers share the costs of insurance and insurers pay medical bills in full), do not make well-reasoned economic decisions in the realm of health care. In other words, when people know that they will get considerably more health care than they pay for on their own, they consent to more medical care than they need. If, according to this theory, Americans were more often forced to pay for service directly and in full, they would reason more efficiently and spend their money more wisely, and prices would fall system-wide as health care providers began to compete for customers on the basis of price.

Another frequently cited reason for the high cost of health care in the United States is the burden placed on hospitals and physicians by frivolous lawsuits. Doctors and facilities pay a great deal of money to insure themselves against malpractice claims, and they pass these costs along to consumers.

As Figure 10.1 shows, in 2014 average annual health care spending per person in the United States was $9,036, compared with $5,200 in Germany, $4,502 in Canada, $4,464 in France, $4,269 in Japan, $3,989 in the United Kingdom, and $3,271 in Italy. The much higher spending on U.S. health care did not translate into better health

FIGURE 10.1

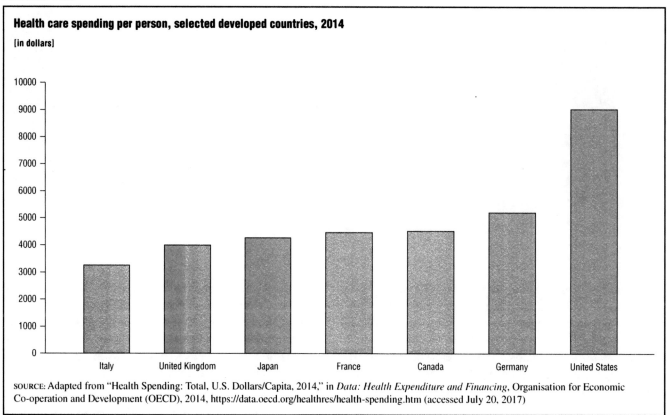

Health care spending per person, selected developed countries, 2014

[in dollars]

SOURCE: Adapted from "Health Spending: Total, U.S. Dollars/Capita, 2014," in *Data: Health Expenditure and Financing*, Organisation for Economic Co-operation and Development (OECD), 2014, https://data.oecd.org/healthres/health-spending.htm (accessed July 20, 2017)

outcomes across the population, however. In 2014 life expectancy at birth in the United States was 76.5 years for men and 81.3 years for women, compared with 78.7 years for men and 83.6 years for women in Germany, 79.5 years for men and 86 years for women in France, 80.5 years for men and 86.8 years for women in Japan, 79.5 years for men and 83.2 years for women in the United Kingdom, and 80.7 years for men and 85.6 years for women in Italy. (See Table 10.1; note that no data were available for Canada in 2014.)

The International Federation of Health Plans, the global health insurance industry's leading trade group, conducts an annual survey of health care costs worldwide. In *International Federation of Health Plans 2015 Comparative Price Report: Variation in Medical and Hospital Prices by Country* (2016, http://www.ifhp.com/s/2015-Comparative-Price-Report-090916.pdf), the group notes that for virtually every variety of medical service and treatment, from routine office visits to major surgery, the average price that insurers paid to health care providers was significantly higher in the United States in 2015 than in other developed countries. For example, in 2015 the average cost of one day in a hospital was $5,220 in the United States, compared with $2,142 in New Zealand, $765 in Australia, and $424 in Spain. Humira, a drug commonly prescribed to treat rheumatoid arthritis, cost an average of $2,669 per month in the United States, compared with $1,362 in the United Kingdom and $1,253

in Spain. The cost of bypass surgery (commonly used to reduce the risk of death from heart disease) averaged $78,318 in the United States, $32,480 in New Zealand, $28,888 in Australia, $24,059 in the United Kingdom, and $14,579 in Spain. (The International Federation of Health Plans notes that although its figures for the United States are based on averages from 370 million claims paid by multiple insurers, its numbers for other countries are based on one plan per country and thus may not reflect the overall average in those countries.)

These prices represent costs paid by insurers (including government insurance programs). In the United States and elsewhere, however, insurers may pay only part of the total cost of health care. Depending on the type of health plan someone is enrolled in, they may be expected to pay a premium (a set fee) on a regular schedule in order to be covered by insurance at all. Some insurance plans feature co-payments, meaning that their members must pay a portion of the total cost of whatever services they do use. Deductibles, which are also a feature of many health plans, require plan members to pay a certain amount of health care costs themselves each year before the insurer will step in to cover any remaining expenses. Premiums, co-payments, and deductibles are not exclusive to the U.S. health care system, but they are very common features of health insurance plans there. This means that the relatively high cost of care borne by insurers in the United States is also being passed on to consumers to some degree.

TABLE 10.1

Life expectancy at birth and at age 65, by sex, selected developed countries, 2014

[Data are based on reporting by OECD countries]

Country	Life expectancy, in years (2014)	
	Male	**Female**
At birth		
Canada	NA	NA
France	79.5[b]	86.0[b]
Germany	78.7[b]	83.6[b]
Italy	80.7	85.6
Japan	80.5	86.8
United Kingdom	79.5[a]	83.2[a]
United States	76.5	81.3
At 65 years		
Canada	NA	NA
France	19.7[b]	24.0[b]
Germany	18.2[b]	21.4[b]
Italy	19.2	22.8
Japan	19.3	24.2
United Kingdom	18.8[a]	21.3[c]
United States	18.0	20.6

OECD = Organisation for Economic Co-operation and Development

NA = data not available

[a]Data are estimated.

[b]Break in series.

[c]Until 1990, estimates refer to the Federal Republic of Germany; from 1995 onward data refer to Germany after reunication.

Notes: Differences in life expectancy may reflect differences in reporting and calculation methods, which can vary by country, in addition to actual differences in mortality rates. Therefore, ranks are not presented and comparisons among countries should be made with caution. Some estimates for selected countries and selected years were revised and differ from previous editions of *Health, United States*.

SOURCE: Adapted from "Table 14. Life Expectancy at Birth and at Age 65, by Sex: Organisation for Economic Co-operation and Development (OECD) Countries, Selected Years 1980–2014," in *Health, United States, 2016: With Chartbook on Long-term Trends in Health*, Centers for Disease Control and Prevention, National Center for Health Statistics, 2017, https://www.cdc.gov/nchs/data/hus/hus16.pdf (accessed July 16, 2017)

Additionally, many in the United States have no insurance coverage at all. Such individuals must pay their medical fees in full when they receive care. Payment in full of health care expenses, however, is beyond the means of many people in the United States, so many people without health insurance forgo health care except in emergency situations. Emergency medical care is much more expensive than routine preventive care, which can often treat illnesses before a patient's condition becomes critical. Unlike nonemergency physicians' offices, however, in the United States most emergency medical facilities are legally obliged to care for anyone in need, whether or not they can pay for the care that they receive. State and federal funds are typically used to reimburse hospitals for the emergency treatment of uninsured people. The cost of such treatment, which is passed on to taxpayers, is another significant driver of overall health care spending in the United States.

As Table 10.2 shows, health care spending in the United States has risen much faster than the population

has grown. Total national health expenditures stood at $27.2 billion in 1960, when the population was 186 million. By 2015 the population had grown by a factor of more than 1.7, reaching 321 million, but health expenditures had risen by a factor of nearly 118, to $3.2 trillion. In 1960 health care spending represented 5% of the gross domestic product (GDP; the total value of all goods and services produced in the country in a given year); by 2015 health care spending represented 17.8% of GDP.

Over this period the cost of health care has not only increased relative to previous eras but also relative to the costs of other goods and services. As measured by the consumer price index (CPI), a numerical value meant to quantify the cost of an average "basket of goods" for the purposes of measuring changes in prices, the cost of health care has risen more rapidly since the late 20th century than all other basic goods and services Americans typically purchase. (See Table 10.3.) Between 1960 and 2012 the cost of medical care as measured by the CPI rose by a factor of nearly 19, from 22.3 to 414.9. By contrast, the price of the next-most costly set of goods ordinarily purchased—energy (including both fuel for automobiles and electricity and gas for the home)—rose by a factor of just less than 11 during the same period. The prices of other goods, such as food and housing, while substantially more expensive in 2012 than in 1960, likewise rose much more slowly than the price of medical care.

By 2012 health care spending was a major financial burden for many families. Robin A. Cohen and Whitney K. Kirzinger of the National Center for Health Statistics report in "Financial Burden of Medical Care: A Family Perspective" (*NCHS Data Brief*, no. 142, January 2014) that 16.5% of U.S. families had trouble paying medical bills at some point in 2012 and 8.9% had medical bills that they were completely unable to pay at the time they were surveyed. More than one in four families (26.8%) reported that medical care represented a financial burden for their households, and 21.4% of families had made arrangements to pay medical debts over time. The financial burden of health care was, understandably, most pressing for those families with the least amount of income. Cohen and Kirzinger also examine the prevalence of financial burdens related to medical care according to income level. The poverty level is an income threshold below which a household is considered officially poor, according to the federal government. Those families making below 250% of the federal poverty level (FPL) were substantially more likely to have trouble paying their medical bills than those who made more than that amount. Sizable percentages of families making between 250% and 400% of the FPL struggled to pay their medical bills as well. Even among those with an income exceeding the FPL by 400%

TABLE 10.2

National health expenditures, selected years 1960–2015

Item	1960	1970	1980	1990	2000	2001	2002	2003	2004	2005	2006	2007	2008	2009	2010	2011	2012	2013	2014	2015
												Amount in billions								
National health expenditures	$27.2	$74.6	$255.3	$721.4	$1,369.7	$1,486.8	$1,629.2	$1,768.2	$1,896.3	$2,024.2	$2,156.5	$2,295.7	$2,399.1	$2,494.7	$2,596.4	$2,687.9	$2,795.4	$2,877.6	$3,029.3	$3,205.6
Health consumption expenditures	24.7	67.0	235.5	674.1	1,286.4	1,399.4	1,532.4	1,664.4	1,784.9	1,904.5	2,031.4	2,157.3	2,251.1	2,355.7	2,453.7	2,538.4	2,642.2	2,724.5	2,878.4	3,050.8
Personal health care	23.3	63.1	217.0	615.3	1,162.0	1,261.9	1,367.6	1,477.7	1,588.0	1,696.2	1,804.7	1,918.8	2,010.7	2,114.2	2,194.6	2,272.6	2,365.9	2,435.6	2,562.8	2,717.2
Government administration and net cost of health insurance	1.1	2.6	12.1	38.7	81.3	90.7	112.6	132.5	142.0	151.1	165.9	172.6	168.9	167.4	183.6	191.7	199.0	211.0	236.6	252.7
Government public health activities	0.4	1.4	6.4	20.0	43.0	46.8	52.2	54.2	54.9	57.2	60.8	65.9	71.5	74.1	75.5	74.2	77.2	77.9	79.0	80.9
Investment	2.5	7.5	19.9	47.3	83.3	87.4	96.8	103.7	111.4	119.7	125.2	138.4	148.0	139.0	142.7	149.5	153.2	153.0	150.9	154.7
U.S. population[a]	186	210	230	254	282	285	287	290	293	295	298	301	304	306	309	311	314	316	318	321
Gross domestic product[b]	$543	$1,076	$2,863	$5,980	$10,285	$10,622	$10,978	$11,511	$12,275	$13,094	$13,856	$14,478	$14,719	$14,419	$14,964	$15,518	$16,155	$16,692	$17,393	$18,037
												Average annual percent change from previous year shown								
National health expenditures		10.6%	13.1%	10.9%	6.6%	8.5%	9.6%	8.5%	7.2%	6.7%	6.5%	6.5%	4.5%	4.0%	4.1%	3.5%	4.0%	2.9%	5.3%	5.8%
Health consumption expenditures		10.5	13.4	11.1	6.7	8.8	9.5	8.6	7.2	6.7	6.7	6.2	4.3	4.6	4.2	3.5	4.1	3.1	5.6	6.0
Personal health care		10.5	13.2	11.0	6.6	8.6	8.4	8.0	7.5	6.8	6.4	6.3	4.8	5.1	3.8	3.6	4.1	2.9	5.2	6.0
Government administration and net cost of health insurance		9.4	16.4	12.4	7.7	11.5	24.2	17.7	7.2	6.4	9.8	4.0	–2.1	–0.9	9.6	4.4	3.8	6.0	12.1	6.8
Government public health activities		13.8	16.9	12.0	8.0	8.7	11.6	3.9	1.3	4.1	6.4	8.3	8.5	3.6	1.9	–1.8	4.2	0.9	1.4	2.4
Investment		11.6	10.2	9.1	5.8	4.9	10.8	7.2	7.4	7.5	4.5	10.6	6.9	–6.1	2.7	4.7	2.5	–0.1	–1.4	2.6
U.S. population[a]		1.2	0.9	1.0	1.1	1.0	0.9	0.9	0.9	0.9	1.0	0.9	0.9	0.9	0.8	0.7	0.8	0.7	0.8	0.8
Gross domestic product[b]		7.1	10.3	7.6	5.6	3.3	3.3	4.9	6.6	6.7	5.8	4.5	1.7	–2.0	3.8	3.7	4.1	3.3	4.2	3.7
												Percent distribution								
National health expenditures	100.0%	100.0%	100.0%	100.0%	100.0%	100.0%	100.0%	100.0%	100.0%	100.0%	100.0%	100.0%	100.0%	100.0%	100.0%	100.0%	100.0%	100.0%	100.0%	100.0%
Health consumption expenditures	90.8	89.9	92.2	93.4	93.9	94.1	94.1	94.1	94.1	94.1	94.2	94.0	93.8	94.4	94.5	94.4	94.5	94.7	95.0	95.2
Personal health care	85.5	84.6	85.0	85.3	84.8	84.9	83.9	83.6	83.7	83.8	83.7	83.6	83.8	84.7	84.5	84.5	84.6	84.6	84.6	84.8
Government administration and net cost of health insurance	3.9	3.5	4.7	5.4	5.9	6.1	6.9	7.5	7.5	7.5	7.7	7.5	7.0	6.7	7.1	7.1	7.1	7.3	7.8	7.9
Government public health activities	1.4	1.8	2.5	2.8	3.1	3.1	3.2	3.1	2.9	2.8	2.8	2.9	3.0	3.0	2.9	2.8	2.8	2.7	2.6	2.5
Investment	9.2	10.1	7.8	6.6	6.1	5.9	5.9	5.9	5.9	5.9	5.8	6.0	6.2	5.6	5.5	5.6	5.5	5.3	5.0	4.8
												Per capita amount								
National health expenditures	$146	$355	$1,108	$2,843	$4,857	$5,220	$5,668	$6,098	$6,481	$6,855	$7,233	$7,628	$7,897	$8,141	$8,404	$8,638	$8,915	$9,110	$9,515	$9,990
Health consumption expenditures	133	319	1,022	2,657	4,562	4,914	5,331	5,741	6,100	6,450	6,814	7,168	7,410	7,687	7,942	8,158	8,427	8,625	9,041	9,508
Personal health care	125	300	942	2,425	4,121	4,431	4,758	5,097	5,427	5,744	6,053	6,376	6,619	6,899	7,103	7,303	7,546	7,711	8,050	8,468
Government administration and net cost of health insurance	6	13	52	153	288	318	392	457	485	512	556	573	556	546	594	616	635	668	743	787
Government public health activities	2	6	28	79	153	164	182	187	188	194	204	219	235	242	244	238	246	247	248	252
Investment	13	36	86	187	295	307	337	358	381	405	420	460	487	453	462	480	489	484	474	482
												Percent								
National health expenditures as a percent of gross domestic product	5.0%	6.9%	8.9%	12.1%	13.3%	14.0%	14.8%	15.4%	15.4%	15.5%	15.6%	15.9%	16.3%	17.3%	17.4%	17.3%	17.3%	17.2%	17.4%	17.8%

[a] U.S. Bureau of the Census. Census resident-based population less armed forces overseas and population of outlying areas.
[b] U.S. Department of Commerce. Bureau of Economic Analysis.
Note: Numbers and percents may not add to totals because of rounding. Dollar amounts shown are in current dollars. Percent changes are calculated from unrounded data.

SOURCE: "Table 1. National Health Expenditures; Aggregate and per Capita Amounts, Annual Percent Change and Percent Distribution: Selected Calendar Years 1960–2015," in *National Health Expenditure Data: Historical*, Centers for Medicare and Medicaid Services, 2016, https://www.cms.gov/Research-Statistics-Data-and-Systems/Statistics-Trends-and-Reports/NationalHealthExpendData/NationalHealthAccountsHistorical.html (accessed July 24, 2017)

TABLE 10.3

Consumer price index and average annual percentage change for all items, selected items, and medical care components, selected years 1960–2012

[Data are based on reporting by samples of providers and other retail outlets]

Items and medical care components	1960	1970	1980	1990	1995	2000	2005	2011	2012
	Consumer Price Index (CPI)								
All items	29.6	38.8	82.4	130.7	152.4	172.2	195.3	224.9	229.6
All items less medical care	30.2	39.2	82.8	128.8	148.6	167.3	188.7	216.3	220.6
Services	24.1	35.0	77.9	139.2	168.7	195.3	230.1	265.8	271.4
Food	30.0	39.2	86.8	132.4	148.4	167.8	190.7	227.8	233.8
Apparel	45.7	59.2	90.9	124.1	132.0	129.6	119.5	122.1	126.3
Housing	—	36.4	81.1	128.5	148.5	169.6	195.7	219.1	222.7
Energy	22.4	25.5	86.0	102.1	105.2	124.6	177.1	243.9	246.1
Medical care	22.3	34.0	74.9	162.8	220.5	260.8	323.2	400.3	414.9
Components of medical care									
Medical care services	19.5	32.3	74.8	162.7	224.2	266.0	336.7	423.8	440.3
Professional services	—	37.0	77.9	156.1	201.0	237.7	281.7	335.7	342.0
Physician services	21.9	34.5	76.5	160.8	208.8	244.7	287.5	340.3	347.3
Dental services	27.0	39.2	78.9	155.8	206.8	258.5	324.0	408.0	417.5
Eyeglasses and eye care[a]	—	—	—	117.3	137.0	149.7	163.2	178.3	179.9
Services by other medical professionals[a]	—	—	—	120.2	143.9	161.9	186.8	217.4	219.6
Hospital and related services	—	—	69.2	178.0	257.8	317.3	439.9	641.5	672.1
Hospital services[b]	—	—	—	—	—	115.9	161.6	241.2	253.6
Inpatient hospital services[b,c]	—	—	—	—	—	113.8	156.6	236.6	248.8
Outpatient hospital services[a,c]	—	—	—	138.7	204.6	263.8	373.0	546.9	574.0
Hospital rooms	9.3	23.6	68.0	175.4	251.2	—	—	—	—
Other inpatient services[a]	—	—	—	142.7	206.8	—	—	—	—
Nursing homes and adult day care[b]	—	—	—	—	—	117.0	145.0	182.2	188.8
Health insurance[d]	—	—	—	—	—	—	—	105.5	118.3
Medical care commodities	46.9	46.5	75.4	163.4	204.5	238.1	276.0	324.1	333.6
Medicinal drugs[e]	—	—	—	—	—	—	—	105.5	108.6
Prescription drugs[f]	54.0	47.4	72.5	181.7	235.0	285.4	349.0	425.0	440.1
Nonprescription drugs[e]	—	—	—	—	—	—	—	98.6	99.3
Medical equipment and supplies[e]	—	—	—	—	—	—	—	99.3	100.6
Nonprescription drugs and medical supplies[a,g]	—	—	—	120.6	140.5	149.5	151.7	—	—
Internal and respiratory over-the-counter drugs[h]	—	42.3	74.9	145.9	167.0	176.9	179.7	—	—
Nonprescription medical equipment and supplies[i]	—	—	79.2	138.0	166.3	178.1	180.6	—	—
	Average annual percent change from previous year shown								
All items	...	2.7	7.8	4.7	3.1	2.5	2.5	3.2	2.1
All items less medical care	...	2.6	7.8	4.5	2.9	2.4	2.4	3.2	2.0
Services	...	3.8	8.3	6.0	3.9	3.0	3.3	1.7	2.1
Food	...	2.7	8.3	4.3	2.3	2.5	2.6	3.7	2.6
Apparel	...	2.6	4.4	3.2	1.2	−0.4	−1.6	2.2	3.4
Housing	...	—	8.3	4.7	2.9	2.7	2.9	1.3	1.6
Energy	...	1.3	12.9	1.7	0.6	3.4	7.3	15.4	0.9
Medical care	...	4.3	8.2	8.1	6.3	3.4	4.4	3.0	3.7
Components of medical care									
Medical care services	...	5.2	8.8	8.1	6.6	3.5	4.8	3.1	3.9
Professional services	...	—	7.7	7.2	5.2	3.4	3.5	2.3	1.9
Physician services	...	4.6	8.3	7.7	5.4	3.2	3.3	2.7	2.1
Dental services	...	3.8	7.2	7.0	5.8	4.6	4.6	2.3	2.3
Eyeglasses and eye care[a]	...	—	—	—	3.2	1.8	1.7	0.9	0.9
Services by other medical professionals[a]	...	—	—	—	3.7	2.4	2.9	1.4	1.0
Hospital and related services	...	—	—	9.9	7.7	4.2	6.8	5.6	4.8
Hospital services[b]	...	—	—	—	—	—	6.9	6.2	5.1
Inpatient hospital services[b,c]	...	—	—	—	—	—	6.6	6.8	5.2
Outpatient hospital services[a,c]	...	—	—	—	8.1	5.2	7.2	5.1	5.0
Hospital rooms	...	9.8	11.2	9.9	7.4	—	—	—	—
Other inpatient services[a]	...	—	—	—	7.7	—	—	—	—
Nursing homes and adult day care[b]	...	—	—	—	—	—	4.4	2.9	3.6
Health insurance[d]	...	—	—	—	—	—	—	−1.1	12.1
Medical care commodities	...	−0.1	5.0	8.0	4.6	3.1	3.0	3.0	2.9
Medicinal drugs[e]	...	—	—	—	—	—	—	3.1	3.0
Prescription drugs[f]	...	−1.3	4.3	9.6	5.3	4.0	4.1	4.2	3.6
Nonprescription drugs[e]	...	—	—	—	—	—	—	−1.3	0.7
Medical equipment and supplies[e]	...	—	—	—	—	—	—	0.3	1.2
Nonprescription drugs and medical supplies[a,g]	...	—	—	—	3.1	1.2	0.3	—	—
Internal and respiratory over-the-counter drugs[h]	...	—	5.9	6.9	2.7	1.2	0.3	—	—
Nonprescription medical equipment and supplies[i]	...	—	—	5.7	3.8	1.4	0.3	—	—

($92,200 for a family of four in 2012) or more, 16.6% considered themselves financially burdened due to medical care and 14.9% were paying medical bills in installments.

TABLE 10.3

Consumer price index and average annual percentage change for all items, selected items, and medical care components, selected years 1960–2012 [CONTINUED]

[Data are based on reporting by samples of providers and other retail outlets]

— Data not available.
... Category not applicable.
ªDecember 1986 = 100.
ᵇDecember 1996 = 100.
ᶜSpecial index based on a substantially smaller sample.
ᵈDecember 2005 = 100.
ᵉDecember 2009 = 100.
ᶠPrior to 2006, this category included medical supplies.
ᵍStarting with 2010 updates, this index series will no longer be published.
ʰStarting with 2010 updates, replaced by the series, Nonprescription drugs.
ⁱStarting with 2010 updates, replaced by the series, Medical equipment and supplies.
Notes: CPI for all urban consumers (CPI-U) U.S. city average, detailed expenditure categories. 1982–1984 = 100, except where noted. Data are not seasonally adjusted.

SOURCE: "Table 113. Consumer Price Index and Average Annual Percent Change for All Items, Selected Items, and Medical Care Components: United States, Selected Years 1960–2012," in *Health, United States, 2013: With Special Feature on Prescription Drugs,* Centers for Disease Control and Prevention, National Center for Health Statistics, 2014, https://www.cdc.gov/nchs/data/hus/hus13.pdf (accessed July 24, 2017)

The Affordable Care Act

It was in large part to relieve some of these financial burdens that President Barack Obama (1961–) made it a legislative priority to reform the U.S. health care system during his first term in office. The resulting Patient Protection and Affordable Care Act (commonly called the Affordable Care Act, or the ACA), which Obama signed into law in 2010, had provisions outlawing the insurance industry practice of denying coverage to those who were ill or otherwise in need of care, offering subsidized insurance policies to households making less than 400% of the FPL, and expanding Medicaid, the federally funded, state-administered program of health care coverage for low-income Americans. The Medicaid expansion was designed to offer coverage to all adults and children making less than 138% of the FPL, building on Medicaid's traditional mission of serving needy families with dependent children, pregnant women, the disabled, and other selected groups of low-income people (with variations in eligibility occurring at the state level).

The ACA reached full implementation in January 2014, but its success at expanding health care coverage to those in need remained mixed in the years that followed. One limit on the expansion of coverage came in the form of state opposition to the Medicaid expansion. As of July 2016, 18 states had chosen not to expand Medicaid. (See Figure 10.2.) Additionally, unrelenting opposition from Republicans and other opponents of the law had a significant effect on public perceptions of the ACA, possibly depressing the numbers of enrollees. Despite political resistance to the ACA, the U.S. uninsured rate experienced a steady decline between 2013 and 2015. (See Figure 10.3.) In *Health Insurance Coverage in the United States: 2015* (September 2016, https://www.census.gov/content/dam/Census/library/publications/2016/demo/p60-257.pdf), Jessica C. Barnett and Marina S. Vornovitsky of the U.S.

Census Bureau report that, during this span, the states that had expanded Medicaid coverage under the ACA saw more substantial declines in uninsured rates than did states that had not expanded Medicaid.

Although government subsidies and coverage expansions under the ACA were likely to relieve some of the financial burden felt by a number of poor and middle-class families, it was unclear what effect the law would have on overall health care costs at the national level. In spite of representing a significant enhancement of the government's role in the health care system, the ACA's reforms did not bring about a centralized system such as those that were in place in other wealthy countries. Private health care businesses—such as hospitals, insurance companies, and physicians' offices—were subject to new government regulations, but they remained central players in the health care marketplace.

MEETING THE END-OF-LIFE HEALTH CARE NEEDS OF THE ELDERLY

Kenneth D. Kochanek et al. of the National Center for Health Statistics note in "Deaths: Final Data for 2014" (*National Vital Statistics Reports,* vol. 65, no. 4, June 30, 2016) that out of the 2.6 million people who died in 2014, 1.9 million (73.1%) were aged 65 years and older. Most of these people were covered by Medicare, the federal government program offering universal health care coverage to those aged 65 years and older. As a major source of health care funding for the impoverished and disabled, Medicaid also plays a significant role in end-of-life care for Americans of all ages. Health programs under the U.S. Department of Veterans Affairs and the U.S. Department of Defense also pay for terminal care for some Americans. In addition, many older Americans make substantial out-of-pocket payments toward their medical expenses.

FIGURE 10.2

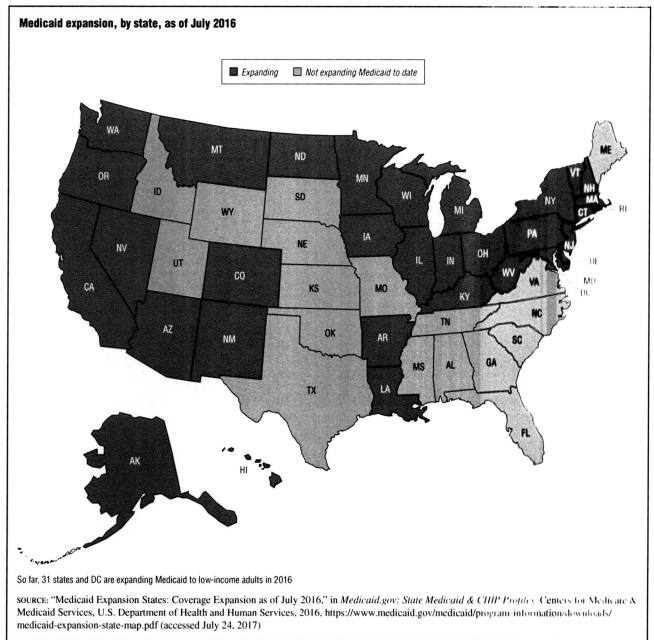

Medicaid expansion, by state, as of July 2016

Expanding   Not expanding Medicaid to date

So far, 31 states and DC are expanding Medicaid to low-income adults in 2016

SOURCE: "Medicaid Expansion States: Coverage Expansion as of July 2016," in *Medicaid.gov: State Medicaid & CHIP Profiles,* Centers for Medicare & Medicaid Services, U.S. Department of Health and Human Services, 2016, https://www.medicaid.gov/medicaid/program-information/downloads/medicaid-expansion-state-map.pdf (accessed July 24, 2017)

Medicare

Medicare is a major player in the overall medical marketplace and is among the primary sources of funding for end-of-life care, Medicare consists of a base program that is free for all eligible individuals as well as supplemental forms of fee-based coverage. Medicare's viability as a program has been brought into question as a result of rising health care costs and the rapid growth of the elderly population.

Enacted in 1965 as part of an amendment to the Social Security Act of 1935, Medicare went into effect in 1966 and has been subject to numerous additions and amendments since that time. As of 2017 Medicare was divided into two primary components: part A, or hospital insurance; and part B, or supplementary medical insurance. Part A covers costs related to hospital stays, temporary stays in skilled nursing facilities, home health care, and hospice care. Part A is free for all eligible individuals, although there are coverage limits beyond which participants may be required to share costs. Part B covers a range of preventive medical services and other medically necessary care not covered under Part A; most of these services and forms of care, by contrast with Part A, are delivered on an outpatient basis. Part B is optional for as long as participants have other health coverage through an employer or a spouse's employer, but thereafter individuals are subject to penalties if they do not participate in a Part B plan. Participants must reach a deductible under Part B coverage, beyond which Medicare pays for 80% of costs.

FIGURE 10.3

Uninsured rate by age, 2013–15

[Civilian noninstitutionalized population]

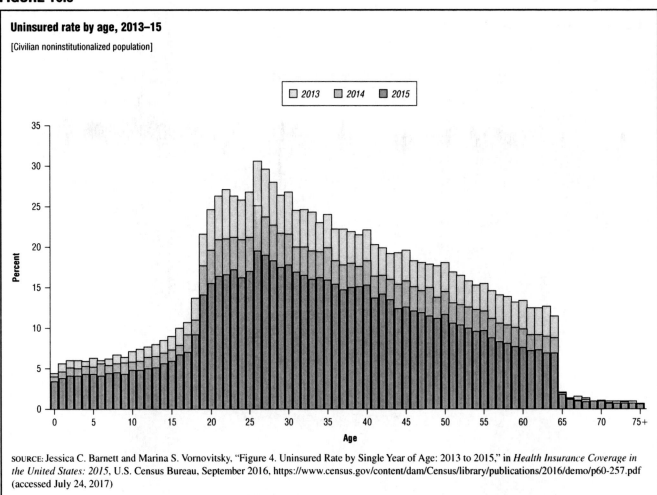

SOURCE: Jessica C. Barnett and Marina S. Vornovitsky, "Figure 4. Uninsured Rate by Single Year of Age: 2013 to 2015," in *Health Insurance Coverage in the United States: 2015*, U.S. Census Bureau, September 2016, https://www.census.gov/content/dam/Census/library/publications/2016/demo/p60-257.pdf (accessed July 24, 2017)

There is also a Medicare Part D, introduced in 2003 by the George W. Bush administration and implemented in 2006, which covers prescription drugs. Part D is significantly smaller, as a percentage of total costs, than Parts A and B, but it has rapidly become a major element of the overall Medicare effort. Additionally, there is a Medicare Part C, which consists of health plans offered by private insurers but managed under Medicare regulations. Part C is not truly separate from Parts A and B but represents, rather, a different way of accessing the benefits other people access under Parts A and B. Besides these basic components of Medicare, program participants may purchase Medigap insurance, a form of supplemental coverage that pays for services not covered under Parts A and B. Medigap policies are private insurance, not a government program.

As Table 10.4 shows, the number of Medicare enrollees increased by 171% between 1970 and 2015, from 20.4 million to 55.3 million. Medicare's board of trustees, who provide an annual report to Congress on the financial status of the program, predict that the number of Medicare enrollees will more than double between 2015 and 2085, rising to 112.6 million. (See Figure 10.4.)

The combination of rapidly rising prices for health care and a growing elderly population has resulted in massive increases in overall Medicare spending. In 1970 the total cost of providing seniors with health care coverage under Medicare was $7.5 billion; by 2015 the cost was $647.6 billion. (See Table 10.4.) The elderly have a disproportionate need for medical care, relative to the population as a whole. Those aged 65 years and older accounted for a little over 13% of the U.S. population in 2010. (See Figure 1.5 in Chapter 1.) Just five years later, in 2015, Medicare accounted for 22% of total health care spending in the United States. (See Figure 10.5.)

Medicare spending, like health care spending in general, has risen more rapidly than U.S. GDP since the 1970s. Between 1975 and 2005 Medicare spending grew from 1% of GDP to 2.6% of GDP. (See Figure 10.6.) Over the next decade continued growth of the elderly population together with the addition of the Part D prescription drug benefit drove accelerated spending, and by 2015 Medicare spending stood at 3.6% of GDP. Medicare's trustees projected that by 2085 Medicare spending will grow to 6% of GDP.

TABLE 10.4

Medicare enrollees and expenditures, by Medicare program and type of service, selected years 1970–2015

[Data are compiled from various sources by the Centers for Medicare & Medicaid Services]

Medicare program and type of service	1970	1980	1990	1995	2000	2005	2010	2012	2013	2014	2015[a]
Enrollees					Number, in millions						
Total Medicare[b]	20.4	28.4	34.3	37.6	39.7	42.6	47.7	50.9	52.5	54.1	55.3
Hospital insurance	20.1	28.0	33.7	37.2	39.3	42.2	47.4	50.5	52.1	53.7	54.9
Supplementary medical insurance (SMI)[c]	19.5	27.3	32.6	35.6	37.3	—	—	—	—	—	—
Part B	19.5	27.3	32.6	35.6	37.3	39.8	43.9	46.5	48.0	49.4	50.7
Part D[d]	—	—	—	—	—	1.8	34.8	37.4	39.1	40.5	41.8
Expenditures					Amount, in billions						
Total Medicare	$7.5	$36.8	$111.0	$184.2	$221.8	$336.4	$522.9	$574.2	$582.9	$613.3	$647.6
Total hospital insurance (HI)	5.3	25.6	67.0	117.6	131.1	182.9	247.9	266.8	266.2	269.3	278.9
HI payments to managed care organizations[e]	—	0.0	2.7	6.7	21.4	24.9	60.7	70.2	73.1	74.0	78.5
HI payments for fee-for-service utilization	5.1	25.0	63.4	109.5	105.1	156.6	183.3	189.2	184.7	186.4	191.5
Inpatient hospital	4.8	24.1	56.9	82.3	87.1	123.3	136.1	138.9	134.2	136.2	139.2
Skilled nursing facility	0.2	0.4	2.5	9.1	11.1	19.3	27.0	28.4	28.4	28.5	29.7
Home health agency	0.1	0.5	3.7	16.2	4.0	6.0	7.1	6.8	6.8	6.5	6.6
Hospice	—	—	0.3	1.9	2.9	8.0	13.1	15.0	15.2	15.2	15.9
Other programs[f]	—	—	—	—	—	—	—	2.8	3.5	3.7	2.6
Home health agency transfer[g]	—	—	—	—	1.7	—	—	—	—	—	—
Medicare Advantage premiums[h]	—	—	—	—	—	—	0.2	0.2	0.3	0.3	0.3
Accounting error (CY 2005–2008)[i]	—	—	—	—	—	-1.9	—	—	—	—	—
Administrative expenses[j]	0.2	0.5	0.9	1.4	2.9	3.3	3.8	4.3	4.7	4.9	5.9
Total supplementary medical insurance (SMI)[c]	2.2	11.2	44.0	66.6	90.7	153.5	274.9	307.4	316.7	344.0	368.8
Total Part B	2.2	11.2	44.0	66.6	90.7	152.4	212.9	240.5	247.1	265.9	279.0
Part B payments to managed care organizations[e]	0.0	0.2	2.8	6.6	18.4	22.0	55.2	66.0	72.7	85.7	93.8
Part B payments for fee-for-service utilization[k]	1.9	10.4	39.6	58.4	72.2	125.0	154.3	170.3	170.8	175.8	181.5
Physician/supplies[l]	1.8	8.2	29.6	—	—	—	—	—	—	—	—
Outpatient hospital[m]	0.1	1.9	8.5	—	—	—	—	—	—	—	—
Independent laboratory[n]	0.0	0.1	1.5	—	—	—	—	—	—	—	—
Physician fee schedule	—	—	—	31.7	37.0	57.7	63.9	69.5	68.6	69.2	70.3
Durable medical equipment	—	—	—	3.7	4.7	8.0	8.3	8.2	7.2	6.3	6.8
Laboratory[o]	—	—	—	4.3	4.4	6.9	8.4	9.2	9.1	8.2	8.5
Other[p]	—	—	—	9.9	13.6	26.7	34.2	38.4	38.3	39.5	41.1
Hospital[q]	—	—	—	8.7	8.1	18.7	27.6	33.6	36.2	41.5	43.7
Home health agency	0.0	0.2	0.1	0.2	4.5	7.1	12.0	11.4	11.4	11.1	11.1
Home health agency transfer[g]	—	—	—	—	-1.7	—	—	—	—	—	—
Medicare Advantage premiums[h]	—	—	—	—	—	—	0.2	0.2	0.3	0.3	0.4
Accounting error (CY 2005–2008)[i]	—	—	—	—	—	1.9	—	—	—	—	—
Administrative expenses[j]	0.2	0.6	1.5	1.6	1.8	2.8	3.2	4.0	3.4	4.1	3.3
Part D start-up costs[r]	—	—	—	—	—	0.7	—	—	—	—	—
Total Part D[d]	—	—	—	—	—	1.1	62.1	66.9	69.7	78.1	89.8
					Percent distribution of expenditures						
Total hospital insurance (HI)	100.0	100.0	100.0	100.0	100.0	100.0	100.0	100.0	100.0	100.0	100.0
HI payments to managed care organizations[e]	—	0.0	4.0	5.7	16.3	13.6	24.5	26.3	27.5	27.5	28.2
HI payments for fee-for-service utilization	97.0	97.9	94.6	93.1	80.2	85.6	73.9	70.9	69.4	69.2	68.6
Inpatient hospital	91.4	94.3	85.0	70.0	66.4	67.4	54.9	52.1	50.4	50.6	49.9
Skilled nursing facility	4.7	1.5	3.7	7.8	8.5	10.6	10.9	10.7	10.7	10.6	10.7
Home health agency	1.0	2.1	5.5	13.8	3.1	3.3	2.9	2.6	2.6	2.4	2.4
Hospice	—	—	0.5	1.6	2.2	4.4	5.3	5.6	5.7	5.6	5.7
Other programs[f]	—	—	—	—	—	—	—	1.1	1.3	1.4	0.9
Home health agency transfer[g]	—	—	—	—	1.3	—	—	—	—	—	—
Medicare Advantage premiums[h]	—	—	—	—	—	—	0.1	0.1	0.1	0.1	0.1
Accounting error (CY 2005–2008)[i]	—	—	—	—	—	-1.0	—	—	—	—	—
Administrative expenses[j]	3.0	2.1	1.4	1.2	2.2	1.8	1.5	1.6	1.8	1.8	2.1

In 2015 spending was almost identical on Medicare Part A ($278.9 billion) and Part B ($279 billion), while Part D accounted for the remaining $89.8 billion in spending. As Figure 10.7 shows, the components of Medicare spending have shifted over time. For example, in 2006 inpatient hospital treatment was the single largest category of Medicare spending, accounting for 31% of the total. That year, managed care was the second-largest expense to the program, accounting for 16% of all spending. Physician fees were the third-largest expense (15%), and Part D prescription drugs were the fourth-largest expense (11%). In 2015 spending on managed care was the largest expense (27%), followed by inpatient hospital care (22%), Part D prescription drugs (14%), and physician fees (11%).

Although most Medicare beneficiaries are aged 65 years and older, some nonelderly disabled people and nonelderly people with end-stage renal disease qualify for benefits. (End-stage renal disease is the final phase

TABLE 10.4

Medicare enrollees and expenditures, by Medicare program and type of service, selected years 1970–2015 [CONTINUED]

[Data are compiled from various sources by the Centers for Medicare & Medicaid Services]

Medicare program and type of service	1970	1980	1990	1995	2000	2005	2010	2012	2013	2014	2015[a]
Total supplementary medical insurance (SMI)[c]	100.0	100.0	100.0	100.0	100.0	100.0	100.0	100.0	100.0	100.0	100.0
Total Part B	100.0	100.0	100.0	100.0	100.0	99.3	77.4	78.2	78.0	77.3	75.6
Part B payments to managed care organizations[e]	1.2	1.8	6.4	9.9	20.2	14.3	20.1	21.5	22.9	24.9	25.4
Part B payments for fee-for-service utilization[k]	88.1	92.8	90.1	87.6	79.6	81.5	56.1	55.4	53.9	51.1	49.2
Physician/supplies[l]	80.9	72.8	67.3	—	—	—	—	—	—	—	—
Outpatient hospital[m]	5.2	16.9	19.3	—	—	—	—	—	—	—	—
Independent laboratory[n]	0.5	1.0	3.4	—	—	—	—	—	—	—	—
Physician fee schedule	—	—	—	47.5	40.8	37.6	23.2	22.6	21.7	20.1	19.1
Durable medical equipment	—	—	—	5.5	5.2	5.2	3.0	2.7	2.3	1.8	1.8
Laboratory[o]	—	—	—	6.4	4.8	4.5	3.1	3.0	2.9	2.4	2.3
Other[p]	—	—	—	14.8	15.0	17.4	12.4	12.5	12.1	11.5	11.1
Hospital[q]	—	—	—	13.0	8.9	12.2	10.0	10.9	11.4	12.1	11.9
Home health agency	1.5	2.1	0.2	0.3	4.9	4.6	4.4	3.7	3.6	3.2	3.0
Home health agency transfer[g]	—	—	—	—	−1.9	—	—	—	—	—	—
Medicare Advantage premiums[h]	—	—	—	—	—	—	0.1	0.1	0.1	0.1	0.1
Accounting error (CY 2005–2008)[i]	—	—	—	—	—	1.2	—	—	—	—	—
Administrative expenses[j]	10.7	5.4	3.5	2.4	2.0	1.8	1.2	1.3	1.1	1.2	0.9
Part D start-up costs[r]	—	—	—	—	—	0.4	—	—	—	—	—
Total Part D[d]	—	—	—	—	—	0.7	22.6	21.8	22.0	22.7	24.4

CY = calendar year.

NA = category not applicable or data not available.

[a]Preliminary estimates.

[b]Average number enrolled in the hospital insurance (HI) and/or supplementary medical insurance (SMI) programs for the period.

[c]Starting with 2004 data, the SMI trust fund consists of two separate accounts: Part B (which pays for a portion of the costs of physicians' services, outpatient hospital services, and other related medical and health services for voluntarily enrolled individuals) and Part D (Medicare Prescription Drug Account, which pays private plans to provide prescription drug coverage). The Medicare Modernization Act, enacted December 8, 2003, established within SMI two Part D accounts related to prescription drug benefits: the Medicare Prescription Drug Account and the Transitional Assistance Account. The Medicare Prescription Drug Account is used in conjunction with the broad, voluntary prescription drug benefits that began in 2006. The Transitional Assistance Account was used to provide transitional assistance benefits, beginning in 2004 and extending through 2005, for certain low-income beneficiaries prior to the start of the new prescription drug benefit. The amounts shown for Total Part D expenditures–and thus for total SMI expenditures and total Medicare expenditures—for 2006 and later years include estimated amounts for premiums paid directly from Part D beneficiaries to Part D prescription drug plans.

[e]Medicare-approved managed care organizations.

[f]Includes Community-Based Care Transitions Program ($0.1 billion in each of 2011–2015) and Electronic Health Records Incentive Program ($0.7 billion in 2011, $2.7 billion in 2012, $3.4 billion in 2013, $3.6 billion in 2014, and $2.5 billion in 2015).

[g]For 1998 to 2003, data reflects annual home health HI to SMI transfer amounts.

[h]When a beneficiary chooses a Medicare Advantage plan whose monthly premium exceeds the benchmark amount, the additional premiums (that is, amounts beyond those paid by Medicare to the plan) are the responsibility of the beneficiary. Beneficiaries subject to such premiums may choose to either reimburse the plans directly or have the additional premiums deducted from their Social Security checks. The amounts shown here are only those additional premiums deducted from Social Security checks. These amounts are transferred to the HI trust and SMI trust funds and then transferred from the trust funds to the plans.

[i]Represents misallocation of benefit payments between the HI trust fund and the Part B account of the SMI trust fund from May 2005 to September 2007, and the transfer made in June 2008 to correct the misallocation.

[j]Includes expenditures for research, experiments and demonstration projects, peer review activity (performed by Peer Review Organizations from 1983 to 2001 and by Quality Review Organizations from 2002 to present), and to combat and prevent fraud and abuse.

[k]Type-of-service reporting categories for fee-for-service reimbursement differ before and after 1991.

[l]Includes payment for physicians, practitioners, durable medical equipment, and all suppliers other than independent laboratory through 1990. Starting with 1991 data, physician services subject to the physician fee schedule are shown. Payments for laboratory services paid under the laboratory fee schedule and performed in a physician office are included under Laboratory beginning in 1991. Payments for durable medical equipment are shown separately beginning in 1991. The remaining services from the Physician/supplier category are included in Other.

[m]Includes payments for hospital outpatient department services, skilled nursing facility outpatient services, Part B services received as an inpatient in a hospital or skilled nursing facility setting, and other types of outpatient facilities. Starting with 1991 data, payments for hospital outpatient department services, except for laboratory services, are listed under Hospital. Hospital outpatient laboratory services are included in the Laboratory line.

[n]Starting with 1991 data, those independent laboratory services that were paid under the laboratory fee schedule (most of the independent laboratory category) are included in the Laboratory line; the remaining services are included in the Physician fee schedule and Other lines.

[o]Payments for laboratory services paid under the laboratory fee schedule performed in a physician office, independent laboratory, or in a hospital outpatient department.

[p]Includes payments for physician-administered drugs; freestanding ambulatory surgical center facility services; ambulance services; supplies; freestanding end-stage renal disease (ESRD) dialysis facility services; rural health clinics; outpatient rehabilitation facilities; psychiatric hospitals; and federally qualified health centers.

[q]Includes the hospital facility costs for Medicare Part B services that are predominantly in the outpatient department, with the exception of hospital outpatient laboratory services, which are included on the Laboratory line. Physician reimbursement is included on the Physician fee schedule line.

[r]Part D start-up costs were funded through the SMI Part B account in 2004–2008.

Notes: Estimates are subject to change as more recent data become available. Totals may not equal the sum of the components because of rounding. Estimates are for Medicare-covered services furnished to Medicare enrollees residing in the United States, Puerto Rico, Virgin Islands, Guam, other outlying areas, foreign countries, and unknown residence. Estimates in this table have been revised and differ from previous editions of Health, United States. 0.0 represents the quantity more than zero but less than 0.05.

SOURCE: "Table 107. Medicare Enrollees and Expenditures and Percent Distribution, by Medicare Program and Type of Service: United States and Other Areas, Selected Years 1970–2015," in Health, United States, 2016: With Chartbook on Long-term Trends in Health, Centers for Disease Control and Prevention, National Center for Health Statistics, 2017, https://www.cdc.gov/nchs/data/hus/hus16.pdf (accessed July 16, 2017)

of irreversible kidney disease and requires either kidney transplantation or dialysis, a medical procedure in which a machine performs the diseased organ's functions.)

As Figure 10.8 shows, 82.7% of those in the Medicare population in 2013 were aged 65 years and older, while 16.3% were disabled and 0.9% had end-stage renal

FIGURE 10.4

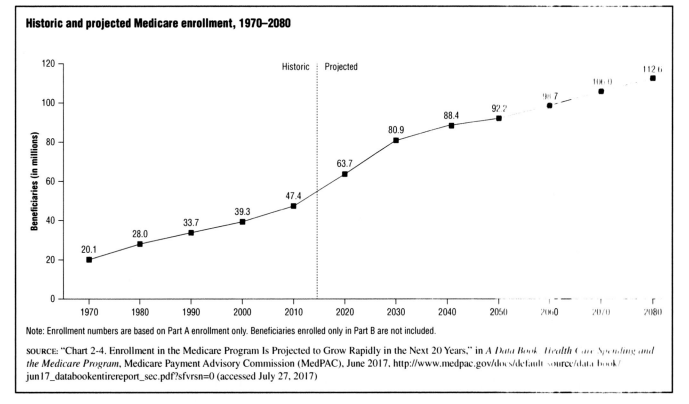

Historic and projected Medicare enrollment, 1970–2080

Note: Enrollment numbers are based on Part A enrollment only. Beneficiaries enrolled only in Part B are not included.

SOURCE: "Chart 2-4. Enrollment in the Medicare Program Is Projected to Grow Rapidly in the Next 20 Years," in *A Data Book: Health Care Spending and the Medicare Program,* Medicare Payment Advisory Commission (MedPAC), June 2017, http://www.medpac.gov/docs/default-source/data-book/jun17_databookentirereport_sec.pdf?sfvrsn=0 (accessed July 27, 2017)

disease. The beneficiaries with disabilities accounted for a slightly disproportionate amount of spending (18.5%) relative to their share of the overall Medicare population, and those beneficiaries with end-stage renal disease accounted for a significantly disproportionate amount of spending, at 5.6% of the total. By age, the costliest groups to cover under Medicare in 2013 were those under the age of 65 years (who were either disabled or had end-stage renal disease) and those aged 75 years and older. (See Figure 10.9.) Those aged 65 to 74 years accounted for 45.9% of the Medicare population but only 34.7% of total spending.

Elderly Medicaid Beneficiaries

Medicaid is not primarily a program for the elderly, but some impoverished people aged 65 years and older are covered by both Medicare and Medicaid. These beneficiaries tend to be unable to afford supplemental Medicare coverage, and they are among the most expensive of Medicaid patients to insure. As Table 10.5 shows, those aged 65 years and older accounted for 5.6% of Medicaid's 73.7 million beneficiaries in 2013. Although the average yearly payment per Medicaid beneficiary was $5,094, the average payment per elderly Medicaid beneficiary was $15,194.

Hospice Care

In 1982 Congress created a Medicare hospice benefit program, via the Tax Equity and Fiscal Responsibility Act, to provide services to terminally ill patients with an anticipated

six months or less to live. In 1989 the U.S. General Accounting Office (GAO; now called the U.S. Government Accountability Office) reported that only 35% of eligible hospices were Medicare certified, in part due to the Health Care Financing Administration's low rates of reimbursement to hospices. That same year Congress gave hospices a 20% increase in reimbursement rates through a provision in the Omnibus Budget Reconciliation Act.

Under the Balanced Budget Act (BBA) of 1997, Medicare hospice benefits are divided into three benefit periods:

- An initial 90-day period

- A subsequent 90-day period

- An unlimited number of subsequent 60-day periods, but only if a patient continues to satisfy the program eligibility requirements

At the start of each period the Medicare patient must be recertified as terminally ill. After the patient's death, the patient's family receives up to 13 months of bereavement counseling.

Statistics on Medicare and Medicaid usage are published annually by the Centers for Medicare and Medicaid Services (CMS), and are aggregated on the agency's "CMS Statistics Reference Booklet" (November, 23, 2015, https://www.cms.gov/Research-Statistics-Data-and-Systems/Statistics-Trends-and-Reports/CMS-Statistics-Reference-Booklet/) website. According to the 2015 and

FIGURE 10.5

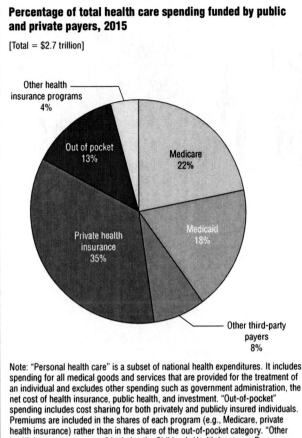

Percentage of total health care spending funded by public and private payers, 2015

[Total = $2.7 trillion]

- Other health insurance programs 4%
- Out of pocket 13%
- Medicare 22%
- Private health insurance 35%
- Medicaid 18%
- Other third-party payers 8%

Note: "Personal health care" is a subset of national health expenditures. It includes spending for all medical goods and services that are provided for the treatment of an individual and excludes other spending such as government administration, the net cost of health insurance, public health, and investment. "Out-of-pocket" spending includes cost sharing for both privately and publicly insured individuals. Premiums are included in the shares of each program (e.g., Medicare, private health insurance) rather than in the share of the out-of-pocket category. "Other health insurance programs" includes the Children's Health Insurance Program, Department of Defense, and Department of Veterans Affairs. "Other third-party payers" includes worksite health care, other private revenues, Indian Health Service, workers' compensation, general assistance, maternal and child health, vocational rehabilitation, other federal programs, Substance Abuse and Mental Health Services Administration, other state and local programs, and school health.

SOURCE: "Chart 1–1. Medicare Was the Largest Single Purchaser of Personal Health Care, 2015," in *A Data Book: Health Care Spending and the Medicare Program*, Medicare Payment Advisory Commission (MedPAC), June 2017, http://www.medpac.gov/docs/default-source/data-book/jun17_-databookentirereport_sec.pdf?sfvrsn=0 (accessed July 27, 2017)

2016 reports, in 2015 there were 4,302 Medicare-certified hospices serving nearly 1.4 million patients in the United States. At that time Medicare paid most of the cost of hospice care. Patients receiving care in a hospice incurred lower Medicare costs than those being cared for in a hospital or skilled nursing facility. For example, in fiscal year (FY) 2015 Medicare paid $16.1 billion in benefits for 1.4 million hospice patients, an average of $11,500 per patient. By comparison, Medicare paid $29.9 billion in benefits to 1.8 million patients living in skilled nursing facilities ($16,611 per patient) and $136.4 billion in benefits to 6.6 billion people receiving inpatient hospital care ($20,666 per patient).

Home Health Care

The concept of home health care began as postacute care after hospitalization, an alternative to longer, costlier hospital stays. The CMS explains in "Home Health PPS" (August 23, 2017, https://www.cms.gov/Medicare/Medicare-Fee-for-Service-Payment/HomeHealthPPS/index.html) that in the 21st century Medicare's home health care services provide medical help, prescribed by a doctor, to home-bound people who are covered by Medicare. Having been hospitalized is not a prerequisite. There are no limits to the number of professional visits or to the length of coverage. As long as the patient's condition warrants it, the following services are provided:

- Part-time or intermittent skilled nursing and home health aide services

- Speech-language pathology services

- Physical and occupational therapy

- Medical social services

- Medical supplies

- Durable medical equipment (such as walkers and hospital beds, with a 20% co-pay)

The CMS notes in *2016 CMS Statistics* that there were 12,149 Medicare-certified home health agencies in 2015. However, Medicare coverage of home health needs tends to be temporary. Those patients who have a protracted need for constant medical attention in the home must typically find other funding sources.

Long-Term Care

Longer life spans and improved life-sustaining technologies have created an increasing need for long-term care, usually defined as care that is continuously ongoing for an average of three years. The Kaiser Family Foundation (KFF) estimates in "A Short Look at Long-Term Care for Seniors" (*Journal of the American Medical Association*, vol. 301, no. 8, August 28, 2013) that 70% of all adults aged 65 years and older will need long-term care before their deaths, and that 20% will require long-term care that lasts for five years or more. Of the 12 million Americans who needed long-term care in 2010, 87% received it from family members on an unpaid basis. The KFF estimates the annual value of unpaid labor devoted to long-term care at $450 billion as of 2009, and it projects that the number of Americans requiring long-term care will more than double by 2050, increasing from 12 million to 27 million.

Although Medicare covers some home health care and temporary care in skilled nursing facilities (which are similar to nursing homes), it typically does not cover long-term care, whether that care is delivered in the home or in an institution such as a nursing home. Medicaid, however, does cover long-term care for those impoverished elderly adults who meet the program's eligibility criteria. According to the KFF, among long-term-care recipients who were paying for that care in 2011, Medicaid

FIGURE 10.6

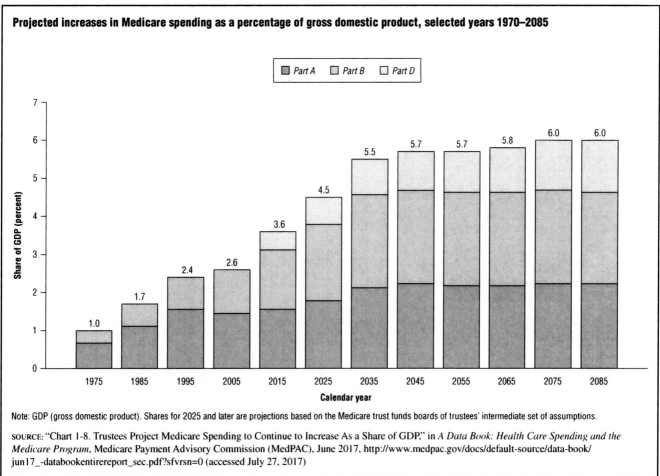

Projected increases in Medicare spending as a percentage of gross domestic product, selected years 1970–2085

☐ *Part A*　☐ *Part B*　☐ *Part D*

Note: GDP (gross domestic product). Shares for 2025 and later are projections based on the Medicare trust funds boards of trustees' intermediate set of assumptions.

SOURCE: "Chart 1-8. Trustees Project Medicare Spending to Continue to Increase As a Share of GDP," in *A Data Book: Health Care Spending and the Medicare Program*, Medicare Payment Advisory Commission (MedPAC), June 2017, http://www.medpac.gov/docs/default-source/data-book/jun17_-databookentirereport_sec.pdf?sfvrsn=0 (accessed July 27, 2017)

was the single largest source of funding, accounting for 40% of the total $357 billion spent on long-term care that year. Another 21% of total long-term-care expenditures were paid for under Medicare's post-acute care coverage, 15% was paid out-of-pocket by patients and their families, 7% was paid for by private insurers, and 18% was paid for by other private and public sources.

As Medicare does not cover long-term care and Medicaid covers only people who are poor, Americans who are not impoverished must either have private insurance that covers long-term care, the assets to pay for long-term care out-of-pocket, or family members who are able and willing to provide them with long-term care. Otherwise, the costs of such care will exhaust whatever funds they do have, driving them into poverty and the Medicaid program. In spite of the fact that most people will require long-term care at the end of life, only 35% of people aged 40 years and older have set aside money to pay for such care, according to the KFF.

NURSING HOMES. Among long-term-care options, nursing homes are by far the most costly. For those who require labor-intensive, round-the-clock care, however, nursing homes may be the only viable option. Nursing

homes provide terminally ill residents with end-of-life services in a variety of ways:

- Caring for patients in the nursing home

- Transferring patients who request it to hospitals or hospices

- Contracting with hospices to provide palliative care (care that relieves the pain but does not cure the illness) within the nursing home

Since the 1990s the number of people being cared for in nursing homes has declined at the national level, with some variations at the state level. (See Table 10.6.) Growth of the home health care industry is likely partly responsible for the decline in nursing home populations, as home health care is a less costly option for those needing long-term care. Another factor is likely the increased popularity of assisted-living and continuing-care retirement communities, which offer alternatives to nursing home care for those people who need less than round-the-clock assistance, and which cost less on average than nursing home care. There is also a trend toward healthy aging—more older adults are living longer with fewer disabilities. Finally, the high cost of nursing home care is a prohibitive factor for many older Americans.

FIGURE 10.7

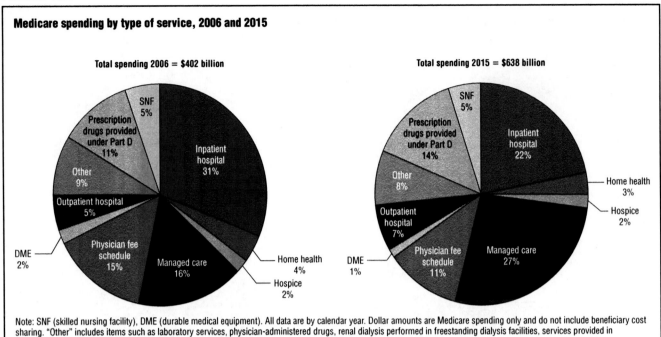

Medicare spending by type of service, 2006 and 2015

Note: SNF (skilled nursing facility), DME (durable medical equipment). All data are by calendar year. Dollar amounts are Medicare spending only and do not include beneficiary cost sharing. "Other" includes items such as laboratory services, physician-administered drugs, renal dialysis performed in freestanding dialysis facilities, services provided in freestanding ambulatory surgical center facilities, and ambulance. Totals may not sum to 100 percent due to rounding.

SOURCE: "Chart 1–2. Medicare Spending Is Concentrated in Certain Services and Has Shifted over Time," in *A Data Book: Health Care Spending and the Medicare Program,* Medicare Payment Advisory Commission (MedPAC), June 2017, http://www.medpac.gov/docs/default-source/data-book/jun17_-databookentirereport_sec.pdf?sfvrsn=0 (accessed July 27, 2017)

FIGURE 10.8

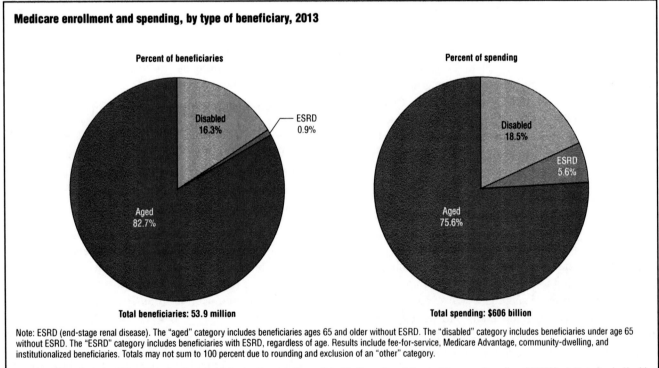

Medicare enrollment and spending, by type of beneficiary, 2013

Note: ESRD (end-stage renal disease). The "aged" category includes beneficiaries ages 65 and older without ESRD. The "disabled" category includes beneficiaries under age 65 without ESRD. The "ESRD" category includes beneficiaries with ESRD, regardless of age. Results include fee-for-service, Medicare Advantage, community-dwelling, and institutionalized beneficiaries. Totals may not sum to 100 percent due to rounding and exclusion of an "other" category.

SOURCE: "Chart 2–1. Aged Beneficiaries Accounted for the Greatest Share of the Medicare Population and Program Spending, 2013," in *A Data Book: Health Care Spending and the Medicare Program,* Medicare Payment Advisory Commission (MedPAC), June 2017, http://www.medpac.gov/docs/default-source/data-book/jun17_databookentirereport_sec.pdf?sfvrsn=0 (accessed July 27, 2017)

In 2015 there were 15,656 nursing homes in the United States with a combined occupancy of just under 1.7 million beds. (See Table 10.6.) Slightly fewer than 1.4 million adults were nursing home residents in 2015,

FIGURE 10.9

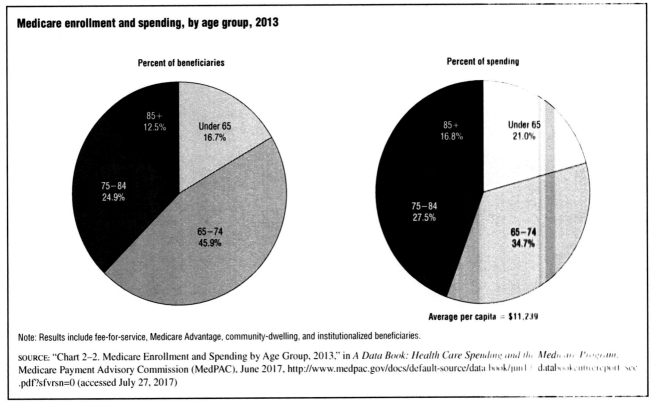

Medicare enrollment and spending, by age group, 2013

Percent of beneficiaries

85+ 12.5%
Under 65 16.7%
75–84 24.9%
65–74 45.9%

Percent of spending

85+ 16.8%
Under 65 21.0%
75–84 27.5%
65–74 34.7%

Average per capita = $11,239

Note: Results include fee-for-service, Medicare Advantage, community-dwelling, and institutionalized beneficiaries.

SOURCE: "Chart 2–2. Medicare Enrollment and Spending by Age Group, 2013," in *A Data Book: Health Care Spending and the Medicare Program,* Medicare Payment Advisory Commission (MedPAC), June 2017, http://www.medpac.gov/docs/default-source/data book/jun17 databookentirereport sec .pdf?sfvrsn=0 (accessed July 27, 2017)

for an overall occupancy rate of 80.3%. The lowest occupancy rates were in Oregon (60.1%), Utah (63.9%), and Indiana (64.3%). The highest occupancy rates were in North Dakota (92.7%), the District of Columbia (91.8%), Rhode Island (91.4%), South Dakota (91.4%), and Alaska (90.3%). According to the *Genworth 2016 Cost of Care Survey* (June 2016, https://www.genworth .com/about-us/industry-expertise/cost-of-care.html), a comprehensive annual survey of long-term-care costs produced by Genworth Financial (a public company that offers long-term-care insurance), the median rate paid by nursing home residents in 2016 was $225 per day (or $82,128 per year) for a semiprivate room and $253 per day (or $92,376 per year) for a private room.

PATIENTS WITH TERMINAL DISEASES
Acquired Immunodeficiency Syndrome

Acquired immunodeficiency syndrome (AIDS) is a set of signs, symptoms, and diseases that occur together when the immune system of a person who is infected with the human immunodeficiency virus (HIV) becomes extremely weakened. Advances in treatment during the mid- to late 1990s made it possible to slow the progression of HIV infection to AIDS, which led to dramatic decreases in AIDS deaths. Whereas an HIV diagnosis represented a death sentence in the 1980s, by the early 21st century HIV-infected individuals were able to manage their conditions and live relatively normal lives,

provided that they had access to high-quality health care and drug treatments.

Among the poor, however, HIV infection retains much of its deadly force. The disease is more common, more likely to develop into AIDS, and more likely to lead to premature death among those who live in poverty or who do not have reliable access to health care. Medicaid has historically played a major role in providing for the care of the HIV-positive population in the United States. Even before the ACA expanded Medicaid eligibility, many HIV patients qualified for coverage because the disease had permanently disabled them. Besides those who are poor at the time that they contract HIV, many patients become impoverished because of the condition, and Medicaid then becomes their primary recourse for health care coverage. For example, people in whom the disease progresses are often forced to discontinue working. If these people have private health insurance through their employers, they lose their coverage when they become too ill to work.

It was uncertain, as of 2017, how the ACA would affect the HIV-positive population, but the Medicaid expansion guarantees coverage to many more low-income Americans with the infection. Additionally, the ACA prohibits insurers from denying people coverage based on preexisting medical conditions. This makes it less likely that people living well above the poverty line

TABLE 10.5

Medicaid recipients and payments, by basis of eligibility, and by race and Hispanic origin, selected fiscal years 1999–2013

[Data are compiled by the Centers for Medicare & Medicaid Services from the Medicaid Data System]

Basis of eligibility and race and Hispanic origin	1999	2000	2005	2008	2009	2010	2011[a]	2012[a]	2013[a]
Beneficiaries[b]					Number, in millions				
All beneficiaries	40.1	42.8	57.7	58.8	62.6	65.7	71.4	71.6	73.7
Basis of eligibility:					Percent of beneficiaries				
Aged (65 years and over)	9.4	8.7	7.6	7.1	6.7	6.5	5.7	5.7	5.6
Blind and disabled	16.7	16.1	14.2	14.8	14.4	14.3	13.1	13.2	13.0
Adults in families with dependent children[c]	18.7	20.5	21.8	22.0	23.1	23.7	18.9	19.5	19.0
Children under age 21[d]	46.9	46.1	47.2	47.8	47.7	48.3	40.5	40.6	40.4
Other Title XIX[e]	8.4	8.6	9.1	8.4	8.1	7.2	9.6	8.7	9.8
Separate CHIP[f]	NA	NA	NA	NA	NA	NA	12.2	12.3	12.1
Race and Hispanic origin:[g]									
White	NA	NA	39.3	38.1	38.2	38.9	37.2	37.2	36.1
Black or African American	NA	NA	21.5	21.1	20.7	20.6	19.8	20.1	19.5
American Indian or Alaska Native	NA	NA	1.2	1.3	1.2	1.2	1.1	1.1	1.1
Asian or Pacific Islander	NA	NA	3.5	3.5	3.6	3.6	3.6	3.8	3.8
Asian	NA	NA	2.5	2.6	2.7	2.7	2.8	2.9	3.0
Pacific Islander	NA	NA	0.9	0.9	0.9	0.9	0.9	0.8	0.8
Hispanic or Latino	NA	NA	20.6	21.7	22.3	22.3	17.4	17.4	17.4
Multiple race or unknown	NA	NA	13.9	14.3	14.0	13.3	20.9	20.4	22.0
Payments[h]					Amount, in billions				
All payments	$153.5	$168.3	$274.9	$296.8	$326.0	$339.0	$368.6	$363.9	$375.3
					Percent distribution				
Total	**100.0**	**100.0**	**100.0**	**100.0**	**100.0**	**100.0**	**100.0**	**100.0**	**100.0**
Basis of eligibility:									
Aged (65 years and over)	27.7	26.4	23.1	20.6	19.7	19.4	16.6	16.7	16.7
Blind and disabled	42.9	43.2	43.4	43.5	43.4	43.4	40.8	41.2	41.0
Adults in families with dependent children[c]	10.3	10.6	11.8	12.7	13.9	14.2	12.6	13.3	13.1
Children under age 21[d]	15.7	15.9	17.2	19.2	19.6	19.8	18.1	18.2	18.4
Other Title XIX[e]	3.4	3.9	4.6	4.0	3.3	3.1	4.5	3.5	3.5
Separate CHIP[f]	NA	NA	NA	NA	NA	NA	7.4	7.2	7.4
Race and Hispanic origin:[g]									
White	NA	NA	53.0	50.2	50.0	50.2	48.1	48.3	47.5
Black or African American	NA	NA	19.8	20.6	20.7	20.5	20.3	20.8	20.3
American Indian or Alaska Native	NA	NA	1.2	1.3	1.2	1.3	1.2	1.3	1.3
Asian or Pacific Islander	NA	NA	2.7	2.9	3.1	3.0	3.1	3.2	3.5
Asian	NA	NA	1.9	2.1	2.3	2.3	2.4	2.5	2.7
Pacific Islander	NA	NA	0.8	0.8	0.8	0.7	0.7	0.7	0.7
Hispanic or Latino	NA	NA	12.2	13.7	14.2	14.2	9.9	9.7	10.1
Multiple race or unknown	NA	NA	11.1	11.4	10.8	10.8	17.4	16.7	17.4
Payments per beneficiary[h]					Amount				
All beneficiaries	$3,819	$3,936	$4,768	$5,051	$5,209	$5,160	$5,159	$5,082	$5,094
Basis of eligibility:									
Aged (65 years and over)	11,268	11,929	14,427	14,742	15,337	15,286	15,073	14,862	15,194
Blind and disabled	9,832	10,559	14,531	14,843	15,670	15,695	16,104	15,825	16,115
Adults in families with dependent children[c]	2,104	2,030	2,583	2,912	3,144	3,095	3,443	3,460	3,503
Children under age 21[d]	1,282	1,358	1,732	2,035	2,145	2,122	2,300	2,281	2,315
Other Title XIX[e]	1,532	1,778	2,380	2,407	2,104	2,219	2,402	2,030	1,803
Separate CHIP[f]	NA	NA	NA	NA	NA	NA	3,125	2,979	3,083
Race and Hispanic origin:[g]									
White	NA	NA	6,422	6,657	6,809	6,663	6,677	6,598	6,691
Black or African American	NA	NA	4,397	4,928	5,216	5,142	5,308	5,266	5,314
American Indian or Alaska Native	NA	NA	4,626	5,218	5,382	5,421	5,461	5,649	5,824
Asian or Pacific Islander	NA	NA	3,710	4,133	4,402	4,300	4,483	4,365	4,585
Asian	NA	NA	3,624	4,123	4,386	4,307	4,482	4,383	4,575
Pacific Islander	NA	NA	3,947	4,161	4,448	4,275	4,484	4,302	4,624
Hispanic or Latino	NA	NA	2,822	3,175	3,322	3,276	2,944	2,821	2,958
Multiple race or unknown	NA	NA	3,816	4,014	4,025	4,173	4,298	4,161	4,025

will be financially devastated by a disease such as HIV. In the event that a middle- or high-income person with HIV is forced to stop working, that person no longer becomes immediately uninsurable.

THE RYAN WHITE COMPREHENSIVE AIDS RESOURCES EMERGENCY ACT. The Ryan White Comprehensive AIDS Resources Emergency (CARE) Act is a federal program that provides funds for the care, treatment, and support of

TABLE 10.5

Medicaid recipients and payments, by basis of eligibility, and by race and Hispanic origin, selected fiscal years 1999–2013 [CONTINUED]

[Data are compiled by the Centers for Medicare & Medicaid Services from the Medicaid Data System]

NA = Data not available.

aStarting with 2011, a new tabular methodology was used. Therefore, estimates may not be comparable to earlier data and caution should be used with trend analysis.

bBeneficiaries include those who were enrolled or received services through Medicaid or the Children's Health Insurance Program (CHIP). Beneficiary counts for 2011 and subsequent years were derived from MSIS claims files. Separate CHIP beneficiaries are included for 2011 and subsequent years.

cIncludes adults who meet the requirements for the Aid to Families with Dependent Children (AFDC) program that were in effect in their state on July 16, 1996, or, at state option, meet more liberal criteria (with some exceptions). Includes adults in the Temporary Assistance for Needy Families (TANF) program. Starting with 2001 data, includes women in the Breast and Cervical Cancer Prevention and Treatment Program and unemployed adults.

dIncludes children (including those in the foster care system) in the TANF program.

eIncludes some participants in the Supplemental Security Income program and other people deemed medically needy in participating states. Excludes foster care children and includes unknown eligibility. Prior to 2001, includes unemployed adults.

fCHIP is Children's Health Insurance Program. CHIP provides federal funds for states to provide health care coverage to eligible low-income, uninsured children who do not qualify for Medicaid. Some states use CHIP funds to expand Medicaid. For 2012 data, all states except Colorado and Idaho had separate CHIP beneficiaries.

gRace and Hispanic origin are as determined based on the last best eligibility record of the beneficiary. Categories are mutually exclusive. Starting with 2001 data, the Hispanic category included Hispanic persons, regardless of race. Persons indicating more than one race or missing race information were included in the multiple race category.

hPayments for 2011 and subsequent years were derived from MSIS claims files. Medicaid payment data for 2010 and earlier excluded disproportionate share hospital (DSH) payments ($14.7 billion in fiscal year 2010) and DSH mental health facility payments ($2.9 billion in fiscal year 2010).

Notes: Data are for fiscal year ending September 30. Colorado and Idaho had not reported 2012 data as of the date 2012 data were accessed. Colorado, District of Columbia, Idaho, and Rhode Island had not reported 2013 data and Kansas had only reported partial 2013 data as of the date accessed.

SOURCE: "Table 109. Medicaid and Children's Health Insurance Program Beneficiaries and Payments, by Basis of Eligibility, and Race and Hispanic Origin: United States, Selected Fiscal Years 1999–2013," in *Health, United States, 2016: With Chartbook on Long-term Trends in Health*, Centers for Disease Control and Prevention, National Center for Health Statistics, 2017, https://www.cdc.gov/nchs/data/hus/hus16.pdf (accessed July 16, 2017)

---

low-income, uninsured or underinsured people with AIDS. It is the largest federally funded program for helping people with AIDS. The act is named after an Indiana teenager who had AIDS and worked against AIDS-related discrimination. The act was initially passed in 1990 and has since been reauthorized numerous times. According to the U.S. Department of Health and Human Services (HHS), in "Clarifications Regarding Use of Ryan White HIV/AIDS Program Funds for Premium and Cost-Sharing Assistance for Medicaid" (June 6, 2014, https://hab.hrsa.gov/sites/default/files/hab/Global/pcn1306medicaidpremiumcostsharing.pdf), "The RWHAP will continue to be the payer of last resort and will continue to pay for Ryan White HIV/AIDS Program services not covered, or partially covered, by Medicaid." In "About the Ryan White HIV/AIDS Program" (October 2016, https://hab.hrsa.gov/about-ryan-white-hivaids-program/about-ryan-white-hivaids-program), the HHS notes that the program served 52% of all Americans diagnosed with HIV, and had a budget of $2.3 billion in FY 2016.

Cancer

Cancer, in all its forms, is expensive to treat. Compared with most other diseases, there are more options for cancer treatment, more adverse side effects that require additional treatment, and a greater potential for unrelieved pain. In *Cancer Facts and Figures 2017* (2017, https://www.cancer.org/content/dam/cancer-org/research/cancer-facts-and-statistics/annual-cancer-facts-and-figures/2017/cancer-facts-and-figures-2017.pdf), the American Cancer Society (ACS) estimates that in 2014 the direct medical cost of cancer in the United States were $87.8 billion. More than half (58%) of this amount was dedicated

to hospital outpatient or office-based health care provider services, while just over one-quarter (27%) covered inpatient hospital visits.

The ACS notes that cancer costs are generally higher for those who are uninsured: "Uninsured patients and those from many ethnic minority groups are substantially more likely to be diagnosed with cancer at a later stage, when treatment is often more extensive, costlier, and less successful." Cancer is also, like AIDS, likely to leave individuals unable to continue with their careers as the disease progresses. Thus, those who have health insurance through their employers may end up losing coverage. The ACA's prohibition of coverage denials based on preexisting conditions was expected to be helpful to cancer patients who were able to afford private insurance coverage. The expansion of coverage through Medicaid and subsidies was also potentially helpful in enabling previously uninsured Americans to access preventive care that would allow for earlier diagnoses of cancer, bringing down costs and increasing the chances of survival.

Alzheimer's Disease

Alzheimer's disease is a form of dementia that is characterized by memory loss, behavior and personality changes, and decreasing capacity for clear thought. The disease is terminal, and it worsens over time. The chances of developing Alzheimer's increase with age. Thus, it is a particularly pressing concern in countries with rapidly expanding populations of people who live longer into old age.

In *2017 Alzheimer's Disease Facts and Figures* (2017, https://www.alz.org/documents_custom/2017-facts-and-figures.pdf), the Alzheimer's Association estimates that 5.5 million people in the United States had Alzheimer's

TABLE 10.6

Nursing homes, beds, residents, and occupancy rates, by state, selected years 1995–2015

[Data are based on a census of certified nursing facilities]

State	Nursing homes				Beds			
	1995	2000	2014	2015	1995	2000	2014	2015
					Number			
United States	**16,389**	**16,886**	**15,643**	**15,656**	**1,751,302**	**1,795,388**	**1,693,943**	**1,694,777**
Alabama	221	225	226	227	23,353	25,248	26,388	26,506
Alaska	15	15	18	18	814	821	693	693
Arizona	152	150	147	145	16,162	17,458	16,605	16,523
Arkansas	256	255	229	228	29,952	25,715	24,558	24,463
California	1,382	1,369	1,217	1,213	140,203	131,762	119,866	119,046
Colorado	219	225	214	217	19,912	20,240	20,431	20,560
Connecticut	267	259	229	229	32,827	32,433	27,673	27,608
Delaware	42	43	46	45	4,739	4,906	4,876	4,791
District of Columbia	19	20	19	19	3,206	3,078	2,766	2,766
Florida	627	732	689	689	72,656	83,365	83,545	83,668
Georgia	352	363	357	358	38,097	39,817	39,975	39,857
Hawaii	34	45	46	46	2,513	4,006	4,213	4,313
Idaho	76	84	78	79	5,747	6,181	5,951	5,977
Illinois	827	869	761	762	103,230	110,766	98,348	98,489
Indiana	556	564	528	541	59,538	56,762	59,555	61,048
Iowa	419	467	443	442	39,959	37,034	31,950	31,843
Kansas	429	392	345	344	30,016	27,067	25,730	25,756
Kentucky	288	307	287	289	23,221	25,341	26,300	27,060
Louisiana	337	337	280	279	37,769	39,430	35,066	34,537
Maine	132	126	105	103	9,243	8,248	6,953	6,904
Maryland	218	255	228	228	28,394	31,495	28,115	28,013
Massachusetts	550	526	416	413	54,532	56,030	48,320	47,990
Michigan	432	439	433	437	49,473	50,696	46,521	46,669
Minnesota	432	433	377	377	43,865	42,149	30,319	29,934
Mississippi	183	190	205	204	16,059	17,068	18,434	18,426
Missouri	546	551	512	512	52,679	54,829	55,273	55,245
Montana	100	104	83	80	7,210	7,667	6,732	6,693
Nebraska	231	236	219	217	18,169	17,877	16,005	15,961
Nevada	42	51	52	54	3,998	5,547	6,040	6,256
New Hampshire	74	83	76	76	7,412	7,837	7,501	7,525
New Jersey	300	361	361	365	43,967	52,195	52,051	52,538
New Mexico	83	80	71	73	6,969	7,289	6,869	7,070
New York	624	665	628	626	107,750	120,514	117,131	116,666
North Carolina	391	410	422	423	38,322	41,376	45,088	45,221
North Dakota	87	88	81	80	7,125	6,954	6,131	6,009
Ohio	943	1,009	954	959	106,884	105,038	90,653	90,667
Oklahoma	405	392	309	305	33,918	33,903	28,962	28,580
Oregon	161	150	137	137	13,885	13,500	12,210	12,274
Pennsylvania	726	770	699	699	92,625	95,063	88,236	88,133
Rhode Island	94	99	84	84	9,612	10,271	8,720	8,720
South Carolina	166	178	188	187	16,682	18,102	19,631	19,758
South Dakota	114	114	111	111	8,296	7,844	6,945	6,893
Tennessee	322	349	321	319	37,074	38,593	37,268	36,719
Texas	1,266	1,215	1,212	1,222	123,056	125,052	136,000	137,396
Utah	91	93	99	100	7,101	7,651	8,577	8,639
Vermont	23	44	37	37	1,862	3,743	3,174	3,174
Virginia	271	278	288	286	30,070	30,595	32,497	32,447
Washington	285	277	221	220	28,464	25,905	21,286	21,145
West Virginia	129	139	127	126	10,903	11,413	10,888	10,858
Wisconsin	413	420	389	388	48,754	46,395	33,959	33,800
Wyoming	37	40	39	38	3,035	3,119	2,965	2,950

disease in 2017, 5.3 million of whom were aged 65 years and older. The remaining 200,000 were younger people suffering from a specific subset of the disease known as younger-onset Alzheimer's. The organization went on to state that 10% of adults aged 65 years and older had Alzheimer's and that 32% of adults aged 85 years and older had the disease.

Of the 5.3 million elderly adults in the United States who had Alzheimer's in 2017, 3.3 million (62.3%) were women. The Alzheimer's Association indicates that "the prevailing view has been that this discrepancy is due to

the fact that women live longer than men on average, and older age is the greatest risk factor for Alzheimer's.... However, researchers have recently begun to revisit the question of whether the risk of Alzheimer's could actually be higher for women at any given age due to biological or genetic variations or differences in life experiences."

Because of the deterioration of their mental faculties, Alzheimer's patients require round-the-clock supervision and can be extremely demanding. Compared with other older people who require daily care, Alzheimer's patients

TABLE 10.6

Nursing homes, beds, residents, and occupancy rates, by state, selected years 1995–2015 [CONTINUED]

[Data are based on a census of certified nursing facilities]

State	Residents				Occupancy rate*			
	1995	2000	2010	2011	1995	2000	2010	2011
				Number				
United States	**1,479,550**	**1,480,076**	**1,368,667**	**1,360,970**	**84.5**	**82.4**	**80.8**	**80.3**
Alabama	21,691	23,089	22,731	22,721	92.9	91.4	86.1	85.7
Alaska	634	595	612	626	77.9	72.5	88.4	90.3
Arizona	12,382	13,253	11,428	11,588	76.6	75.9	68.8	70.1
Arkansas	20,823	19,317	17,688	17,655	69.5	75.1	72.0	72.2
California	109,805	106,460	102,245	102,674	78.3	80.8	85.4	86.2
Colorado	17,055	17,045	16,309	16,290	85.7	84.2	79.8	79.2
Connecticut	29,948	29,657	24,250	24,018	91.2	91.4	87.6	87.0
Delaware	3,819	3,900	4,314	4,253	80.6	79.5	88.5	88.8
District of Columbia	2,576	2,858	2,539	2,540	80.3	92.9	91.8	91.8
Florida	61,845	69,050	73,487	73,492	85.1	82.8	88.0	87.8
Georgia	35,933	36,559	33,930	33,399	94.3	91.8	84.9	83.8
Hawaii	2,413	3,558	3,663	3,568	96.0	88.8	86.9	82.7
Idaho	4,697	4,640	3,841	3,881	81.7	75.1	64.5	64.9
Illinois	83,696	83,604	72,563	71,952	81.1	75.5	73.8	73.1
Indiana	44,328	42,328	38,893	39,267	74.5	74.6	65.3	64.3
Iowa	27,506	29,204	24,859	24,585	68.8	78.9	77.8	77.2
Kansas	25,140	22,230	18,337	18,204	83.8	82.1	71.3	70.7
Kentucky	20,696	22,730	23,008	23,453	89.1	89.7	87.5	86.7
Louisiana	32,493	30,735	25,854	25,722	86.0	77.9	73.7	74.5
Maine	8,587	7,298	6,239	6,199	92.9	88.5	89.7	89.8
Maryland	24,716	25,629	24,430	24,572	87.0	81.4	86.9	87.7
Massachusetts	49,765	49,805	41,255	40,794	91.3	88.9	85.4	85.0
Michigan	43,271	42,615	39,374	39,275	87.5	84.1	84.6	84.2
Minnesota	41,163	38,813	26,695	25,725	93.8	92.1	88.0	85.9
Mississippi	15,247	15,815	16,129	16,026	94.9	92.7	87.5	87.0
Missouri	39,891	38,586	38,326	38,418	75.7	70.4	69.3	69.5
Montana	6,415	5,973	4,619	4,466	89.0	77.9	68.6	66.7
Nebraska	16,166	14,989	12,043	11,938	89.0	83.8	75.2	74.8
Nevada	3,645	3,657	4,821	4,827	91.2	65.9	79.8	77.2
New Hampshire	6,877	7,158	6,767	6,706	92.8	91.3	90.2	89.1
New Jersey	40,397	45,837	45,185	44,998	91.9	87.8	86.8	85.6
New Mexico	6,051	6,503	5,439	5,502	86.8	89.2	79.2	77.8
New York	103,409	112,957	105,390	104,684	96.0	93.7	90.0	89.7
North Carolina	35,511	36,658	37,058	36,612	92.7	88.6	82.2	81.0
North Dakota	6,868	6,343	5,664	5,571	96.4	91.2	92.4	92.7
Ohio	79,026	81,946	76,325	75,523	73.9	78.0	84.2	83.3
Oklahoma	26,377	23,833	19,108	18,854	77.8	70.3	66.0	66.0
Oregon	11,673	9,990	7,343	7,379	84.1	74.0	60.1	60.1
Pennsylvania	84,843	83,880	79,598	78,822	91.6	88.2	90.2	89.4
Rhode Island	8,823	9,041	8,011	7,966	91.8	88.0	91.9	91.4
South Carolina	14,568	15,739	16,773	16,830	87.3	86.9	85.4	85.2
South Dakota	7,926	7,059	6,381	6,301	95.5	90.0	91.9	91.4
Tennessee	33,929	34,714	28,897	28,246	91.5	89.9	77.5	76.9
Texas	89,354	85,275	93,170	93,316	72.6	68.2	68.5	67.9
Utah	5,832	5,703	5,515	5,518	82.1	74.5	64.3	63.9
Vermont	1,792	3,349	2,686	2,628	96.2	89.5	84.6	82.8
Virginia	28,119	27,091	28,486	27,874	93.5	88.5	87.7	85.9
Washington	24,954	21,158	17,005	16,969	87.7	81.7	79.9	80.3
West Virginia	10,216	10,334	9,535	9,471	93.7	90.5	87.6	87.2
Wisconsin	43,998	38,911	27,485	26,804	90.2	83.9	80.9	79.3
Wyoming	2,661	2,605	2,364	2,268	87.7	83.5	79.7	76.9

*Percentage of beds occupied (number of nursing home residents per 100 nursing home beds).

Notes: Annual numbers of nursing homes, beds, and residents are based on the Centers for Medicare & Medicaid Services' reporting cycle. Starting with 2013 data, a new editing rule was used for number of beds. For the U.S., the number of beds decreased by less than 1%. For most states, this caused little or no change in the data. The change in the number of beds also caused a change in some occupancy rates. Because of the methodology change, trends should be interpreted with caution.

SOURCE: "Table 92. Nursing Homes, Beds, Residents, and Occupancy Rates, by State: United States, Selected Years 1995–2015," in *Health, United States, 2016: With Chartbook on Long-term Trends in Health*, Centers for Disease Control and Prevention, National Center for Health Statistics, 2017, https://www.cdc.gov/nchs/data/hus/hus16.pdf (accessed July 16, 2017)

---

are more likely to need help getting in and out of bed, dressing, using the toilet, bathing, and eating. Likewise, the progression of the disease is slow compared with other terminal conditions, so caregivers often must provide for the needs of patients for longer than caregivers of other older patients. Most care of Alzheimer's patients falls to family members. According to the Alzheimer's Association, 15.9 million family and other unpaid caregivers provided an estimated 18.2 billion hours of unpaid care to U.S. Alzheimer's patients in 2016. The association estimates the value of this care (using a pay rate of $12.65 per hour, which is significantly lower than the hourly pay of most home health care workers) at $230.1 billion.

Alzheimer's patients also receive a substantial amount of paid care. In 2017 an estimated $259 billion was spent on paid care for patients with Alzheimer's or other dementias, according to the Alzheimer's Association. Medicare and Medicaid covered approximately 67% of this total. Alzheimer's patients (and other dementia patients) can be exceptionally expensive to care for. The Alzheimer's Association notes that, in 2016, Medicare beneficiaries with Alzheimer's or other forms of dementia made average per-person payments of $46,786 to cover their health care and long-term care. By contrast, Medicare beneficiaries in the same age group who did not have Alzheimer's or other forms of dementia made average per-person payments of $13,351 for their health care and long-term care. Among the Medicare beneficiaries with Alzheimer's and other forms of dementia, on average $23,497 of their total care was paid for by Medicare (50.2%), while $8,182 (17.4%) was paid for by Medicaid. Out-of-pocket payments covered another $10,315 (22%) of these costs, with the balance being paid for by health maintenance organizations, private insurance, other payers, or going uncompensated.

The Alzheimer's Association expected these costs, and the number of older people requiring treatment for the disease, to grow rapidly through the middle of the 21st century. The organization projected that the cost of paid care for Alzheimer's patients would top $1.1 trillion by 2050.

IMPORTANT NAMES
AND ADDRESSES

AARP
601 E St. NW
Washington, DC 20049
1-888-687-2277
E-mail: member@aarp.org
URL: http://www.aarp.org/

Aging with Dignity
3050 Highland Oaks Terrace, Ste. 2
Tallahassee, FL 32301-3841
(850) 681-2010
FAX: (850) 681-2481
E-mail: fivewishes@agingwithdignity.org
URL: https://www.agingwithdignity.org/

Alzheimer's Association
225 N. Michigan Ave., 17th Floor
Chicago, IL 60601-7633
(312) 335-8700
1-800-272-3900
FAX: 1-866-699-1246
URL: http://www.alz.org/

American Association of Suicidology
5221 Wisconsin Ave. NW
Washington, DC 20015
(202) 237-2280
FAX: (202) 237-2282
URL: http://www.suicidology.org/

American Cancer Society
250 Williams St. NW
Atlanta, GA 30303
1-800-227-2345
URL: https://www.cancer.org/

**American Foundation for Suicide
Prevention**
120 Wall St., 29th Floor
New York, NY 10005
(212) 363-3500
1-888-333-2377
FAX: (212) 363-6237

E-mail: info@afsp.org
URL: https://afsp.org/

**Centers for Disease Control and
Prevention**
1600 Clifton Rd.
Atlanta, GA 30329-4027
1-800-232-4636
URL: https://www.cdc.gov/

Children's Hospice International
500 Montgomery St., Ste. 400
Alexandria, VA 22314
(703) 684-0330
E-mail: Info@CHIonline.org
URL: http://www.chionline.org/

Compassion & Choices
PO Box 101810
Denver, CO 80250
1-800-247-7421
URL: https://www.compassionandchoices
.org/

The Hastings Center
21 Malcolm Gordon Rd.
Garrison, NY 10524-4125
(845) 424-4040
FAX: (845)424-4545
E-mail: mail@thehastingscenter.org
URL: http://www.thehastingscenter.org/

**Health Resources and Services
Administration Information Center**
5600 Fishers Ln.
Rockville, MD 20857
1-877-464-4772
URL: https://www.hrsa.gov/

March of Dimes
1275 Mamaroneck Ave.
White Plains, NY 10605
(914) 997-4488
URL: http://www.marchofdimes.com/

**National Association for Home Care
and Hospice**
228 Seventh St. SE
Washington, DC 20003
(202) 547-7424
FAX: (202) 547-3540
URL: http://www.nahc.org/

National Council on Aging
251 18th St. South, Ste. 500
Arlington, VA 22202
(571) 527-3900
URL: https://www.ncoa.org/

**National Hospice and Palliative
Care Organization**
1731 King St.
Alexandria, VA 22314
(703) 837-1500
FAX: (703) 837-1233
URL: https://www.nhpco.org/

National Institute on Aging
Bldg. 31, Rm. 5C27
31 Center Dr., MSC 2292
Bethesda, MD 20892
1-800-222-2225
E-mail: niaic@nia.nih.gov
URL: https://www.nia.nih.gov/

**National Right to Life
Committee**
512 10th St. NW
Washington, DC 20004
(202) 626-8800
URL: http://www.nrlc.org/

**United Network for Organ
Sharing**
700 N. Fourth St.
Richmond, VA 23219
(804) 782-4800
1-888-894-6361
URL: https://www.unos.org/

RESOURCES

Many of the most authoritative sources of data and information on end-of-life issues are published by various agencies of the U.S. government.

The National Center for Health Statistics, which is affiliated with the Centers for Disease Control and Prevention (CDC), provides a number of annual publications on health-related matters. Among the most useful sources for the topics covered in this book were *Health, United States, 2016: With Chartbook on Long-Term Trends in Health* (2017), as well as several reports published as part of the *National Vital Statistics Reports* series, including "Births: Final Data for 2015" (January 2017, Joyce A. Martin et al.), "Deaths: Leading Causes for 2014" (June 2016, Melonie Heron), and "Deaths: Final Data for 2014" (June 2016, Kenneth D. Kochanek et al.). A number of papers issued as part of the *NCHS Data Brief* series were also helpful, including "75 Years of Mortality in the United States, 1935–2010" (March 2012, Donna L. Hoyert) and "Financial Burden of Medical Care: A Family Perspective" (January 2014, Robin A. Cohen and Whitney K. Kirzinger). Other important CDC sources include the series *Morbidity and Mortality Weekly Report*, in particular the data release "Youth Risk Behavior Surveillance— United States, 2015" (June 2016, Laura Kann et al.).

Numerous data sources from the U.S. Department of Health and Human Services and its subordinate agencies were also instrumental in compiling this book. These include the Organ Procurement and Transplantation Network's (OPTN) online database (https://optn.transplant .hrsa.gov/data/), as well as the OPTN's "United States Organ Transplantation: OPTN & SRTR Annual Data Report 2015" (January 2017); the Department of Health and Human Services' *Child Mortality in the United States, 1935–2007: Large Racial and Socioeconomic Disparities Have Persisted over Time* (2010, Gopal K. Singh); and the Administration on Aging's *A Profile of Older Americans: 2016* (March 2017).

The U.S. Census Bureau provides a wealth of data on the U.S. population in the form of reports as well as freely accessible online data tables. Census Bureau reports used in compiling this book include *Health Insurance Coverage in the United States: 2015* (September 2016, Jessica C. Barnett and Marina S. Vornovitsky), *Projections of the Size and Composition of the U.S. Population: 2014 to 2060* (March 2015, Sandra L. Colby and Jennifer M. Ortman), and *The Older Population: 2010* (November 2011, Carrie A. Werner). The bureau's *2014 National Population Projections: Summary Tables* provided a useful collection of online data tables.

Other important government data sources were *Older Americans 2016: Key Indicators of Well-Being* (August 2016) by the Federal Interagency Forum on Aging Related Statistics, "National Health Expenditure Data: Historical—NHE Tables" (2016) by the Centers for Medicare and Medicaid Services, and *A Data Book: Health Care Spending and the Medicare Program* (June 2017) by the Medicare Payment Advisory Commission.

The mission of the National Hospice and Palliative Care Organization is "improving end of life care and expanding access to hospice care with the goal of profoundly enhancing quality of life for people dying in America and their loved ones." The Hospice Association of America represents hospices, caregivers, and volunteers who serve terminally ill patients and their families. The National Hospice and Palliative Care Organization and the Hospice Association of America both collect data about hospice care that were helpful in addressing this topic.

Journals that frequently publish studies dealing with life-sustaining treatment, medical ethics, and medical costs include *American Family Physician, American Journal of Hospice and Palliative Medicine, American Journal of Nursing, Archives of Disease in Childhood, BMC Medicine, Current Opinion in Critical Care, Journal of the Academy of Nutrition and Dietetics, Journal of the American Medical*

Association, Journal of Medical Ethics, Journal of Neurology, Neurology, New England Journal of Medicine, Pediatrics, Proceedings of the National Academy of Sciences of the United States of America, Psychological Review, Psychological Science, and *Trends in Cognitive Sciences.*

Gallup, Inc., and the Pew Research Center have conducted opinion polls on topics that are related to death and dying; a number of such polls and the reports accompanying them were used to provide perspective on public opinions about controversial end-of-life issues.

The Kaiser Family Foundation provides a wealth of information on health-related topics, including most of the issues raised in this book.

INDEX

B

McCarter, Dorothy, 129
McMath, Jahi, 129
Mechanical ventilation
    clear and convincing evidence for
      removal of, 122
    competent patients' wishes, 117–118
    life-sustaining treatment types, 33, 35
    persistent vegetative state, 16
    Quinlan, Karen Ann, 115–116
Medicaid
    Affordable Care Act, 136
    AIDS, 145
    Alzheimer's disease, 150
    cancer, 147
    expansion, 137f
    long-term care, 142–143
    older adults, 52, 141
    recipients and payments, by race/
      ethnicity, 146t–147t
Medical education, 26, 53, 54
Medical ethics, 25–26, 111
Medical neglect, 79
Medical technology and population aging, 8
Medicare
    aging population, 45
    Alzheimer's disease, 150
    cost of health care, 137–141, 139t–140t
    end-of-life care utilization, 59(f5.13)
    enrollment, 141f
    enrollment and spending, by age group,
      145f
    enrollment and spending, by type of
      beneficiary, 144(f 10.8)
    hospice care, 39
    hospice care coverage, 141–142
    increases in Medicare spending, 143f
    older adults, 51, 52
    spending by type of service, 144(f10.7)
Medigap insurance, 138
Meditations on First Philosophy
    (Descartes), 3–4
Mediums, 5
Mendeleyev, Dmitry Ivanovich, 5
Mesopotamians, 2
Metabolic intoxication, 14, 15
Mexico, 62
Michael J. Satz etc. v. Abe Perlmutter,
    117–118
Michigan, 48
Middle Ages, 3
Middle East, 3
Mind-body dualism, 3–4
Minimally conscious state, 36
Minnesota, 30, 80–81
Mississippi, 30, 93
Missouri Supreme Court, 124–125
Model advance directive, 106, 107t–109t
Montana, 28, 48, 92, 97
Montana, Baxter v., 128–129
More, Thomas, 21

Mortality rates. *See* Death rates
Mount Auburn Cemetery, 4
Muhammad, 23
Multiculturalism, 26–27
Multiple-birth rate, 67, 69t–70t
Mummification, 1–2
Myers, Frederic William Henry, 5

N

National Conference of Commissioners on
    Uniform State Laws, 106
National Hospice and Palliative Care
    Organization (NHPCO), 35, 39–40
National Organ Transplant Act, 37
National Right to Life Committee, 109
Native Americans, 5, 81
Nazis, 93–94
Near-death experiences, 18–20
Negative-pressure ventilators, 35
Nejdl, Robert, 119
Neonatal mortality, 61
Netherlands, 62, 94, 101–102
Neumann, Kara, 80
Neural tube defects, 73, 74–75
Neurocritical Care Society, 16
Neurophysiology and near-death
    experiences, 18, 19
Nevada, 93
New England Centenarian Study, 48
*New England Sinai Hospital, Patricia E.
    Brophy v.*, 119–120
New Hampshire, 108
New Jersey, 48, 92, 115–116
New Jersey Supreme Court, 115–116,
    121–122
New Mexico, 92
New York, 30, 48, 92
New York Appellate Court, 117
New York Court of Appeals, 123
New Zealand, 62, 132
NHPCO (National Hospice and Palliative
    Care Organization), 35, 39–40
Nineteenth century, 4–5
Nolan, Joseph Richard, 120
Nonhospital do-not-resuscitate orders,
    33–34
North Africa, 3
North Carolina, 48
North Dakota, 145
Nursing homes
    advance directives, 111, 112, 112(f8.3)
    costs, 143–145
    do-not-resuscitate orders, 113(f8.4)
    life-sustaining treatment, 121–122
    living wills, 113(f8.5)
    nursing home care, 148t–149t
    site of death, 52
Nutrition, artificial. *See* Artificial nutrition
    and hydration

O

Obama, Barack, 136
O'Connor, Mary, 122–123
O'Connor, Sandra Day, 125, 127–128
Odyssey (Homer), 2
OECD (Organisation for Economic
    Co-operation and Development), 61–62,
    63t, 89
O'Hern, Daniel, 122
Ohio, 48, 108
Oklahoma, 30
Older adults
    advance directives, people with, 112
    Alzheimer's disease, 147–150
    attitudes about death, 7
    characteristics of, 45, 47–50
    chronic health conditions, by sex,
      55(f5.9)
    demographics, 48–50
    disability, 57f
    educational attainment, 52f
    geriatrics, 52–54
    government benefit programs, 136
    health and morbidity, 50–52
    health insurance coverage, 59(f5.12)
    income, 49–50, 53f, 54f
    leading causes of death, 55(f5.8)
    Medicare, 137–141
    population, 11(f1.5)
    population, by state, 49f
    site of death, 59(f5.14)
    suicide, 83, 85–86, 90
Oldest-old, 47–48
Olson, James, 81
Omnibus Budget Reconciliation Act of
    1990, 106
On Death and Dying (Kübler-Ross), 6
Oregon
    advance directives, 108
    Death with Dignity Act, 97–100, 99f,
      100t, 128
    nursing home occupancy rates, 145
    Oregon Medical Association, 97
    physician-assisted suicide, 28, 94
Oregon Death with Dignity Act, 97–100,
    99f, 100t, 128
Oregon Medical Association, 97
Organ donors, 41t–42t
Organ transplantation
    anencephalic infants, 74–75
    heart transplantation, 13
    organ donors, 36–39
    transplantable organs and tissue, 37f
    transplants performed, by organ, 40f
    waiting list, 38f, 39f, 39t
Organisation for Economic Co-operation
    and Development (OECD), 61–62, 63t,
    89
Organ/tissue donor card, 43f
Orthodox Judaism, 23

CPSIA information can be obtained
at www.ICGtesting.com
Printed in the USA
FFOW01n2009140518
46680244-48766FF